FIRST CASUALTY

ALSO BY TOBY HARNDEN

Dead Men Risen:
An Epic Story of War
and Heroism in Afghanistan

Bandit Country:
The IRA & South Armagh

Toby Harnden

FIRST CASUALTY

The Untold Story of the Battle
That Began the War in Afghanistan

WELBECK

Published by Welbeck
An imprint of Welbeck Non-Fiction Limited,
part of Welbeck Publishing Group.
20 Mortimer Street,
London W1T 3JW

First published by Welbeck in 2021

A CIP catalogue record for this book is available from the British Library

ISBN
Hardback – 9781787396449
Trade Paperback – 9781787396432
eBook – 9781787396456

Printed and bound in the UK

10 9 8 7 6 5 4 3 2 1

www.welbeckpublishing.com

For Alexandra

Then I heard the voice of the Lord saying, "Whom shall I send, and who will go for us?" And I said, "Here am I; send me!"

—Isaiah 6:8

We are the Nation's first line of defense. We accomplish what others cannot accomplish and go where others cannot go.

—CIA mission statement

Someone has got to do the things no one else wants to do.

—CIA officer
Mike Spann

CONTENTS

CONTENTS

PREFACE

FOR TWO DECADES, the United States has been engaged in a seemingly endless—and eventually largely forgotten—war in Afghanistan. During this time America and NATO troops suffered over 3,500 fatalities. After the first casualty in 2001, the CIA sustained at least another 18, more than in any other war during the Agency's seventy-three-year history. American deaths reduced to a trickle after 2015, but since then over 10,000 Afghan civilians are have died each year.

The Taliban now controls most of the country and has never cut its ties to Al-Qaeda. Its leaders believe, with justification, that they defeated American forces. With the US withdrawal due to be completed by September 11, 2021, the Taliban is poised to seize power, and a bloody civil war seems inevitable—leaving the few Americans still paying attention to wonder what the war was for.

It was not always like this. On September 11, 2001, Al-Qaeda operatives turned four hijacked planes into missiles aimed at symbols of American power. It was the deadliest terrorist attack in history. Nearly 3,000 people were killed in New York, the Pentagon, and Pennsylvania on 9/11, eclipsing the death toll at Pearl Harbor sixty years earlier. All nineteen of the suicide hijackers had been trained in or had visited Afghanistan, where Al-Qaeda leader Osama bin Laden, given sanctuary by the Taliban government, had orchestrated the 9/11 attacks.

With images of planes hitting the twin towers playing in loops on every TV network, America was united. Mass murder had come to American shores. The perpetrators of 9/11 had to be brought to justice and prevented from launching further attacks. Groups harboring terrorists, including the Taliban, would be swept away. There was anger, certainly, and a desire for vengeance. But the abiding sentiment was one of "Never again." Playing defense was no longer an option. Now Americans were determined to hunt down the enemy on the other side of the world.

In the days after 9/11, Americans embraced the reality that survival meant risk, and more death. The post-Vietnam aversion to casualties was in the past. Within the US government, only the CIA knew Afghanistan. America had abandoned Afghanistan after the Cold War, but a small band within the CIA had vigilantly observed the growing power of Islamic fundamentalists. For more than two years, it had sent small teams into the country to assist leaders of the Northern Alliance, the Taliban's foes and Afghanistan's resistance. The Pentagon had no military plan for Afghanistan, and so it was that in the country's hour of need the Agency was called upon to lead America's response.

First Casualty is the story of Team Alpha, a group of eight Americans who were at the forefront of that response and became the first to fight behind enemy lines after 9/11. It is a rousing tale of the remarkable success they achieved when, for perhaps six weeks, the CIA ran the war. These men brought regional expertise, language skills, and a focus on tribal dynamics and human psychology—as well as a warrior ethos and elite military skills. The power delegated to them took their breath away. This was a war directed on the battlefield, not from 20,000 feet above or 7,000 miles away.

Each day, Team Alpha members lived on a knife edge and made decisions of strategic consequence. Knowing the axiom that in war the first casualty is the plan, they embraced flexibility and improvisation, drawing on the legacy of the wartime Office of Strategic Services (OSS), the forerunner of the CIA. Along with the Green Berets, Team Alpha's officers were insurgents engaging in unconventional warfare "by, with, and through" indigenous allies—a concept that later became part of US military doctrine. They helped the resistance overthrow Afghanistan's oppressors. It was a formula that worked, in a place where historically almost nothing had.

By December 2001, ten CIA teams—including Team Alpha and totalling a few dozen CIA officers—had secured victory across Afghanistan. Fighting alongside them were Special Forces troops operating symbiotically with US air power. Among those troops was a unit from Britain's Special Boat Service (SBS), operating in the tradition of their country's Special Operations Executive (SOE), which inspired the OSS. Jettisoning a directive that restricted their ability to fight, the SBS headed toward the sound of gunfire.

The complexity of Afghanistan was apparent to Team Alpha. False surrenders, switching sides, warlord machinations, prisoner abuse, suicide attacks, and ethnic ferment were facts of life. This was a country—if it was a country at all—that could not be controlled. After the surviving members of Team Alpha left Afghanistan, the US military took over and American forces became occupiers rather than insurgents. Conventional troops poured into the country, and fortified bases were established. The United States sought to impose democracy and a central government in Kabul. Rather than allowing warlord rivalries to play out in a deeply traditional society of ethnic and regional patchworks, the US excluded leaders it found unpalatable. Western standards of morality and fair play were applied, even retrospectively, as the US tried to create a nation in its own image. Early success became a long-drawn-out failure.

First Casualty tells the story of the opening chapter in a new era of history when a resolute America was confident in what could be done, and the CIA seized the opportunity to do it. It is an inspiring story of what was achieved then, and a plaintive one of what might have been since.

WHO'S WHO

CENTRAL INTELLIGENCE AGENCY (CIA)

George Tenet: Director

Cofer Black: Director of Counterterrorism Center (CTC); Africa Division case officer

Hank Crumpton: Chief of CTC/Special Operations (CTC/SO); Africa Division case officer

Rich Blee: Chief of Alec station; Africa Division case officer

Robert Grenier: Chief of Islamabad station; Near East (NE) Division case officer

Charlie Gilbert: Chief of Tashkent station; NE Division case officer

Gary Schroen: Chief of Jawbreaker; NE Division case officer

Team Alpha

J. R. Seeger: Chief; Dari linguist; NE Division case officer

Alex Hernandez: Deputy; Ground Branch paramilitary officer

Scott Spellmeyer: Ground Branch paramilitary; later Team Bravo chief

David Tyson: Uzbek linguist; Central Eurasian (CE) Division case officer

Mike Spann: Ground Branch paramilitary officer; husband of **Shannon Spann,** a CTC officer

Mark Rausenberger: Medic, Office of Medical Services (OMS)

Andy: Ground Branch paramilitary officer
Justin Sapp: Captain; Green Beret detailed to the CIA

Team Bravo

Bob: Dari linguist; NE Division case officer
Glenn: Medic, OMS
Greg: Ground Branch paramilitary officer

US MILITARY

Donald Rumsfeld: Defense Secretary
Paul Wolfowitz: Deputy Defense Secretary
Tommy Franks: General; head of US Central Command (CENTCOM)
Bert Calland: Rear admiral; head of CENTCOM's Special Operations (SOCCENT)
John Mulholland: Colonel; commander, 5th Special Forces Group and Task Force Dagger

Green Berets, 5th Special Force Group

Operational Detachment Charlie (ODC) 53 (Boxer), 3rd Battalion

Max Bowers: Lieutenant colonel; commander
Kurt Sonntag: Major; executive officer
Mark Mitchell: Major; operations officer
Paul Syverson: Captain; adjutant
Anthony Jarrett: Captain; communications officer
Paul Beck: Sergeant first class, communications
Mike Sciortino: Staff sergeant, US Air Force; air controller
Kevin Leahy: Captain; commander of support company
Dave Betz: Master sergeant, support company
Ken Ashton: Sergeant first class, Operational Detachment Bravo (ODB) 580

Operational Detachment Alpha (ODA) 595

Mark Nutsch: Captain; commander
Andy Marchal: Sergeant first class; intelligence sergeant
Steve Bleigh: Sergeant first class; medic
Bill Bennett: Sergeant first class; medic

UK MILITARY

Z Squadron, Special Boat Service (SBS)

Jess: Captain, Royal Marines; team commander
Paul "Scruff" McGough: Sergeant, Royal Marines
Tony: Corporal, Royal Marines
Steph Bass: Chief boatswain's mate; Navy SEAL

NORTHERN ALLIANCE

Jamiat-i Islami (Tajiks)

Ahmad Shah Massoud: Commander of Northern Alliance forces until
    September 9, 2001
Fahim Khan: Commander of Northern Alliance forces after Massoud
Atta Mohammed Noor: Commander of Jamiat forces in Mazar-i
    Sharif area

Hezb-i Wahdat (Hazaras)

Karim Khalili: Commander of Hazara forces in Bamiyan province
Mohammed Mohaqeq: Commander of Hazara forces in Mazar-i
    Sharif area

Jumbesh-i Milli (Uzbeks)

Abdul Rashid Dostum: Commander

Lal Mohammed: Deputy commander
Amir Jan Naseri: Adviser; former Taliban commander; Pashtun
Faqir Mohammed Jowzjani: Unit commander
Ak Yasin: Unit commander
Abdul Sattar: Chief of security
Amanullah: Chief of intelligence in Darya Suf Valley; Tajik
Abdul Salam: Chief of captives in Darya Suf Valley
Sayed Kamal: Chief of intelligence in Mazar-i Sharif

AL-QAEDA AND TALIBAN

Osama bin Laden: Al-Qaeda founder and leader
Mohammed Atta: Leader of nineteen hijackers on 9/11
Mullah Mohammed Omar: Taliban founder and leader
Mullah Mohammad Fazl: Deputy minister of defense; commander of Taliban northern forces
Mullah Norullah Noori: Governor of Balkh province; Taliban political commander of Northern Zone
Mullah Dadullah: Senior Taliban commander
John Walker Lindh: Ansar (Arab) Brigade 055 foot soldier

FIRST
CASUALTY

1

ZERO HOUR

4:35 p.m. (GMT +5), September 11, 2001;
Tashkent International Airport, Uzbekistan

SETTLING IN FOR the journey from Tashkent to Heathrow, the burly, broad-shouldered man traveling alone blended in among the passengers on board Uzbekistan Airways Flight 201. His thick, graying hair framed a friendly, open face with rough-hewn features. He was six feet two and looked like he worked in perhaps engineering or agriculture—hands on rather than in an office. A plaid shirt hung loosely over canvas pants. David Tyson was certainly not one of the sharp-suited businessmen flying from the former Soviet republic in the hope of closing a deal in London.

The Boeing 757, painted in the powder blue, yellow, and green of the national airline, took off on schedule for a flight of seven hours. At precisely the same moment some 6,000 miles and nine time zones away, Mohammed Atta, an Egyptian national, was about to board American Airlines Flight 11 at Boston Logan Airport with four subordinates. There it was 7:35 a.m. and the azure sky was cloudless. Atta was the leader of nineteen hijackers from Osama bin Laden's Al-Qaeda on four planes who were about to launch the most devastating attack on the United States in history. An Al-Qaeda commander had referred to the day of the coordinated terrorist strikes as "zero hour."

3

To anyone on Flight 201 giving David a second thought, it might have been a surprise to learn that he was an American—especially given his ease with the vernacular of various dialects of the Uzbek language. David spoke fluent Russian, Turkish, and Turkmen, and could converse in Kazakh, Tatar, and Azerbaijani. But it was his Uzbek, honed during four years of living in Uzbekistan as a student, that could pass as native. Never seen in a tie, David, as a graduate student in Tashkent, had at one time possessed no shoes. His friends would quip that he had been an Uzbek peasant in another life. By David's own admission, he had once teetered on the verge of going native. The business cards now in his wallet, however, identified him as not just an American but a diplomat, a second secretary serving with the Department of State in the Political-Military section of the US Embassy in Tashkent.

In truth, David was a spy. Aged forty and under diplomatic cover, he was a clandestine operative working at the Central Intelligence Agency's Tashkent station, housed inside the embassy. More specifically, he was a case officer, a member of the CIA's Central Eurasian Division, within its Directorate of Operations. The DO, as it was known, was the CIA's elite clandestine arm. The CIA's analysts, technicians, and support staff were housed in separate directorates and worked overtly. In the DO, by contrast, CIA officers worked undercover, the majority as State Department employees, using aliases in all communications. Their true affiliation was classified and kept secret, often even from their families. Though booked on the flight in his true name, in all diplomatic and intelligence traffic he was referred to by an operational pseudonym. Monitoring bin Laden and Al-Qaeda in Afghanistan had been one of David's principal responsibilities since being stationed in Uzbekistan in 1998. He was traveling to London to discuss his efforts to keep armaments in Afghanistan from falling into terrorist hands.

David was not a typical CIA officer. Agency colleagues may have viewed Uzbekistan as the ass-end of nowhere, but David loved the place. He had joined the CIA in 1996—Tashkent was his first posting—at the age of thirty-five, from graduate school at Indiana University, where he had been lecturing and working toward a PhD. There, he had gained a master's degree with a thesis on "Literacy in Turkistan Prior to Soviet Rule" and become an expert on shrine pilgrimage among the Turkmens.

CIA colleagues had nicknamed him "the Professor." When leaving academia, however, he had known that he was crossing over to what many regarded as the dark side. For well over a year, he had been talking to a middle-aged CIA officer who had identified herself as Sandy Baker—not her real name—about what he had gleaned from his travels in the former Soviet Union. Latterly, she had broached whether he might become a spy. The turning point had been in a freezing parking lot in Bloomington with his wife, Rosann. She hailed from the same small town in Pennsylvania, and they had met when they were undergraduates. The couple had two young children and were struggling to make ends meet. David told her that he had received a job offer from the CIA and they wanted an answer. "Do we leave this life here behind?" he asked. "We need to make a decision." He was entrenched in the small world of Central Asian studies and considered part of his department's family. They had stood looking at each other in the snow and then agreed that he should make the leap. David had strong bonds with his professors, and he knew that joining the CIA would cause some of his colleagues to cut him off. There would be no going back. It had been a close call, with government health insurance tipping the balance.

So far, life as a spy seemed like an endless adventure. David had been on missions in Uzbekistan, Tajikistan, and Afghanistan, often operating alone, armed, using his languages, and employing his newly learned intelligence tradecraft. He had become part of a close-knit band of CIA officers on the edge of what was for most Americans a forgotten Cold War frontier. Though it was a time of peace for the United States, the region where David lived was wracked by war. David had been pushing the CIA for more money and more weapons for US allies, and to take more risks. It was a time before he had a surfeit of all three. It was a time when he had not killed a man, or kicked a bloodied body to check if a friend was still alive. It was a time when he had not run, and shot, and fought for his life. It was a time when he had not lain in the dust beside the staring eyes of a corpse. It was a time when he had no nightmares of being chased by men determined to kill him. It was a time when he could not conceive of any of those things happening.

At age seventeen, David's wanderlust was such that he had written a letter to the French Foreign Legion—he found the address in a school library book—asking if he could join. To his surprise, he received a reply suggesting he report to a recruiting depot outside Marseilles; alas, he had no means of raising the airfare. Instead, David enlisted in the US Army straight out of high school, without telling his parents, rather than take a job in the paper or steel mills surrounding his home in Downingtown, Pennsylvania. After two uneventful years in the field artillery, when he was mostly based in West Germany and played a lot of basketball, he had become a student. David had enrolled at Westchester State University and discovered a talent for languages, beginning with Russian because it seemed the most exotic. During a semester at Columbia University, he had been so short of money that he had started going to a New York homeless shelter to get free soup. Before long, he had become a helper there; then, for free board and a modest paycheck, he worked as a live-in supervisor. Some of the men took him around the New York subway system, introducing him to underground tribes of homeless. David had become so involved in the lives of the men at the shelter, many of them alcoholics or drug addicts, that Rosann had fretted it was distracting him from his studies.

He quit Columbia and moved to a doctoral program at Indiana University, at the same time securing an ROTC commission as an intelligence officer. His second stint in the Army enabled him to use the G.I. Bill to fund his student life. Central Asian studies was a niche area of academia that offered more opportunities than Russian, which was dominated by émigrés. David had grown up in a family with an ethos of modesty, thrift, teetotalism, and staunch Christianity drawn from the Mennonite tradition. Having discovered his aptitude for languages and a fascination with other cultures, he was drawn from these simple roots to explore the obscure and the esoteric.

David's patriotism was understated but deep. His father had served in the aircraft carrier USS *Intrepid* during World War II and survived Japanese kamikaze attacks. Although post-traumatic stress had never been discussed, after the war his father had seemed a changed man and had struggled to stay in jobs, working variously as a carpenter, janitor, preacher, and security guard. David had studied in Leningrad from 1985 to 1986, before the collapse of the Soviet Union, fueling his belief in personal freedom, the rights of the individual versus the state, and America's role as a force for good in the world. He had experienced communism again as a student in Tashkent beginning in 1989, when he was arrested regularly by the Uzbek secret police; he used his time being held, sometimes overnight in the cells, to hone his tenses and bolster his vocabulary.

David's first job at the Agency in 1996 was not glamorous: translating "open source" material such as the Russian newspapers *Izvestia* and *Pravda*. He joked that rather than being recruited as a clandestine operative, as he initially hoped, he had been captured by the nerds. His department, the Agency's Foreign Broadcast Information Service, occupied a nondescript office block seven miles from CIA headquarters in Langley, northern Virginia, just outside Washington, DC. But David's facility with languages meant he was soon plucked from this back-water. After an accelerated course at "The Farm," the Agency's training facility near Williamsburg, Virginia, he was bound for his old stomping ground of Tashkent.

In Uzbekistan, David had impressed his CIA superiors with his thirst for every aspect of his job, barring bureaucracy. A case officer in Pakistan destined for the highest ranks of the CIA had taken him under his wing, teaching him the art of hands-on spying, recruiting assets, and navigating the intrigue of ethnic rivalries. David was not fazed by danger and was happy to take risks. He seemed to be the kind of eccentric who was a perfect fit for the CIA. Colleagues loved to tell the tale of how the Tyson family, with Rosann's parents in the back of the car, had stopped at a gas station in rural Uzbekistan. When Rosann had looked around as the gas was being pumped, her husband had disappeared. Some considerable time later—the exact period depended on who was recounting the story—he returned, puzzled by the fuss over his absence. David had seen an elderly farmer working in a field and walked over to talk to him. The old man had invited David to his home for tea; it would have been rude to refuse.

David had no sense of self-importance and would help anyone. He was also uninterested in professional advancement. It was received wisdom that any new case officer, and especially one who had joined the Agency late, should take a job in headquarters after their first tour. Instead, David had signed up for a second stint in Tashkent. He was where he wanted to be. Having left academia behind, David was now all in with the CIA. He had found his new tribe.

On September 11, David's destination was a hotel close to Grosvenor Square in London's well-heeled Mayfair district. Although he had been in the CIA just three years, David's age, expertise in his region, and air of quiet self-assurance meant that he was being treated as an operative with greater experience. The following day, he was to meet fellow CIA officers inside the Agency's vast London station, where the subject would be Afghanistan.

* * *

Ravaged by war for more than two decades, Afghanistan was one of the poorest and most unstable countries in the world. Its position between Persia, India, and the Arabian Sea made it a strategic crossroads, and for millennia it had attracted a succession of invaders. In 2001, Afghans had a life expectancy of forty-three years and a literacy rate around 25 percent. Some 3.5 million of its population of 23 million were living in squalid refugee camps in Iran and Pakistan. The country was infested with up to 7 million land mines, which killed or wounded more than 1,000 Afghans—many of them children—each year.

Many argued that Afghanistan was not even a country; David tended to agree. With no majority ethnic group, and tribal or regional identities much stronger than nationalism, it seemed forever destined to be engulfed by strife. For most of its history, Afghanistan had been ruled by the Pashtuns, who made up 38 percent of the population and were mostly in the south and east. But Tajiks, 25 percent of Afghans, had ruled from 1992 to 1996 with the help of Hazaras, 19 percent, and Uzbeks and Turkmens, 12 percent.

Afghanistan had become a Cold War battleground in April 1978, when the secular, modernist president Daoud Khan was executed during a bloody coup by Marxists in the army. His killers created the Soviet-backed Democratic Republic of Afghanistan (DRA). The DRA was immediately opposed by Islamic mujahideen fighters, who declared jihad—"holy war"—against the communist infidels. Fearing the DRA would be overthrown, the Soviet Union invaded in December 1979 with 100,000 troops. What the Russians intended to be a short operation to prop up the DRA and its puppet leader, Babrak Karmal, turned into a bloody occupation of more than nine years that cost the lives of over 40,000 Soviet soldiers and 1.5 million Afghans—90 percent of them civilians.

During the war with the Soviets, most of Afghanistan was united against the common enemy. The mujahideen, numbering up to 150,000 fighters, represented all ethnic factions; money, weapons, and supplies poured in from the United States, Iran, Pakistan, China, Saudi Arabia, and the Gulf states. Under President Ronald Reagan, from 1981 to 1987, it was the war in Afghanistan that the CIA conducted that became the biggest clandestine operation in history. Most US aid was adminis-tered through the CIA's counterparts in the ISI, Pakistan's intelligence agency—a relationship that would come back to haunt the CIA. The United States provided $4.5 billion in aid to the mujahideen—a sum matched by Saudi Arabia—and in total the rebels received $10 billion.

Among the most prominent mujahideen leaders were Gulbuddin Hekmatyar, a Pashtun extremist based in Pakistan; Ahmad Shah Massoud, a Tajik based in northern Afghanistan; Abdul Haq, a moderate Pashtun in the east; and Karim Khalili, a Hazara Shia in central Afghanistan. Opposing the mujahideen in alliance with the Russians were Abdul Rashid Dostum and his ethnic Uzbeks in northern Afghanistan. They had strong links with Uzbekistan, then part of the Soviet Union, and feared Pashtun domination. Secular and anti-Pashtun, Dostum opposed Islamic fundamentalism and based his leadership on the interests of ethnic Uzbeks and their autonomous way of life. Over the years to come, Dostum would wield power by switching sides at strategic moments, consistently putting Uzbek tribalism above all else. Pakistan and Saudi Arabia were the principal funders of the Pashtuns, who were fellow Sunni Muslims, while Iran backed their fellow Shia.

While the United States sent everything from Tennessee mules to combat boots and chickpeas, it also supplied lethal aid. From 1986 on, the CIA secretly provided the mujahideen with up to 2,500 shoulder-launched, heat-seeking Stinger missiles that the rebels had requested to neutralize Soviet air power. The CIA also supported the ISI efforts to recruit radical Islamists from around the world and persuade them to flock to Pakistan to fight with the mujahideen. The virulently anti-communist Reagan administration, which sought to stamp out Marxism from the globe, wanted to show that the Muslim world was united against the Soviet Union. It even supplied Korans and anti-Soviet tracts to fighters who would distribute them in Uzbekistan while carrying out guerrilla raids. The United States paid mujahideen leaders handsomely: Massoud, for one, received $200,000 a month, on top of what he was getting from the ISI.

From 1982 to 1992, some 35,000 Islamic radicals from forty-three countries fought with the mujahideen. The Saudis saw the Afghan jihad as a way of promoting the fundamentalist Wahhabi strain of Islam and—as a bonus—took the opportunity to export radicals who might cause trouble in their own kingdom. Among the Saudis who went to

10

Afghanistan was Osama bin Laden, who arrived in 1984 to assist the mujahideen with cash and construction, and later took up arms. At the time, the choice could not have been easier for America. So what if, as one former senior US official argued, the price of ending the Cold War included backing "a few stirred-up Muslims" in a faraway land?

While the United States supported local mujahideen leaders in Afghanistan, it never funded or trained bin Laden or his future Al-Qaeda lieutenants. Bin Laden's "Arab Afghans" did not arrive until seven years after the Soviet invasion, and they were never a major force within the mujahideen. US support for Pakistani and Saudi sponsorship of Islamic fundamentalists in Afghanistan, however, did lead indirectly to the founding of Al-Qaeda—Arabic for *The Base*—in 1988 and, thirteen years later, to the blowback of 9/11.

*   *   *

When the Soviet Union collapsed at the end of 1991, CIA aid to Afghanistan ended. The communist president Najibullah clung to power until April 1992. He resigned and tried to flee the country, but was blocked at Kabul airport by the Uzbek forces of Dostum, previously a loyal ally. Najibullah took refuge in the capital's UN compound. With the Soviets gone, the mujahideen dissolved into competing ethnic and religious factions that waged a bloody, four-year civil war. After the fall of Najibullah, the Tajik forces of Burhanuddin Rabbani and Massoud, supported by Dostum, seized Kabul, marking the first time in 300 years that the Afghan capital had not been under Pashtun control. Hekmatyar laid siege to the Afghan capital, bombarding it mercilessly. Pashtuns supported by Pakistan and Saudi Arabia fought Hazara Shia backed by Iran. In January 1994, Dostum switched sides again, joining Hekmatyar to attack Kabul.

By the end of 1994, the Rabbani government, with Massoud commanding its military forces, still held Kabul, but the country was disintegrating. Warlords ruled their fiefdoms, often brutalizing their people; the economy was in shambles and corruption was rife. In this environment, a new Pashtun group emerged, promising to cleanse Afghanistan. This was the Taliban—fundamentalist Islamic students, or "talibs," many of whom had grown up in refugee camps and been educated in madrassas in Pakistan. They vowed to end abuses of power by re-creating an Afghanistan based on the ideals of the Prophet Mohammed in the 7th century. The Taliban, now backed by Pakistan, seized Kandahar in November 1994, followed by Herat some ten months later. Hekmatyar and Dostum aligned themselves with their former foes Rabbani and Massoud, hoping to fight off this new common enemy together. But it was too late.

On September 26, 1996, Massoud withdrew his forces from Kabul to the Panjshir Valley rather than be wiped out. The Taliban had effectively won the civil war and now established the Islamic Emirate of Afghanistan. The new regime's first act was to make an example out of the hapless Najibullah, who had spent four years at the UN compound. He was beaten, then driven from the compound to the presidential palace, where he was castrated, dragged behind a jeep, and shot dead. The bodies of Najibullah and his brother were hung by wire nooses from concrete traffic posts. Cigarettes had been placed between their fingers and banknotes stuffed in their pockets to symbolize their alleged debauchery and corruption.

Rabbani fled the country and a month later the Northern Alliance was formed, with Massoud, Dostum, Khalili, and some Pashtuns coalescing in one anti-Taliban bloc. Massoud controlled the Panjshir Valley while Dostum held the northern city of Mazar-i Sharif, along with six surrounding provinces. The Taliban had barred women from working, forced men to grow long beards, and banned all games, including chess and kite flying. In contrast, Dostum ran a modern, secular ministate, backed by Russia, Uzbekistan, and Iran. He had his own airline, the markets were filled with French perfumes and Russian vodka, and women wore lipstick and went to university.

Mazar-i Sharif, Afghanistan's fourth-largest city, was an oasis of modernity and tolerance. Once a trading post near the ancient Silk Road, it had become a place where Uzbeks, Tajiks, Hazaras, and even some Pashtuns lived together peacefully. All this came to an end in May 1997, when Dostum's deputy Abdul Malik Pahlawan—who suspected that his brother had been murdered by Dostum—betrayed the Uzbek leader. Malik cut a deal with the Taliban that would allow them to take over Mazar-i Sharif in return for giving him a government post.

Some 2,500 Taliban troops arrived in the holy city, shut down the university, and imposed sharia law, prompting Dostum to flee to Turkey. The city's Hazaras revolted, massacring 600 of the Taliban. Malik, unhappy with the Taliban's offer of only a minor post in their government in exchange for his treachery toward Dostum, changed his mind. Five days after his act of betrayal, he joined the Hazaras against the Taliban. Even considering the history of shifting Afghan allegiances, this was an extraordinary turnaround. Malik then followed up with another zealous interpretation of an Afghan tradition: the slaughter of prisoners. Malik's men were believed to have killed as many as 2,000 Taliban captives, some of whom were thrown alive into wells and gruesomely killed by hand grenades dropped on their heads.

Dostum returned to Mazar-i Sharif from his exile in Turkey in September 1997, and the treacherous Malik soon fled into Turkmenistan. But with the Uzbeks divided, Dostum managed to control the city for only a year. A fresh Taliban offensive on Mazar-i Sharif, which Dostum and his men could not withstand, ended with the Uzbek warlord being driven out—again—in August 1998. Dostum retreated to Bamiyan in central Afghanistan and then left for Iran.

The Taliban, now back in power throughout northern Afghanistan, killed Hazaras with a ferocity stunning even by their own standards. They shot dead some 400 civilians who had sought sanctuary at the Shrine of Hazrat Ali, and blew up the tomb of Abdul Ali Mazari, a Hazara leader killed by the Taliban in 1995, with civilians trapped inside. Mullah Manon Niazi, the new Taliban governor of Mazar-i Sharif, declared that Hazaras, being Shia, were not Muslims and were to be "exterminated." He vowed: "Wherever you go we will catch you. If you go up, we will pull you down by your feet. If you hide below, we will pull you up by your hair." An estimated 8,000 Hazaras were murdered, some by having their throats slit "the halal way"—one swipe of the blade across the throat—others by being shot in the testicles. Human Rights Watch described it as "one of the single worst examples of killings of civilians in Afghanistan's 20-year war." The Taliban raped Hazara women, 400 of whom were kidnapped and taken as concubines. The murder by the Taliban of eleven Iranian diplomats inside their consulate in Mazar-i Sharif prompted an international outcry, and Iran dispatched troops to its border with Afghanistan.

*   *   *

Having narrowly avoided war with Iran, the Taliban faced diplomatic isolation. In the United States, First Lady Hillary Clinton declared: "We must give voice to women in Afghanistan, where women are brutalized and silenced by the Taliban." Mavis Leno, wife of the television comedian Jay Leno, championed the issue among the Hollywood elite. There was also outrage that poppy cultivation and opium and heroin production had skyrocketed since the Taliban had come to power, despite the group's pious words about the evils of narcotics. A State Department report concluded that the Taliban had instituted a 10 percent tax on drugs to enrich itself and was "facilitating major traffickers to move large quantities of morphine base and heroin to the West" in a bid to destabilize the United States and Europe. Yet for all the concerns about the Taliban's medieval system of justice, repression of women, and drug dealing, for the CIA it was only the Taliban's relationship with Osama bin Laden and Al-Qaeda that mattered.

Bin Laden had returned to Saudi Arabia from Afghanistan in 1989 and then broken with his homeland after its royal family allowed US troops to be stationed there during the 1991 Gulf War against Saddam Hussein's Iraq. When American forces stayed on after the war, bin

Laden branded the interior minister, who was a prince, a traitor. Bin Laden left Saudi Arabia in 1992 to take part in the Islamic revolution in Sudan. In 1994, the country of his birth—angered by his continued and vocal criticism—revoked bin Laden's citizenship. After US and Saudi pressure led to his expulsion by Sudan in May 1996, the now-stateless Al-Qaeda leader was given refuge by the Taliban, flying to Afghanistan in a chartered jet along with a large armed entourage, three wives, and thirteen children. Three months later, bin Laden declared jihad against the United States in a thirty-page fatwa. In February 1998 he issued another fatwa, this one stating that "to kill Americans and their allies— civilians and military—is an individual duty for every Muslim."

Six months later, on August 7, 1998, Al-Qaeda operatives bombed US embassies in Kenya and Tanzania, killing 224 and injuring 4,000. These were the deadliest attacks against Americans overseas since the 1983 Beirut bombings by Hezbollah. David Tyson, preparing for his posting to Tashkent, knew that Osama bin Laden had become his country's principal foe. President Bill Clinton responded with seventy-five Tomahawk cruise missiles, which were fired at night on a pharmaceutical factory in Sudan and on Al-Qaeda camps in Khost, northeastern Afghanistan, close to the Pakistan border. Each missile cost around $750,000; the attacks cost the United States over $56 million. Yet they killed no terrorist planners and failed to damage Al-Qaeda's capabilities. It was an anemic response that had handed bin Laden a publicity coup.

2

BLUE SKY

9:10 a.m. (GMT +4.5), October 20, 1999;
Above the Anjuman Pass, Badakhshan province, Afghanistan

DAVID TYSON LOOKED uneasily at the fuel leaking onto the deck of the battered Mi-17, a former Russian transport helicopter provided by Ahmad Shah Massoud. As the aircraft passed over the peaks of the Hindu Kush at 14,500 feet, it began to descend toward Massoud's birthplace of Bazarak. Below him, David saw the rusting wrecks of Soviet aircraft that had been shot down or had crashed into the snowcapped mountains. He was part of a six-man CIA Counterterrorism Center (CTC) team—codenamed Jawbreaker—heading into Afghanistan's Panjshir Valley, a sliver of land north of Kabul nestled between mountain flanks. There, the team would confer with Massoud, the ethnic Tajik and former mujahideen commander who led the anti-Taliban forces of the Northern Alliance. The CIA officers had taken off in the Mi-17 from Dushanbe, the dilapidated, war-torn capital of Tajikistan—a city so riven by crime and gang warfare that the US embassy and CIA station there had been closed.

Massoud—the "Lion of the Panjshir"—was tall and sinewy, with a wispy beard and a ridged nose. Fluent in French, he possessed a vast library and was a student of Persian poetry as well as the guerrilla philosophies of Mao Zedong and Che Guevara. He had been abandoned

16

by the Americans after the Russians left and was skeptical of this new set of CIA men, who told him they were not yet authorized to give him weapons or help his men fight.

Osama bin Laden was waging jihad against the West from Afghanistan. He was a guest of the Taliban, but also their ally and benefactor. Al-Qaeda camps in Afghanistan trained Arabs for its Brigade 055—also known as Ansar—which fought alongside the Taliban. Bin Laden needed to bolster the Taliban so it could provide the territory from which Al-Qaeda could operate. Mazar-i Sharif and the six provinces once held by Abdul Rashid Dostum, Massoud's Uzbek ally in the Northern Alliance, were now in Taliban hands. That meant the fundamentalist regime controlled 90 percent of Afghanistan. Only the Panjshir Valley was holding out, and Massoud was the lone major opposition figure in Afghanistan.

When David had arrived at the CIA's Tashkent station in October 1998 and his new boss had told him that a core part of David's job would be Afghanistan. "We've got the Taliban there and Osama bin Laden's running around," said the station chief, Fred, a grizzled veteran openly contemptuous of the Agency's hierarchy. "Headquarters doesn't give a shit. But I want you to learn about Afghanistan because shit's going to happen there someday." Tapping David on the shoulders, he joked: "I hereby anoint you Afghan *référent*," using the French word for adviser or point of contact. They were the only two CIA operations officers in Tashkent station.

In February 1999, David's wife, Rosann, ran to the porch of their house in Tashkent when she heard an explosion and flung herself to the ground when a second blast—much closer—shattered the windows. The explosions were from six car bombs targeting government officials, killing sixteen and injuring over 120. President Islam Karimov, Uzbekistan's autocratic leader, a secular former communist, narrowly escaped death. Declaring that he was "prepared to rip off the heads of 200 people" to maintain security, he announced a crackdown on the perpetrators, the Islamic Movement of Uzbekistan (IMU), an Islamist group sustained by Al-Qaeda. The IMU was based in Kabul and had a significant presence in Mazar-i Sharif.

Five countries shared major borders with Afghanistan, and in 1998 none looked like a promising partner for the United States to take on Al-Qaeda. Iran was an avowed enemy of the United States, while Pakistan was a sponsor of the Taliban. Turkmenistan still recognized the Taliban government and was aligned with Russia. Tajikistan provided some assistance to the US, but still looked to Moscow. Uzbekistan's President Karimov had a human rights record that made him unpalatable to the US State Department. Geopolitical alignments, however, were shifting.

The East Africa embassy bombings had prompted a reassessment inside CIA headquarters and a fresh focus on bin Laden's sanctuary in Afghanistan. Although the Clinton White House remained disengaged, at the highest levels of the CIA there was an assumption that it was just a matter of time before bin Laden would strike America. Members of Alec station—the twenty-five-strong unit inside CTC that tracked bin Laden—had repeatedly sounded the alarm about Al-Qaeda's intentions. In June 1999 Rich Blee had become Alec station's new leader. The tall, sandy-haired son of a legendary CIA officer needed no persuading about the threat bin Laden posed. As station chief in Algiers, he had witnessed veterans of the Afghan jihad lead an Islamist insurgency and massacre tens of thousands of people. Blee felt in his bones that bin Laden would not stop after the Africa bombings. As a highflier, his appointment was a sign of heightened CIA focus on Al-Qaeda.

Blee had made the case for the CIA's Mi-17 mission into the Panjshir Valley to enlist Massoud in the hunt for bin Laden—and he was leading the six-man Jawbreaker team. The US government was divided over the Northern Alliance commander. The State Department was wary of Massoud's alleged involvement in the narcotics trade and his links to Iran. Despite all contrary evidence, it also believed that the Taliban could be persuaded to give up bin Laden in return for diplomatic recognition. The CIA's Near East (NE) Division, one of the Agency's most powerful and prestigious directorates, tended to side with the State Department. NE Division ran the CIA's Islamabad station—which Blee and his allies regarded as out of touch and in thrall to Pakistan—and believed the Pashtuns, the largest ethnic faction, held the key to Afghanistan's future. Part of this was a bureaucratic turf war. Within the CIA, responsibility for Afghanistan was split, with CTC charged with working against bin Laden, and NE Division dealing with the Taliban. But there was also an important philosophical question involved: should the United States work with Massoud, the only commander fighting the Taliban and Al-Qaeda, or try diplomacy with the Islamists and wait for a Pashtun opposition leader to emerge? For now, CTC had prevailed. "This situation is going to change," Blee told an exasperated Massoud in Bazarak, as David translated. "And then we're going to be looking toward allies. Our policy is stupid—I agree that we're fighting with our hands behind our backs—but I'm working within our system. So, be patient with us."

There were four more Jawbreaker missions over the course of eighteen months as the CIA brought in equipment to help Massoud collect intelligence. David was among the CIA officers who spoke frequently with Massoud's aides over encrypted channels and met with them in Tajikistan. Despite its suspicions of Massoud, NE Division wanted to maintain its own links with him; its Northern Alliance Liaison Team, or NALT, made forays into the Panjshir Valley and met with Massoud in Paris. Blee's hope was that Massoud could pass on intelligence about bin Laden's movements and a Predator drone strike would do the rest. But neither the political will nor the legal authority to kill bin Laden existed in Washington, DC.

In early 2000, Massoud's men mortared Darunta, an Al-Qaeda training base near Jalalabad, which bin Laden was suspected to be visiting. Panic ensued at CIA headquarters—Massoud was acting on intelligence collected with the help of the Agency, but the US government had not authorized lethal force against the Al-Qaeda leader. Blee was forced to tell Massoud that his actions had been illegal and, if repeated, the CIA would cut off aid. Only Blee's frustration outweighed his embarrassment at having to deliver a message that trying to kill bin Laden had been a faux pas.

A CIA plan in May 2000 to snatch bin Laden at Tarnak Farms, his base on the outskirts of Kandahar airport, was shelved due to fears of civilian casualties. To Blee's dismay, the Agency's hierarchy curtailed the Jawbreaker missions out of concern that Massoud's rickety helicopters were unsafe for CIA officers. That prompted the CIA to buy its own Mi-17, painted in Uzbekistan Airways colors. For Alec station, however, it felt like time was running out. In October 2000, 17 American sailors were killed and 39 injured in an Al-Qaeda suicide attack on the USS *Cole* in the port of Aden in Yemen. There was no military response from the Clinton administration.

In late 2000 the CIA laid out its "Blue Sky Memo," a plan to take down the Taliban and go after Al-Qaeda by increasing support to the Northern Alliance and Uzbekistan. The plan was built in part on David's reporting on the Afghan resistance, but he knew that it had been dead on arrival at the White House, with neither the outgoing Clinton nor President-Elect George W. Bush engaged.

David was among those who feared that the CIA had fallen prey to Massoud's magnetism and was failing to court the other groups in the north. He was part of the CIA's liaison with Uzbekistan's intelligence service, helping train commando teams that could be used against bin Laden. The Uzbeks were pushing the CIA to work with the warlord Dostum, their ethnic kinsman, and David agreed that he could be a valuable ally. If Massoud was controversial within the State Department, however, Dostum was beyond the pale. Heavyset, with a powerful physique and features that showed his Mongol heritage, he had a brushlike black mustache and short, graying hair. Dostum had fought with the Russians, then betrayed his benefactor Najibullah. He had shelled Kabul and fought with Hekmatyar against Massoud, only to swap sides again. Few in the US government felt he could be trusted.

Dostum was the son of a peasant, and his schooling had ended at the age of twelve when he was sent to work in the oil and gas fields of Sheberghan in northern Afghanistan. During his national service, it had become clear that he was a natural soldier, and he was sent to the elite 444 Commando Unit in Jalalabad. In 1978—the year he joined the Afghan Communist Army at age twenty-four—he had been given the nom de guerre Dostum, meaning "my friend." Now forty-seven, he had spent almost all his adult life at war. Even in a culture in which cruelty and death were facts of life, Dostum was notorious for his determination to kill and his unwillingness to give any quarter in battle. Dostum drank vodka and did not read poetry. His first wife, Khadija, mother of his four eldest children, had died in bizarre circumstances in 1993. Dostum insisted she was shot twice in the chest by an AK-47 that fell from behind a refrigerator while she was cleaning; a former aide would later claim she was killed on his orders. The Western sophisticates who had gravitated to the soulful Massoud would not be feting Dostum. He was the archetypal Afghan warlord.

When Dostum, at Massoud's urging, returned from exile in Turkey to northern Afghanistan in May 2001, however, David pushed for the CIA to woo him. Like Massoud, Dostum was in the country and fighting the Taliban. While Massoud was relatively safe in his own enclave, the Uzbek warlorrd was operating in the mountains in Taliban-controlled territory. David sensed that the Tashkent station's push to broaden the CIA's links to the anti-Taliban opposition would pay off in due course. But resources and manpower were limited—Afghanistan was low in the Bush administration's foreign-policy priorities—and for now nearly all the eggs had been placed in the Massoud basket.

On September 9, 2001, a Predator drone had arrived at a secret CIA base at Shakhrisabz, 200 miles southwest of Tashkent, ready to be used against bin Laden. But despite the urgent threat warnings emanating from Alec station, US policy toward Al-Qaeda and Afghanistan had moved with glacial speed. The Predator was "weapons system capable," but no authorization had been given for it to be armed. For now, the Hellfire missiles it had been outfitted to carry were stored in weapons lockers. Bill Clinton had treated Al-Qaeda as a problem to be dealt with via legal means, while Bush's new administration was preoccupied with nation-state threats. In the meantime, the Afghans fighting the Taliban and Al-Qaeda were dying as they begged for more American help. Time was about to run out.

* * *

The subject of David's meeting at the CIA's London station was the Agency's secret program to buy back Stingers from Afghan warlords. After the Russian occupation, the CIA had lost track of the missiles it had supplied to the mujahideen, and around 600 remained unaccounted for. Iran had acquired some, while the Taliban reputedly possessed fifty-three. The United States feared the Stingers might be used against civilian targets, but the buyback program had also been a way of engaging, and paying, the Northern Alliance leaders. Massoud had returned some missiles and so had Dostum, via the Uzbekistan intelligence service.

David's first clandestine missions had been to receive Stingers inside Tajikistan. The CIA was offering up to $150,000 apiece. It was not much of a bargain for the US taxpayer, who had already footed the bill for them once, but it had become an important source of income for Massoud and other anti-Taliban fighters.

Events, however, had already overtaken the issue of Stinger buybacks. Two days before, on September 9, Massoud had been slain by Al-Qaeda, who had sent two Tunisians to pose as a television crew and detonate a suicide bomb hidden in a camera. Bin Laden's operatives had exploited Massoud's Achilles' heel—his ego. For years, Massoud had enjoyed giving interviews to journalists who had trekked through the mountains to sit at his feet and absorb his wisdom.

David was stunned by Massoud's death. The personality cult surrounding the "Lion of the Panjshir" meant he had left no obvious heir to lead the Tajiks and unite them with the rest of the Northern

Alliance against the Taliban. Now, the CIA man lamented, the Panjshir, the last stronghold, would fall to the Taliban and refugees would pour into Tajikistan and Uzbekistan. The Taliban would control the whole of Afghanistan, giving bin Laden free rein to plot attacks against America. It was a nightmare, and one that directly affected the Tyson family. If the Taliban took control of land up to Afghanistan's northern border, it would embolden the Al-Qaeda–backed IMU—the Islamist group targeting the Karimov regime—to launch more attacks inside neighboring Uzbekistan, especially against American targets. David pondered the safety of Rosann and their children—Kara, eleven, and Mark, nine—in Tashkent.

All these ramifications flashed through David's mind as Flight 201 headed west over Kazakhstan and then Russia. There were no obvious solutions. But tomorrow, David reasoned as he closed his eyes to try to get some sleep before London, would be another day.

3

THIRD OPTION

8 a.m. (GMT -4), September 11, 2001;
Trumbo Point, Fleming Key, Florida

THE TWO SCUBA DIVERS rolled backward over the side of the Boston whaler into the tropical waters of the Gulf of Mexico. There was no need for wet suits. It was already 83°F and the sea temperature only a few degrees cooler. "Prepare to go subsurface!" the instructor ordered. The divers, tethered together with a buddy line and attached to a buoy, dipped beneath the lapping waves and began to swim toward the shore. Square-jawed with brown hair and blue eyes and a shade under six feet tall, Captain Justin Sapp of the US Army's 5th Special Forces Group was about to turn twenty-nine, an elite soldier in peak physical condition. The four-week Special Forces combat diver course was one of the toughest training courses in the Army and students had no time, even if they had been allowed, to sample the bars and bright lights of nearby Key West. A graduate of Virginia Military Institute (VMI), Justin had been a competitive high school swimmer, and he was one of the outstanding students on the diving course, on track to pass with distinction. He and his Air Force dive partner were breathing via Dräger LAR V closed-circuit oxygen rebreather units strapped to their chests, allowing them to avoid detection by sending no bubbles to the surface.

A minute before Justin entered the water, and almost half an hour into David Tyson's flight to London, American Airlines Flight 11 had taken off from Boston Logan, bound for Los Angeles. The Al-Qaeda hijacker Mohammed Atta was on board. Soon, the Boeing 767 would alter course unexpectedly and head toward New York. More than 1,600 miles to the south of Boston, Justin and his partner were swimming 2,000 meters (1.25 miles) to reach a red marker on the beach. With no underwater terrain features to guide them, it required intense concentration to follow the assigned bearing and balance their speed with minimal exertion to avoid hypoxia.

Justin, seven years into his Army career, had returned from leading Operational Detachment Alpha (ODA) 522 on a training mission to Kuwait and Uzbekistan six weeks earlier. ODAs were twelve-man teams that formed the basic fighting units of Special Forces, made up of hardened sergeants and led by a captain with a warrant officer as his deputy. Commanding an ODA was a test of a young officer's toughness and leadership, and Justin had excelled—as he had with every challenge in his Army career. After the ODA assignment, Justin had initially been picked to lead a counterterrorist diving unit tasked with infiltrating oil rigs or pirate ships. Just before he arrived in Key West, however, his new appointment had been changed. Instead he was to be an S4, or company logistics officer—a dreaded rear-echelon role for a Type A officer determined to be, in Army parlance, at the tip of the spear. Justin had shrugged off the setback. He was a career Army officer who understood that he belonged to a system that would not always cater to his wishes.

Already, Justin had learned to live with the unexpected. His father, Kenneth, had been a case officer in the Agency's NE Division, taking his family with him on postings throughout the Middle East. Kenneth Sapp's obituary would describe him as "a warrior, scholar, patriot, spy." In 1976, a year into the Lebanese Civil War, when Justin was four, the Sapps had been evacuated from Beirut, leaving behind all their furniture and household effects. They had been evacuated again in 1979, this time from Libya, after demonstrators supporting the Iranian revolution set fire to the US Embassy in Tripoli; Justin's father had grabbed the American flag as he fled.

Justin Sapp had wanted to be a soldier for as long as he could remember, growing up with tales of his grandfather, a 101st Airborne sergeant major, fighting at the Battle of the Bulge, and watching the movie *Patton*, for which Francis Ford Coppola won an Oscar. Justin's family had a strong military tradition. His younger brother was at VMI and destined for the 82nd Airborne Division, and their father had served in the Army before joining the CIA.

In Uzbekistan, Justin's ODA 522 had trained Uzbek army special forces, or Spetsnaz, to carry out operations against the Al-Qaeda–backed IMU. During a preliminary visit there in May 2001, Justin had met David Tyson, who had been shuttling visitors from a hotel to the embassy. Justin had chatted with the friendly American driving the Land Cruiser, unaware that he was a CIA officer. David was helping oversee the training of elite Spetsnaz commando units that could be used in a mission to kill bin Laden. During ODA 522's time in Uzbekistan, five Uzbek soldiers had been killed by a mine, and the unit they were training had been called away to deal with an IMU border incursion from Afghanistan.

As a college student at VMI in 1992, Justin Sapp had interned at the CIA—a customary opportunity for the children of Agency officers, and often a first step toward a career as a spy. He had been assigned to the Office of Leadership Analysis, part of the Agency's Directorate of Intelligence. While Justin filed news clippings from South Asian periodicals, he was able to eavesdrop on the Central Asia analysts a cubicle away. They were preoccupied with the actions of Dostum, who had just turned against Najibullah.

Justin had been fascinated by the discussion of Dostum's treachery and the speculation about his next move. Dostum was then at the height of his power, commanding three infantry divisions and one armored brigade; he had 200 T-55 and T-62 tanks at his disposal, as well as 60

MiG-21 fighters and Su-22 fighter-bombers. Despite the subject matter they were debating, Justin had viewed the analysts as far removed from the action. Eager for what he considered real adventure, he redoubled his determination to join the Army. Years later in Uzbekistan, Justin had wanted to see Afghanistan for himself. During his stint with ODA 522, he had tried to visit the Friendship Bridge at Termez, which connected the former Soviet republic with Afghanistan and was the route for the last departing Russian troops in February 1989. The bridge was a controlled military zone, however, and Justin was told that going there was impossible.

At the end of the diving course, Justin was due to report back to the 5th Special Forces Group at Fort Campbell, a sprawling base sixty miles northwest of Nashville that straddled the border between Tennessee and Kentucky. There, he had already been identified as a bright prospect by Colonel John Mulholland, who had arrived as the new 5th Group commander in July. Mulholland, an imposing six feet five with a booming voice, had come from Delta Force, the Army's secret "special mission unit," and had already stamped his outsize personality on the 5th Group. He was disappointed by the state of readiness he had inherited and concerned that Special Forces had been starved of resources for two decades at the expense of Delta Force and the 160th Special Operations Aviation Regiment, the "Night Stalkers" helicopter unit that supported Special Forces. Mulholland also worried about the lack of plans for operations beyond the Middle East but within the 5th Group's area of responsibility. Afghanistan had been ignored in favor of a focus on the threat from countries such as Iraq. The primary responsibility of Justin's ODA 522 had been to build an underground resistance in Kuwait should Saddam Hussein's Iraq invade again. One thing that did satisfy Mulholland, however, was the quality of the officers and NCOs serving in the 5th Group's ODAs.

All this was a world away from Justin's thoughts as he and his dive partner approached the shore of Fleming Key. His entire focus was on the compass he held in front of him; he was oblivious to everything above the waves.

It was 8:44 a.m. and Flight 11, with Egyptian hijacker Mohammed Atta now at the controls, was approaching Manhattan from the north. Amy Sweeney, a flight attendant, had reached an American Airlines manager in Boston by phone and told him the plane had been taken over by Middle Easterners who had slashed the throat of a first-class passenger, stabbed two cabin staff, and stormed the cockpit. They had sprayed Mace and claimed they had a bomb. "Something is wrong," Sweeney said. "We are in a rapid descent…We are all over the place."

*　　*　　*

8:44 a.m. (GMT -4), September 11, 2001;
Giant Food supermarket, Manassas, Virginia

This was not the life that Shannon Spann had expected when she joined the CIA. Holding her three-month-old baby, Jake, with one hand and steering a grocery cart with the other, she had just dropped her step-daughters off: Alison, nine, at Manassas Elementary School, and Emily, four, at preschool. Now she was cruising the aisles of this suburban Virginia supermarket to gather the ingredients for a calzone dinner. Though Shannon had been assessed at the end of her training at The Farm nine months earlier as a CIA officer of high potential, her career was currently on hold.

Slim, pale, and with straight, center-parted black hair framing an angular face, Shannon cut a striking figure. There was a grace and poise about the thirty-two-year-old, even as she had to cope with a baby and two new stepchildren. Shannon was attached to the Agency's CTC, where she'd been assigned at the start of the year after The Farm. Since June 1999, everything in her life had changed. She had met her husband, Mike Spann—a former Marine Corps officer now working as assistant to the chief of the Ground Branch within the Agency's paramilitary

Special Activities Division (SAD). An unexpected pregnancy meant that they had added Jake to their newly blended family. Now, Shannon was on maternity leave.

Mike's then-wife, Kathryn, had delayed their divorce during a bitter custody battle. That meant he had not been able to marry Shannon until the day after Jake was born. The ceremony took place in their townhouse on Lanae Lane in Manassas Park two hours after the couple and their baby arrived home from the hospital. The only witnesses present had been the civil officiant and the three children. Just after the Fourth of July holiday, barely a month after Jake's birth, Mike had been sent to the Balkans on a two-month assignment. He had returned three days earlier, September 8, and was now scheduled to be at home until after Christmas.

At last, life was looking a little clearer for the Spanns. Mike and Shannon had discussed with CIA managers dual postings to Islamabad station. Pakistan, with its support for the Taliban and Al-Qaeda despite its status as a US ally, would be a professional challenge. Islamabad station was considered suitable for officers to be accompanied by families, and there was an American school there for the girls.

Shannon had noticed Mike almost immediately among the several dozen fellow students at The Farm. Both were thirty, born three months apart in 1969, yet on the surface almost entirely different. He was from Alabama and was one of the former military students who made up about 20 percent of the class. She was a civilian, a lawyer from California. He was known as "Silent Mike," a man of intense focus with a serious, almost forbidding mien. She was more outgoing and appeared more carefree. But each had a failed marriage behind them and both were Christian and staunchly conservative. When he was growing up, Mike's Christianity had been cultural and instinctive, while Shannon's was more a matter of doctrine and study. As he got older, however, Mike's faith had deepened. At The Farm, he would slip away to church services in Williamsburg each Sunday—something virtually no other student, including Shannon, made it a priority to do.

Mike was from a prominent family in the Appalachian foothill town of Winfield, which had four stoplights and 4,548 inhabitants. Originally named Needmore, Winfield lacked a movie theater and was in a county where the sale of alcohol had been banned since Prohibition. Mike's father, Johnny, was a real estate agent and developer with an office on Winfield's main street, and his mother, Gail, was a homemaker. Their son was christened Johnny Micheal Spann, the middle name spelled the Irish way in a nod to his mother's ancestry. Mike had two sisters: Tonya, three years younger, and Tammy, six years younger. A solid student but no standout, Mike had lifted weights to bulk up his frame and had become a wide receiver and running back on the Winfield High School football team, playing without apparent fear. He attended Sunday school at the Church of Christ, fished for bass, got in trouble when he shot a cow with a .22 rifle after mistaking it for a deer, and charmed his teachers, who saw in him the archetype of the all-American boy.

During a flying lesson—he went on to gain his pilot's license at age twenty—Mike buzzed his friends on the football team, who whooped and waved. When he graduated in the Class of '87, he was one of only six seniors who selected a Bible verse as his philosophy of life. He chose Proverbs 13:20: "He that walketh with wise men shall be wise; but a companion of fools shall be destroyed." Always intent on a career in law enforcement or the military, Mike had gone on to study criminal justice at Auburn University, where he drove a pickup truck and lived in a trailer to save money. In his senior year, Tonya, who was also studying at Auburn, had telephoned home to grumble about her overprotective brother: "Mother, you've got to do something about him." she said. "I had a date, and Mike was waiting outside the door for my boyfriend."

At twenty-two, Mike had married Kathryn Webb, known in his family as Cissy, from Winfield's neighboring town of Guin. They had met during one of Mike's trips home during college. She was twenty on their wedding day, and their first daughter, Alison, was born seven months later. Mike had then joined the Marines as an artillery officer and trained as a parachutist and diver. During his eight years in the

Marines, he and his young family were stationed in Okinawa, Japan, and at Camp Lejeune in North Carolina. Kathryn had been pregnant with Emily, born in 1997, when she discovered she had ovarian cancer. Mike had been away on Marine Corps duty for eight months of that pregnancy, and by the time they had moved to Virginia for him to join the CIA, the marriage, always troubled, was unraveling. They separated in April 2000 after Mike discovered a love letter that Kathryn had written to a fellow worker at the local post office. Making matters even more complicated, Kathryn's cancer had returned a year after the separation, and she was now undergoing chemotherapy. A court hearing over custody, set to conclude on September 11, 2001, had been postponed because of her treatment.

Shannon Spann, neé Joy, had grown up in Tustin, a former California farm town swallowed by the suburban sprawl of Orange County. She was the middle of three daughters and her father was a mechanical engineer who had worked on the space program for McDonnell Douglas. The race to beat the Soviets to the moon was part of her family's ethos of the primacy of American values in the world. Tustin was conservative and patriotic, its leading lights well-educated but not elitist. Shannon had grown up in a close-knit family, attending church and studying hard at Tustin High School. There she was in the pep squad, elected to a seat in the student senate, and chosen Queen of the Winter Formal. Shannon then studied English and American Studies at UCLA.

While still an undergraduate, she had become Shannon Verleur when she married a man from a prominent local family, who was four years her senior and had been her boyfriend since high school. Next she studied at Trinity Law School, a small Christian college in Orange County, passing the bar in 1995 at age twenty-six. Scarcely a year later Shannon found herself the dean of Trinity Law, then preparing to merge with the evangelical Trinity International University. Driven but somewhat sheltered, she had been on the board of a Bible-translation foundation. Her well-ordered life, however, had become unglued. Her marriage had foundered, and there was a sense of something missing in her life. Restless, and mortified by her divorce, she was eager to escape California.

Flicking through the pages of *The Economist* one day, Shannon's eye had been caught by an advertisement: "Do you have what it takes?" A photograph of a young professional woman with a confident smile had five attributes superimposed: *Integrity, Intellect, Common Sense, Patriotism, Courage.* The ad went on to explain: "You will need to deal with fast-moving, ambiguous, and unstructured situations that will test your resourcefulness to the utmost. This is the Clandestine Service of the CIA."

Overt advertising was a new strategy for the CIA, whose strength had shrunk from more than 20,000 employees to 16,000 after the end of the Cold War. It had traditionally sought out recruits individually, just as David Tyson had been approached several years earlier. After applying on a whim, and undergoing a raft of interviews, Shannon was accepted. She broke her lease—telling the university she was bound for a State Department career—and in June 1999 reported to CIA headquarters in Langley, Virginia, seven miles up the Potomac River from Washington, DC.

Upon her arrival, Shannon, along with Mike and their fellow recruits, was guided into the CIA lobby, crossing the Agency's seal, set in granite in the floor. The students were then shown the Memorial Wall, to the right of the lobby. It was a somber sight for every recruit, bringing home the reality that their career could end by paying the ultimate price. Carved into the white Alabama marble were seventy-eight stars, each marking the death of a CIA officer in the line of duty. The 77th and 78th stars were for Agency officers killed in the Al-Qaeda bombing of the US Embassy in Nairobi in 1998.

At The Farm, Shannon had found herself drawn to "Silent Mike," who exuded strength and applied a laser focus to everything he did. Other students had found it difficult to get past his outward demeanor as a driven and opinionated Southerner. Art Keller, a former Army officer with a degree in international affairs who had studied in Russia and Germany, had been paired with Mike throughout the course and found they disagreed on almost everything. "He was conservative and very black-and-white," Keller later recalled. "He wasn't traditional case-officer material. Case officers live in a world of nuance and gray." During a lecture about the care and nurturing of agents, Keller said, Mike had asked, in essence: "Why won't these fuckers just do what we tell them?" This was, Keller felt, the result of Mike's experience in the Marines, working in a high-caliber military unit in which everyone was held to high standards with a minimum of supervision. The only time Keller had managed to get a smile from Mike was when a classmate had made a mistake and Keller, referring to the police patrol work that Mike had done during his criminal justice course, said: "Mike, I bet it's just like the good old days when you put on your mirrored shades, walked up to someone you just pulled over and be like, 'You just done fucked up, son.'"

Classmates at The Farm also noticed a shadow hanging over Mike that seemed to stem from his divorce. He said little about it but let slip to Keller that Kathryn was trying to use his new career against him in their child custody case, claiming he was a CIA assassin. Mike displayed a burning intensity at times. In one exercise in which a Farm instructor played a CIA asset being recruited, marks were deducted because the instructor felt that Mike had been about to reach across the table and throttle him.

There was more to Mike, however, than the monochromatic front he often presented. Soon, one of his closest friends on the course was Amy, a Californian who had run a nightclub in Southeast Asia before taking a master's degree in public policy. The military aspects of the course were anathema to Amy, but Mike quietly helped her—without ever revealing that he had done so. Mike was trying to figure out how he could work for the CIA and look after his daughters. Divorce and single fatherhood hadn't been part of the life he had expected. Amy, who had backpacked and lived with tribes in Africa, was not from his world, so he opened up to her. One evening Amy asked him, "Are you ever going to date?" Mike confessed that he was attracted to Shannon, citing her polish and sophistication. Amy laughed. "Dude, she's so out of your league," she told him. "There's no way. Mike, she's a lawyer, she's from California. I just don't see that happening."

But Shannon was attracted to qualities in Mike Spann that might not have been readily apparent to others. Beneath the seriousness and the pain of his divorce was a wry, quirky sense of humor and humility, even vulnerability. Shannon and Mike, along with Amy, had become part of a small group determined to enjoy the residential course despite its all-consuming relentlessness.

Shannon found herself wanting to impress Mike. He had gently mocked the "civilians" in the class, so when the trainees were required to take the Army Fitness Test in preparation for parachute jumping, she became determined to achieve 100 percent. When she did, he took note.

Mike was a practical joker, and Shannon had let it slip that she was afraid of insects. The students had been split into two barracks. Mike and Amy hatched an elaborate plan for a prank on their rivals, who included Shannon. They ordered 10,000 live crickets from a farm store, and then arranged for another student to collect the insects and hide them under a pile of leaves in a forest. The pair sneaked out of class, jumped on bicycles, and rode into the forest to retrieve the crickets.

As they were speeding back, dressed in camouflage gear and laughing at the ridiculousness of it all, Amy called out, "You know we might get kicked out for this?" Mike shouted back, "I don't care, Amy. It was totally fucking worth it." When Shannon opened her room to find it swarming with crickets, she managed to suppress her panic, which prompted further admiration from Mike.

Dating, however, did not interest Shannon. Her plan was to move overseas and avoid entanglements. She had told herself that she did not need people—that she should be alone and celibate. When Mike asked if she'd like to go for a movie or dinner sometime, she had refused, adding, "I hope I haven't ruined our chance to be friends, because I enjoy spending time with you." That, Mike later said, was "like twisting the knife."

Shannon wanted to keep things professional and casual between them. Soon, however, she realized she was falling in love, and feared she had blown her chance. Several weeks after the rebuff, Mike asked Shannon to lunch at an Indian restaurant in Williamsburg. Assuming it was a group meal, she arrived to discover it was just the two of them. After that they were a couple—under the radar at first, then more openly. The Farm was a fishbowl of CIA officers being trained in surveillance and situational awareness, so subterfuge would probably have been futile.

Right away, the relationship turned serious. Neither was interested in a fling. Almost immediately, they began talking about how to merge their lives. About two months before the end of the course, Shannon learned she was pregnant. Amy watched Shannon dealing with the news with an almost serene acceptance and a determination to press forward and make everything work. Amy had concluded that Mike and Shannon, despite their obvious differences, were ultimately two sides of the same coin. Each felt lucky that the other was offering them a second shot at life. When Art Keller realized that Mike and Shannon were a couple, he began to wonder if he'd misjudged the former Marine—there must be a lot more to him than the Southern gunslinger stereotype if he had managed to win Shannon.

It would take time for Shannon to bond with Mike's family in Winfield. As a lawyer from California who took her tea hot and unsweetened, she felt like an alien in Alabama. Her appearance on the scene, the swift pregnancy, had been like a record scratch for Mike's parents, who had yet to take down their photographs of Kathryn.

The person at The Farm who Mike had known the longest was Brian, who had served with him as a Marine officer in Okinawa and Camp Lejeune. Both had been specialist fire support officers in the Air Naval Gunfire Liaison Company (ANGLICO). Brian knew that Mike wanted to strive for more than the Marines could offer. Though he loved the

Marines, Mike had not been interested in staff jobs or training billets. Brian also knew Mike had earned the respect of enlisted Marines— not an easy feat for a young lieutenant—because there was no bluster or self-aggrandizement about him. Mike was thinking beyond military tactics and considering strategic questions. Although both he and Brian were paramilitary officers, they shared an ambition to become case officers, learn languages, and do much more than just fight.

Mike had a keen sense that Al-Qaeda was a growing threat. In early 2001, he was on a training course with Brian when the subject of the USS *Cole* bombing came up. "What would we be doing right now as a country if the *Cole* had snapped in half and gone to the bottom of the Gulf of Aden?" Mike asked. "Would we be on a training course?" The crew of the *Cole* had battled valiantly to save their ship. Mike suspected that their success in doing so had let the politicians off the hook. But it would be only a brief respite. Mike learned more about the Al-Qaeda threat during a temporary assignment to Uzbekistan, where he met David Tyson, who was struck by his seriousness and intensity. Mike helped train commandos that he hoped might one day be the CIA's partners in hunting down Osama bin Laden.

Shannon's maternity leave would soon be over, and she would return to the CIA to begin her career as a spy in earnest. A family and professional adventure in Pakistan beckoned. She had already achieved a lot of the things she had planned for in her life. But perhaps, she reflected as she headed for the Giant Food checkout line, the best things were the ones that weren't planned. It was around 8:46 a.m. by the time she reached the cashier.

"Oh my God, we are way too low," Amy Sweeney, the flight attendant onboard Flight 11 had just told the Boston manager. Those were her last words as the plane plunged into the North Tower of the World Trade Center in New York between floors 93 and 99.

*   *   *

At the checkout, the clerks were chatting about an accident in New York. They'd heard that an aircraft had flown into the World Trade Center. "Gosh, that's terrible," Shannon thought. "It must have been an accident." As she drove the three or four minutes to get home, she heard on the radio that it was a small private plane. But Shannon knew that early reports were often wrong; she had been trained to be skeptical.

When she turned on the television at home and saw the startling gash in the north face of the World Trade Center's North Tower, she felt certain it was an airliner.

At 9 a.m., on board United Airlines Flight 175, heading from Boston to Los Angeles, Peter Hanson, a passenger, called his father to tell him that hijackers armed with knives and Mace had taken over the plane, and that he thought they intended to fly it into a building. "Don't worry, Dad," he said. "If it happens, it'll be very fast—my God, my God." As the call ended abruptly, his father heard a woman scream.

Shannon watched as Flight 175 punctured the south face of the World Trade Center's South Tower between floors 77 and 85 at 9:03 a.m. She knew immediately that this was a coordinated terrorist attack—and that the only group with both the intent and the capability to pull it off was Osama bin Laden's Al-Qaeda. Inside CIA headquarters, Mike, at his desk in the Special Activities Division, had reached the same conclusion. The couple spoke briefly on the phone to check that each other was safe—a conversation between not just a wife and husband but also two counterterrorism officers who grasped the magnitude of a 21st-century Pearl Harbor.

At 9:16 a.m., Barbara Olson, a conservative commentator and wife of Theodore Olson, the Bush administration's solicitor general, called her husband from American Airlines Flight 77, telling him it had been hijacked. When he warned her that two planes had been flown into the World Trade Center, she asked him: "What can I tell the pilot? What can I do? How do I stop this?" She had delayed her flight to Los Angeles for a day because September 11 was her husband's birthday. At

9:37 a.m., Flight 77 slammed into the western side of the Pentagon, nine miles east along the Potomac River from CIA headquarters.

At 9:55 a.m., passengers aboard United Airlines Flight 93 banded together to storm the cockpit and wrest control of the plane from the hijackers; Todd Beamer was heard by a ground operator saying, "Are you guys ready? Let's roll." They were the first Americans to fight back against Al-Qaeda, their lives ending in a field in Pennsylvania.

*   *   *

Within CTC, there was a fear that the CIA would be next. Analysts remembered that Ramzi Yousef, the mastermind of the 1993 World Trade Center bombing, had been part of a plot to fly an explosives-laden plane into CIA headquarters. At 10 a.m., the word EVACUATE flashed in red on every computer screen in the building. Mike, already enraged by the mass murder he had just witnessed, was now fuming that he was being ordered to desert his post. "Why are we leaving when we can stay and do something?" he asked colleagues. At 10:03 a.m., Flight 93, the fourth and last hijacked plane in the air, crashed in Shanksville, southeast of Pittsburgh. The hijackers had sent it into a dive as Beamer and the other passengers were about to breach the cockpit door. Al-Qaeda's plan had been to fly the plane into the White House or the US Capitol in Washington. "This is so stupid," Mike vented to Shannon on the phone. "We're the CIA. We're not supposed to go home."

Only CIA personnel deemed "essential" that day were to remain on duty. Mike did not view himself as surplus to requirements. There may have been little for him to do immediately, but he knew that would soon change. The Special Activities Division's motto was TERTIA OPTIO, or "Third Option." a reference to covert action as a third option after diplomacy and military force. The first thing Mike said when he walked through the door at Lanae Lane an hour later was "It's war."

In her fourth-grade classroom at Manassas Park Elementary School,

Alison Spann was confused as to why children were being sent home. By recess, she knew something was wrong because she was one of only three pupils left. No explanation was given for fear of upsetting the children, many of whose parents had jobs at the Pentagon or in other government facilities. Alison had been told that her father worked at the State Department, his official cover. CIA officers were advised not to tell young children of their true affiliation in case of playground chatter.

Eventually, Alison caught the school bus home and was greeted at the bus stop by a friend, who told her excitedly, "Someone flew a plane into the Empire State Building!" Alison was taken aback when her father answered the door at home—he was never there before 6 p.m. When she blurted out that the Empire State Building had been attacked, Mike told his daughter that she was mistaken, and he would explain.

They watched footage of the attacks together before sitting down to eat the calzones Shannon had shopped for that morning. Mike explained that bad men known as terrorists had flown planes into buildings in New York and the Pentagon while another aircraft had crashed in rural Pennsylvania after brave passengers had fought back. Soon, he told Alison, other Americans would be sent to find the terrorists who had carried out the attacks and stop them from striking again.

* * *

9:10 a.m. (GMT -4), September 11, 2001;
Trumbo Point, Fleming Key, Florida

Justin Sapp and his dive partner had been in the water for around seventy minutes when they reached the shore of Fleming Key. They emerged just twenty yards from the red marker they had been aiming for. The instructor logging the results for each pair gave them a thumbs-up as they walked up the beach to the freshwater station to wash out their Drägers. They were in high spirits. There would be classroom work for the rest of the morning, then afternoon and evening dives.

At the freshwater station, a dozen or so student divers were cleaning their rebreathing apparatus. The mood was light and there was banter about who had missed their marker by the farthest. As he rinsed his equipment, a laborious process, Justin heard two instructors talking about a terrorist attack. His mind flitted back to Osama bin Laden and Uzbekistan, which he had left in July. There, he had seen matchbooks produced by the State Department offering a $25 million FBI reward for information leading to the capture of the Al-Qaeda leader. The thought had barely formed when another instructor told him, "Hey, your girlfriend called." Justin thought: "That's strange. I never gave her the number of the school. Why would she be calling me on a Tuesday morning?" The instructor asked, "Haven't you heard about New York?"

The students were told to grab their kit and run up to the classroom; within minutes, a sergeant was pushing a cassette into the VHS player. The picture on the screen flickered, then came video footage of the second plane slamming into the World Trade Center. "Gentlemen, the nation is under attack," the sergeant told them. "We await our orders. In the interim, we're suspending training and your task is to guard the dive facility from further attack." Justin's mind raced. In the next few minutes, he learned that the Pentagon had also been hit and that a fourth plane had come down in Pennsylvania. Who knew when the next attack would come? Justin thanked his lucky stars that he was not already behind the company S4's desk at Fort Campbell. That meant he was available. Whatever happened, he vowed, he was going to be in this fight.

*　　*　　*

8:05 p.m. (GMT +1), September 11, 2001;
London Heathrow Terminal 2

David Tyson descended the steps of the airport bus that had taken him and his fellow passengers from the Uzbekistan Airways gate to the main terminal and immigration. After sleeping only fitfully on the flight, he felt a little groggy. It was just after 2 a.m. in Tashkent. In the United States, it was past 3 p.m., but there had been no announcements during his flight about the horrific events in New York, Washington, and Pennsylvania. When he got into the terminal, the waiting areas were unusually empty. All flights from Heathrow had been suspended. Crowded around televisions suspended from the ceilings, knots of people watched quietly as footage of the jets flying into the World Trade Center and occupants of the towers jumping to their deaths was played again and again.

While most Americans focused solely on the atrocities on the country's East Coast, David's mind glided to Afghanistan. At last, he reasoned, the CIA would be able to go after bin Laden. The two years of mounting frustration, pleading for resources, issuing warnings, begging for permission to help Massoud, pushing to meet with Dostum—all that was over.

David grapsed that the 9/11 attacks were a strategic gift to the Northern Alliance. Without Al-Qaeda's assault on America, the Taliban would have recaptured the Panjshir Valley and Afghanistan would have fallen. Now, the strategic landscape had been transformed. David had no doubt that American teams would be sent into the north of the country. He was the CIA's only Uzbek linguist, and one of a handful of officers with current Afghanistan experience. He would be going in. He called the CIA's London station. The embassy was locked down and the Stinger meeting had been canceled. He had to return to Tashkent as soon as possible.

4

SHOWTIME

6:15 a.m. (GMT -4), September 12, 2001;
9413 Lanae Lane, Manassas Park, Virginia

THERE WAS NEVER any question in Mike Spann's mind that he would be part of America's response to the Al-Qaeda attack on 9/11. He had left the Marines because the prospect of staff jobs and more training exercises failed to excite him. Mike was recently remarried with a baby son, and two daughters whose mother was gravely ill. No one would have criticized him if he had stayed behind. Shannon Spann briefly wondered whether it was right that he should go, before concluding that this was what her new husband had joined the CIA to do.

For Mike, the choice between country and family was a false one. By protecting his country, he was protecting his family. In his application to join the CIA, Mike had written: "I am an action person that feels personally responsible for making any changes in this world that are in my power because if I don't no one else will." Six months into his career at the Agency, Mike had emailed a dozen pieces of advice to a member of a church youth group he had taught. Among them were "Don't be a follower. Dread naught and NEVER quit" and "Spread the Christian and conservative message through your actions and deeds. ALWAYS do the right thing, in the end all you have is your character. Remember to always vote Republican."

At The Farm, Mike had expressed his views in Manichean terms. He was open about his conservatism and had little interest in engaging in political back-and-forth. Now, the country was experiencing a swelling patriotism, a yearning for vengeance, and an acknowledgment that there would be sacrifices. The self-indulgent complacency of the 1990s was over. There was evil in the world, and Americans had to be sent to faraway lands to stamp it out so it did not reach home shores again. Mike had always felt this way. Suddenly, America was a lot more like him. It was as if God had placed him on the earth for this moment.

In the higher echelons of the CIA, the man of the hour was Cofer Black, director of CTC and Shannon Spann's ultimate boss. Standing six three, with a slicked-back, receding hairline and a bulky, looming presence, the fifty-one-year-old reminded some colleagues of the actor Jack Nicholson. He was a legendary case officer from Africa Division who had reveled in working the streets of the world's hellholes. The pinnacle of his career thus far had been as Khartoum station chief in Sudan, a failing state that was a magnet to outlawed groups, which he referred to as a "superbowl of terrorism." In Khartoum he had overseen the tracking down of Carlos the Jackal, who had been ambushed by the French, bundled into a small plane, and flown to Paris for a trial. After Black's role in that operation was revealed, most likely by Sudanese sources, bin Laden targeted him for assassination or kidnapping, dispatching Al-Qaeda surveillance teams to plot his movements.

The son of a Pan Am pilot, Black had first visited sub-Saharan Africa as a young boy, being dropped off at airfields in Nigeria, Gambia, and Liberia and allowed to roam freely. Before boarding school in Connecticut, he had attended a preparatory school in Sunningdale, Berkshire, just outside of London. Vestiges of an English accent remained in his voice. Renowned for having the courage to take risks and for the vivid, portentous turns of phrase that he used to express hard truths, Black retained the swagger of his years in the field but now dressed formally and wore shirts with French cuffs. Many accomplished case officers felt out of their element in headquarters, but Black had mastered the politics—displaying, as one protégé noted, "a rare mix of prudence and fearlessness."

In the two years and three months he had been leading CTC, Black repeatedly warned the Clinton and Bush administrations that Al-Qaeda planned to attack America. That message had been amplified by Black's boss, George Tenet, the cigar-chomping CIA director whose route into the intelligence world had been as a senior aide on Capitol Hill. Tenet, who had never been a spy, was a backslapping master at maintaining relationships and navigating Washington, DC. Tenet was the only member of Bill Clinton's Cabinet who had been kept on by George W. Bush. Underneath Black was Rich Blee—the Alec station chief who was monitoring the bin Laden threat.

Black had concluded that the White House viewed the *Cole* attack as the cost of doing business; many more body bags would be required to prompt any action. Clinton later insisted that he had "tried to take Mr. Bin Laden out of the picture for the last four years-plus I was in office," claiming that the CIA had been given the authority it needed. But the CIA's legal advice had been that Black and his officers were authorized to capture bin Laden; only if a capture operation went wrong could he be killed. Otherwise, CIA officers could face felony charges for assassinating the Al-Qaeda leader. Black felt that a political trap had been laid for the Agency. "This is sometimes a corollary of service in the CIA," he observed later. "If it's successful, they [the White House] did it. If there's a problem, it's all you, baby." He insisted, therefore, that orders had to be written and signed.

In practical terms, little had changed under the George W. Bush administration. After eight years out of office, Republicans still viewed terrorism as little more than an irritant, which had been the consensus at the end of the George H. W. Bush administration in 1993. Vice President Dick Cheney and Defense Secretary Donald Rumsfeld were preoccupied with missile defense, nuclear treaties, and rivalries with China and Russia. They were stuck in a Cold War mindset.

Tenet later testified that by the summer of 2000 the threat-warning system was "blinking red." On July 10, 2001, in the face of overwhelming indications that an attack was imminent, Tenet, Black, and Blee were prompted to deliver an emergency briefing for National Security Adviser Condoleezza Rice at the White House that day. When Rice asked how best to respond to the threat, Black replied, banging his fist on the table, "This country's got to get on a war footing now!" The advice went unheeded.

On August 6, Bush's Presidential Daily Brief from the CIA carried the headline BIN LADEN DETERMINED TO STRIKE IN US and mentioned the possibility of Al-Qaeda hijacking planes. Nine days later, Black told a classified counterterrorism conference at the Pentagon, "We are going to be struck soon. Many Americans are going to die, and it could be in the US." Blee blurted out at a CIA meeting chaired by Tenet, "They're coming here. They're coming to America."

When the attack came on 9/11, Black was bracing for it. In an odd coincidence, Captain Kirk Lippold, commanding officer of the USS *Cole,* had been visiting Black in his CTC office when the second plane hit the World Trade Center. "So, this has been really interesting, but I've got to cut it short," Black told Lippold. "We have to go to war now." The CDC chief delivered a stirring address to his staff while standing on the desk of his secretary. He had already thought through what needed to be said when America's darkest day came.

Though much of the Washington area was in a state of catatonic shock, Black was psychologically prepared. When Tenet decided that the CIA should be evacuated, Black pushed back, urging that CTC personnel remain at their posts—and if that meant they would die, so be it. As far as Black was concerned, CTC officers were now America's first line of defense; it was inconceivable that they would retreat while the country was under attack.

When Black was summoned to the seventh floor, where Tenet and his top lieutenants had their offices, the scene reminded him of the Tokyo subway system, as people scurried to cram themselves into the director's suite. Black knew that only CTC could lead the fight against

Al-Qaeda. As he walked in, the throng parted and he took his place in the sole empty chair, directly across the conference table from Tenet. "Guess what?" Black told himself. "It's showtime."

* * *

The Jawbreaker and NALT missions into the Panjshir Valley from 1999 onward, coupled with the two-year process of trying to get the legal authorities to kill bin Laden, meant that Black had a plan for Afghanistan in place. The CIA had laid it out in its "Blue Sky" document less than a year earlier.

At 9:30 a.m. on September 13, President Bush convened his National Security Council (NSC) in the White House Situation Room. The NSC had met several times over the two days since the attacks, but this would be the first discussion of the details of America's response. After Tenet described the contours of the CIA plan, Black was given the floor to explain exactly how Agency teams and US Special Forces could take down the Taliban and expel Al-Qaeda from Afghanistan. Roughly 20,000 fighters from the Northern Alliance, drawn principally from four rival ethnic groups—Tajiks, Hazaras, Uzbeks, and Turkmens—would do most of the fighting. In support would be CIA teams of about eight men with a mix of paramilitary, regional, and linguistic expertise; these would act as pathfinders for the Green Berets.

Black had a penchant for theatrics, and he saw this as a moment of high drama—a chance to propel the CIA into the forefront of the fight. He felt the presentation was, as he put it later, "the whole ballgame." Black warned: "Many Americans could die." Bush responded, "That's war." Al-Qaeda fighters would blow themselves up rather than surrender or negotiate, Black said. He recounted what Massoud had told him in Tajikistan: "We've been fighting these guys for four years and I've never captured one of these bastards." So the aim, Black told the president, should be to kill: "When we're through with them, they will have flies walking across their eyeballs."

Black was not certain how Bush—an untested president with scant foreign-policy experience—would react, though he had judged that Bush was inclined toward swift, decisive action rather than the Pentagon approach of a slow, deliberate buildup and overwhelming force. When Black finished, Bush asked him how long it would take for the Taliban regime to fall. "Once we're fully deployed on the ground, it should go in weeks," he replied. There was silence in the room. Even Tenet thought the timeline ambitious. Bush stared, unblinking, at the wall at the far end of the Situation Room for more than ten seconds, perhaps fifteen. It seemed like a lifetime to Black, who began to wonder if he had overdone it. Then Bush turned to him and asked, his voice laced with incredulity, "Cofer, can you really do this?"

Black thought to himself, "The President needs to know that this is not another PowerPoint presentation with no connection to reality." The CTC chief realized this was no time to hedge or add caveats. Leaning forward with his elbows on the table, Black looked Bush in the eye and paused for several seconds before answering, "Mr. President, there isn't a doubt in my mind." That was enough for Bush, who told the room in his Texas drawl, "That's what I'm talking about. Go get 'em."

The next day, Congress authorized Bush to use "all necessary and appropriate force" against the perpetrators of the 9/11 attacks and those who harbored them; 518 members voted in favor, with Representative Barbara Lee, a Democrat from California, the lone dissenter. That morning, Bush had vowed in a national prayer service to "rid the world of evildoers in this crusade, this war on terrorism." Hours later, he used a bullhorn to tell rescue workers at the World Trade Center site, "I can hear you, the rest of the world hears you, and the people who knocked these buildings down will hear all of us soon." In the meantime, the FBI released the names of the 9/11 hijackers. It later emerged that Mohammed Atta had met with Osama bin Laden in Afghanistan, and that all nineteen hijackers had been to the country.

On the morning of September 15, a Saturday, the Afghanistan war plan was finalized at Camp David, the presidential retreat in Maryland. Tenet delivered his brief, stressing that Americans would be insurgents rather than invaders, helping Afghans rid their country of the foreign occupiers of Al-Qaeda. Cofer Black, who was there as Tenet's backup and knew his pitch had already been accepted by Bush, surreptitiously rolled a tennis ball for Barney, the president's Scottish terrier. When Tenet finished, Rumsfeld suggested that if the new War on Terror was going to be global, military action against Iraq should be considered. Rumsfeld's deputy, Paul Wolfowitz, chipped in that Saddam Hussein could well have been involved in 9/11, and that perhaps it was time to "cut the head off the snake" by attacking Iraq.

Black's brain was screaming. "I can't believe what I'm hearing," he thought. The CTC director felt he could not remain silent. He raised his hand and said, "Mr. President, we were attacked on September 11 by Osama bin Laden and Al-Qaeda in Afghanistan. Saddam Hussein and Iraq have nothing whatsoever to do with this." Bush told everyone to move on, and it seemed that the notion of going after Iraq had been dismissed.

Black's dramatic "flies walking across their eyeballs" phrase was something he had picked up when he was in Kinshasa, the capital of Zaire, supporting anti-communist forces during the civil war in neighboring Angola. Black had spent his career assessing people and calculating how to persuade them to side with him; he had read the president correctly. Colin Powell later reflected on the impact Black's September 13 presentation had on Bush: the president wanted to kill somebody. Black had ensured that the CIA and not the Pentagon would run the war. He had also made it a fait accompli that CTC, champions of the Northern Alliance, the only Afghan group that had been fighting the Taliban and Al-Qaeda all along, would be in the lead. NE Division and its Islamabad station, with their leanings toward the Pashtuns and Pakistan, had been sidelined. Now, Black concluded, the CIA would be given the authority to do what it did best: go where no one else could go, and do what no one else would do, alongside allies no one else was prepared to work with. These allies would be the Northern Alliance, including the Uzbek warlord Dostum.

With Tajiks, Hazaras, and Uzbeks making up 50 percent of the Afghan population—Pashtuns were 38 percent—the Northern Alliance represented a majority. The Pashtun south was a much tougher proposition than the north because no one there was fighting the Taliban. Hamid Karzai—who had met with CIA officers, including David Tyson, before 9/11—and Abdul Haq were both promising prospective allies. But they were exiles, with no known following inside the country. There was no Southern Alliance in Afghanistan.

The US military had been caught flat-footed. The Pentagon, which had plans for almost every conceivable contingency, lacked an Afghanistan war plan. General Tommy Franks, the head of US Central Command, or CENTCOM—which covered Afghanistan—had already told Rumsfeld that it would take months to prepare conventional ground troops for an invasion. Rumsfeld later remarked acidly that the "shock of 9/11 had not provoked much originality or imagination" from his military staff. A month after 9/11, Rumsfeld chastised his generals: "I am seeing nothing that is thoughtful, creative or actionable. How can that be?" The Pentagon was at least eight times as big as the CIA and its business was war, yet the Agency was in charge.

Though seething, Rumsfeld had little choice but to embrace the CIA's initial concept of using Special Forces. From the CIA's point of view, Rumsfeld would see to it that the Pentagon would drag its feet until he was officially in charge.

* * *

On a remote mountainside some seventy miles south of Mazar-i Sharif, General Abdul Rashid Dostum discussed the implications of 9/11 with his commanders. Now, he promised them, the Americans would come. Afghanistan would be the venue for a war between the United States and Al-Qaeda. The United States had no interest in the

Taliban, but they wanted to avenge 9/11 by killing bin Laden and crushing Al-Qaeda. To do that, the Taliban had to be defeated. And to remove the Taliban, the United States would need the Northern Alliance—and Dostum. He was not an educated man, but Dostum understood power and vengeance. He knew the United States would choose him even before the Americans themselves were certain they would.

Although the Tajiks had a foothold in the Panjshir Valley, north of Kabul, Dostum saw that Mazar-i Sharif could be the key to toppling the Taliban government. The Taliban had held the city for only three years; its Pashtun forces were loathed by the Uzbeks, Tajiks, and Hazaras who made up the majority there. Mazar-i Sharif was a holy city, site of the Shrine of Hazrat Ali, the cousin and son-in-law of the Prophet Mohammed. Ali, the fourth caliph of Islam, was reputedly buried there. Forty miles south of the border with the former Soviet Union, the city held the key to northern Afghanistan.

Capturing Mazar-i Sharif would mean controlling six surrounding provinces—a huge swath of territory—and opening a land bridge to Uzbekistan, from where the US could drive in supplies and equipment. It had two airfields and was strategically placed on National Highway 01, the ring road linked to Kabul and Kandahar. Losing Mazar-i Sharif would also be a major psychological blow to the mullahs.

Dostum had been in northern Afghanistan for four months uniting Uzbeks and Turkmens against the Taliban. Alongside him were the Hazaras—their leaders Mohammed Mohaqeq and Karim Khalili had been lobbying for outside support and had aligned themselves with Dostum within the Northern Alliance. Along the Darya Suf, or River of Caves, Dostum had been moving among scattered bands of dozens of his men. A British officer had noted in 1893 that the terrain "lends itself in a marked manner to guerrilla warfare."

Barely forty-eight hours before the 9/11 attacks, Dostum had been contemplating the fall of Afghanistan to the Taliban—and even his own death. He had been told by his Tajik allies that Massoud had been wounded and was being treated in Dushanbe. But he quizzed them about the suicide attack mounted by the Arab journalists: was it inside or outside? Informed that the blast had occurred in Massoud's reception room, Dostum turned to his security commander, Abdul Sattar, shaking his head. Dostum and Massoud had fought against each other as rivals for power in the north, but the oppression of the Taliban had bound them together. They had come to need one another, and now Massoud was gone.

Low on ammunition and leading a depleted force of no more than 200 Uzbeks fighting on horseback against a Taliban equipped with jets and rocket launchers, Dostum was in retreat. He handed Sattar a fistful of bullets and told him what he must do when they were overrun by the Taliban: "I want you to shoot me in the head and then use the next bullet for yourself," he instructed. "I will turn away, so you do not have to look into my eyes."

In his 2000 book on the Taliban, the Pakistani author Ahmed Rashid had claimed that during a visit to Dostum's headquarters at Qala-i Jangi—"the Fort of War"—he had seen gore on the ground of the 19th-century citadel. He had been told that "a man had been tied to the tracks of a Russian-made tank, which then drove around the courtyard crushing his body to mincemeat, as the garrison and Dostum watched." Rashid had added that the Uzbeks were "noted for their love of marauding and pillaging" and had painted Dostum as "a bear of a man with a gruff laugh, which, some Uzbeks swear, has on occasion frightened people to death." In demand by everyone preparing for war in Afghanistan, Rashid's book was selling out in Washington, DC. The evocative tale of the tank execution was already being retold and embellished. It would be forever tied to Dostum.

Before 9/11, opinion on Dostum within the CIA had been mixed at best. David Tyson had been lobbying to be allowed to meet with the Uzbek warlord, but the Agency had not yet authorized any of its officers to do so. The pre-9/11 intelligence reports from Tashkent station, however, had helped establish the case for Dostum's value to the United

States. David, now back in Tashkent after returning from his canceled meeting in London, was about to be given the green light.

During the Situation Room meeting, Bush had asked Cofer Black about the Northern Alliance leaders. Massoud's assassination had left a vacuum, Black explained, and intensified rivalries between leaders for whom shifting alliances were a way of life. Not wanting to sugarcoat things, Black cited Dostum as the most notoriously fickle of the leaders, relating how the Uzbek warlord had fought for the Soviets, and then joined with Massoud before turning against him. At various junctures Dostum had taken money from Russia, Iran, Turkey, India, and the CIA—sometimes simultaneously. But Black was not looking for choirboys. If Dostum had the will and the capability to take the fight to the Taliban and seize territory, that was good enough for him.

Dostum did have one American friend: Charlie Santos, whose interest in Afghanistan had first been piqued in the mid-1980s as a graduate student working part-time for the National Automobile Dealers Insurance Trust in Washington, DC. One of his fellow clerks in that humdrum office had been governor of Zabul province before fleeing when the communists took over in 1978. The Afghan was more than three decades older than Santos, but the pair became fast friends. Soon Santos was meeting almost every major Afghan figure who wasn't in the government or the mujahideen.

By the 1990s Santos was in and out of Afghanistan, working for the United Nations at a time when the United States had all but lost interest in the country. He first met Dostum in 1993. He grew to admire the Uzbek leader and to believe strongly in a decentralized Afghanistan in which the minority ethnic groups ran their own affairs. Santos went on to work on behalf of Unocal, a Houston-based energy corporation that from 1995 to 1998 sought to build a trans-Afghan oil and gas pipeline from Turkmenistan to Pakistan, which involved wooing the Taliban as well as the Uzbeks in the north. Now in his midthirties, Santos was a balding, garrulous adventurer who loved Afghanistan and was unconstrained by the rules that kept CIA officers from ranging freely and courting danger. Maybe it had something to do with Massoud's people accepting a $1 million payment from Unocal's Argentine rival, but Santos was intensely skeptical of the Tajiks in the Panjshir. In 1996 he had arranged for Dostum and other Afghan leaders to visit Washington, New York, and Texas—the only time the warlord had been to the United States.

On September 12, Dostum had called his friend Santos, who had been in Manhattan on 9/11, on his satellite phone from the Darya Suf Valley. Dostum had a message for the US government: he told Santos that he and the United States shared a common enemy, and that he had "the means for the Americans to achieve their vengeance on the Al-Qaeda slaughterers of both our people's women and children." He asked for American support to mount an offensive from the Darya Suf Valley north into Mazar-i Sharif, stating that seizing the city would be a fatal blow to the Taliban. Santos relayed the message to a contact at the Pentagon. The next day, two Defense Intelligence Agency officers knocked on his apartment door. Two days later Santos was flown to Tampa to advise CENTCOM, juggling phone calls with Dostum, Mohaqeq, and Khalili. There, it became apparent that the US military feared that Dostum would turn on American troops. "Look, he's not going to kill your guys," Santos reassured senior officers.

The first CIA team, Jawbreaker, would go into the Panjshir because that was the place the Agency knew best—and the Tajiks, even without Massoud, were then viewed as the key to victory in the north. The Tajiks, moreover, controlled territory that was denied to the Taliban while Dostum and isolated Hazara commanders were operating behind enemy lines. Black selected Gary Schroen, a veteran NE Division officer and former Islamabad station chief who had been dealing with Afghanistan since the 1980s, to lead Jawbreaker; at fifty-nine, he had been in the process of retiring. Jawbreaker's team medic was Dave Phillips, fifty-five, who had been an "18 Delta"—a Special Forces combat medical sergeant—in Vietnam, where he'd been wounded, before joining the Agency. He had been part of a CIA team working on the Predator program in Uzbekistan. The team had been flying home on 9/11 via Frankfurt when their plane had been diverted to Gander in Canada. They had been separated from their luggage, in which was the key to the weapons locker containing the Hellfire missiles for the Predator. Stranded in Gander for days, Phillips eventually managed to get out; he had a war to fight.

Dostum's readiness to wage war and his promise to gather 2,000 troops for a push toward Mazar-i Sharif was greeted with delight within CTC. For now, at least, the time for queasiness about the past conduct of warlords was over: any armed enemy of the Taliban was America's friend. Indeed, every CIA station in the world was now in the business of trying to find Afghans who would help the United States. For more than a decade, almost no Afghan had succeeded in getting the US government to show an interest in them. Now, any Afghan could. To David Tyson's surprise, he read a cable from the CIA's Ankara station proposing that the US pay Abdul Malik Pahlawan $100,000 to return to Afghanistan. This was the same treacherous Malik who had betrayed Dostum in 1997 and allowed the Taliban to enter Mazar-i Sharif. The scheme was swiftly rejected by CTC.

On September 14, David called Dostum on an Inmarsat phone from inside the Tashkent station. After the two men exchanged greetings in Uzbek, David told the warlord that Americans would soon be on their way into the Darya Suf Valley and wanted to link up with him. "How many men and tanks will you bring?" Dostum asked. David replied, "Well, it'll just be me and six or seven other guys, but don't worry—we'll bring our sleeping bags." Dostum was taken aback, but he was used to improvising. Picking up on David's humor, he responded: "Well, I have no armored personnel carriers or heavy guns. All I've got is horses, mules, and donkeys. So, I suppose we are even."

Still, there were doubters within the CIA. Dostum lacked the cachet of the Tajiks, even with their leader Massoud dead. He certainly did not have the network that the Pakistanis enjoyed, which had allowed them to press the Pashtun case within the heart of the United States government. In the Islamabad station and NE Division, the staff suffered from what CTC leaders viewed as a bad case of "clientitis," with many officers echoing the analysis of the ISI, Pakistan's intelligence agency, that the Northern Alliance was a sideshow run by corrupt warlords and drug dealers.

For years the State Department, in sync with NE Division, had been cajoling the Taliban to renounce Al-Qaeda and hand over bin Laden. US diplomats hoped that 9/11 would force Pakistan to abandon its double game and persuade the Taliban to take that leap. Black viewed this as a blind alley that would lead only to delay. Tenet saw no harm in testing the proposition, dubious as it seemed, but time was short, and he made it clear that military action would not be delayed.

Late in the evening of September 15, in a small hotel in Quetta in Pakistan's Baluchistan province, Robert Grenier, the CIA's Islamabad station chief, was meeting with the Taliban. A dapper, Dartmouth-educated NE Division officer, Grenier had a reputation for exquisitely crafted cables replete with literary allusions. He did not hide his disdain for CTC or its leaders, whose operational experience was in Africa. Considering them overpromoted, he resented what he saw as their "aggressive philistinism" and their ignorance of Pakistan and Afghanistan.

Grenier was in Quetta to urge Mullah Osmani, the Taliban's Southern Zone commander, to give up Osama bin Laden. He was getting nowhere as he tried to play the role of respectful intermediary, telling the black-turbaned cleric that war would be "a disaster for everyone, victor and vanquished alike," and that it would spell the end of the Taliban movement. "If you attack us, we will defeat you!" Osmani ranted. "Just as we defeated the Soviets!"

At the conclusion of the five-hour meeting, Osmani agreed to take the bin Laden proposal to Mullah Omar, the one-eyed Taliban leader. Unbeknown to Grenier, however, his preferred way forward was already a dead end in both Washington and Quetta.

As Grenier met with Osmani, half a world away at Camp David there was a break in Bush's war council. The president was conferring with Black, Michael Morell—who was Bush's CIA briefer—and a senior State Department official who suggested that America's first response to 9/11 should be a diplomatic overture to the Taliban. After the official had walked away, Bush turned to the CIA men and said, "Fuck diplomacy. We are going to war."

5

KILL BOX

5:45 a.m. (GMT -4), September 27, 2001;
CTC/SO, CIA Headquarters, Langley, Virginia

COFER BLACK CHOSE Hank Crumpton to run the war in Afghanistan. Crumpton had just taken over as chief of Canberra station but was recalled from Australia to head the newly formed Counterterrorism Center/Special Operations—CTC/SO. Blee, who had led Alec station for more than two years, would oversee the campaign against Al-Qaeda in the rest of the world. A slim, black-haired man of few words and Southern charm, Crumpton was the Zen counterweight to Black's in-your-face assertiveness. But he too did not suffer fools. His eyes could bore through anyone who defied him.

Crumpton had a fierce temper and a determination to cut through red tape. Like Black and Blee, he was an Africa Division hand, used to working in fluid and morally ambiguous environments that demanded unorthodox approaches. As a CTC deputy, Crumpton had met Massoud in the Panjshir in early 2000 and flown to Yemen to liaise with the FBI after the *Cole* attack. He knew what Al-Qaeda was and burned with a moral indignation, even a killing rage, over 9/11. Crumpton relished his new role, which he likened to reconstituting the OSS, the CIA's forerunner, in a week. He was left to get on with it. "Tenet and Cofer gave him a blank check," recalled one CTC/SO officer.

If Hank Crumpton did not select the right officers for the first CIA team going behind enemy lines, he knew they could render the US war in Afghanistan a debacle. Jawbreaker had helicoptered into the Panjshir Valley, which was controlled by the Northern Alliance, on September 26. Now there would be "alphabet teams," from Alpha to Juliet, assigned to different regions and warlords. Team Alpha, made up of eight men, was about to be earmarked for Dostum in the Darya Suf Valley. It would be the first CIA team to land in Taliban territory.

Crumpton was inundated with volunteers, but the number of officers qualified for the task was limited. The teams would generally be headed up by a senior Agency hand with linguistic and regional expertise, with an experienced paramilitary officer as his deputy. Medical and communications specialists were needed, and some teams would have a Green Beret attached to provide current knowledge of procedures used by the Special Forces teams. Green Berets would also offset the paucity of CIA paramilitary officers; some senior figures in the Agency had tried to get the CIA out of the killing business, starving the Special Activities Division of personnel and resources. A second linguist on each team was essential because the teams would sometimes be required to split up. The CIA teams would have responsibility for vast swaths of territory. Team Alpha's writ was to extend over Samangan, Balkh, Faryab, Jowzjan, and Sar-e Pol, five of Afghanistan's thirty-four provinces. This was a land area of over 30,000 square miles—slightly larger than the state of South Carolina.

The initial campaign would be centered around a "kill box" between the four cities of Mazar-i Sharif, Taloqan, Kabul, and Bamiyan. Team Alpha's part of that was Mazar-i Sharif. The holy city was key to the broader campaign because of its proximity to Uzbekistan and the Friendship Bridge land connection just forty miles away. Once Mazar-i Sharif was captured, Uzbek, Hazara, and Tajik forces of the Northern Alliance led by Dostum could move east to Taloqan. There they would link up with Tajik forces of the Northern Alliance led by Fahim Khan, Massoud's successor, on the Shomali Plains north of Kabul. US air power would destroy the enemy in the kill box, preventing Taliban and Al-Qaeda forces from escaping to the south. Team Bravo would augment Team Alpha at a time and place to be determined, with the two teams merging in Mazar-i Sharif. For the time being, the campaign was all about the northern half of Afghanistan; the south would have to come later.

At first it was intended that CIA and Special Forces teams would be inserted into Afghanistan together. But military bureaucracy and aversion to risk were already bogging down the Special Forces. US military doctrine dictated that aircraft could not fly unless there was a Combat Search and Rescue (CSAR) plan in place; basing and overflight agreements had yet to be negotiated. There were also debates about whether Green Berets should be in uniform. Crumpton didn't need CSAR plans for his CIA teams, nor did he care about uniforms. He told General Franks, "Look, we've got our Jawbreaker team and we're going with Alpha and Bravo. And we're going to put them in as fast as we can. We need you with us. But we're not waiting." Later, Crumpton was incandescent when a Green Beret medic was blocked at the last minute from joining a CIA team, wondering if "these dickheads" were "more concerned about their administrative prerogative than saving the lives of our men on the battlefield."

Team Alpha's leader was J. R. Seeger, a former 82nd Airborne officer. As an NE Division recruit at The Farm, he had been trained by Kenneth Sapp, Justin's father. He was fluent in Dari, the lingua franca of Afghanistan, as well as Farsi and Tajik. At forty-seven, he was six months younger than Dostum and an expert on Afghanistan's tribes. J.R. had been in California on 9/11, working out of the CIA's San Francisco station and liaising with the FBI on counterterrorism. Had he not been stranded on the West Coast when US airspace was shut down after 9/11, J.R. might have been on Gary Schroen's Jawbreaker team. But leading a unit behind enemy lines seemed a better fit for J.R., whose reverence for the Green Berets was not shared by some in the CIA who regarded them as knuckle-draggers. A keen soccer player, J.R. was a goalkeeper—

a lonely position of great responsibility that requires composure and an ability to read the game as it plays out, often at quite a distance.

J.R. was from a blue-collar background in western New York, with few pretensions, an easy manner, and a fondness for practical rather than academic solutions. He had degrees in ancient history and social anthropology and had worked as an archaeologist before joining the Army in 1979. As his Army commission was ending, he received a cold call from a CIA recruiter that led both J.R. and his wife to join the Agency, where they became a "tandem couple"—the path on which Mike and Shannon Spann were embarking. After Dari language training, his first CIA posting was to Islamabad station, where he worked with Pashtun mujahideen groups in Afghanistan fighting the Russians as the Soviet occupation came to its ignominious end. Alongside his Afghan specialization, J.R.'s Army background led him to liaison roles with the military. During the 1990 run-up to the Gulf War he was sent to Saudi Arabia to provide counterterrorist support to the military—and found himself the target of Saddam Hussein's Scud missiles.

Although a GS-15 in the CIA, the equivalent of a colonel, J.R. described himself as just a foot soldier. But as a student of the 19th-century Great Game—in which Afghanistan was the buffer state between the Russian Empire and British India—he knew that he would be the 2001 equivalent of the colonial officer on whose shoulders the future of a different empire could rest.

The Team Alpha deputy was Alex Hernandez, forty-nine, a vastly experienced former 10th Special Forces Group sergeant major who had completed a storied Army career before joining the CIA as a paramilitary officer. Alex, a Mexican-American, had grown up in the Chicago suburbs and joined the infantry to go to Vietnam, but just missed out as the US withdrawal began. A specialist diver and parachutist, he became the first Green Beret to be a Navy SEAL training instructor, then worked in a Cold War undercover antiterrorist and sabotage unit based in Berlin. At thirty-seven, Hernandez had been selected for a "special mission unit," liaising with the CIA in Somalia at the start of the US intervention there in late 1992. He knew all about the horrors and unpredictability of war.

In Somalia, Alex had been first on the scene after Lawrence "Gus" Freedman, a legendary CIA paramilitary who rejoiced in the nickname "Super Jew," had been killed when his vehicle hit a land mine, catapulting his torso into a tree. Freedman had become America's first casualty in Somalia and the 68th star on the CIA's Memorial Wall. Alex had been married for twenty years and, like J.R., had no children. Cautious, unflappable, and adept at managing risk, he told Team Alpha members to make sure they took out $1 million life-insurance policies.

Third in command of Team Alpha was Scott Spellmeyer, thirty-three, a former US Army Ranger. From upstate New York, he was the deputy in Alex's paramilitary team before 9/11 and had been three years ahead of Justin Sapp at VMI. He, too, had seen action in Somalia. As an Army lieutenant in 1993, Scott had taken a piece of shrapnel or a bullet fragment in the thigh during the Battle of Mogadishu. He had been leading a weapons platoon of twenty-five men when they were ambushed, suffering two killed and thirteen wounded. The battle was depicted in Mark Bowden's book *Black Hawk Down* in 1999, adapted as a movie and released four months after 9/11.

Scott had been aiming to apply for Delta Force when a woman who was helping him type up his résumé gave him a telephone number for the CIA. By 9/11, he had already been identified as having potential for the highest ranks of the Agency; J.R. planned to use him to lead a smaller group should Team Alpha be broken down. On 9/11, Scott and his wife had been thousands of miles away in a foreign courtroom, finalizing the adoption of their eighteen-month-old son. As with Mike, recent fatherhood had not dissuaded Scott from pushing to go to Afghanistan. Before leaving, he had updated what he called his "kill file" at home, which detailed everything to be done in the event of his death—including the music to be played at his funeral.

The team medic was Mark Rausenberger, also thirty-three, a by-the-book former soldier who had been posted to Somalia after the Battle of Mogadishu. He had joined the Agency's Office of Medical Services (OMS) after qualifying as a physician's assistant, a course he enrolled in when he left the Army. Mark's dour manner and deep, monotone voice—which earned him the nickname Dark Mark—disguised a mordant wit. Raised in Davenport, Iowa, he was a man of straightforward tastes and a blunt manner.

Improbably, Mark was also a published author. His *Somalia Journal*— a sergeant's account of "what happened in the trenches" as a medic in "the Mogue" (Mogadishu) projected the image of a jaundiced but good-hearted grunt distrustful of the government, the media, and the top brass. Amid caustic reflections such as "God has more planned for me than getting waxed in a third world country for Bill Clinton" were flashes of patriotism and a determination to hone his medical skills.

Mike Spann had fought hard to get on Team Alpha, reminding everyone he knew in CTC and the Special Activities Division that his experience calling in air strikes as a Marine Corps officer made him a natural fit. Andy was a former enlisted Special Forces weapons specialist in his early thirties. Nicknamed "Cousin Andy" because of his roots in rural West Virginia and to differentiate him from a senior paramilitary officer known as "Uncle Andy," he had graduated from The Farm just a month before 9/11. On joining Alex's paramilitary team, he had been tasked with making an inventory of every piece of communications equipment in Ground Branch. By default, Andy would be the comms man on Team Alpha. He invariably had a smile on his face and would joke that the extent of his communications knowledge was that it was all "FM"—Fucking Magic. Greg, a former enlisted Navy SEAL, had been on the same course at The Farm as Andy. He had been heading for a new posting in South America when his commercial flight was canceled; the next day he was selected for Afghanistan. The eighth and final member of Team Alpha would be a Green Beret.

The men of Team Alpha embodied America's desire to strike back after 9/11. On September 20, President Bush, in an address to a joint session of Congress, described the United States as "a country awakened to danger and called to defend freedom," declaring: "And in our grief and anger we have found our mission and our moment." That day his Gallup approval rating reached 90 percent—higher than that of President Franklin Roosevelt after Pearl Harbor.

* * *

After two days spent guarding the Special Forces diving school at Key West after 9/11, Justin Sapp and his classmates resumed their course. There had been no word from the 5th Special Forces Group, and Justin began to worry he might miss the war after all. Not until September 20—the last day of diver training—did he begin to sense he might get his chance. That morning, as the divers were about to start their final exercise in the pitch-black, an instructor broke open a chemical light and announced, "Well, it looks like some of you guys are going to be infiltrating for real."

Justin chuckled to himself. He had just spent six weeks learning how to dive, one of three men to pass the course from an initial ten at the pre-selection, and now he might be off to a landlocked country. When he got to his tiny apartment at Fort Campbell, there was a message on his answering machine: "Captain Sapp, you are to be in the battalion commander's office tomorrow at 0900 to discuss matters of urgent importance."

The next morning, Justin, who had barely slept, was greeted by the battalion commander, Lieutenant Colonel Chris Haas. "Good news, bud," Haas said. "I need you to go see the group commander at 1100. I'm probably not going to see you for at least six months. We'll high-five in Kabul on the top of a T-55." Haas—whom Justin regarded as the Special Forces version of the bluff, hearty American football coach— knew that he would be going to Afghanistan too. This was the big game for both of them. The group commander was Colonel Mulholland, the former Delta Force operator, who had been chosen to lead Task Force Dagger—the Joint Special Operations Task Force (JSOTF) being stood up at Karshi-Khanabad air base, known as K2, in Uzbekistan. Dagger would oversee all military activities in northern Afghanistan.

When Justin got to Mulholland's office, he found four others had been ordered there too: another captain, Jim, a contemporary; and three warrant officers, junior in rank but senior in age and experience. Characteristically, Mulholland got straight to the point. He had a lot on his plate. He had already fought off a bid from 10th Group, which specialized in mountain warfare, to lead the Special Forces in Afghanistan. As with CTC and NE Division within the CIA, a turf war was often the first element of any planning process. "Right," Mulholland told the five Green Berets. "I need to form a pilot team to go into Afghanistan. Once you're assigned, you'll be seconded to the Agency."

A pilot team was Special Forces terminology for the pathfinder unit that scouts out the terrain for an ODA, the twelve-man team that was the linchpin of a mission. The colonel stared at the men in front of him, who had dreamed of a moment like this, and added: "But first I've got to pick three of you." Mulholland asked about their experience; each had to sell himself without openly knifing his rivals. Justin's pitch was that he knew the CIA. His father was a retired CIA officer, and Justin himself had worked at the Agency for a summer nine years earlier. It wasn't much, Justin thought, but it was something. Mulholland was unconvinced. "But that was analytical work, not operations," he said. Justin thought he might have blown it. "I was a college sophomore," he thought. "Give me a break. There were no operations interns." Mulholland said, "Come back at 1500 and I'll let you know."

When Justin returned that afternoon, only he, Jim, and one of the warrant officers were present. "So, you three guys are going to be detailed," Mulholland said. "Good luck to you. I want you to go to Washington next week and come back and brief me on what their plan is." As he walked out of Mulholland's office, Justin felt the hairs on the back of his neck stand up. The 5th Group headquarters looked over a field of young oak trees, each one planted in memory of a Green Beret who had died in the line of duty. Certainly, Justin thought he might be killed. But this was one of the plum appointments in the entire US military after 9/11. He turned to Jim and the warrant officer and said: "You know, it's an honor to be working with you guys."

CIA headquarters was a whirlwind of activity. Three floors below ground level, CTC had been a warren of cubicles, with the rabbit runs between them dubbed "Hezbollah Highway" and "Bin Laden Boulevard." Now, the cubicles had been cleared away and tables set up to form a large rectangle in the center of the room. There was a fierce urgency to everything. When a logistics officer told Crumpton that a supply drop into Afghanistan had not taken place because the request had been lodged only twelve hours earlier, the new CTC/SO chief ripped into him: "I don't give a flying fuck when the request came in! I want those supplies there now!"

Work was around the clock. Some officers dozed in sleeping bags beneath their desks. With no food available in the middle of one night, peckish CTC/SO officers cut the chains off the cafeteria padlock and helped themselves. After that, the cafeteria went into a 24/7 routine. When a fire-alarm test interrupted a CTC meeting, Frank Archibald, a hulking former Marine and veteran SAD officer who was a deputy to Crumpton, stood up and disabled it by ripping the wires out.

For many, 9/11 was intensely personal. Crumpton had worked on the USS *Cole* investigation in Yemen with John O'Neill, an FBI agent who had subsequently retired to become security chief at the World Trade Center. O'Neill had perished when he went back into the South Tower to direct its evacuation. His body was found on September 21 beneath twelve feet of debris. A retired CIA officer and father of Diane Killip, a key figure in Alec station, had died of a heart attack while watching the 9/11 attacks on television. She took a day off for his funeral, then went right back to work.

When Justin Sapp arrived at CIA headquarters, he was given a temporary badge; he felt even the admin staff looked down on him. A coin toss meant that he was assigned to Team Alpha, with his 5th Group colleague Jim headed to the Panjshir. Welcomed to the team by

Alex Hernandez, Justin learned that his first job would be to oversee the weapons. To conceal the team's origins, Justin was told he could take no military kit or equipment with him, so he went to REI with a government credit card and bought $3,000 worth of gear—everything from cargo pants, wick-dry shirts, and camping towels to binoculars and a reverse osmosis water pump.

Justin took his 5th Group colleague Jim to visit Justin's parents in nearby Herndon, Virginia. The two young Special Forces officers obeyed the order to keep their mission secret, saying only that they were heading to an unknown country for temporary duty. Kenneth Sapp, who had retired from the Agency four years earlier, was having none of it. They were watching CNN news when he asked: "So, which one of you guys is going into the Panjshir?"

Upon first joining Special Forces, Justin had told his father that he was considering 5th Group, covering CENTCOM's area of responsibility in the Middle East. His father had replied, "Well, if you want to go where the policymakers are focused, where the oil is, and where all the conflict is, CENTCOM is probably the right choice." Now he was stoic about what his son would soon face. "This is what you wanted," he told him. "They say be careful what you ask for. You got it, Justin. You got it."

J. R. Seeger had flown ahead to the CIA station in Tashkent. Soon after he arrived, it was confirmed that Team Alpha would link up with Dostum. David Tyson could have gone back into the Panjshir, but with Massoud dead he sensed that the Tajik Afghans would be in disarray. The Tajiks, moreover, were more refined and political than the Uzbeks. Except for Massoud and a few others, David viewed them as reluctant warriors, some of whom were principally interested in lining their own pockets. He knew from Uzbek intelligence that Dostum would fight without the prodding and coddling the Tajiks would require. Besides, David was the only Uzbek speaker in the CIA, with current expertise on Afghanistan as well as experience on Jawbreaker missions. He wanted to go into the Darya Suf Valley.

J.R. was delighted. "I'm taking Dave," the Team Alpha leader told

Charlie Gilbert, who had become Tashkent station chief days before 9/11. That meant dropping one of the original eight. Alex told a dismayed Greg, the former SEAL, that he had drawn the short straw. "But don't worry," Alex said. "You'll be on another team and in Afghanistan soon enough."

At CIA headquarters, the mood was resolute. Crumpton's new deputy, John Massie, had been due to retire but changed his mind after 9/11, spending days digging through the rubble of the World Trade Center and then heeding Crumpton's call to return to headquarters. Massie, a devout Catholic, told one team before they left for Afghanistan, "You men need to realize that what you will be involved in may well bear on the salvation of your very soul. It is important that you are at peace with yourself and with God and with the actions you take."

Amy—the cricket-releasing classmate of Mike and Shannon at The Farm—had been preparing for a posting to Southeast Asia. Without seeking permission, she pulled herself out of language training and called Crumpton. "Hey, I'm working for you," she told him. "Got it," Crumpton responded. "We've got a lot of chiefs, but we need some Indians." Amy went to work on logistics, helping to prepare the teams that would be going into Afghanistan. She would be a crucial link between Mike and Shannon.

As Team Alpha's departure for Uzbekistan neared, the Spann family— Mike, Shannon, Alison, Emily, and Jake—drove down to Williamsburg for the weekend. They also visited nearby Yorktown, site of the 1781 British surrender and birthplace of American independence. The trip had been arranged long before, and Mike was not going to miss it. But the timeline for the team leaving was fluid, and he'd been told the date could be moved up at short notice. "No matter what happens, do not leave without me," he told Alex. For two days the Spanns took in the sights of colonial Williamsburg, the couple reminiscing about the times they had spent there while at The Farm—already that seemed like a lifetime ago. Unlike many military operators before a deployment, Mike had not detached mentally. Shannon felt he was fully present—giving the girls piggyback rides, holding Jake whenever he could, and pushing the stroller, which he had dubbed the JTV—Jake Terrain Vehicle.

Despite the steely image he projected at the CIA, Mike was an involved parent. Shannon was breastfeeding, and he encouraged her to pump milk so he could feed Jake from a bottle. He washed Jake's baby clothes and organized them in the nursery, blow-dried Emily's hair, read bedtime stories, and packed school lunches. Shannon had found that Mike, in the swing of being a single father before she met him, had a system for everything.

Mike loved American military history, particularly the Civil War, and had told Alison that Ulysses S. Grant, the Union general and later US president, was one of his heroes. On Memorial Day of that year, with Shannon nearly nine months pregnant, they had taken the girls by Metro to visit Arlington National Cemetery. It was a sacred place to Mike, and a day to teach his children the importance of respect for America's fallen.

By then he and Shannon knew they were going to be welcoming a baby boy, and Mike was ecstatic to be having a son. He would pat Shannon's middle and ask how "my little Marine" was doing. When the girls tried to give their baby brother silly nicknames—Moochie or Boo-Boo Bear—Mike would respond, "Uh, why don't we just call him Jake?" It was important to teach Jake to be a real man, Mike would say, or the Marine Corps would do it for him.

Their life together was busy and chaotic, but Mike and Shannon had been working hard to carve out time for each other. On March 28 he had emailed her, "It seems I can never find the words to fully tell you how much I sincerely love you. The simple fact is, there are no words worthy enough for you. You certainly [were] God's gift to a hardened and broken-down heart when I needed it most."

Mike had been tasked with coordinating the paperwork for Team Alpha. He told Justin to update his life insurance and nominate five people to carry his casket if he was killed. But the Green Beret captain wasn't thinking about dying; he felt like a surfer riding a tsunami and trying not to wipe out. Justin's greatest fear was doing or saying the wrong thing and being dropped from the team.

As for Mike, if he worried about the danger of the mission, he didn't show it. Meticulous to a fault, on the morning of October 5 he and Shannon went to a lawyer's office in Manassas to sign his will, which designated her as the guardian of Alison and Emily. His main assets were a 1997 Geo Metro and the Lanae Lane townhouse, which he had bought for $128,000 two years earlier. As a GS-10 officer in his third year at the CIA, his annual salary was $43,059.

After a discussion with Shannon, Mike emailed Amy. "I don't mean to sound dramatic," he wrote. "I'm sure this will be a piece of cake, but if anything happens to me, I want you to be the one who tells Shannon. I don't want her to hear it from someone she doesn't know." Amy made sure to place that email in Mike's personnel file.

America was at war, and the CIA was leading the campaign, but the reality hit Amy for the first time: people close to her might die. Mike believed there would be more American casualties, and that Al-Qaeda should be given no quarter. "What everyone needs to understand is these fellows hate you," he wrote in an email to his parents. "They hate you because you are an American. Support your government and your military, especially when the bodies start coming home."

On the evening of October 5, Shannon Spann, with the three children in the car, drove her husband the forty minutes from Manassas Park to CIA headquarters. Before they left, she took a photograph of a smiling Mike standing outside their home on Lanae Lane, flanked by his daughters and clutching baby Jake to his chest with both arms. Mike was thirty-two, his full head of dark-brown hair already dusted with gray, on course to be silver by the time he was forty. Shannon feared he might never come back, but she had promised herself she wouldn't cry.

The couple did not know how often—or even whether—they would be able to communicate. Shannon told him she would always trust that he was safe until she received definitive evidence otherwise. Alison, having seen the footage of 9/11, was beside herself that her father was going to the place where the terrorists had planned the attacks. He had explained to her that he couldn't tell the US government he was unable to go: "What if every daddy said that? Who would there be to protect you?"

Shannon and Mike kissed and hugged, and she told him she loved him and was proud of him. She supported what he was doing and wanted him to succeed, she said, for the sake of his family and his country. Then, carrying his bags, he walked into the CIA headquarters building where they had both arrived as recruits just over two years earlier. Inside, a huge American flag had been hung in honor of the victims of 9/11. The automatic doors swished open and Mike, not looking back, disappeared into the lobby. Shannon returned to the car and wept.

6
TALISMAN

11:20 p.m. (GMT +5), October 15, 2001;
Karshi-Khanabad Air Base, Uzbekistan

OUT ON THE runway of the crumbling former Soviet air base of K2 in southeastern Uzbekistan, the turbine engines of two MH-60L Black Hawk helicopters whirred into action. There had been four days of delays due to poor weather and debates among Task Force Dagger staff over different routes to get the CIA into the Darya Suf Valley to link up with General Dostum. Before settling on Black Hawks, crossing into Afghanistan on foot had been considered. Team Alpha had also been told that they might be parachuted into Afghanistan from a plane launched from an aircraft carrier in the Arabian Sea. "You might have to wear a burqa," Justin Sapp had been informed. Another plan had been to swim across the Amu Darya from Uzbekistan and be met on the Afghanistan side by a smuggler who would drive the team to Dostum.

The team had been split into two groups of four, configured so that each could operate if one of the Black Hawks crashed into the mountains. Accompanying them to the Afghanistan border would be a Chinook helicopter, also from the 160th Special Operations Aviation Regiment, the Night Stalkers. The Chinook's role was to provide emergency refueling should the Black Hawks be unable to refuel from a Hercules tanker that would rendezvous with them just inside

Uzbekistan. Earlier that day, Team Alpha had posed for a photograph in front of one of the Black Hawks. Stenciled on the side of the helicopter were words adapted from the 1987 movie *The Untouchables,* about Al Capone: "Don't Bring a Knife to a Gunfight." Seven of the team were married; Justin was the only single man. Three had children: David, Mike, and Scott, who had just adopted a toddler. Andy's wife was pregnant with their first child.

Team Alpha was about to be the first CIA team behind Taliban lines. At the Pentagon, there had been intense frustration with the delays, increasing the pressure to get into Afghanistan. Intelligence reports of Taliban fighters positioning shoulder-launched missiles just south of the Uzbekistan border and concern about helicopter performance at such high altitude had to be set aside. At the end of the mission brief in an old Soviet aircraft bunker, the 160th chaplain had asked God to "bless these crews and bless these machines." Justin was poised to become the first American service member among the almost 1.4 million in uniform to enter enemy territory in Afghanistan after 9/11. He felt the weight of history and national expectations on his shoulders.

In Justin's pocket was a silver ring etched with the Special Forces motto, DE OPPRESSO LIBER—to liberate the oppressed. A former Green Beret had stopped him in a corridor at CIA headquarters to ask him to take it into Afghanistan with him. Justin carried no identification apart from a silk "blood chit" offering a reward to anyone who might help him. In Pashto, Dari, Uzbek, Farsi, and Urdu, it stated: "I am an American and do not speak your language. I will not harm you! I bear no malice toward your people." On his right shoulder was an infrared chemical light. These had been given to each member of the team to distinguish them from Afghans should a firefight erupt after they landed.

Mike Spann had spent time at K2 with Brian, the fellow former Marine who had been in his class at The Farm. Brian was bound for the Panjshir Valley to link up with Jawbreaker and the Tajiks, while Mike was going in with Team Alpha. As ANGLICO officers, they had called in hundreds of air strikes in training. Now they would be doing the real

thing in war. It felt like there was an element of destiny in their joining these missions. They discussed escape and evasion routes, quickly
agreeing that with just one CIA helicopter the only option if disaster
struck would be to head north for the border. "There isn't much of a
Plan B," Mike deadpanned.

Justin was whispering a prayer to himself on the runway as Colonel
John Mulholland arrived to bid farewell to the CIA men. Now sporting
a bushy mustache, Mulholland had named the K2 base "Stronghold
Freedom" and given his Task Force Dagger the motto STRENGTH AND
HONOR. But the intensely patriotic and normally loquacious commander
seemed to be grasping for something stirring to say. Struggling to make
himself heard over the din of the Black Hawks, the towering colonel
leaned down to shout into the young captain's ear: "Don't get fucking
killed!" This wasn't exactly poetry, Justin thought. "I'll try not to let you
down, sir!" he responded. It was clear that Mulholland thought some,
perhaps all, of Team Alpha would not make it back. Alex had tried to
dampen that fear among the team, telling them in their final briefing,
"No one dies on this mission."

The Black Hawks, with the call signs Sponge 05 and Sponge 06,
were Direct-Action Penetrators, known as DAPs and configured as
gunships to support Special Forces troops in action. The very presence
of DAPs in Uzbekistan was a closely held secret because the Karimov
government had not authorized combat missions to be launched from
the country. The cover story was that they were regular Black Hawks,
on standby for CSAR.

Given first pick of call signs, the Chinook pilots had chosen Razor,
allocating to the Black Hawks the rather less warlike moniker of
Sponge. But for now, the Black Hawk pilots had had the last laugh
in this rivalry: their smaller, lighter craft had been chosen for the first
insertion because of the threat from Taliban antiaircraft fire and Stinger
missiles. The Chinook had a greater heat-and-noise signature, while
the Black Hawk had been fitted with defensive systems that used chaff
and flares.

Normally, a DAP would have carried an array of weaponry such as 30mm cannons, heavy machine guns, and Hellfire missiles. But the extremely high altitudes of Central Asia's mountain ranges affected lift power, and the requirement to carry passengers and their kit meant everything possible had to be sacrificed to bring down the weight. There were no seats; most of the CIA men sat on Pelican cases while Andy perched on a large green sack stuffed with $3 million in nonsequential $100 bills. Each man except David Tyson had been given a new Romanian-made AKMS rifle—a version of the Kalashnikov with a folding metal shoulder stock—and a 9mm Glock 17 pistol. The rifle's collapsible stock made it easier to conceal and easier to fire from inside a vehicle.

David, added to the team late, had no rifle. Instead of a Glock, he had drawn a 9mm Browning Hi-Power pistol from Tashkent station. The pistol had been a running joke among CIA officers in Tashkent: its serial number ended in 007. David, who was an unlikely James Bond, had traveled with it many times before.

Inside the Pelican cases were satellite radios, power cables, folding antennae, Panasonic Toughbook laptops, and an assortment of American and Soviet military maps. No body armor or helmets would be worn by Team Alpha. The rule was the same for the ODAs; the reasoning was that it would be harder for the Americans to win over Afghan tribesmen if they were more heavily armed and better protected than their indigenous allies.

The only weapons fixed to each Black Hawk for the flight of two hours and thirty minutes were two six-barrel, rotating M134 miniguns, along with 8,000 rounds of 7.06mm ammunition. Chief Warrant Officer Ross Childs, senior pilot in Sponge 05, was leading the mission. Chief Warrant Officer Alan Mack was senior pilot in Razor 03, the lone Chinook. Each of the three helicopters had two pilots. Inside Sponge 05 was an American flag that would later be presented by the crew to President Bush with the pledge "We will not stop until this war is won."

Team Alpha had arrived in Uzbekistan on October 7, just as the US bombing of Afghanistan began and the US campaign was given the name Operation Enduring Freedom. A central aim of the strikes was to cripple the Taliban's antiaircraft capability, making it safer to insert the teams of CIA and Green Berets. The first missile to be launched was a Hellfire, fitted to a CIA Predator after a new key had been found to open the weapons locker. Chalked on the Hellfire was the name of Barbara Olson, the wife of Solicitor General Theodore Olson, who had been killed on Flight 77 on 9/11 when it hit the Pentagon minutes after she had called her husband to tell him her plane had been hijacked. Theodore Olson later said his late wife would have been delighted that her name had been on a US missile fired into Afghanistan. "Barbara was a warrior, so she would have wanted to fight back."

Mike and Justin had been checking into Tashkent's high-rise Sheraton Hotel just as footage of the air strikes appeared on televisions in the lobby, where a group of journalists had gathered. Justin wasn't having much luck with being clandestine: a receptionist at the hotel desk had greeted him with a cheery "Hello, Justin!" During his posting to Uzbekistan with ODA 522, the young women working at the hotel—invariably outfitted in miniskirts and high heels—had flirted with the visiting Green Berets, and he had played along.

Justin hadn't fared much better with the Black Hawk crew, not all of whom knew who their passengers were. "So who are you guys with?" one crewman asked Justin. "State Department" came the terse reply from the Green Beret, who had a Kalashnikov slung over his shoulder and was clearly not a diplomat. A few minutes later the skeptical crewman asked another team member, who replied: "CIA." The crewman flashed Justin a withering look.

Before the flight, Team Alpha had received an Afghanistan familiarization from J. R. Seeger and medical instruction from Mark Rausenberger. Alex was concerned about David's relative lack of military experience. David had taken a CIA pistol training course four years earlier, but Justin, in charge of the weapons, had taken him to an unventilated, underground range in Tashkent to teach him how to fire a Kalashnikov.

"Whatever you do in the heat of the moment," Justin told him, "always bring the selector all the way down to semiauto. If you go halfway down—one click—you're going to be on full auto, the muzzle will climb to the right, and you'll miss."

The night was clear and moonlit. Flying east toward Tajikistan, the trio of helicopters had to thread their way through an 8,000-foot-high pass in the Baisun-Tau mountain range, nicknamed "the Bear" because of its shape. The crew doors were open so the miniguns could fire, making the cabin freezing cold. To avoid Taliban antiaircraft sites, the circuitous flight route cut due east into Tajikistan, passing south of the 15,000-foot-high peak Khazret Sultan on the border and skirting the Tajik capital of Dushanbe. Some of the CIA men were mystified by the military Rules of Engagement (ROE), which stipulated that these Taliban sites could be destroyed only once the enemy had opened fire.

As the helicopters turned south toward Afghanistan and began to descend, a Hercules suddenly appeared above and slightly behind Sponge 06. The Hercules moved forward and to the right of the Black Hawk; then, with both aircraft maintaining a lumbering 120 knots, the Hercules reeled out a hose with a funnel-shaped end, known as a drogue. A fourteen-foot-long probe was then extended from the nose of the Black Hawk to meet the drogue, the two devices coupling so fuel could be transferred.

This was a tricky maneuver in the daytime, never mind at night in unfamiliar conditions. David, sitting next to a door gunner, watched with fascination through the open door of the helicopter and on the pilots' night-vision screens. Once the refueling was complete, Sponge 05 followed suit. The two Black Hawks then peeled away, leaving the Hercules and Razor 03, the Chinook, to return to K2. "Congratulations, gentlemen" came an ethereal voice from the Hercules cockpit. "You just completed the first combat in-air refueling for the 160th Regiment. Good luck and Godspeed."

Andy thought of how his father had flown into Vietnam in 1965 as one of the first troops in the buildup of US forces in the country. Now, more than thirty-five years later, Andy had found himself part of the start of another war. He had applied to the CIA three times before they accepted him; he had to pinch himself that he wasn't dreaming. Around midnight, the scattered lights of Uzbekistan disappeared. The darkness below was broken only by the moon's reflection on the Amu Darya, known in antiquity as the Oxus River and now marking the eighty-nine-mile-long international border. "Welcome to Afghanistan," said Childs, prompting Andy to slap Justin on the thigh in exhilaration.

* * *

Of the eight members of Team Alpha, David Tyson was perhaps the least seized by the momentousness of this mission. Having been outside the United States on 9/11, he had been insulated from the national outpouring of grief and thirst for retribution. The rest of Team Alpha had traveled from Virginia to Tashkent via Germany in a Gulfstream, a luxurious US government VIP jet. To them, the stripped-down Black Hawk was unnervingly austere. David, however, had flown into Afghanistan on cold, dilapidated Mi-17s several times in the past two years, and if he closed his eyes this was little different.

Although his wife, Rosann, knew where he was going, back in Tashkent David had told his children he was taking another trip to Tajikistan—a regular occurrence. His daughter, Kara, eleven, had sensed there was something unusual about her father's trip. Without telling anyone, she had placed in his backpack a homemade Native American sacred bundle. The talisman was made of feathers, a rock, a beetle's head, and an Uzbek evil eye charm. David and Kara had discussed Native American lore, and they shared a sense of the mystic and the spiritual. He would not discover it until he reached the Darya Suf Valley; it would stay close to him for the next forty days in Afghanistan.

The first fifty miles or so of Taliban-controlled land was flat with crested sand dunes, almost like the Sahara. The weather forecasters back at K2 had predicted clear conditions over the border, but a sand-storm soon hit the helicopters and visibility shrank to less than half a mile. The pilots could see the stars above, but the sandstorm was 10,000 feet high. Using their forward-looking infrared radar (FLIR) to pick out the rugged landscape ahead, the pilots pressed forward.

South of Mazar-i Sharif—the prize sought by Dostum and Team Alpha—the Black Hawks flew "nap of the earth," a low-altitude course using valleys as cover to avoid Taliban antiaircraft guns or Stingers. There were occasional glimpses of orange below from fires inside mud huts. A few times, tracer fire was visible as the Taliban, hearing a helicopter, shot blindly into the air. Rising to 8,000 feet as the two heli-copters entered the Hindu Kush, they drew close to the Landing Zone (LZ) at Kamach, fourteen miles south of the village of Dehi. Dostum had said the LZ would be marked by a small fire. Instead, it looked like the Afghans had gathered every light bulb and extension cord in north-ern Afghanistan and attached them to a portable generator. The lights were so bright that some of the Team Alpha men took off their night-vision goggles (NVGs). "This is a good sign," thought Andy. "They've overperformed here. This is like Shea Stadium." Crowded around the LZ were more than 100 Afghans, with their horses and vehicles. "Hey, J.R.," Childs told him from the cockpit, "I think we're here."

Sponge 05 stopped moving forward, then descended like an eleva-tor. On each side, the CIA men could see sheer rock faces. "Man, I hope you know what you're doing," thought Justin Sapp, wondering how much clearance there was between the rock and the rotors as the Black Hawk landed on a plateau at the bottom of a canyon. J.R., who had agreed with the pilots that he would be the only one to get out of the helicopter initially, had two preoccupations. One was to pull the lever that opened the door, not the nearby one that jettisoned it. The other was to remember to take off his headset before stepping out of the helicopter. As Sponge 05 settled gently on the ground, kicking up a swirl of dust, Sponge 06 hovered overhead.

It was 2 a.m. on October 17—thirty-six days after the 9/11 attacks.

The CIA was now behind enemy lines inside Afghanistan. It was Day 1 of Team Alpha's mission to topple the Taliban regime in the north and dislodge Al-Qaeda.

*   *   *

Mike Cuthbert, one of the Sponge 06 pilots, looked down at the men and horses gathered in the canyon, bathed in the green light of his NVGs. Sponge 06's miniguns were angled downward in case of an ambush. "There's so many people down there, there's nothing we can do if they decide to start taking Americans out," Cuthbert thought. J.R. removed his headset, safely opened the door, and stepped out. His next concern was that the Black Hawk's rotor blades might decapitate the prospective allies. The Afghans, wearing heavy chapan coats, turbans, and pakol hats, began to approach. Alarmed, J.R. shouted in Dari, "Stop—it's dangerous!" There was no hope of them hearing him over the whine of the engines, so he raised his palms in front of his face, then bent down on one knee. To his bemusement, the Afghans, thinking this was an American greeting, mimicked his actions.

Having established that these were indeed Dostum's people, J.R. gave the thumbs-up to the other three CIA men in the helicopter, and they climbed out. After around six minutes—much longer than Black Hawk pilots prefer to stay on an LZ—Sponge 05 took off and Sponge 06 landed.

As gear was being unloaded from the second helicopter, the Afghans moved forward once more, intending to help. Again J.R. put his hands up, then crouched down—and again the Afghans followed suit. As soon as J.R. turned his back, however, the Afghans stood up and began moving toward the helicopter once more. To end this strange minuet, J.R. ran forward and grabbed the nearest Afghan by his chapan and pulled him to the ground; he then took a knee once more. Observing this, the rest of the Afghans also knelt.

They remained in those positions until the Black Hawks had been unloaded. Only when the second helicopter had lifted off, leaving an eerie silence, did J.R. stand up. The Afghan whose chapan he had been grasping stood up too. Pulling down the turban wrapped around his face, he was instantly recognizable as Abdul Rashid Dostum. The warlord addressed the CIA officer using the honorific for father or wise old man. "Baba Jan," he said. "Welcome to Afghanistan. You must have some tea."

It was clear that Dostum inspired unquestioning loyalty from his men, who viewed him with a combination of love, fear, and awe. Noting his powerful frame and gruff demeanor, Team Alpha members nicknamed him Bluto, after the cartoon sailor and rival to Popeye. Loud, jovial, and impatient, Dostum was determined to launch a new push against the Taliban, whose front lines were less than a mile away. "Baba Jan, I know you," he told J.R. "In the 1980s, you tried to kill me. Now we're on the same side." The pair had in fact never met, but Dostum had heard of the six-four blue-eyed American who spoke Dari with a northern Afghan accent and had helped the mujahideen. Though it was an exaggeration that J.R. had tried to kill Dostum, it was certainly true the CIA man had collected intelligence on the warlord fighting for the communist Democratic Republic of Afghanistan. Now, they were on the same side. "Welcome to the team," J.R. said, handing Dostum a bag containing $1 million as his initial payment from the CIA.

When Dostum asked J.R. his deputy's name, the Team Alpha leader replied, "Iskandar"—Dari for Alexander. Dostum's eyes widened, and a reverent silence descended over his aides. J.R. turned to Alex Hernandez. "Holy shit," he said. "The only Iskandar they know is Alexander the Great. There's no room for weakness or failure here."

It was impressive enough for an American to be fluent in Dari, but the Afghans were astonished by David Tyson's command of Uzbek. Many had never met anyone from the United States, and none of them imagined that an American could speak their language. Referred to as Daoud Aka, or Older Brother David, he began a running joke with the

Afghans that he was an Uzbek who had moved to America later in life and was now returning to his homeland. A few believed the jest.

David felt comfortable with these Afghan Uzbeks in a way that no other Team Alpha member ever would. Able to engage in wordplay and subtle humor in their own language, the CIA man was able to connect with them on a deeper level. He understood that the brutal nature of the Jumbesh—the name used for Dostum's political party and warriors—and their practice of switching sides was part of their need to survive. These were a tough, unsentimental people who were nevertheless open-hearted and generous to their guests and allies.

J.R., by contrast, was intensely suspicious of Dostum. In part this stemmed from his responsibilities as team leader. One of J.R.'s principal duties was to keep the CIA men safe—and that meant taking nothing for granted. Before the first meeting with Dostum, in a concrete hut, David argued that the CIA men should leave their Kalashnikovs outside, along with their boots, as a sign of trust. J.R. disagreed. "No disrespect," he said. "We're in Afghanistan and Dostum doesn't exactly have the reputation of Mother Teresa." The Americans went inside with their weapons, but no boots.

"Some tea" turned out to be a council of war among the CIA, Dostum, and Mohammed Mohaqeq, the local Hazara leader, who had some 3,000 Hezb-i-Wahdat fighters at his disposal. Relations between Dostum and Mohaqeq—a cleric who had fought with the mujahideen—were on a firm footing: the Uzbeks and Hazaras were long-established brothers-in-arms. Notably absent was Atta Muhammad Noor, an ethnic Tajik from Massoud's Jamiat-i Islami party, whose fighters were essential if Mazar-i Sharif was to be captured. As was the way in Afghanistan, Atta had been Dostum's deadly rival as well as his ally of convenience. It was J.R.'s job to use appeals to anti-Taliban principles, money, or the threat of US retribution—or any combination of the three he felt necessary—to ensure that Atta was with Dostum for this fight.

Dostum did most of the talking. He made it plain he wanted to fight, and that his main wish was for American air power. His Uzbek horse-mounted troops were valiant warriors, he explained, but their AK-47s and RPGs were no match for the Taliban's tanks, armored vehicles, truck-borne ZU-23-2 automatic cannons, and towed artillery pieces. J.R., David, Mike, and Justin sat cross-legged on the floor with the Afghans. Among Dostum's senior aides was Amir Jan Naseri, a mysterious former Taliban commander who had recently switched sides and defected to Dostum. A Pashtun and ex-mujahideen fighter from the ancient city of Balkh, he had been a Taliban leader in Mazar-i Sharif. Naseri prompted deep suspicion among several of the Uzbek commanders—as well as within Team Alpha. Dostum, however, seemed to trust him, and would use him to glean intelligence on enemy movements and to make overtures to Taliban commanders.

Also present at the meeting was a man Dostum introduced as "my Iranian friend." He was a member of the Quds Force, later designated by the United States as a terrorist group. After a brief discussion between Dostum and J.R., the Iranian was asked to leave. As a Shia state, Iran opposed the Taliban, who were Sunni; nonetheless, the US was the enemy of the fundamentalist mullahs in Tehran, who viewed America as the "Great Satan."

Cofer Black's concept of the CIA operation after 9/11 was to push authority downward, granting extraordinary freedom of action to those on the ground. Thus, he had placed Hank Crumpton in charge of running the war; Black would deal with the Washington politics. Crumpton had delegated responsibility for much of northern Afghanistan to J.R.; the two spoke by satellite phone daily, but J.R. had almost carte blanche to make tactical decisions, even if they had strategic implications. There was no second-guessing from CIA headquarters.

In the morning, the Afghans drove the CIA men in a truck along a dry riverbed that doubled as the road to Dehi, where Dostum had set up a temporary base. Along the way were deserted Hazara villages that had been ethnically cleansed by the Taliban. Afghans leading donkey caravans were forced to the shoulder by the truck. The donkeys would speed up as the truck approached, quickening their short steps as their riders beat them feverishly with sticks. The riders would then jump off while the donkeys were still in motion, herding the animals away from the truck's path. David was entranced.

The base was a fifty-yard-square courtyard surrounded by high mud walls and flanked by mud huts, with a stone cistern in the center. It looked like something out of the old American West; J.R. nicknamed it the Alamo. Team Alpha's initial role was to pave the way for the twelve-man ODA 595. The plan was for the Green Berets to assist the Afghans in fighting the Taliban. The CIA, meanwhile, would seek out intelligence—particularly on Al-Qaeda—and manipulate the tribal politics. Both Team Alpha and ODA 595 would remain with Dostum all the way to Mazar-i Sharif.

7

TWO CADILLACS

THE ARRIVAL OF the CIA meant that Dostum needed to coordinate his forces throughout the Darya Suf Valley for the campaign to drive the Taliban north and out of the mountains. Radio communications were patchy and Dostum had not heard from one of his principal commanders, who had the nom de guerre Tufan, meaning "hurricane," for almost two weeks. Late on their first day in Afghanistan, Andy, Mark Rausenberger and David Tyson—the latter carrying one of the new AK-47s that had been delivered to Dostum's forces—were driven south to link up with Tufan.

When they arrived at the hamlet of Besh Qariya, they learned that Tufan had been wounded in a skirmish with the Taliban eleven days earlier. They were warned that his injuries were shocking. Andy told David that whatever he saw when they were taken in to meet Tufan, it was important not to react. Confronted by the grisly sight of the commander, his turban still on his head, lying down, stricken and moaning, in a dark, filthy room, however, David forgot the advice. "Oh my God!" he exclaimed. Tufan's jaw and the lower part of his face had been torn off by three bullets. His intact tongue was hanging loose over exposed bone and a few teeth—all that remained of his mouth. He could not speak. Tufan's elderly father was with him, feeding him by forcing a tube into his throat and pouring broth down it. Tufan was emaciated, and though his father had been cleaning the massive wound daily, there had been no medication available. Mark gave Tufan some Motrin for the pain and told David that the commander would die if he did not receive hospital treatment soon.

Wide-eyed from shock, Tufan gazed at the Americans. A medical evacuation was out of the question. The Army was not flying in the day-time, and it had been mandated that only American casualties would be brought back to K2. David debated whether he should tell Tufan, in front of his father, that he was almost certain to die. The CIA man wanted to buoy their spirits, but decided he had to deliver the truth. "There is nothing we can do for you unless you are in a hospital, and that's impossible," David said. "I'm very sorry. We are surrounded by Taliban and it is not safe to bring in a helicopter."

David had never seen a man shot before, or had to tell someone they would die. More than anyone else on Team Alpha, he felt as if he had now joined this Afghan tribe that would be eating, sleeping, and fighting together for weeks, perhaps months. But he was an American, and they were Afghans—and he realized there was a tacit acceptance on both sides that his life counted for more.

Justin Sapp, tasked with setting up LZ Albatross for ODA 595, chose a tilled field adjacent to the Alamo for the site. ODA 595 was supposed to leave K2 late on October 17, twenty-four hours after Team Alpha. Another ODA, however, was given priority. That night, a Chinook captained by Chief Warrant Officer Andy Sentiff took ODA 555—known as Triple Nickel—over the Bear and toward the Panjshir Valley, where they were to link up with Gary Schroen's Jawbreaker team. At 21,000 feet, however—battling freezing conditions, and with the radar inoperable—they turned back.

On the night of October 18—Day 2 for Team Alpha—the same thing happened. Captain Joe, the mission commander, was apoplectic that the weather forecast had once again been wildly off. A former Delta Force operator who had become a Chinook pilot, Captain Joe had grown up in rural Virginia and was a combat veteran of Panama and the Gulf War. Storming into the operations room on his return from this second aborted insertion, he grabbed an Air Force captain by the collar and told him, "If you ever fucking lie to me again, I will literally take you at gunpoint, strap you to my aircraft, and take you with me!"

Alan Mack, due to take in ODA 595, was also raging. If Sentiff kept turning back, Mack feared, the ODA missions might be taken away from the Chinooks. Sentiff was convinced he would die if he kept being forced to fly this way. He shared a joke with another pilot about emptying his M4 rifle into aircraft on the runway so he would be hauled off to the military psychologist. But this cut no ice with Mack. Three days earlier, he and Sentiff had shared an illicit cup of Jack Daniel's and talked about the perils of high-altitude flying in Afghanistan; now they were on the brink of a fistfight. Mack called Sentiff a "pussy" and a "sissy," and soon the two men were shoving each other and squaring off. Another aviator stepped between them as someone in the background repeated a line from the 1964 movie *Dr. Strangelove*: "Gentlemen, you can't fight in here. This is the War Room!"

In Washington as well as at K2, the pressure to get American troops into Afghanistan after 9/11 was reaching fever pitch. Donald Rumsfeld, the US Defense Secretary, had been bending the ear of Mulholland, the Task Force Dagger commander. The colonel had been alerted by a friend in the Pentagon that Rumsfeld was considering firing him. Mulholland, who had endured Pentagon staff officers telling him he should parachute ODAs into Afghanistan, was at peace with being relieved of command. Rumsfeld was livid that the Pentagon was beholden to the CIA. "The Department of Defense is many times bigger than the CIA, and yet we are sitting here like little birds in a nest, waiting for someone to drop food in our mouths," he told General Tommy Franks. On October 16, the day Team Alpha had left K2 for Afghanistan, Rumsfeld had railed during an NSC meeting: "This is the CIA's strategy…you guys are in charge. You guys have the contacts. We're just following you in."

On October 19—Team Alpha's Day 3 in Afghanistan—Franks phoned the Defense Secretary to say that because "it appears that you no longer have confidence in me…you should select another commander." Rumsfeld demurred, but shortly afterward, early in the morning in Uzbekistan, a 160th staff officer at K2 received a call from the Pentagon. "Please hold for the Secretary," said a female voice. Seconds later, another voice came on the line: "This is Donald Rumsfeld. Who am I speaking to?" There was no discussion. Rumsfeld directed that ODAs 595 and 555 were to be inserted into Afghanistan that night, no matter what the weather. Already irked that the CIA had unveiled a war plan when the Army had none, and that its officers had arrived in Afghanistan before the Green Berets, the famously irascible Pentagon chief had had enough.

That night, ODA 595 boarded Alan Mack's Chinook, bound for the Darya Suf. After traversing the Bear and refueling, Mack hit a sandstorm. Having ripped into Sentiff for not being prepared for the weather, Mack was now struggling to see. He switched to his Multi-Mode Radar (MMR) system, which allowed him to fly in Terrain Following (TF) mode by staring at a gauge the size of a silver dollar and adjusting the controls to keep two inverted triangles from touching each other. Mack reasoned that he might not be able to see the mountains, but that meant no one in the mountains with a heat-seeking missile could see him either. Both Mack and Sentiff got their Chinooks into Afghanistan that night.

None of the Green Berets spoke Dari, and they had been told by Colonel Mulholland's staff that Dostum's forces might kidnap them. Their intelligence profile of the Uzbek warlord was much less accurate than the information the CIA had gathered and lacked the insights that Charlie Santos had been able to provide CENTCOM. The Green Berets had expected Dostum to be frail and several decades older than his forty-seven years. A combination of the pressure of being at the forefront of America's response to 9/11, the long wait at K2, and the impression made by briefers stressing worst-case scenarios meant that some of the men feared they were on a suicide mission and would be killed or captured within minutes of landing. Watching them emerge from the dusty LZ at 2 a.m., weapons at the ready, David Tyson was afraid they might open fire on their Afghan hosts.

"Welcome to the Stone Age," Justin greeted them. Andy Marchal, the intelligence sergeant on ODA 595 and a native of the backwoods of West Virginia, replied, "Don't worry—I'm used to it." The Green Berets slept in a stable, surrounded by a security perimeter maintained by a constant two-man guard. The CIA men shrugged and bedded down in the mud rooms of the Alamo. It was ironic, David thought, that the spies were more trusting than the soldiers.

Dostum was due to appear at the Alamo at 8:30 a.m. Perhaps to test the newest Americans, he turned up an hour early with more than fifty horsemen, their arrival heralded by an advance guard of seven riders. Dostum sat astride his white horse, Surkun, flanked by turbaned fighters with bandoliers across their chests and brandishing rifles, machine guns, and RPGs. The scene reminded David of *Genghis Khan,* the 1965 movie in which Omar Sharif plays the legendary Mongol emperor. Indeed, Dostum and his men proudly traced their lineage to the hordes of Khan, one of history's greatest conquerors. Apart from the firearms the Uzbek warriors carried, battle tactics had not changed much in the intervening 800 years.

Captain Mark Nutsch was compact, blue-eyed, and gap-toothed, with light-brown hair and a sandy goatee. The thirty-two-year-old had grown up on a Kansas ranch and was fortuitously an expert horseman. Dostum was the physical opposite of what the Green Berets had expected—stronger, younger, and much friendlier. Nutsch made a mental note to ignore the intelligence he'd been given on Dostum, much of it gleaned from faded copies of *National Geographic* and books about Soviet combat tactics in Afghanistan more than a decade earlier. Dostum greeted the man he would come to revere as "Commander Mark," then led him into the Alamo and spread out a huge, hand-drawn map. With no bedding available, Justin had tried to keep warm by sleeping under the map the night before. "This is what I want to do today," Dostum announced.

Nutsch spoke what he described as "caveman-level Russian," and this helped him converse with Dostum, who had learned the language while fighting for the Soviets. Like all Green Berets during his initial Special Forces training—the Q Course, or Qualifying Course—Nutsch had completed an "unconventional warfare" exercise in North Carolina called Robin Sage, set in the fictional republic of Pineland. He had been required to shadow and build a rapport with the guerrilla chief—or "G-Chief"—counseling and supporting him while steering him toward accomplishing American aims and adhering to the laws of war. Though trainees often believed the exercise was unrealistic, Nutsch now realized that he had stepped into a real-life Robin Sage in which Dostum was the G-Chief. Like Team Alpha's Andy, several of the Green Berets hailed from Appalachia. They quickly grasped that the occupants of the Darya Suf Valley shared traits with the bygone clans of West Virginia, where extended families had lived in isolated hollers and formed alliances, pursued rivalries, and nursed grievances for generations.

Dostum explained to J.R. and Nutsch that the enemy occupied most of the villages in the Darya Suf Valley, which led into the larger Balkh Valley, also controlled by Taliban forces. His plan was to use a combination of US air power and cavalry charges to overwhelm the Taliban, then push north through the Balkh Valley to the Tang-i Cheshme Shifa Pass—literally the Narrows of the Medicinal Spring and known to the Americans as the Tangi Gap. Dostum could then recapture Qala-i Jangi—the fort that had been his headquarters and was now in the hands of the Taliban—and, seven miles farther east, Mazar-i Sharif. "Now we will go and kill the Taliban," Dostum announced. "We leave in fifteen minutes."

Only then did it dawn on the CIA officers that the route was too rough for vehicles. The only way to get there was on horseback. They would be riding to war. ODA 595, however, was not traveling light. As well as their M4 rifles, pistols, grenades, and ammunition, they carried food, water, and M86 Pursuit Deterrent Munitions—antipersonnel mines for use when being chased by enemy forces. Everything had to be loaded on the horses, strapped down and carefully balanced. The impatient Dostum rode off, telling David that the Green Berets could catch up later. Ahead of them lay a two-hour ride north to Dostum's mountain headquarters, next to the Taliban front line.

With Dostum still out ahead, the Green Berets, accompanied by Justin and David, rode through the Dehi bazaar. Dostum's men had warned them to be wary of the Hazara village, so Nutsch instructed his five Green Berets, "Smile and wave with one hand, and grip your weapon tight with the other, ready to fire." The male villagers, dirty and dressed in little more than rags, peered out from their stalls and workshops or thronged the street to catch a glimpse of these seemingly futuristic warriors. As the Americans moved through the back streets, children and veiled women came out to stare. The children, standing on walls and roofs, looked like miniature adults—some of the boys wearing hats, the hair of the girls matted and unkempt. A few small boys ran barefoot down a stony hillside.

David had been given a brown horse called Turug, which was calm and steadfast as he crossed deep streams and navigated irrigation ditches. They passed a man on a horse, his AK-47 slung over his shoulder, who regarded the Americans with curiosity, as if trying to establish whether they were Russians or other invaders he might have seen before—and whether he could trust them. Some ten yards behind, sitting sidesaddle on a mule and clad in a burqa that covered her from head to foot, was one of his wives; Afghans were permitted up to four.

After Dehi came a steep incline, the wind whipping up dust as the horses climbed higher. Turug slipped twice, squealing and clopping his hooves as he regained his footing. At points the trail narrowed to three feet. Turug jumped or crouched whenever they descended into dips, forcing David to grip the reins.

Dehi now lay far below; beyond it stretched a breathtaking vista of snow-peaked mountains beneath a clear blue sky. The American group caught up with Dostum, and David rode beside the warlord, who complimented him on the tastiness of the humanitarian meals that had arrived in a US airdrop the night before. A Green Beret sergeant was struggling to control his horse, which reared up and galloped ahead before racing back, seemingly oblivious to its rider. Watching the powerless sergeant cling fast for dear life, Dostum roared with laughter: "Surely he is the greatest horseman in Afghanistan!"

Dostum's command position, well fortified with bunkers and trenches, occupied a barren, windswept hilltop just south of Cobaki. His bunker was carpeted and had a stove, from which the Americans were served Uzbek pilaf rice. Nutsch's team used a GPS receiver to fix their own position and calculate the distance to a Taliban position just visible through binoculars five miles to the north. They then radioed the coordinates to a B-52 bomber some 20,000 feet overhead.

The B-52, which had flown thirteen hours from the Indian Ocean island of Diego Garcia, carried six 2,000-pound bombs, known as JDAMs—Joint Direct Attack Munitions—after their precision-guidance systems. The first two JDAMs landed a mile west of the position; the third detonated about 200 yards away. Nutsch and Justin watched dozens of Taliban fighters emerge to inspect the crater. The Green Berets radioed the B-52, trying to talk the plane onto the target, but with no distinctive landmarks it was a fruitless task. The next three bombs landed more than two miles away. Dostum did not seem to mind they were astray, and his Uzbek soldiers giddily rejoiced as the bombs landed. "That's it!" shouted Dostum as the munitions exploded. Over the radio, David could hear Taliban fighters screaming in Pashtun and Uzbek commanders reporting that the enemy was running in panic. Dostum had paraded the Green Berets through Dehi, and the Taliban surely knew that American bombers had arrived in the Darya Suf Valley. "I am here, and I have brought the Americans with me," Dostum boasted over the radio.

On the way back to the Alamo, David was assigned a different horse. The saddle—a rough, carpet-covered wooden frame, built for Afghans much thinner and lighter than Americans—was too far forward and the stirrups too high, causing his legs to bump constantly into the horse's shoulders. While David was still on the hilltop, the new horse bolted down the slope and ran in small circles while three Uzbeks hurried over to help. David's confidence with riding was shattered, and the ride was intensely painful—his groin hit the front of the saddle and his feet grew numb as they lost circulation. When he got back to the Alamo, David jumped down from the saddle and almost fell over as his legs buckled beneath him. J.R. had grown up riding in western New York and Mike had owned a Shetland pony as a child, but no one was prepared for this kind of riding. The most expert horseman on Team Alpha was Andy, who had ridden extensively in Appalachia. He soon found, however, that Afghan horses were different; not only were they smaller but they fought with one another and had been trained to run toward gunfire rather than away.

Mike had called Shannon from K2 and told her that he was writing down his reflections on recent events so he could share them with her when he got back. Sitting at home on Lanae Lane shortly after Mike got to Afghanistan, Shannon wrote: "The house is quiet, and so I'm here speaking to my favorite person. I miss you so much, especially in the evenings. However, even though we're a bit sick, we're all doing quite well, I should say. Emily had to do a little homework for school, a picture of a tree, and we were supposed to decorate it as a family tree, and so we made leaves and printed out pictures of all of our faces, and it made me so happy to see all of our family on one page. I can't wait until we're all together."

Shannon let him know she had been reading St. Paul's Epistle to the Philippians: "Finally, brethren, whatever is true, whatever is honorable, whatever is right, whatever is pure, whatever is lovely, whatever is of good repute, if there is any excellence and if anything worthy of praise, dwell on these things." She told him: "That verse made me feel special because it made me think of you, my husband: true, honorable, bright, pure, lovely, of good repute, excellent and worthy of praise. All words that describe you, my dear." The word "lovely," she elaborated, described his love for her and the children. She signed off: "Now I shall go to bed a lucky girl, and dwell on these things and the happiness of belonging to you."

*　　*　　*

"I need to see Atta," J.R. told Dostum. The Tajik leader commanded substantial forces in the Darya Suf Valley and was a crucial link to the Northern Alliance leadership in the Panjshir Valley—the only Afghan territory currently denied to the Taliban, where the CIA's Jawbreaker team was embedded. "Well, there's a problem with that," Dostum said. "He's refusing to see you." J.R. discussed the issue with Gary Schroen, the Jawbreaker team leader, who in turn raised it with the new Northern Alliance leader, Fahim Khan—Massoud's heir and Atta's commander. Grudgingly, Atta agreed to meet J.R.

The meeting took place on October 22, Day 6 for Team Alpha. Atta was in a compound just outside Dehi—he could easily have met the the Americans earlier. Brooding and with a heavy, inky-black beard that made him resemble the *Tintin* character Captain Haddock, the Tajik warlord received J.R. with a bare minimum of politeness. Although he spoke English, Atta pretended not to—a maneuver to slow down the conversation and give him time to scheme and deliberate before answering questions. He also insisted on addressing the Team Alpha leader in a literary form of Farsi. J.R. himself spoke what he characterized as "barracks Farsi," because he was used to conversing with fighters and tribesmen. But Atta was more interested in posturing and trying to get the upper hand than in communicating effectively.

For this meeting J.R. was sporting a pakol hat, favored by the Tajiks but not the Uzbeks. But Atta faulted the way J.R. was wearing it and directed an aide to rearrange the pakol for the American. Atta's performance was for the benefit of his aides, who doubtless would describe the encounter to Fahim in the Panjshir Valley.

Atta accused the CIA of supporting Dostum and Mohaqeq against the Tajiks. J.R. flatly rejected this. The United States, he said, had no interest in taking sides in Afghanistan and would work with anyone who could help overthrow the Taliban and expel Al-Qaeda. J.R. was correct, though that would soon change and the United States would spend much of the next two decades choosing sides. Atta was contemptuous of US military efforts thus far: "You have been bombing for almost fifteen days," he told J.R. "But you have not captured any significant areas yet."

While Atta was prepared to be a military ally in the push north to Mazar-i Sharif, he viewed himself as more important than Dostum and wanted the Americans to validate that. In agreement with Fahim, he had given himself the title of General Commander of Resistance Against the Taliban in the North. It was clear to J.R. that Atta was already trying to position himself for the post-Taliban settlement. Bundles of US dollars, weapons, and other supplies came with the CIA and the Green Berets, and hatred of the Taliban was a common cause. But competition for American cash and impending new power only fueled old enmities.

J.R. found this tedious, but he would play the game. Atta's stance was ludicrous; both men knew that the Americans possessed the military might needed to end Taliban rule. Atta groused about the several hundred thousand dollars J.R. had brought him. Not averse to a power play himself, J.R. pointed out that this was in addition to the $250,000 given to Fahim for transfer to Atta. Atta's crestfallen look confirmed J.R.'s hunch that Fahim had kept the money for himself. The warlord swiftly acknowledged that of course he recognized this was an additional sum.

The CIA man's greatest fear was that Atta would launch a military attack against Dostum if he felt he was being left out in the cold by the Americans. The CIA knew that internecine warfare could strangle in the cradle any attempt to overthrow the Taliban. The challenge was huge: to get three military commanders from rival ethnic groups to fight the Taliban and not one another—or, in the worst-case scenario, the Americans. J.R. calculated that Team Alpha would have to split up at times to support different factions, and that Atta's forces had to be supplied independently with weapons and food. Alex expressed his concerns about Atta to J.R.: "We've got Americans here risking their lives and he's still playing this tribal politics bullshit?"

For the time being, Dostum was all in with the Americans. After finishing a conversation in Russian on his satellite phone, the warlord turned to J.R. "That was Vladimir Putin's interpreter," he said. "He asked me to come to a meeting of Central Asia leaders in Dushanbe. I told him I have some new friends and I am a little busy." But Dostum knew that the alliance between him and the US was one of convenience. Dostum loved MREs (Meals Ready to Eat—US military rations) and often chatted with David as he ate. One evening, the two men discussed the future. "We're going to use you and you're going to use us until we get to Mazar," David told him. "After we get to Mazar, I have no idea what's going to happen." Dostum nodded. He was a practical man and this was what he had presumed.

*　　*　　*

Osama bin Laden had calculated that the Americans would leave Afghanistan as soon as they sustained casualties, as they had in Lebanon in 1983 and Somalia a decade later. Dostum was working off a similar assumption. He wanted US air power and money, but no American blood spilled. "Five hundred of my men can die," he said, "but not one American can even be injured, or you will leave."

Intelligence sources from Dostum's network claimed that Pakistani hit teams had been sent in to kill Americans and that Al-Qaeda bounties had been placed on their heads. Dostum took the reports seriously. When Justin tried to go for a walk outside the Alamo, he found himself being followed by Abdul Sattar, Dostum's security commander. "I'm just going for a walk," Justin told Sattar. "I don't need anyone with me." The Afghan replied, "No, you don't understand. If you get hurt, General Dostum will cut my head off. He'll kill me." Sattar was a brute of a man—a squat, barrel-chested former wrestler with a rough beard—but he clearly feared Dostum. Justin reckoned that bodyguards were also a way for Dostum to track what the Americans were doing: trust went only so far.

Dostum's reluctance to let ODA 595 get close to the enemy was a major headache for Captain Nutsch and his men. As they had discovered at Cobaki, five miles was too far for effective air strikes. In subsequent days, F-14 and F-18 fighters from the aircraft carrier USS *Enterprise* in the Arabian Sea occasionally failed to find enemy targets on which to drop their bombs. On the radio, the frustration was evident in the voices of the US Navy pilots. In late October 2001, returning to an aircraft carrier with bombs still strapped on was not the outcome the crew desired or expected.

Dostum was growing frustrated that the Americans had yet to kill any enemy fighters. ODA 595 had arrived in the Darya Suf Valley without a US Air Force air controller—a specialist at calling in air strikes—or a Special Operations Forces Laser Acquisition Marker (SOFLAM). A box and viewfinder mounted on a tripod and resembling a movie camera, the SOFLAM could paint a target with a laser beam, which a missile could then lock on to. To Alex's frustration, the two SOFLAMs he had arranged to be sent to K2 for Team Alpha had been diverted to the Panjshir Valley for Jawbreaker.

J.R. encouraged Alex to sit down with ODA 595 to discuss Dostum's fear of an American getting killed. "Listen, guys, I've had these experiences, too," Alex told the Green Berets over dinner. "If you need to break down into smaller teams, you can leave your gear here and I'll get it to you. But if Dostum won't bring you the horses, you have a responsibility to start walking."

After some persuasion, Dostum took Nutsch to within two miles of the Taliban, who were defending the village of Beshcam. The ensuing air strike was a direct hit on a group of Taliban pickup trucks, reducing them to twisted metal and scattered body parts. Nutsch then watched cavalry charges from waves of Dostum's men, firing RPGs and AK-47s from horseback before dismounting and fighting hand to hand. Further air strikes took out Taliban tanks and artillery pieces before the final American pilot, low on fuel, had to withdraw, leaving Dostum's 300 men fighting a rearguard action against a Taliban counterattack.

Work had to be done on coordinating bombing. But the combination of 21st-century American technology and Afghans fighting much as they had in the 19th century was taking shape. Beshcam fell to Dostum on October 23. Within days, SOFLAMs and two air controllers were dispatched to ODA 595. They transformed the battlefield in the Darya Suf Valley and would hasten the fall of Mazar-i Sharif.

*   *   *

On the side of a mountain near Dehi, several hundred Afghan fighters, Uzbeks, Turkmens, and Hazaras were gathered, dressed in chapans and turbans, their horses snorting and whinnying beside them. These were Dostum's men. For J. R. Seeger, the scene drove home the contrast between Dostum and Fatim—the hardened mountain fighters versus the Tajiks biding their time north of Kabul. Rallying his troops, the larger-than-life Uzbek warlord implored them to fight like men possessed, and to slaughter the enemy. The Taliban deserved no mercy, he thundered. They should feel honored to die at the hands of Dostum's army.

Dostum's speech reminded the Team Alpha leader of the blood-thirsty, profane address in the opening scene of *Patton,* the same movie that had inspired Justin as a boy. In the film, the general tells his men: "We're not just going to shoot the bastards. We're going to cut out their living guts and use them to grease the treads of our tanks." Dostum, who already stood accused of committing atrocities with tank treads, spoke in a similarly savage fashion. A little later, Dostum finished a satellite-phone interview with the BBC, in which he had delivered a more nuanced message. He turned to J.R. "You know, Baba Jan," he said. "I suspect that while you were watching me today, talking to the soldiers, you were thinking, 'This man is a barbarian.' I can see why, but you have to understand that this is a persona I have to adopt when I'm talking to my men, so that they will follow me and fight." J.R. nodded. Then Dostum leaned over, looked the CIA man straight in the eye, and said: "But I'm a sophisticated guy. I've owned a Cadillac. I've actually owned *two* Cadillacs." J.R. didn't know whether to laugh or feign awe.

Dostum liked to regale J.R. with his war stories, which were brimful with bravado. During a night staying in a cave next to his command post at Cobaki, Dostum told J.R.: "You know, they tried to kill me last month. Fired artillery on this position. Buried me alive in this cave. But did I die? Of course not—because *I am Dostum!*" J.R. wondered quietly about his own decision to spend the night in the cave, given that he was not Dostum.

Back at CTC/SO, Hank Crumpton had directed that the CIA officers should follow Lawrence of Arabia's dictum: "Do not try to do too much with your own hands. Better the Arabs do it tolerably than that you do it perfectly. It is their war, and you are to help them, not to win it for them." Hyper-conscious of Team Alpha's safety, J.R. and Alex told the CIA men that their weapons were to be used only in extremis. Alex was the only Team Alpha member who had opened fire in the first few days; venturing too far forward with the Green Berets, he had been caught in a Taliban ambush. The Americans had beaten a hasty retreat, firing their rifles to keep the enemy at bay. Alex hadn't mentioned this to the rest of the team. The message from the two leaders was that if CIA officers opened fire, they had failed; it meant they were not collecting intelligence.

Justin and Mike chafed against this; they were young men eager for combat, but they accepted the chain of command. David Tyson was different. His academic background, facility with languages, and years of assimilation in Central Asia made him the outlier among the eight members of Team Alpha. He acted with an independence and a confidence regarding the Afghans that led to animated debates with J.R. David's Uzbek language skills meant he was often alone with the Afghans, miles separating him from the other Americans. The CIA had issued no Rules of Engagement about when its officers were permitted to open fire. If he was with Afghans pursuing the Taliban and Al-Qaeda, David wanted to be part of the posse.

On October 23, Day 7, David and Mark, the Team Alpha medic, rode to a nearby village to receive an airdrop of supplies, including crates of AK-47s bought by the CIA in Eastern Europe. Escorting them was Abdul Sattar, who struck David as Dostum's alter ego—an Uzbek Afghan embodiment of the US Marine Corps mantra NO BETTER FRIEND, NO WORSE ENEMY. With an AK-47 slung across his back, a bandolier across his chest, and a knife in his belt, Sattar made it easy to believe the rumor that he had thrown Taliban prisoners to their deaths from a mountain ledge before the Americans arrived. One Afghan told David, "All he has to do is look at someone and they will beat themselves."

Airdrops had become a major headache. They always occurred in the middle of the night, depriving everyone of sleep, and they almost invariably missed the designated drop zone—sometimes by a wide margin. In addition, the poverty of the locals meant they would do almost anything to reach the supplies before Americans or Afghan soldiers could. The US Air Force was unwilling to risk an aircraft being hit by Taliban surface fire, remote though that possibility was. C-17 Globemaster crews, flying from Ramstein Air Base in Germany, dropped boxes from a lofty 29,000 feet.

Humanitarian drops, which had begun on October 7, the night the bombing campaign started, were a core part of the Bush administration's promise to deliver $320 million in aid to the Afghan people. Weapons, ammunition, communications equipment, and horse feed were also dropped—these were for the Americans and Dostum's troops. Even lower-altitude drops went wrong. At 2 a.m. on October 21, Day 5, four 500-pound bundles dropped from a C-130 landed more than 1,000 yards from the drop zone. Two of the packages splashed into the Darya Suf; the other two came to rest on its opposite bank. By the time the Americans reached the bundles, nothing was left but barley for horses—which turned out to be infested with insects. Two days later, bundles of wheat burst open when they hit the ground, scattering the grain over the wet soil. On other drops, Dostum's men beat the locals with sticks and rifle butts to keep them away from the supplies.

The drop on Day 7 was near a Hazara village, whose occupants had been warned by Sattar and his men not to touch the supplies. As usual the drop went astray, with pallets spread across a hillside. As the two Americans and Sattar approached, they saw an elderly Afghan clambering over the pallets. They dismounted some twenty yards away, whereupon Sattar raised his AK-47 and shot the old man, who fell to the ground, gasping. Grabbing his medical bag, Mark ran toward the man. The stricken Afghan had a sucking chest wound that would almost certainly be fatal. Instinctively, Mark began to treat the victim, but Sattar raised his rifle butt as if he intended to strike the CIA officer. "Don't waste your equipment on this guy," Sattar said. "He was stealing our stuff."

Reality was already tempering David's initial euphoria at being inside Afghanistan. He felt he was part of a noble mission. He was doing everything he had joined the CIA to do, using his languages and his years of experience and cultural assimilation in Central Asia. But this was no longer just an exciting adventure. People were dying. Callousness existed alongside camaraderie. David admired Sattar and the other Uzbeks. He respected their confidence, their toughness, and the fact that they did not resent the Americans for being different and well-off. Unlike the Tajiks in the Panjshir Valley, they neither complained nor proselytized, and they willingly embraced what was new. But David could also see what years of conflict had done to them. "Their suffering, endurance, and will are incredible," he scrawled in his diary, a spiral-bound notebook. "That said, all this has contributed to their being relentless and even cruel fighters who are forced to put their humanity aside."

Both Dostum's men and the CIA officers were experiencing a jarring culture shock. The Afghans marveled at the size of the Americans, their soft hands, and all the gear they had brought with them. The Afghans improvised with everything. Once the airdrops started, the parachute straps and bundle ties were fashioned into bridles and reins for the horses. "The Uzbeks let nothing go to waste and think of their horses first," David noted in his diary. They had, however, failed to calculate for the stretch factor in the nylon parachute cords. Andy laughed as he watched the saddles slip off, leaving the rider hanging underneath the horse.

Most of the Americans were ill at ease around horses—an endless source of mirth for Dostum's men. When David dismounted from his horse because of an aching knee and two other Americans followed suit, the Uzbek fighters were alarmed. "No men of such stature should walk!" one chided. Each morning when Commander Lal, Dostum's deputy, spied David mounting his horse, he would approach with his own steed, which would bite David's. As the two horses sparred, David routinely fell off as laughing Afghans crowded around. Whereas the Americans spoke of distances and elevations as absolute values, the Afghans could describe things only in relation to the landscape. Dostum could read a map; most of his men could not.

In a nearby village, Sattar was strong-arming a local herder into handing over some of his sheep when David intervened with a $100 bill— more than six months' income for the average Afghan, but the only unit of currency the CIA carried. Sattar gave David a pitying look, then tossed him a blunt knife, pointed at the sheep, and asked, "Okay, what time's dinner?" David could not bring himself to slit the animal's throat. After that, Afghan banter with David included the gibe "I see that your ability to slaughter the sheep is very impressive." Another barb from the Afghans, who squatted to urinate, was: "You're standing up to piss. I wonder, is this an ancient cultural tradition of the infidel?" Dostum's men were bawdy and few were religious. One fighter among them who prayed several times a day was teased as "Taliban." When Ramadan came, Dostum would often arrange a "meeting" with the Americans so he could surreptitiously break his fast by munching on MREs.

Team Alpha members noticed that when one of them was nudged

to get up for guard duty or to collect an airdrop, the man being woken would instantly reach for his pistol, or even lash out. The sense of danger was becoming ingrained. "We are changing a bit, it seems," David wrote in his diary.

*   *   *

On October 24, Day 8 for Team Alpha, David accompanied Commander Faqir, a tall, powerfully built man with a heavy mustache. Faqir, half-Arab and half-Uzbek, was the most trusted of Dostum's younger lieutenants. Standing beside the CIA man on a hillside, Faqir peered through binoculars and caught the glint of windshields in the far distance. "That's Al-Qaeda," the commander said. "Brigade 055." Also known as Ansar—"the helpers"—or the Arab Brigade, 055 was an Arab foreign legion of holy warriors trained in Osama bin Laden's camps. David was surprised that Faqir knew about them. With no US aircraft nearby—and only thirty horsemen at his disposal—Faqir opted to retreat. Almost immediately, however, the Arabs spotted Faqir and his men. The enemy sped toward Faqir's force in six Toyota Hilux trucks, skidded to a halt, and jumped out.

Some of Faqir's men opened fire. David joined them, using his AK-47 to shoot at the rapidly advancing enemy. Emboldened by David's eagerness to fight, Faqir changed his mind and ordered his men to mount a cavalry charge. As the Arabs continued to press forward, David—flat on his stomach in the sparse vegetation—found himself just 150 yards from the Al-Qaeda men, with a clear view of them. Aiming through the iron sight, he picked off enemy fighters one by one, shooting three of them in the center of their body mass. It was the first time he had killed.

With lethal fire incoming from their flank, the Arab fighters were powerless to stop Faqir's charging horsemen, who killed more than half of them in their first pass before turning back to finish off the rest—some at close quarters with knives. The engagement ended with several dozen Al-Qaeda dead, no survivors, and only a handful of casualties among Faqir's men. The commander was ecstatic to see an American fight, and kill.

David had reflexively shot the first Al-Qaeda fighter in the chest without comprehending the enormity of what he was doing. It was not something he had planned, but his instinct was that if the Afghans were shooting, he should be too. In the split second after the man fell, he asked himself: "What the fuck did you just do?" David had grown up hunting. He remembered helping his father pick up roadkill to take home, cut up, and eat. But a human death, by David's own hand, was of far greater magnitude. "Wow," he thought. "You did it. You just killed someone."

As Faqir's men battled one another for the sneakers worn by the dead Al-Qaeda jihadists—slapping each other in the Afghan way of fighting—David wandered over and looked at the first man whose life he had taken. The victim was in his twenties, with a light, wispy beard. Strapped to the dead man's side was a vintage Enfield bayonet, stamped with the year of its manufacture—1913. David took it as a souvenir. The CIA officer felt neither guilt nor elation, but a sense of power. More than anything, David Tyson realized how easy it was to kill.

8

WILD THING

7:15 a.m. (GMT +4.5), October 25, 2001 (Day 9);
near Yakawlang, Bamiyan province, Afghanistan

IN HIS MOUNTAIN redoubt, Karim Khalili waited for the CIA. The leader of the Hazaras in central Afghanistan, he felt a connection with the Americans. In 1996, he had been among the group of Afghan leaders hosted in the United States by Charlie Santos and Unocal. Walking through Manhattan, Khalili was struck by the fact that the narrow streets and skyscrapers were like the steep valleys and high mountains of central Afghanistan. After 9/11, he had been astonished when Dostum told him via satellite phone that Al-Qaeda—allies of the Taliban, whom Khalili had been battling for the five years since his visit to the United States—had brought down the World Trade Center towers.

Yakawlang—"Place of Shining Light"—in the central highlands of Afghanistan had seen mass murders by the Taliban, whose Al-Qaeda brothers had now slaughtered thousands of Americans. From exile in Iran, Khalili had been certain that the kinship he felt with New Yorkers would soon be forged in war. He secretly returned to Afghanistan, which he considered to be "an inferno" under the Taliban. Now America, too, was ablaze. "It seems best to fight fire with fire," he said.

A scholarly cleric of fifty-one, Khalili had been a fearsome mujahideen fighter against the Russians. He still carried shrapnel in his back and chest from a Soviet bombardment. When doctors had recommended removing it, he told them he wanted the fragments to remain in his body so that on meeting Allah in the afterlife they would prove he had fought the communists. Dostum and the Uzbeks were viewed by the Taliban as godless and debauched, but they were still Sunnis. As Shia, Khalili's Hazaras were the lowest caste in Afghanistan. To the Sunni fundamentalist Taliban, they were infidels—even subhuman.

In January 2001, around 180 Hazaras had been massacred in Yakawlang. Some of the victims were tortured with bayonets and knives. One eyewitness reported seeing people skinned alive with a scalpel, after which the Taliban performed a traditional Pashtun dance. Among those who had orchestrated the massacre by radio was Mullah Mohammad Fazl, now Deputy Minister of Defense and commander of Taliban forces in the north. The world had largely been indifferent to the ethnic cleansing of Hazaras, but international outrage erupted in March 2001 when two 6th-century statues of Buddha were blown up. The Taliban had decided they violated Islamic rulings on idolatry.

By October 25, Day 9 for Team Alpha, the Americans were already losing faith in Fahim Khan, Massoud's replacement as Northern Alliance leader. Despite his broken nose and brutish appearance, he lacked presence and did not inspire his soldiers. Jawbreaker had been in the Panjshir Valley since September 26, but Tajik forces were not moving from there, and Fahim appeared more intent on slowing down Dostum than on seizing territory himself.

Team Alpha and Jawbreaker vied for air power and supplies. With Fahim demanding more and more as his price for fighting, Schroen and J.R. locked in almost nightly battles over which American team should get what. Schroen far outranked J.R., and Alex was growing concerned that Fahim's inaction was hobbling and endangering Team Alpha. J.R. and Alex had jelled as Team Alpha's leaders. Theirs was the classic relationship of the officer with a broad vision who was respected and protected by the trusted senior NCO with greater military experience.

The Jawbreaker team was fixed in place. They had ordered bags of Starbucks coffee from CIA headquarters, which arrived along with two percolators. Schroen had taken to sitting on a patio chair with a mocha to watch the sunrise each day. The cushy conditions enjoyed by Jawbreaker were a running joke among Team Alpha, in denied territory in the mountains, who were dealing with lice and urinary-tract infections as well as injuries from horseback riding.

For Team Alpha, moreover, there was constant danger. One night J.R. slept in a tent next to the burned-out ruins of a Hazara village that had been destroyed by the Taliban. The next morning, he went to use the hole in the ground that had been designated as the toilet. As he walked back, there was a massive explosion. An Afghan fighter who had gone to use the hole after him had stepped on an antipersonnel mine planted there by the Taliban for any Hazaras who tried to return.

Alex was alarmed that the Taliban occupied high ground nearby and were likely preparing to assault Dostum's forces. He believed that momentum in war was everything, and he was sure that the dominoes would begin to topple once Dostum started winning. The Team Alpha deputy was taciturn and loyal, but he felt he had to intervene. Alex called Hank Crumpton in CTC/SO. "Sir, you've got to get Gary Schroen off our back. We can't wait. The war needs to start here today. The Taliban are massing. We're getting pressed and we're not in a position to fight a defensive war. We have to do something."

In Washington, too, frustration was mounting that events were not moving more swiftly. On October 25, Rumsfeld circulated a startlingly pessimistic report produced for him by the Defense Intelligence Agency. It stated: "Northern Alliance forces are incapable of overcoming Taliban resistance in northern Afghanistan, particularly the strategic city of Mazar-i Sharif." The report was equally downbeat about the prospects of capturing Kabul or making inroads in the south. It concluded: "Barring widespread defections, the Northern Alliance will not secure any major gains before winter." Rumsfeld had berated General Franks, who had in turn passed the flak down to Mulholland.

The same day as the DIA report was circulated, a peeved Captain Nutsch typed out an explanation of "some of the realities on the ground" in response to questions "about us and the Northern Alliance just sitting around and doing nothing." The combination of US air power and the tenacity of Dostum's horsemen, he insisted, was defeating the Taliban. Channeling General Patton, he signed off: "We killed the bastards by the bushel-ful today, and we'll get more tomorrow." Steve Bleigh, an ODA 595 medical sergeant, proofread the message and told Nutsch: "This is probably going to end your career." In fact, Nutsch's commentary would soon be celebrated by the very policymakers whose misplaced impatience had triggered it.

The ultimate objective for the Americans was Kabul, but there was more than one route to the Afghan capital. The problems in the Panjshir Valley and Dostum's strength, underscored by Alex, led to a shift of strategy by Crumpton. Cajoling Fahim and the Tajiks would continue, but in the meantime the focus would be on Mazar-i Sharif. Pressure on Kabul could be ratcheted up by helping the Hazaras in central Afghanistan, to Team Alpha's south. With around 3,000 Hazaras under his command, Khalili was an obvious candidate for help from the CIA and the Green Berets. Recapturing Bamiyan, 180 miles west of Kabul, would open another front against the Taliban.

J.R. told Crumpton that Atta, the Tajik warlord, needed his own CIA team and ODA, to ensure that he did not move against Dostum and to strengthen the push to take Mazar-i Sharif while Fahim was stalled. To do this, J.R. decided, he needed to send a three-man pathfinder team to link up with Atta. J.R. selected Scott as team leader, David—who could speak some Dari—and Andy to trek west to Atta. In addition, J.R. and Crumpton agreed to send a second three-man team to be Khalili's path-finders in Yakawlang, sixty miles west of Bamiyan. Khalili would also be getting a CIA team and an ODA. The pathfinder who would liaise with Khalili and prepare the way for the CIA's Team Delta and ODA 553 would be led by Mike; he would take Mark and Justin with him.

Sending away two three-man teams would leave just J.R. and Alex with Dostum. "We're really getting thin now," Alex told J.R. He resented giving Atta anything, and was concerned that Team Alpha was overextended. He knew from experience that splitting up into smaller teams greatly increased risk and invited communications problems. Mike, afraid he would miss out on the battle for Mazar-i Sharif, begged not to go to Bamiyan. Alex sympathized, but told him there was no other option. When he had been in Special Forces, Alex's mantra had been that while perfection was not necessary, he would not do "stupid things." Now, he reflected, he was having to adjust his red line to not doing "*incredibly* stupid things." Everything Team Alpha did was a risk.

Dostum's aggressiveness and willingness to go all in with the Americans was a stark contrast to the wary hesitancy of Fahim and Atta. That meant he now the key to defeating the Taliban nationally. With the weather about to get much colder, however, there was little time to spare. J.R. told Steve Bleigh that this was a pivotal moment. "We have to get out of these mountains before the first snow falls because if we don't, we're going to be up here all winter and it's just going to be a survival exercise," J.R. said. "If we can push these different groups to take Mazar-i Sharif real quick, it will force Fahim and the other Afghans to get off their asses and Kabul will fall."

As Mike and David prepared to depart for their separate missions, word came back from Dostum that prisoners had been captured and needed to be questioned by the CIA. There were about forty of them in Dostum's mountain prison at Bazar-i Sukhta. Mike told J.R., "I want to do this." The Team Alpha commander judged that Mike's by-the-book military approach and David's language skills made them a good pair to deal with captives; Justin would accompany them because, as the young Green Beret officer joked about his role, he was "Mr. Gun Guy" on the team.

On the eve of the trip to interrogate the prisoners, Mike stayed up all night writing down, in his tiny, neat script, scores of questions to ask them. This would be the first large group of Taliban combatants to be questioned by Americans since the 9/11 attacks, and he left nothing to chance. David watched Mike as he wrote and reflected that this was a man who felt a higher calling than simply being a CIA officer carrying out his job professionally.

* * *

The CIA was concerned about how Dostum's men were treating their prisoners. Abdul Salam was in charge of the captives; he was a small, dour man who always seemed to be angry. Early on, Salam brought some to the Alamo one or two at a time. Seemingly out of defiance toward the Americans, he would abuse the prisoners, smashing them in the face with his rifle butt, knocking out teeth or shattering a cheekbone. Appalled, the CIA men told Salam that this was unacceptable, as well as counterproductive. But Salam persisted. One petrified Taliban prisoner, from Helmand province in the south, shook uncontrollably after Salam warned him the CIA was about to execute him. David told Salam to stop the abuse or he would inform Dostum.

Salam reacted with fury. "I was a prisoner of the Taliban in Kandahar for three years before Dostum paid a ransom to get me out!" he shouted at David. "I was tortured and beaten every day with a cable on my legs, my buttocks, and the soles of my feet." David had seen such a cable—heavy and with a metal ball at the end—after Dostum's men had seized it from the Taliban. It had been used to beat women for supposed breaches of Islamic law, such as displaying their ankles or trying to see a doctor. Another Uzbek soldier joined the debate and said that he too had been a Taliban prisoner. "The Taliban beat the meat off my bones," he said. To David's bewilderment, the soldier dropped his pants and bent over, showing his bottom. In place of the flesh on his right buttock was only a disfigured hollow covered in scars.

David thought about the suffering Salam had endured, and the brutality it had instilled in him. "His eyes showed little compassion," David wrote in his diary. "His time with the Taliban probably sucked him dry of such feelings. When the Talib prisoner came by earlier that day, Salam was one of the men who took pleasure in watching him become frightened...I know why Salam did this. His humanity had been beaten out of him."

David was beginning to grasp the shifting nature of war in Afghanistan:

villages fought villages, traitors became allies, comrades became enemies. He had read about the barbarity of the Japanese in the Pacific and, studying Native Americans, had been seized by the 19th-century notion of the "savage." The Comanches, he had learned, had tortured their prisoners, in part because they did not consider them human beings. Yet the layer upon layer of brutality in Afghanistan was something that David realized he would never comprehend or become inured to. The violence was fed by ethnic identity, tribes, clans, feuds, honor, and vengeance. For all his languages and cultural understanding, David concluded, he would always be an interloper in the Afghan world.

On the morning of October 26, Day 10, David, Mike, and Justin set out for the mountain prison. During the forty-minute ride they passed through two Hazara villages that the Taliban had burned to the ground. The three CIA men were accompanied by Amanullah, an ethnic Tajik who was Dostum's intelligence chief and oversaw the prison. David soon came to view Amanullah as a beacon in a moral wasteland—the opposite of Abdul Salam. Remarkably, Amanullah had also been a Taliban prisoner, and two of his brothers remained in captivity. He had been released in a prisoner exchange just two months earlier and his reaction to his experience had been the reverse of Salam's—Amanullah impressed on his men the need to treat captives humanely.

The prison was in a compound built into a mountainside, where two caves had been carved out of the sandstone hundreds of years earlier. The forty captives, reeking and barefoot, were in a single cave measuring about twenty feet by twenty huddled together in the dark, their heads between their knees. When the makeshift wooden cave door swung open and light poured in, they looked up at the Americans holding Kalashnikovs and flinched.

They expected to be shot dead, but the detainees were instead led out one by one for questioning. Some wore fetters on their ankles. David agreed with Amanullah that they were local foot soldiers—Afghans, not Arabs—and that many had been pressed into fighting. One prisoner related that after being handed an AK-47 and ten bullets, he had hidden in a bomb crater when the fighting started. Another, an impoverished farmer, had been told by the Taliban at gunpoint, "You're coming with us. If you don't, we'll kill your family and then you."

As David asked questions, Mike took copious notes. One interview ended early because of the stench from the prisoner's wounds. More prisoners arrived that night, so the CIA men returned early on Day 11 to question them. The ten new captives were Turkmens. David felt they were some of the simplest people he had ever encountered—almost incapable of lying. Amanullah explained that Turkmens were considered among the worst fighters in Afghanistan, surrendering, defecting, or running away as soon as they could. They had been pressed into service just two days earlier. David, who eight years earlier had cowritten a Turkmen-language manual for the Peace Corps, was entranced by the vividness of the prisoners' descriptions. One of them told him that when the American bombs exploded, the Taliban were "so scared that their balls popped out of their scrotums."

Justin felt sorry for them. "If this is the caliber of the enemy, victory might be swift," he thought. Mike, however, showed scant sympathy for men who had been fighting with the terrorists who perpetrated 9/11. He judged them lucky not to have been killed on the battlefield. Dogged and reluctant to make any assumptions, Mike asked David how he could be so sure the prisoners were insignificant conscripts. David explained that he spoke Turkmen, had lived in Turkmenistan, and knew the chances were slim that an ethnic Turkmen would be Al-Qaeda. "But how do you *know* that?" Mike persisted. "Well, I've studied it for ten years," David replied.

Amanullah later asked David if the prisoners could be given blankets; the CIA officer duly ordered some for the next airdrop. When the bedding arrived, David impressed upon Amanullah that they were for the prisoners only—they were not to be taken to the market. Several days later, David and Mike returned to the prison caves on horseback. It was early in the morning, and they found Amanullah still asleep in his hut. David's heart sank at the sight of Amanullah stretched out on the dirt floor, covered only by his unwrapped turban. David thought the bedding must have been sold. "Where's your blanket?" he asked. Amanullah looked bewildered. "I've given them all to the prisoners," he replied.

* * *

Mike, Justin, and Mark departed for Bamiyan in a battered Hilux truck on October 27, Day 11 for Team Alpha. The route led 140 miles along rocky tracks and riverbeds, the terrain having changed little since 1893, when a British surveyor noted that it "may be considered practicable by mules." As with so much that Team Alpha did, the journey was dangerous. Ideally, two Green Berets would have accompanied them for security. But ODA 595 had split into four three-man teams and was coordinating with Dostum's men. With air controllers about to arrive, J.R. reckoned that the Green Berets and the Uzbek warlord would soon be an unstoppable force. He could not risk stalling progress toward that.

The three CIA men were keenly aware of the hazards they faced on this trek. Taliban on the road, or a double cross by the Hazaras—not impossible in a land of murky intrigue and changing allegiances—could spell doom. "We could have our throats slit," thought Justin. "We'll end up as bleached bones in the middle of nowhere."

No US planes were available, so calling in air strikes was not an option. The only mobile communications equipment they had was a PRC (Portable, Radio, Communication), a handheld survival radio designed for downed pilots. At times Justin sat in the truck bed, marveling at the azure lakes of Band-e Amir—"The Commander's Dam" in Dari—separated by natural barriers of travertine and surrounded by jagged cliffs of red, brown, and gray. At a lakeside at around 10,000 feet, they stopped at a dilapidated shrine. At 12,000 feet the CIA men and their Afghan guides had to push the truck, which could not get enough oxygen to labor up the thirty-degree incline.

As dawn broke, the group drove through a narrow pass and descended into the Yakawlang Valley. Once in Karim Khalili's compound, they slept on carpeted floors—there was no furniture—and were welcomed by the Hazara leader, who outlined his plan for retaking Yakawlang and using the town as a springboard to recapture the city of Bamiyan. The American assistance was a way for the Hazaras to win a conflict they were already fighting. Khalili proposed a two-pronged attack on Bamiyan, with 1,500 men assaulting from the southwest and a group of similar size moving in from the northwest. Mike felt that his career had reached a new level. Leading a pathfinder team deep in enemy territory, he was debating military strategy with an Afghan warlord. Communications were a headache. The Medium Gain satellite antenna failed to function. It was the only time in Afghanistan that Justin witnessed Mike becoming nervous. Thankfully, a backup antenna eventually worked when the clouds cleared.

During the Bamiyan mission, Mike opened up to Justin, recounting his divorce and his whirlwind romance with Shannon. He expressed his hopes for his two daughters and his joy at having a son. The pair decided they should name the arrival point for the helicopter LZ Jake. When a functionary in CIA headquarters questioned the propriety of naming an LZ in a war zone after a child, Mike pushed back hard. "There are no rules here," he said. "We're making the decisions and it's going to be called LZ Jake."

Justin and Mark bonded over their mutual fondness for J.R.R. Tolkien, deciding that one of the Afghan hosts was Grima Wormtongue, the sycophantic liar from *The Lord of the Rings*. They also traded dialogue from the movie *Pulp Fiction*. Quentin Tarantino's twisted humor seemed a fit for Afghanistan.

A Chinook from K2 arrived at Yakawlang on October 30, Day 14, with the CIA's Team Delta and a large portable generator on board. Justin, swinging an infrared strobe on a rope to create a signal halo, had to dive to one side to dodge the descending helicopter. The next day, the Green Berets of ODA 553 arrived, split between two Chinooks to reduce the helicopter load in the high-altitude conditions.

The Bamiyan mission was complete. On November 1—Day 16—the three CIA men bade farewell to Khalili and set off to rejoin the main group of Team Alpha and ODA 595, which was now moving north toward the Tangi Gap and Mazar-i Sharif.

* * *

Accompanied by five of Atta's men and two Uzbeks, Scott, David, and Andy set off midmorning for the long horse ride west to the village of Sarob. It was October 29, Day 13 of Team Alpha's mission. There was no road to Sarob, where Atta had set up a temporary headquarters, and the trip to link up with the Tajik warlord was every bit as dangerous as the other team's mission to Bamiyan. Initially, the terrain was rolling hills punctuated by deep washes and ravines. The farther west they ventured, however, the rougher the trail got. One ravine was nearly four miles long, populated by goats that ran bleating alongside the riders.

David was spent. His horse was also tiring—it was small and its stirrups too high. Atta's lead guide swapped the CIA man's steed for his own horse, which was large and powerful. The respite was short; soon David's legs, knees, and crotch were aching again. A heavy box of gear kept slipping off one of the other horses, forcing everyone to dismount and reposition it, which made David even more depleted. As dusk approached, they halted at an Uzbek village to drink water. Fringing the village were man-made caves that had served as bunkers during the mujahideen's war with the Soviets.

David had now been in the saddle for six hours, his body feeling every second of it. Had he known Sarob was still seven hours away, he probably would have given up. As night fell, they descended into a rocky canyon, the horses stumbling on the stones. Mercifully, it was almost a full moon: no one had NVGs. Suddenly, an artillery round exploded some distance away, echoing through the canyon. Atta's lead guide ordered they continue on foot.

Andy walked in front of David for a while and they discussed Johnny

Cash. This led David to think about his father, who had died eighteen years earlier. Soon, David was talking to his father to spur himself on. Back on his horse, he reflected on his childhood in Pennsylvania—the simple goodness of the way he'd been raised, and the stoicism instilled in him, and on which he now drew. They dismounted once more as the canyon narrowed and the moon disappeared behind the rock faces. David's horse zigzagged precariously up what seemed like a vertical ascent. When the adrenaline rush wore off, it was replaced by fatigue, pain, and dizziness. David struggled to remount his horse, finally doing so by climbing on top of a boulder. He relieved himself in the saddle three times, much as the Chinook pilots did in their seats during long missions. David heard an American plane overhead and envied the pilot's ability to escape Afghanistan so quickly, heading for a warm bed in Europe or in an aircraft carrier. A Taliban antiaircraft gun opened fire less than two miles away, but the plane was out of range. When he finally reached Sarob, David was too bone-tired to be happy.

The next night, while waiting for Atta to appear, the CIA men rode up through sleet and snow to the drop zone to receive supplies. It was pitch-black, and the reins had cut and chapped David's hands. As he made his way up the mountainside, one of his Gore-Tex gloves slipped off. The horse was moving and there was no way of turning back. David cursed and wondered how things could get any worse—the gloves had been the sole protection for his aching hands. Lamenting the lost glove, he spotted figures moving along the mountainside. The supplies had been dropped, and Afghans were ferrying the boxes of ammunition, weapons, and food down to the road for transportation back to Sarob. David could see they were teenagers and younger.

As he got closer, David realized that the children clambering up and down the mountain were barefoot. He thought of how upset he was over a lost glove, juxtaposed with the lives of these shoeless young Afghans, and instantly felt warmer. Before leaving for Afghanistan, David had watched the 1997 movie *GI Jane*, starring Demi Moore, with his daughter, Kara. The story of a young woman becoming a Navy SEAL had delighted the eleven-year-old girl. Now, a poem recited at the end of the film by a SEAL Master Chief, played by Viggo Mortensen, came into David's mind. It was D. H. Lawrence's "Self-Pity":

> *I never saw a wild thing*
> *sorry for itself.*
> *A small bird will drop frozen dead from a bough*
> *without ever having felt sorry for itself.*

Atta's first objective was the village of Aq Kupruk, where Taliban commander Mullah Amir Mohamed had up to 2,000 fighters, along with ZSU guns, BMP fighting vehicles, and BM-21 truck-mounted rocket launchers. Some of the Taliban fighters might be induced to switch sides if their commanders were paid enough, and Atta could use whatever equipment he captured for the coming battle over the city of Mazar-i Sharif. Once Aq Kupruk had fallen, Atta would push northeast down the Balkh Valley while Dostum's forces fought in parallel through the Darya Suf Valley. They would rendezvous at the confluence of the Balkh and Suf rivers before moving on the city.

On November 2, Day 17 for Team Alpha, two Chinooks brought ODA 534 and the three CIA officers of Team Bravo to Sarob, landing at LZ Mustang. Noting the rapport that Scott had built with the recalcitrant Atta, J.R. decided the former Ranger should remain behind to take command of Team Bravo, which could be folded into Team Alpha once Mazar-i Sharif fell. The three new CIA men were Bob, a case officer and fluent Farsi linguist; Greg, the former Navy SEAL who had been pulled from Team Alpha at the last minute to make room for David; and Glenn, a former Special Forces medic. Atta felt he was now being treated equally with Dostum: he had been given the supplies and personnel he needed.

The Uzbeks, Hazaras, and Tajiks in the Darya Suf Valley were finally united—and intent on taking Mazar-i Sharif. David and Andy returned to Team Alpha on the Chinook that had brought in ODA 534 and Bravo. Instead of an agonizing thirteen-hour horse ride back, the journey to LZ Burro at Team Alpha's new position in the village of Chapchal took twenty minutes.

The three Bravo officers were raring to go. Waiting at K2, Glenn recalled the British Special Air Service (SAS) motto: WHO DARES WINS. He itched to get into Afghanistan and kill Osama bin Laden. If that meant he died trying, so be it.

Bob, a lifelong contrarian, had joined the CIA to work in the field—the farther away from Agency headquarters the better. He had reputedly learned Farsi as a teenager on the streets of Los Angeles from gangs of Iranian immigrants. His comfort with other cultures was second only to David Tyson's. Greg was still smarting from losing his spot on Team Alpha to David. Supremely fit and a trained Tier One operator, his military prowess was unquestioned.

To his disgust, Glenn—six feet one, with a bushy ginger beard—had been assigned to the Balkans after 9/11. Like Team Alpha's Mark, he was a qualified physician's assistant and attached to the Agency's OMS. He had bumped into Mark at CIA headquarters and circumvented his bosses by walking into CTC/SO and telling them his skills would be needed in Afghanistan. Once Glenn had secured his spot, he was placed in a team due to be flown into Pakistan from an aircraft carrier in the Indian Ocean, before crossing the border into Afghanistan on camels, and then heading to Kandahar. Glenn had protested that this would be suicide. Indeed, several days later Abdul Haq—the Pashtun commander and mujahideen veteran who had been vying to lead Afghanistan—died attempting much the same route to reenter Afghanistan. He was caught by the Taliban, hanged, and his body riddled with bullets. To Glenn's relief, the camel scheme was eventually abandoned by the CIA.

Helicopter delays prompted a short-lived plan for Team Bravo to parachute into Sarob. Greg had completed 1,300 jumps as a SEAL, while Glenn had about forty under his belt. Bob had no military experience and had never parachuted, but he immediately agreed to the idea; Glenn thought, "That's original OSS [Office of Strategic Services] gravitas right there." It all felt chaotic and improvised to Glenn, but the imperative to get teams into Afghanistan before winter set in meant this had become the Agency's new modus operandi. Cofer Black and Hank Crumpton put immense pressure on their officers, trusting that they would work out the kinks on the ground in situ.

Glenn, a habitual pessimist, believed he had a fifty-fifty chance of surviving the mission. Some of Atta's own men were equally downbeat. Before he left Sarob, Commander Mir Rahmat told David about his family in the city. In his forties, Rahmat had four wives and so many children, he joked, that he could not count them all. "Daoud," he told the CIA man, "we've been fighting for so long we're never going to make it to Mazar." David replied, "Sure we are. I'll make you a bet. When we get to Mazar, you're going to invite me to your house and serve me dinner, and I'm going to take pictures of your family." Rahmat laughed, and the two men shook hands on the wager.

The first task of the newly arrived Americans at Sarob was to show the skeptical Atta what they could do. Team Bravo and ODA 534 took him up to a ridgeline, separated by a valley from where the Taliban were dug in. One of the Green Berets invited Atta to look through the SOFLAM, which they had set up next to a DShK machine gun. Peering through the device, Atta saw a bunker flying the Taliban flag. As he watched, an F-14 released a 2,000-pound JDAM that landed squarely on the fortification, leaving only a smoking crater behind.

Atta smiled. It seemed like a light had gone on inside the Tajik warlord's head. Scott was buoyed that Atta seemed to have put his rivalry with Dostum aside and was now focused on fighting. Dismissing the doubts of Mir Rahmat, the Tajik warlord told Scott, "Once we take Mazar, it will be city after city until Spin Boldak!" Scott thought, "Great! Now where's Spin Boldak?" A Pashtun town southeast of Kandahar on the Pakistan border, Spin Boldak would be one of the Taliban's last redoubts. Finally, Atta had gotten with the CIA program—and soon Mazar-i Sharif would be in sight.

9

DEVIL'S WATER

9:05 a.m. (GMT +4.5), November 4, 2001 (Day 19);
Cobaki, Samangan province, Afghanistan

AN EXHAUSTED DAVID Tyson was napping in the sun at Dostum's command post. Beside him, the warlord monitored radio channels, giving instructions to his commanders and eavesdropping on the Taliban. Dostum was fascinated by the potency of air strikes—not just to kill, but to break the enemy's spirit. He loved the SOFLAM. Sometimes Dostum tried to buy off the Taliban commanders, offering them $10,000 to surrender. On other occasions, he mocked and threatened them, a crude version of what the CIA and military termed psyops—psychological operations.

A lot had happened during the four days David was in Sarob. The final straw with Fahim Khan for the Americans had come on October 30, Day 14 for Team Alpha in Afghanistan. In the back of a US Air Force C-17 on an airstrip in Dushanbe, the Tajikistan capital, Fahim had met with Hank Crumpton, running the war for the CIA, and General Tommy Franks, his military counterpart. Despite the 20,000 men at his disposal, Fahim was still not taking on the enemy. Instead he was demanding US air power everywhere—and a salary of $7 million a month. Mazar-i Sharif didn't matter, Fahim insisted; the Americans needed to help him get to Kabul. Franks had stood up, glared at the interpreter, and said: "This is bullshit. Translate that."

The same day, Dostum and ODA 595 had captured Chapchal. With the Taliban now in retreat, Dostum's and Atta's forces were poised to sweep north toward Mazar-i Sharif. It didn't matter what Fahim, or even Jawbreaker, wanted. Crumpton and Franks were agreed that US air power should be concentrated on the Darya Suf and Balkh Valleys. Mazar-i Sharif was the priority; the Panjshir Valley and Kabul would come afterward.

David was surprised to find a new group of Green Berets at Chapchal, bivouacked in caves in the mountainside, separate from the compound Team Alpha and ODA 595 occupied. Whereas the CIA had stayed lean, the US Army was adding layers of battalion commanders—lieutenant colonels—and their staffs in Afghanistan. By late October, Defense Secretary Rumsfeld had become concerned that junior officers appeared to be running the Pentagon's war in Afghanistan. "Are you sure those Special Forces teams have senior-enough officers in command?" Rumsfeld asked General Tommy Franks. "It seems to me the Northern Alliance generals won't really listen to young captains and majors." Franks had then pressured Mulholland to dispatch higher ranking Special Forces officers from K2, threatening to install brigadier generals from the regular army if he did not.

To the dismay of Captain Mark Nutsch, his battalion commander—Lieutenant Colonel Max Bowers—and an eight-man command-and-control team code-named Boxer had landed the night David and Andy had returned from Sarob. Nutsch had developed a close bond with Dostum. While David had been in Sarob, the pair had perfected how to synchronize air strikes and cavalry charges. Taliban forces were now being decimated each day. The initial US bombing campaign after October 7 had been ineffectual, largely because of a lack of targets stemming from the Taliban's limited infrastructure. But it was now apparent that using air power to support Northern Alliance troops on the ground, as Nutsch and Dostum were doing, was the key to winning the campaign against the Taliban.

With this formula in place, Nutsch was outraged that his relationship with the warlord was about to be undermined. Adding to the friction, Bowers was known to brook no dissent or even attempts at compromise; within the 5th Special Forces Group, his 3rd Battalion was known as the Third Reich. Bowers, silver-haired and conscious of his appearance, was nicknamed Cinemax—because, it was said, he made everything a big production and acted as if he was always on camera. Inside his backpack, Bowers carried a small piece of charred steel taken from the smoldering ruins of the World Trade Center. He intended to bury it in the soil of Afghanistan.

Within hours of his arrival, Bowers reported back to Task Force Dagger that Boxer was on the ground and "prepared to conduct combat operations." He signed off his message: "Our eyes are on Mazar-e-Sharif. Strength and Honor." The next day, Bowers criticized General Tommy Franks to Mulholland, asking why a resupply had not taken place: "CINC CENTCOM [Franks] promised Gen. Dostum weapons and ammo. It is imperative that Gen. Dostum's forces receive the promised supplies ASAP. Why does the CINC promise things he can't deliver?"

Dostum was confused that "Commander Mark" had been superseded, and he bristled when Bowers declared himself the new point of contact for the Green Berets. The morning after his arrival, Bowers posed for photographs, his arm around a nonplussed Dostum as an anguished Nutsch looked on. Afterward, Bowers sent Mulholland a summary: "Conducted initial meeting with Gen. Dostum. Have successfully established rapport. See attached JPEG file." While the attitude of Nutsch had been that Dostum was in charge and the Green Berets were advisers, Bowers seemed to treat Dostum as a subordinate. The awkwardness of the situation was palpable.

Staff Sergeant Steve Tomat, a newly arrived air controller, was irked when Bowers began suggesting targets he should bomb. Tomat, operating as close as 700 yards from the Taliban, already had his hands full as he prioritized air strikes. When a Boxer staff officer told Tomat that Bowers wanted a T-55 tank hit, the Air Force man replied: "Sir, please respectfully tell Bowers to go fuck off. I've already identified all the targets on the battlefield. I've either engaged the T-55 or I'm getting ready to."

* * *

David was woken from his slumber by a sharp kick from Dostum. He heard the warlord using the Uzbek word "ibna," meaning hermaphrodite. David looked around to see who Dostum might be referring to. "No," Dostum said, pointing at a dot on the horizon. "Up in the air."

The CIA man listened to the radio net and heard a female US Navy F-18 Hornet pilot talking to the air controller. "That's a woman," he told Dostum. This was inconceivable to the warlord. "You have a *woman* flying a plane?" But it took him only seconds to see the possibilities. "Give me the handset," he told David. "Here's what I want you to do." A small crowd of Dostum's men had gathered. "Tell the woman to recite some poetry," he continued. David spoke to the F-18 pilot on the radio and explained what Dostum had requested. "I don't know any fucking poetry," the pilot said. "Over." David relayed this to an exasperated Dostum. "She doesn't know any poetry?" he marveled. "Well, get her to sing a song, then."

After some negotiation, the pilot agreed to sing *Anchors Aweigh*, the Navy fight song. "Tell her to sing loudly when I give the signal," Dostum instructed David. Next, Dostum told his radioman to tune in the channel for Commander Mahmoud, the nearest Taliban leader. "Mahmoud," Dostum said into the radio. "The Americans have a woman flying their plane, and you need to listen to what she's going to do to you." The pilot sang: "Roll up the score, Navy, anchors aweigh, Sail Navy down the field, and sink the Army, sink the Army grey."

David hoped that the pilot was a better aviator than she was a singer, but the performance seemed to do the trick for Dostum. "Commander Mahmoud, did you hear that?" the warlord demanded. "You are stupid and don't speak English, so I will translate. 'I am going to fuck you up,' she is telling you. 'I am going to drop my bombs on top of your men. They are so weak and have such tiny dicks that even a woman can kill them.'"

Dostum's men laughed and cheered as the air controller took over, using a SOFLAM to direct the F-18 to where it should bomb the Taliban position. It was vintage Dostum: he had an intuitive grasp of how to use the Americans to torment the Taliban and motivate his men. As the Taliban massed to defend Baluch, Dostum knew the momentum was about to shift irreversibly against the enemy. "I'm going to capture this area," he taunted a Taliban commander by radio on the night of November 4. "If you do, that means you capture the whole north," the commander responded. Through bribery and threats, Dostum had secured agreements with other Taliban commanders that they would switch allegiance and hand over their Pakistani and Arab fighters once he took Shulgareh.

On November 5, Day 20 for Team Alpha, Northern Alliance forces gathered for the decisive battle. With dedicated air support all day, the four three-man teams from ODA 595—Alpha, Bravo, Charlie, and Delta—fanned out among Dostum's commanders. Delta called in an air strike that killed Taliban commander Mullah Abdul Razzaq and 150 of his men in a bunker system. Razzaq had been the Taliban's corps commander in Mazar-i Sharif, based at Qala-i Jangi.

In one cavalry charge, Commander Lal, Dostum's deputy, mistook Nutsch's signal for "Get ready" as the command for "Go." It was a heart-stopping moment. JDAMs might land on Dostum's horsemen. Fortunately, the bombs exploded just ahead of them, blowing some of the first wave off their horses but allowing the second and third waves to charge through the smoke and finish off the Taliban. BLU-82 bombs—weighing 15,000 pounds and with daisy-cutter fuses that made them explode aboveground to maximize their killing power—were dropped at Aq Kupruk and Baluch. Steve Tomat, the air controller, opted for a BLU-82 for the psychological effect it would create. Watching a mushroom cloud rise, he imagined, the Taliban would believe they'd been hit by an atomic bomb and conclude: "The Americans are here to do some business. Let's defect or get away from here."

True to his word, Atta had moved decisively on Aq Kupruk, which became the first majority-Pashtun town in Afghanistan to fall to the Northern Alliance. Atta, with the help of CIA cash, had persuaded hundreds of Taliban to switch sides. Scott had come in from a mission a few days earlier ready to confer with Greg, the former SEAL. Before Scott could do so, Atta ushered him in to meet some guests. The Team Bravo leader sat down next to three black-turbaned mullahs, who were already seated with Greg. "Hey, Scott," said Greg. "This is a powwow with the Taliban. Atta's negotiating their surrender." Atta then gestured to Scott and Greg and told the mullahs, "If you do not surrender, these Americans will kill you."

After US aircraft bombarded Aq Kupruk, Atta sent in his forces and the last Taliban fighters surrendered. Team Bravo followed Atta into the town along a dry riverbed. Glenn's mules stopped as they approached a canyon about fifty feet wide and 150 feet high. "How many Russians were killed here?" Glenn asked himself. He recited Psalm 23:4 as he tried to catch up with the others: "Yea, though I walk through the valley of the shadow of death, I will fear no evil."

On the far side of the canyon, more than 200 Taliban—armed with RPGs, AK-47s, and PK machine guns—were lined up beside a walled compound. Atta rode past them like a medieval king, and the Taliban glared at the Americans. There was no time to turn back, let alone ask why these prisoners had not been disarmed. The CIA men rode past knowing they could all be killed at any moment and there was nothing they could do about it.

By nightfall on November 5, Baluch and Aq Kupruk had fallen and the Taliban were in full retreat. Razzaq's deputy, Mullah Daoud, was shot in the right forearm and captured. Daoud, shaking with fear as he was treated by an American medic, was ordered by Dostum to get on the radio and tell his fellow Taliban to give up and go home.

Since their arrival, American medics had often treated enemy wounded, to the bemusement of many of Dostum's men. Mark Rausenberger felt that this was part of his duty—and that it signaled to other Taliban that surrender did not mean death—but he made sure the enemy fighters knew he hated them. He entertained the rest of Team Alpha by treating a wounded Taliban fighter while asking the translator to inform the fanatical Muslim, "This is an Israeli bandage." Mark was Jewish and had asked other team members not to talk about this given the Muslim sensibilities of their hosts. David's advice was that if religion was discussed, the Americans should say that they believed in God and leave it at that.

Back at CIA headquarters, Glenn had been contemptuous of the surgical equipment he had been given, and argued that it was woefully inadequate. Sure enough, as Team Bravo swept through Aq Kopruk, Glenn was faced with daunting injuries while carrying a medical kit that was better for little more than first aid. He had, however, brought his own multi-tool—a piece of gear beloved by outdoorsmen and survivalists. Glenn's Schrade Tough Multi-Tool had 21 functions, including a wire cutter, sheepsfoot blade, and woodsaw. He used it to perform three amputations. The most complicated operation was removing the mutilated foot of a young Afghan who had stepped on a mine. "I need a little coaching on how to do this," Glenn told Scott. Using the satellite phone, Scott called CIA headquarters in Virginia and was told a surgeon would call him back shortly. The light was fading, so Atta's men brought a generator to power a 40-watt bulb.

Ten minutes later, the satellite phone buzzed and a CIA officer told Scott he would be patched through to the chief orthopedic surgeon at Landstuhl in Germany, the largest American military hospital outside the United States. Scott passed the phone to Glenn. "Okay, I've got to cut this guy's foot off," Glenn told the surgeon. "How do I do it?" The Army doctor explained the procedure, which involved cutting beneath the skin to saw off the foot bones, connected to tendons, while tying off or cauterizing blood vessels. In a scene reminiscent of American Civil War surgery, the operating table was a ladder placed on top of ammunition crates. One Afghan's job was to wield a stick to keep the village dogs away from the pieces of flesh and bone that dropped on the ground as Glenn sawed them off.

The Northern Alliance captured the town of Keshendeh on November 7, Day 22 for Team Alpha in Afghanistan. The following afternoon, Dostum's and Atta's forces met at Pol-e Baraq, where the Suf and Balkh rivers converged. Team Alpha had acquired a rusting, light-green ten-ton Soviet truck with yellow soccer-ball stickers on its doors—named the Magic Bus by J.R. after the 1968 song by the Who. It doubled as sleeping quarters for J.R. and Alex, and the Team Alpha leader—fastidious about laundry when the opportunity presented itself—hung his washing from it. On November 8 the Hazara driver took the bus up a narrow, snaking road as the CIA men looked down on a valley hundreds of feet below. "At least I'm not on a horse," thought David. They passed the battlefield of the day before, scarred with bomb craters, scorched buildings, wrecked tanks, and other vehicles. Charred horses and dead Taliban lay transfixed in what seemed like contorted pain.

After Pol-e Baraq, the combined forces of Dostum and Atta turned north to take Shulgareh, which had been abandoned by the Taliban. From there, thirty miles of open plains led to the Tangi Gap, gateway to Mazar-i Sharif. Finally, Team Alpha and the Green Berets were out of the mountains. Dostum, Atta, and Mohaqeq met in an old fort to plan an assault on the gap. Victory was within their grasp.

Back in Washington, by contrast, despondency was setting in. At a White House meeting on November 9, Day 24 for Team Alpha, Rumsfeld briefed Bush that the CIA-led campaign was stalling. Citing the DIA paper he had circulated two weeks earlier, he warned that was it unlikely that Dostum's Northern Alliance would take Mazar-i Sharif until 2002. He even cited a *New York Times* article reporting that the word "quagmire" was gaining traction and floating the notion that Afghanistan was the new Vietnam. Without missing a beat, Hank Crumpton looked at Bush and said, "Mazar will fall in the next twenty-four to forty-eight hours." CIA director George Tenet was weary of the negativity of Rumsfeld and the Pentagon, but he wondered whether Crumpton should have added a caveat. Shifting in his seat, he thought, "Well, let's hope that happens."

Robert Grenier, the CIA station chief who had earned the sobriquet "Islamabad Bob" in CENTCOM headquarters in Tampa, had continued to make his case vociferously for prioritizing the Pashtuns over the Northern Alliance. But he had lost the argument to CTC: Cofer Black and Hank Crumpton were simply too busy running the war to continue the debate. In CIA headquarters, Crumpton had begun derisively referring to Grenier as "Taliban Bob." The Pashtun regions of southern Afghanistan were Grenier's responsibility, but he had achieved no movement with the tribes there. At the White House meeting, Tenet admitted, "We don't have anything working in the south." Pashtuns would be needed to finish off the Taliban, and almost certainly to apprehend bin Laden. For the time being, however, Dostum, outnumbered but winning, was the only game in town.

There was still some fierce fighting, but movement toward Mazar-i Sharif was now swift. One night Ak Yasin, one of Dostum's commanders, came to David to tell him that his hands were shaking and he needed medicine. David offered him a Tylenol—the panacea in the field for Afghan fighters, who viewed the capsules as akin to magic. But this was not what Ak Yasin wanted. After some coaxing—and David swearing to secrecy—the Afghan whispered that he needed "devil's water."

David had to talk to Charlie Gilbert, the Tashkent station chief, about the next supply drop. After paying for a string of Taliban defections, the initial $3 million was running low, so David asked Gilbert for $3 million more. In addition, David said, he wanted some vodka. Not a problem, Gilbert told him. Turning to Alex, the team deputy, David asked, "Anything else?" "Three mil in cash and a consignment of vodka sounds like a pretty good party," quipped Alex, adding, "How about some condoms?" Alex obviously wasn't serious, but David laughed and put the order in anyway. When the drop arrived, the cash, the vodka, and the condoms were all included. David discreetly called in Ak Yasin and gave him a tot of Uzbek vodka. The commander drank it down and immediately declared himself cured. Before he left, however, Ak Yasin made David promise never to tell anyone he had drunk alcohol. An hour later another commander knocked on David's door, also seeking devil's water. Throughout the evening the commanders materialized one by one for their medicinal vodka, each acting as if this was a personal secret between him and the American.

The Uzbek condoms turned out to be a bigger problem. David decided to distribute them to the Afghans to put on their rifle muzzles— a World War II practice to keep out dust and water. But the package bore a photograph of a scantily clad woman in a suggestive pose, so the soldiers asked him to explain its contents. When David outlined the principal use of a condom, the Afghans were astounded. They had never heard of such a thing, nor had any notion of why a man would want to use one.

Before long, some Afghans were inflating the prophylactics like balloons, stretching them, and even trying them on. Some accosted David and told him the condoms were against Islam. David needed to end the commotion before it got out of hand. He gathered the Afghans together to tell them that he had been playing a joke: the condoms were merely rifle covers, and he was sorry he had concocted the ridiculous story that they could be used for anything else.

On the same day Rumsfeld briefed Bush, Alex and David drove forward to the front in a truck full of fighters. They stopped just south of the Tangi Gap, where Dostum had set up a command post in the roof garden of a newly constructed house owned by a carpenter. Dostum was jubilant as he prepared to set off with Green Berets from ODA 595 to call in air strikes from the mountaintop. It would be the death blow to the Taliban.

Soon after they left, the road into the pass was hit by a Taliban counterattack of about fifteen BM-21 rockets—which resembled flying telegraph poles—causing enormous explosions that shook the ground. One of Dostum's men had his legs sliced off as a rocket killed his horse beneath him. Locals panicked, running for cover and jumping on horses. Abdul Sattar, Dostum's trusted guard chief, told the two CIA men to run for the hills to the west to escape the next volley. David started to sprint away.

"What the fuck are you doing?" Alex called after him. The Team Alpha deputy was a picture of calm amid the chaos. "I don't know," admitted David. Alex, bringing his colleague back to earth, said, "Well, think for yourself." There was no second volley. As Uzbek fighters streamed out of the pass in retreat, Sattar cajoled and threatened them to turn around and return to the front.

The battle for the Tangi Gap—a narrow, mile-long pass hemmed in by 3,000-foot-high cliff faces—was on. The dead and wounded were brought back by horseback or slung into vehicles. One Turkmen fighter, with a shrapnel wound in his head and gravel embedded in his back, screamed "Infidel!" at the Green Beret medic who treated him. The next patient had ridden over an anti-tank mine, which had blown his horse to pieces and mangled the fighter's left foot. Blood spurted everywhere as the medics clamped and sealed the arteries. David watched as the man, whose foot had just been amputated, moaned only slightly. Once again, the CIA officer could hardly believe how tough the Afghans were.

Overlooking the pass, Dostum pointed out a convoy of thirty vehicles lined up along the highway heading west of Mazar-i Sharif. Those are escaping Taliban, he told Master Sergeant Bart Decker. "Do you want bombs on?" Decker asked him. Minutes later, a US Navy F-14 Tomcat arrived overhead from the USS *Theodore Roosevelt*. Lieutenant (Junior Grade) Sara Stires, the radar-intercept officer, bombed the lead and rear trucks, bringing all enemy vehicles to a halt. Her wingmen then destroyed every vehicle in between, killing an estimated 150 Taliban.

Another large Taliban convoy was spotted by F-18s, heading southeast from Mazar-i Sharif to Kabul. The vehicles were more than 50 miles from the city, with no American troops or CIA officers nearby. The report from the F-18s was passed back to Task Force Dagger and routed to CTC/SO, where a US army general sat liaising with CIA officers. The general confirmed with Hank Crumpton's staff that no Agency assets were in the area and ordered: "Take them out."

In 1998, the Taliban had lost 12,000 men while taking Mazar-i Sharif. Northern Alliance casualties in this battle, by contrast, amounted to fewer than 100, with an estimated 1,500 Taliban killed. Thousands more had fled east toward Kunduz. The Taliban's last stand to protect Mazar-i Sharif had failed. A delighted Dostum grabbed his satellite phone and called CNN's Turkish network to announce, "We have overrun the city."

Most of Team Alpha drove through the Tangi Gap in the Magic Bus. Some of the Green Berets rode in on horses. In the narrow pass they found burned-out Taliban vehicles and the mangled remnants of the BM-21 rocket launcher that had targeted the Afghans. Steve Tomat, the air controller, saw the decapitated corpses of Taliban fighters killed by bombs he had called in. He had no regrets about what he had done, but drew the line at Green Berets taking photographs of the bodies. "They're dead," he thought. "What are you doing?" Andy gazed at a burned torso amid the body parts of horses and enemy fighters; it had only a blackened arm attached to it, reaching up to the sky. It was an image that never left him.

Team Bravo members were in a jinga truck—a brightly painted vehicle from Pakistan—that was soon crammed with Afghans hitching a ride. After weeks sleeping rough, the CIA men stank. Their personal-hygiene regimen had amounted to baby wipes and the occasional splash of water. The Afghans now pressed up against them and sitting on their laps smelled no better. As Glenn, the Team Bravo medic, grimaced, one of the Green Berets told him, "It's a unique aroma. We call it *faba*." Glenn had never heard the term, so the Green Beret deciphered: "It stands for feet, ass, balls, and armpits."

Justin and Mike, racing back from Bamiyan, caught up with the rest of the CIA team just after the Tangi Gap. They drove in a Soviet UAZ truck past bloated Taliban corpses. As they crossed the Balkh River at Pol-e Baraq, water rose up through the floor and the vehicle began to fishtail; Justin feared he might have to put his diving skills to the test. The unfazed Hazara driver pressed forward to the other side.

That night, Atta broke the agreement with Dostum to pause before Mazar-i Sharif and enter the city together. To Dostum's fury, the Tajik warlord drove straight in to stake his claim as the liberator of the north. Not for the first or last time, J.R. counseled Dostum to remain calm and see the bigger picture. As J.R. had assured him, Dostum ended up benefiting. Atta had sneaked into Mazar-i Sharif under the cover of darkness, almost unnoticed. Dostum, by contrast, drove into the city the next day standing atop a white Toyota Land Cruiser and was filmed waving to crowds pouring into the streets. Wearing a gray waistcoat and a thick brown guppi—Uzbek tunic—with a turban swathing his face, Dostum was mobbed and youths jumped onto the hood of the vehicle. Some threw money in the air for good luck. There was no doubt which man was viewed as the conqueror of Mazar-i Sharif.

Inside the city, a sea of people swept Dostum along the streets. Though he was not a religious man, he headed straight for the Shrine of Hazrat Ali, passing the arch where the Taliban had carried out public executions. The shrine was revered primarily by Shia, and the Sunni fundamentalists had banned New Year celebrations there, barred women from worshipping, and walked across its marble floors with their boots on. Some in Mazar-i Sharif believed that whoever controlled the shrine had permission from Allah to rule over all of Afghanistan. When Dostum arrived, there were women at the shrine for the first time in three years. Tears streaked his face as he knelt to pray.

10

THE FORT

10:10 a.m. (GMT +4.5), November 10, 2001 (Day 25);
Mazar-i Sharif, Balkh province, Afghanistan

EXUBERANT CROWDS THRONGED the streets as the Magic
Bus drove through the outskirts of Mazar-i Sharif. After three years of
Taliban rule, the Pashtuns had fled from northern Afghanistan's biggest
city—and with their retreat, oppressive regulations were cast aside.
Music played, many men had shaved their beards, and a few women—
their burqas discarded—emerged from their homes. Mazar-i Sharif had
changed hands many times before, but this occasion seemed especially
momentous. For members of Team Alpha, who had been in Afghanistan
for twenty-five days, it was a scene akin to the 1945 liberation of Europe.

Rising sixty feet above the fields on the western edge of Mazar-i
Sharif stood a fort that looked like a fantasy conjured from the pages
of *The Arabian Nights*. "Qala-i Jangi, the old fortress we've heard so
much about," David narrated, as he videoed the citadel. "Eighteenth
Divisional Headquarters of the Taliban." Dostum and the Green Berets
had decided against bombing the city because reports indicated the
Taliban had already fled, leaving it empty. Now, it would become the
first American base in northern Afghanistan.

Built of mud and wood, Qala-i Jangi's nine walls were topped by a six-
foot-high crenellated parapet with firing slits. Six triangular bastions,

designed to deflect artillery and give the defenders a panoramic view, made it Afghanistan's only "star fort." It had been the pride of Abdur Rahman, the 19th-century "Iron Amir," the first ruler to unite the country. The twenty-foot-high outer walls were surrounded by a dusty forty-five-degree slope and two dry moats. Used by the Soviets in the 1980s and Dostum until 1998, more recently it had been a Taliban base. A pair of disused World War II ZiS-3 anti-tank guns, left behind by the Russians after their occupation ended in 1989, flanked the whitewashed main gate.

Qala-i Jangi had always been a place of treachery and death. Even before the foundations were laid in 1889, a town governor had been tortured there for days and then beheaded. His decapitated corpse was thrown into an unmarked grave beneath the walls of the fort, and his head presented to the general who had ordered his murder. Locals had been outraged, and months later his killer was captured by the governor's brother. The killer's scalp was shaved, and he was paraded through the streets of Mazar-i Sharif on a donkey before being mutilated and thrown alive into a cauldron of boiling fat.

Rahman, a brutal Pashtun ruler, established the citadel because Mazar-i Sharif had replaced Balkh as the capital of Afghan Turkistan. The fort was designed by British military engineers and reputedly took 18,000 workers a dozen years to construct. Rahman was a puppet of the British in the era of the Great Game, subjugating the Uzbeks and Tajiks of the north and massacring Hazaras. The use of forced labor to build the fort led to the imprisonment, exile, or death of so many people that Balkh province was said to be "nearly depopulated" by the spring of 1890.

Qala-i Jangi, then known as Dehdadi after the village nearby, was built with British funds and intended both to defend against Russian invasion and to suppress revolts by Uzbek tribes. Rahman described it as "the largest and strongest fort that had ever been built in Afghanistan." He installed Krupp and Hotchkiss naval cannons, multiple-barrel Nordenfelt guns, and Maxims, the world's first fully automatic machine guns. But it was the design of Qala-i Jangi that made it unique. "The fortifications of this stronghold are hidden underground, making it impossible for any heavy guns to damage the fort," Rahman claimed. Lieutenant Colonel Lavr Kornilov, a Russian military intelligence officer who disguised himself as a Turkmen, visited the fort in 1899. He noted that its strongest features included its command of "all the country lying in front of the most threatened faces," and "the solidity and thickness of the earthen rampart." By then 800 cavalrymen and 2,400 infantry men were stationed at the fort.

Soviet forces secretly entered Afghanistan in 1929 to support the deposed king Amanullah, who had been friendly to Moscow. They were dressed in native garb and led by Vitaly Primakov, a former Soviet military attaché in Kabul, who pretended to be a Caucasian Turk named Ragib-bey. Some 300 Russian troops found themselves besieged inside the fort by 20,000 Turkmens. The Russian incursion lasted thirty-seven days; more than 8,000 Afghan defenders and 120 Soviet troops were killed, doubtless some of them at Qala-i Jangi. Primakov described the operation in terms that foreshadowed the mission of Team Alpha and the Green Berets seventy-two years later: "An action by a small cavalry detachment that in the process of combat activity would be reinforced with local formations."

The name Qala-i Jangi was probably not given to the fort until the 1940s. The Russians, with Dostum's support, occupied it again after their 1979 invasion. Mujahideen attacked Qala-i Jangi in 1981, ousting 170 pro-Soviet Afghan soldiers—some of whom then switched sides—and looting two weapons depots inside. The raiders made off with ammunition and more than 500 guns.

Little of Qala-i Jangi's blood-soaked history was known to the Americans who arrived there on November 10, 2001, and the fort seemed the logical place to stay. Once inside, they discovered that it was two sections, north and south, divided by a twenty-foot wall with a gate just to the east of its center. The northern compound was landscaped with a tree-lined avenue that led at the northern end to the building previously used by Dostum as his headquarters, centered between the northwestern and northeastern towers, which had ramps leading up to them. The two-story headquarters building contained offices and reception rooms and had a fortified roof and an open courtyard in its center. It had a colonnade and an old radio room filled with obsolete Russian equipment. There was a courtyard in the fort's entrance on the east side, part of a walled pentagon that connected the eastern and northeastern towers. Several old Soviet BTR-60 armored personnel carriers gathered dust. The hatch of one had been decorated with a pastoral scene of a couple gazing over a tranquil lake, probably painted by a homesick Russian conscript more than a decade earlier. Freshly dried blood spattered the walls and floor of one room; the Taliban had apparently used it for torture. Other rooms, however, were habitable, particularly in the headquarters building.

In the southern compound, the main building was a one-story structure decorated in salmon-colored stucco, with powder-blue window frames. Built by the Soviets, it was fifty feet square and had been used for classrooms. The Americans called it the Pink House. Underneath it was a cellar of seven rooms, which in the 1990s Dostum had strengthened with concrete so it could be used as an explosives store. From the cellar room on the northeastern corner, a narrow underground passageway led thirty feet to the east and a ground-level entrance with a locked iron gate. Outbuildings were dotted around the inside of the southern compound; there were stables on the southeastern side of the center wall. Several twenty-foot-long Sealink shipping containers were in the southern compound; they were stacked with weapons, including Springfield and Lee-Enfield rifles dating back a century or more. Wooden boxes of PPSh-41s—Russian submachine guns with drum magazines—appeared to have been packed more than fifty years earlier. RPGs, BM-21s, mortar rounds, old munitions, and rusting weapons were stacked high in some rooms. David found a pile of old bayonets, all of them stamped "1913" like the one he had taken from the Al-Qaeda fighter he had killed in the Darya Suf Valley.

By the time the Americans arrived at Qala-i Jangi, Dostum was already hosting a group of local leaders—some of whom had been aligned with the Taliban just days earlier—to decide how to administer the city. Among the group was the Iranian Quds Force officer who had been present at Team Alpha's initial meeting with Dostum in the early hours of October 17.

Before Team Alpha could settle in, Dostum learned that several hundred Chechen fighters were holed up in the city. They were inside the empty Sultan Razia school, two blocks west of the Hazrat Ali Shrine in the city center. It was a girls' school—named after a 13th-century female Muslim ruler of the Delhi Sultanate—that had been shuttered by the Taliban and turned into a military barracks. Two religious men, holding copies of the Koran, had been sent in as emissaries to negotiate a surrender to Atta's forces. They had been shot dead.

J.R. dispatched David to accompany three Green Berets and Steve Tomat, the US Air Force air controller. They needed a linguist to talk to elders who feared the holy shrine would be damaged by bombs. The Americans rode through the city on the back of a truck. It then took David thirty minutes to persuade the elders that the Americans could bomb the school with pinpoint accuracy. Seeking to assert his own authority over Mazar-i Sharif, Atta had told Dostum the school should not be bombed before the possibility of surrender had been exhausted. Dostum, however, was in no mood to humor Atta after the Tajik leader had entered Mazar-i Sharif ahead of the Uzbek fighters. Having briefly found common cause in fighting the Taliban up to the Tangi Gap, the two warlords were now rivals for control of the city.

It turned out that the fighters were not Chechens—a term often used as a catchall for feared foreign fighters—but Pakistanis abandoned by the fleeing Afghan Taliban. Far from being fearsome Al-Qaeda fighters, many were old and around 250 were boys, some as young as twelve. They had been in Mazar-i Sharif for just two days before the city had been recaptured by the Northern Alliance and had little idea of where they were. Nearly all were from the district of Malakand in northwestern Pakistan and had been recruited by an orange-bearded cleric named Sufi Muhammad who used loudspeakers mounted on trucks to urge: "Those who die fighting for God don't die! Those who go on jihad live forever, in paradise!"

Unbeknown to David or the other Americans with him, Atta had eight of his men inside the school still trying to negotiate with the Pakistanis. Members of ODA 534 were about to head to the school and had no idea other US forces were nearby. The conditions were in place for a disaster. Inside the school, many of the boys cheered as they heard gunfire, shouting out that the Taliban was attacking American planes. One boy corrected them, saying they were all doomed: "No, those weren't Taliban bullets. It's the people in the city, celebrating."

David and the Green Berets set up position with a SOFLAM on the roof of a five-story apartment block. It was 340 meters (372 yards) from the school—within 500 meters of friendly forces and therefore designated as Danger Close. Tomat, the air controller, found that the best map of the city they had was Russian, and not reliable enough to confirm GPS coordinates. That ruled out using a GPS-guided JDAM. The second option was a laser-guided bomb; Tomat used the SOFLAM to paint a laser spot on the school for it to lock onto. After one pass, however, the F-18 pilot reported that he could not pick up the laser spot. Either his laser tracker was malfunctioning or buildings were impeding it. A second pass yielded the same result. Tomat therefore opted for the third option, a "talk on" with the pilot, who would identify the school visually and use his aircraft's guidance system to drop the bomb. To do this, the aircraft had to "break the deck"—descend below the minimum altitude and become visible to the ground. Within Danger Close range and with civilians everywhere in the center of a city, a "talk on" was fraught with risk.

The Taliban saw the jets overhead and realized there must be Americans on the ground, flooding the streets in search of them. Tomat spoke to the F-18 pilot while the Green Berets picked off Taliban fighters below. The air controller feared a *Black Hawk Down* scenario in which a low-flying aircraft was hit by ground fire. With the Green Berets focused on firing down into the streets, David worried that Taliban soldiers would rush up the stairs; Afghan fighters popped out of the stairwell to report enemy fighters were on the building's ground floor. David told the Afghans to go down and guard the stairs, but he had no guarantee they would. He grabbed his AK-47 and looked at the scene below. When he saw Taliban fighters running between the buildings, he shot them. At a range of less than 150 yards, his fire was accurate even though he had little more than the tops of their heads to aim at. Several fighters crumpled and lay still.

It took Tomat fifteen minutes to talk the first F-18 onto the school. It dropped a 1,000-pound bomb right into the center of the building, killing around 150 Taliban and sending black smoke billowing over the city. The second F-18 followed, but its bomb failed to release. "I'm going to have to RTB [Return To Base]. I got bombs hung," the pilot told Tomat. "Well, brother, we just stirred up a hornets' nest," Tomat replied. "We're getting shot at right now because they know we're here. I need you to come in and figure out some way to get those bombs off the rack." The first F-18 returned for a second run. "No problem," the pilot reassured Tomat as he released all three of his bombs at the same time, destroying the roof. Tomat yelled in triumph and high-fived David and the Green Berets. The air controller was not usually given to displays of emotion, but he had coordinated the most complex air strike of the war thus far, with a flawless result.

Some of the Taliban fighters ran out screaming and on fire. Dozens emerged stunned and tried to escape, only to be grabbed by local Hazaras and beaten to death with shovels and sticks. Some feared capture more than death, urging Dostum's men, "Don't take my gun—kill me!" Atta's eight men inside Sultan Razia had been killed, along with a total of around 400 Taliban fighters. Scott apologized to the Tajik warlord, but the incident deepened Atta's rift with Dostum.

The school had been decimated, with body parts everywhere and corpses buried beneath the rubble. Once again, David had killed enemy fighters. In the Darya Suf Valley, he had said nothing to J.R. about taking part in the firefight with Faqir's men. This time, however, he had been with Green Berets, so he drafted a cable describing the events and his actions. David had previously calculated there were some things the Team Alpha leader need not know. Now, J.R. decided that CIA headquarters did not have to be informed of everything; he never sent the cable.

*　　*　　*

Inside Qala-i Jangi that afternoon, Dostum summoned David. He wanted the CIA man to see the Taliban commanders who had surrendered. The enemy leaders were standing in the southern compound, unrestrained and not wearing the fetters that Amanullah had used on the prisoners in the Darya Suf Valley. A mixture of Uzbeks, Tajiks, and Pashtuns, they smiled sheepishly as Dostum introduced them by name and extolled their qualities. Dostum was demonstrating his power and underscoring their surrender by introducing them to an American. The fight for Mazar-i Sharif had been one of life and death, but in victory and defeat it seemed like part of an elaborate game played by Afghan rules. At Dostum's insistence, David shook hands with the captives, reminding himself that a few days ago these men had been desperate to kill him—and, given the chance, would try to do so again.

Some 200 Pakistanis survived the bombing of the Sultan Razia school and the wrath of the local Hazaras. They were divided among Dostum, Atta, and Mohaqeq and held in locations spread across the city. Prisoners were a commodity in Afghanistan, their freedom obtainable via a ransom payment. Arabs—particularly those from the Gulf states—were the most valuable and could command tens of thousands of dollars via the hawala system of money brokers. Some were kept in outbuildings in walled compounds, others inside a cotton barn.

David and Mike were tasked with questioning groups of Sultan Razia captives. Accompanied by Green Berets, they tracked down reports of prisoner locations and tried to identify which of the captives might be Al-Qaeda. David met several dozen Pakistani prisoners who had been crammed into a shipping container—a common Afghan mode of keeping and transporting prisoners.

Many of the captives were old men. As they emerged from the container, David heard a young Pakistani speaking English in a British accent. "Mate, please help me," the prisoner asked the CIA man. "I'm in a big pickle here." He beckoned for a pen, then scratched out an American phone number with a 917 area code—New York. For a moment David imagined a connection to the 9/11 plot, but then told himself these were "jihad tourists," not hardcore Al-Qaeda. It turned out the young Pakistani's brother was a taxi driver in Brooklyn. Those with relatives closer to home would be allowed to call them and inform them what their ransom was; a Pakistani might fetch $1,500. If the money was received via the hawala system, the prisoner would be driven to a prearranged spot and handed over.

More darkly, the prisoners also had a sexual value. Some of the younger, more handsome captives would be kept so they could be raped. This was a long-standing Afghan practice, even among the leaders viewed as more palatable to the West. In the 1980s, a hard-bitten CIA officer was shocked by a British intelligence report of Ahmad Shah Massoud's lieutenants gang-raping a Russian prisoner. The MI6 officer who witnessed the rape had told the CIA man that forcibly sodomizing an infidel invader was part of the ingrained Afghan code of revenge. Once in Mazar-i Sharif, Team Bravo members were disgusted to find that some of Atta's commanders were raping young subordinates; it was a part of Afghan warrior culture that they could not fathom.

Team Alpha formed Counterterrorism Pursuit Teams (CTPTs), groups of Dostum's or Atta's men who would help them root out the remnants of Al-Qaeda around Mazar-i Sharif. One of Dostum's sources reported an Al-Qaeda compound in the mountains north of Balkh. Looking at the map, David could see this was a Shia area, making any Al-Qaeda presence implausible. The story kept shifting as he and Mike got closer to the village. After the compound tale was abandoned, they were told a handful of Al-Qaeda holdouts remained in the area. By the time the CIA men reached the village, it turned out that ten foreign prisoners were being held as sex slaves until they could be ransomed. The CIA was offering $5,000 a head for Al-Qaeda fighters, but a ransom from a family in Saudi Arabia could be ten times that amount.

David worked through these layers of untruth, thinking of it as peeling the Afghan onion. Nothing could be taken at face value and his skills as an intelligence officer were constantly being tested. This was true of the treatment of prisoners more than any other aspect of the war. The CIA's theory was that America's role was to support Afghans waging their own war. Custody of prisoners, unless they were Al-Qaeda, was therefore not a US responsibility. There was little desire to interfere with centuries-old practices, no matter how disturbing, or to get sidetracked by human-rights issues.

Neither the CIA nor TF Dagger had given much thought to the practicalities of dealing with prisoners, even those from Al-Qaeda. Of all those on Team Alpha and ODA 595, David had been the most trusting of Dostum and the Afghans. Thus far, nothing had gone wrong and no American had been killed or even wounded. Many of the other Americans remained intensely wary, however. Andy Marchal, the veteran Green Beret, worried that large groups of prisoners were being kept together close to the CIA officers. "You need to segregate these guys," he told David. "They're telling lies, they're whispering to each other. And there's always a chance some of them will jump on you."

*   *   *

Shannon Spann was relieved to learn of Team Alpha's arrival in Mazar-i Sharif. It meant there were more opportunities to talk to Mike, and it seemed that the most dangerous phase of his mission was over. Over the previous month, her status as a CIA officer had allowed her to visit CTC/SO and read classified cables about Afghanistan, so she was privy to much more information than almost any other spouse. She sent emails to Amy that could be printed off and sent, along with photos of Jake and his half-sisters, in care packages included in Team Alpha airdrops along with ammunition, cash, and other supplies.

Mike's favorite candies, Charleston Chews and ZERO bars, were added to the packages for good measure. Amy teased that these were "weird, old-people candy bars from the South," yet she succeeded in finding a local store that stocked them. They were far superior, Mike said, to the candy from MREs, which he always gave to David. Mike's four-year-old daughter, Emily, had recently learned the Pledge of Allegiance at school; now she recited it proudly over the satellite phone. It made Mike's heart swell—this highlighted why he was in Afghanistan.

But Shannon often felt overwhelmed and isolated. Alison and Emily missed their father and were confused and distraught at how sick their cancer-stricken mother, Kathryn, was becoming. The girls had known Shannon for barely a year and she was struggling with the transition from single woman in California to de facto single mother of three on the East Coast. Shannon was stolid and without self-pity. Thousands had died on 9/11, the country was at war, and Mike, whom she loved, had been blessed with the opportunity to serve and protect. She would not have dreamed of complaining about any of it. Separated from family and from the support system and camaraderie of work, however, she felt lonely. Amy worried about her.

*   *   *

There was euphoria in Washington, DC, that a major Afghan city had been liberated and Northern Alliance forces would turn next to Kabul. On the day Mazar-i Sharif fell, President Bush spoke at the United Nations, close to what he described as the "tomb of rubble" left at the World Trade Center by the 9/11 attacks. "The Taliban's days of harboring terrorists, and dealing in heroin, and brutalizing women are drawing to a close," he declared. Donald Rumsfeld had been incensed by the delays inserting the ODAs into Afghanistan and highly critical of the initial slow progress through the Darya Suf Valley; now, he was exultant.

The fall of Mazar-i Sharif had freed up American jets to switch their focus to the Shomali Plains north of Kabul. After weeks of procrastination, Fahim Khan's Tajiks were finally prepared to move. On November 11, twenty-five air strikes on the plains killed an estimated 2,000 Taliban and destroyed twenty-nine tanks and six command bunkers. As darkness fell on Kabul on November 12, around a dozen Taliban leaders met and decided to withdraw immediately, slipping across the border to Pakistan or south to Kandahar, the Taliban's spiritual birthplace and its last stronghold.

By dawn on November 13, Day 28 for Team Alpha, the Taliban were gone from Kabul, five years after they had taken control. Within the Bush administration, there was hand-wringing that the Northern Alliance would exact reprisals inside the capital, triggering a civil war. George Tenet had been quizzed before the fall of Mazar-i Sharif about why the Northern Alliance was moving so slowly; now, the CIA chief was being urged to hold the same forces back from Kabul.

The debate in Washington about the Afghan capital was moot. The Northern Alliance was going into Kabul regardless, and the CIA would have to be with them. At 6 p.m. on November 14, Gary Berntsen, who had taken over as Jawbreaker leader from Gary Schroen, drove past the US Embassy in Kabul, last occupied by the Americans in 1989. President Ronald Reagan's official photo still hung in the lobby. The embassy had been vandalized, but the CIA station, secured within, had never been breached. The same evening, the CIA's Team Echo and ODA 574 entered southern Afghanistan to support the Pashtun exile Hamid Karzai. Less than a month after Team Alpha's arrival, there were now six CIA teams and nine ODAs in Afghanistan. At last, moreover, the Americans were operating in the Pashtun south.

11

GOAT RODEO

7:10 p.m. (GMT -4), November 14, 2001;
Washington, DC

STANDING BENEATH a neon-and-glass sculpture in the atrium of
the Ronald Reagan Building, Paul Wolfowitz, Donald Rumsfeld's deputy,
gloried in the exploits of the Green Berets. In an after-dinner speech
to 450 of the great and the good of Washington's national-security
establishment, he read out parts of Captain Mark Nutsch's October 25
dispatch. He included Nutsch's Pattonesque declarations and added the
embellishment that US Special Forces had been wielding swords. The
text of the message was released by the Pentagon the same night.

Two days later, in response to a reporter's prearranged question
about "Special Forces participating in saber charges on horseback,"
Rumsfeld held up a photograph showing General Dostum on his white
horse, Surkun, with other riders—including Alex Hernandez and Max
Bowers—ranged across a hillside. Together, the letter and the photograph planted in the popular imagination the legend of the horse
soldiers in Afghanistan, without any mention of the CIA.

It had been just over two months since 9/11, and the image of
a band of American heroes riding into Mazar-i Sharif was a neat fit
for the national mood. On November 17, Day 32 for Team Alpha in
Afghanistan and three days after Wolfowitz spoke, the fall of Kandahar

signaled the final collapse of the Taliban government. Now, the American focus turned to installing a successor. Already, the CIA and State Department were looking toward Hamid Karzai.

Even had he lived, Ahmad Shah Massoud would probably not have been chosen by the United States as the new leader of Afghanistan; he was a Tajik. NE Division, which still held sway over CTC within the CIA on matters beyond the war, and the State Department—as well as Pakistan—wanted a Pashtun. With the exiled Pashtun commander Abdul Haq dead, Karzai was the only moderate nationalist Pashtun who fit the bill.

Team Echo and ODA 574, which had been due to link up with Haq, had been diverted to Karzai. Though no warrior, Karzai spoke English fluently and had a cultured manner that reflected his family's ties to Afghan royalty. His father had been murdered by the Taliban in 1999. Karzai had been in exile since 1994, when he had broken with the Rabbani government. He had limited support and no forces inside Afghanistan, but he was acceptable to the Northern Alliance. With the US by his side and a yearning for a new beginning after the Taliban, he was seen as the leader who could unify a new Afghanistan.

The fall of Mazar-i Sharif had been like a dam breaking; the Northern Alliance flooded into cities and towns across the north as the Taliban fled. Dostum embarked on a victory tour of his home province of Jowzjan and neighboring Faryab. J.R. and Justin accompanied him in his Land Cruiser, with Dostum riding shotgun. In the warlord's lap was an AKSU-74, the shortened Kalashnikov automatic that Osama bin Laden often posed with in photographs.

After looking out over the ancient walled city of Balkh, where Alexander the Great had set up camp in 329 BC, the trio headed to the village of Khoja Doko. Dostum had been born there in 1954, in a three-room domed house of clay bricks that lacked running water or electricity. It was in Khoja Doko that Dostum had completed his schooling at twelve to work in the fields, developing a reputation as a brawler and a skilled practitioner of buzkashi, the horse-mounted game in which teams battle over a headless calf. Though Dostum had left Khoja Doko for the gas fields, where he became a union boss, and later the Army, he was greeted there as a favorite son. After joining a village elder for tea, the warlord and the two CIA officers headed for Sheberghan, Dostum's adopted home.

Dostum's walled compound in Sheberghan—which included a small shopping arcade, a swimming pool, and a rose garden with peacocks—had been occupied by the Taliban. Remarkably, the peacocks had survived, though the rose bushes had been neglected and Dostum's gardener was already busy restoring them. The swimming pool was full of algae, the furniture was riddled with bullet holes, and the gym had been turned into a mosque. The Taliban had referred to the building, which had a faux marble facade and frosted-glass windows, as "Dostum's Castle" and used it to host visiting foreigners.

J.R. and Justin stayed in Dostum's nearby guesthouse, a large two-story building with a courtyard outside. An outsize pastoral painting of a forest, deer, and a pond decorated one of the walls. Hewing to their strict Islamic interpretation that the depiction of living things was forbidden, the Taliban had used razor blades to cut out the faces of the people and animals. As if to thumb his nose at the Taliban, Dostum opened a bottle of Johnnie Walker Red Label whisky and shared a toast to a new Afghanistan with J.R. and Justin. Despite his reputation for drunkenness, it was the first time either of them had seen Dostum touch alcohol. His home was still being cleaned up, so he stayed in the guesthouse with the CIA officers.

The CIA men were told that Mullah Fazl, the commander of Taliban forces in northern Afghanistan, had hosted bin Laden at this very guesthouse. As Justin slept fitfully in what had been described as bin Laden's room, he heard Dostum next door on his Inmarsat making call after call, barking orders, cajoling, and wheeling and dealing. Politicians, generals, and warlords the world over, Justin reflected, were all workaholics.

The next day, a large chair for Dostum was set up in the courtyard outside. Displayed next to him was a huge carpet depicting the warlord's visage and scenes of him leading his people, along with images of Taliban Hilux trucks falling off a cliff. It seemed like a cross between Afghan lore, Soviet-style propaganda, and the Bayeux Tapestry. Snaking around the courtyard were lines of men meekly waiting for a brief audience with the conquering warlord. They paid homage to Dostum and presented him with documents and requests, many of them prepared by street transcriptionists who would write for the illiterate. Dostum reveled in this ritual of subservience and patronage.

Maymana, the capital of Faryab province, was the final stop on the tour. Almost halfway from Mazar-i Sharif to Herat, this was the southwestern extent of Dostum's Uzbek domain. The scene upon arrival reminded Justin of the Beatles being mobbed in 1964 when they visited the United States for the first time. People leaped onto the vehicles in Dostum's cavalcade. Some hugged and kissed the warlord. A small boy fell off the Land Cruiser, ripping off a side mirror as he tumbled onto the road, his friends laughing.

The destination was the city's soccer stadium, where the Taliban had staged public executions, amputations, and floggings. Afghans had been ordered to attend those, but this time thousands came of their own accord. They heard Dostum announce that this former site of murder and terror would be used for sport once again now that the city had been liberated with the help of the Americans. J.R., wearing a turban and sunglasses, and Justin, with a floppy desert hat and camouflage chest rig, looked on from seats of honor. The speech was received with such enthusiasm that Justin was afraid people would be crushed to death by the surging crowd, which Dostum's guards beat back. After the stadium gathering, the CIA men visited a Taliban recruiting depot that had been bombed by American jets in October. They gagged at the stench of rotting flesh as they scooped ledgers and other documents into a trash bag to be sent back to CIA headquarters for analysis.

*   *   *

Around Mazar-i Sharif, almost imperceptibly, things were beginning to change as the heady excitement of the early days of victory subsided. The CIA and Dostum were receiving a steady trickle of reports that Taliban elements were infiltrating the outskirts of the city. It was debatable whether Taliban forces had surrendered—or even been fully defeated. Instead, they had just melted away. Surrender had always been a nebulous concept in Afghanistan: when defeat seemed inevitable, troops would switch sides, or be allowed simply to go home, usually without being disarmed.

It was becoming apparent that the Taliban were preparing to return to the conflict. In Mazar-i Sharif itself, the atmosphere was benign. David felt like royalty when he visited the Shrine of Hazrat Ali amid friendly crowds and children vying to speak to this strange American who spoke fluent Uzbek. He had been assigned four Soviet-trained Uzbek security guards, wearing sunglasses and leather jackets, who agreed to pretend he was an Uzbek Muslim so he could view the shrine itself. He prayed there as the throng looked on and one woman shouted, "Amriko Zinda Bosh!"—"Long live America!" in Dari.

Across the city, the Americans were celebrities and objects of awe. Captain Anthony Jarrett, a newly arrived communications officer for the Green Berets, attracted particular attention because he was the first black man most people had seen. "African?" he was asked again and again by confused Afghans. "No," Jarrett laughed. "I'm American."

Each day at Qala-i Jangi, Dostum held public meetings to explain how the Taliban had been defeated and to outline his plans for Mazar-i Sharif. As in Sheberghan, he also receive petitions and requests. David often attended and was introduced. One day Dostum turned to him and said he was tired—and that David should give the talk instead. Suddenly the CIA man faced some 200 Afghans waiting for him to speak. He took a deep breath and launched into an explanation of American foreign policy and the desire of the United States to help rebuild Afghanistan. The Afghans listened with hushed respect.

Afterward, David was congratulating himself on how he'd managed to get all the right points across when he was approached by a Turkmen with a snowy beard and a white turban, walking slowly with the aid of a stick. "Where are you from again?" the old man asked him through rotten teeth. David was puzzled; he had spoken for forty minutes. "America," he answered. "It's across the ocean, very far away." The Turkmen confessed: "I don't know much about America. Who is your village elder?" David told him that his elder was President George W. Bush, but that did not ring any bells. The CIA man mentioned George Washington and Franklin Roosevelt—still no sign of enlightenment. David brought up the Taliban knocking down the buildings in New York on 9/11, but the old man knew nothing about that. Touching on the war with the Soviet Union failed to take things much further; nearly everyone had fought against the Russians, the Turkmen said.

As David wondered whether his speech had registered at all, the old man said, "You speak strange Uzbek. What tribe are you from?" The Turkmen then began to run through the names of Uzbek tribes. Again, David said, he was American. This time there was a hint of recognition. "Merkit?" the old man asked. The Merkit were a Mongol tribe that had battled Genghis Khan. Eventually the Turkmen asked, "Is America west or east of Herat?" Finally, this was a question David could answer. "It's west of Herat," the CIA man said. That satisfied the old man, for whom Herat—450 miles toward Iran to the west—was the most distant place he could imagine. If David came from farther away than that, there was probably little they could talk about.

David tracked down Mir Rahmat, Atta's commander, to collect on the hospitality bet they'd made in Sarob. Rahmat duly invited him to dinner and before eating, the Tajik brought out his four wives for a photograph. They were covered from head to toe in turquoise burqas. David ribbed the Afghan, telling him this invalidated the bet, which had included a photo of his family. The wives' faces had to be visible, David insisted. Rahmat said this was "haram"—forbidden—but eventually relented and sent his wives off to get ready. David waited an hour, then began to worry that the wives would not return. After two hours, he grew concerned that he might have misjudged things and offended

Rahmat. Just then the wives reappeared, wearing makeup and vivid dresses. David went back to Qala-i Jangi that night and joked that the final picture he'd taken was his greatest achievement in Afghanistan.

In contrast to the city itself, when David visited Pashtun towns to the north of Mazari-i Sharif, Dostum's men told him the situation was not safe. Villages that had been open to Dostum and the Americans just a few days earlier were now judged no longer friendly. Ramadan, which meant a month of fasting from sunrise to sunset for Muslims, had began on November 16, heightening the volatility, with more frequent nighttime gunfire and escalating rumors of Taliban resistance.

The Taliban's last stand in the north was shaping up to be in its stronghold of Kunduz, a city 105 miles east of Mazar-i Sharif, where Pashtuns were the largest ethnic group. Meanwhile, more American soldiers and supplies arrived in Mazar-i Sharif. Packed carefully inside some of the supply pallets dropped by parachute were boxes of Cuban cigars, Scotch whisky, and *Playboy* magazines—gifts from K2 to be distributed among the Green Berets. Dozens of saddles materialized from Tennessee and Virginia; though too late for use in the mountains, they made ideal gifts for warlords. The influx of personnel and stores, however, was a trickle rather than a stream.

At the start of the US bombing campaign, American jets had laid waste to two airstrips, one at the main airport east of the city and the other at Dehdadi, close to Qala-i Jangi. Until the craters were filled in and live ordnance removed, only helicopters could land. In addition, President Karimov of Uzbekistan had withstood intense US pressure to reopen the Friendship Bridge at Termez, north of Mazar-i Sharif. It had been closed since May 1997, when the Taliban had first captured Mazar-i Sharif, and Karimov feared the Al-Qaeda-backed IMU or fleeing Taliban might use it to enter his country. For now, even humanitarian aid had to be transported across the Amu Darya by barge.

On November 13, David, Justin, and members of ODA 595 accompanied Dostum to the bridge for a meeting with Uzbek intelligence officers. They sat in the sunshine around a low wooden table in the middle of the iron span for a meal of kebabs and pilaf as Uzbekistan army soldiers peered through barbed wire from their side of the border. Built by the Russians in 1982, the bridge had been given its Orwellian name by the Soviets: its purpose had been to funnel troops and heavy weapons into Afghanistan. Now, the Americans were clamoring to do the same.

Juma Namangani, an IMU leader who had operated around Mazar-i Sharif, was killed in a US air strike around November 18, but Karimov continued to drag his feet. The Uzbek intelligence men told David that an agreement over the bridge would have to be forged in Tashkent. Reopening the Friendship Bridge was a principal American war aim in northern Afghanistan and would cement the capture of Mazar-i Sharif. Until that happened, however, the small number of American forces in the city were vulnerable.

* * *

For the Green Berets, the initial phase after the capture of Mazar-i Sharif was over. Their focus in the city turned toward stability operations across northern Afghanistan—designated by Task Force Dagger as Sector Viper. After nine days in Qala-i Jangi, Team Alpha and Boxer moved to a new headquarters on the east side of Mazar-i Sharif—an eighty-room, five-story high school that had been funded by the government of Turkey. It was named Boxer Base, and the CIA was given the top floor. The Turkish school was surrounded by a ten-foot-high wall and set back from the road. Though US Army lawyers had fretted that occupying a school might violate the Geneva Convention, they gave the go-ahead because the Taliban had closed it weeks earlier.

Most of the Americans had fallen sick at the fort, which had no running water and much of which had been left covered in feces by the Taliban. There was another reason for the move: The military believed that remaining at Qala-i Jangi showed favoritism to Dostum. Although there had been no declared change in policy, the US military had ceased to treat Atta and Mohaqeq as subordinate to Dostum. Instead, they had decided to "negotiate objectively" between them.

Dostum had been the victor in the Darya Suf Valley and Mazar-i Sharif, lauded by the CIA and Green Berets who had fought alongside him. Now he was being marginalized by the broader US government. Dostum had offered to form a CTPT—one of the CIA-sponsored counter-terrorism teams—to pursue Osama bin Laden, marching through Pashtun lands in the east to track down the Al-Qaeda leader. After all, he argued, the Russians had put him in command of 40,000 men and used his Jowzjani Division as far afield as Kandahar. But the proposal was dismissed out of hand in Washington DC.

On the final day in the fort for the Americans, an Afghan threw a cigarette butt into a shipping container filled with ordnance. Rockets whistled through the air and grenade fragments showered the southern compound. In the northern compound, David took cover as Mike and Andy laughed and goofed around in front of the fireworks display on the other side of the center wall. As the team medic, Mark was always alert to the potential for injury. He yelled: "I'm not going to waste bandages on your stupid asses!" Alex, for whom safety of the team was the top priority, arrived to see Mike jumping in the air with explosions in the background as someone took a photograph. "What the hell are you doing, Mr. Hollywood?" Alex shouted at him. "What happens when rockets hit you?" David videoed the plume of black smoke rising. "That's just life in Mazar-i Sharif and Afghanistan for us," he said, as the Green Berets around him laughed. "We see accidents like this. Well, Afghanistan is an accident waiting to happen, I believe." The fire was so intense that the metal container eventually melted.

On November 19, Day 34 after Team Alpha's arrival in Afghanistan, the Americans left Qala-i Jangi. That night, David reflected on how significantly things were changing. More and more Americans were flowing into Mazar-i Sharif—most were support personnel and many appeared to have no clear role. Dostum was preoccupied with his uphill task of securing a political role in the new Afghanistan. The Green Berets who had been Team Alpha's brothers-in-arms in the Darya Suf Valley now had other missions. David knew that it was progress—he would never forget the discomfort he had felt in the Darya Suf Valley, that bruising thirteen-hour horseback ride to Sarob, the dust everywhere. "We moved tonight from our nasty, shit-infested Qala-i Jangi fortress to a big Turkish-Afghan school in town," he wrote in his diary, noting that the Turkish school was equipped with electric lights and running water. But he was conflicted. "I already miss the fortress," he continued. "We are getting farther and farther away from our Uzbek companions and guardians and more isolated. We've got this 20-man Army contingent with us. They're all new and don't compare a lick to our Special Forces buddies. I'll miss them too. They're great guys. ODA 595, Fort Campbell, Kentucky."

* * *

On November 20, General Tommy Franks arrived, cocooned by all the pomp and circumstance befitting a four-star American general. The Chinook pilots had been advised to circumvent Mazar-i Sharif, but they flew right over the city, shooting out flares, before landing at Dehdadi. The general's sergeant major waddled out of the helicopter wearing almost every conceivable cold-weather item, looking like he'd been sent to defend an Arctic pipeline against the Russians. It was 55°F, and Justin wondered if the man might become a heat casualty.

Franks had a staff of about twenty attending to his every whim. There was a Green Beret reception committee, and Northern Alliance fighters lined up to provide security. French officers had been brought in to survey the runway. A Jordanian officer was accidentally left stranded at the airfield. The situation was what Justin called a "goat rodeo." He chuckled to himself at the preposterousness of it all. "What has everyone got to be nervous about?" he thought. "We're the heroes. He's just some guy who's been sitting in Tampa coming to see us."

Franks climbed into a Land Cruiser and was whisked off to Dostum's guesthouse, a gaudy mini-palace decorated with plastic chandeliers. The guesthouse was in Kodi Barq—literally "Fertilizer Electric"—an affluent suburb west of Mazar-i Sharif that the Soviets had developed around Afghanistan's only fertilizer factory. Inside the guesthouse, Franks held court, heaping elaborate praise on Dostum, Atta, and Mohaqeq as they sat listening to J.R. translate the general's words. Justin, nibbling on sugar-coated almonds, was struck by how meek the three warlords seemed before the effusive, six-foot-three American, who hailed from Midland—the same West Texas town as President George W. Bush. When Franks finally yielded the floor, Dostum tentatively outlined his plans for peace and reconciliation in Mazar-i Sharif and Kunduz. It was time for the Taliban to give up their weapons and go home, he said, so everyone in Afghanistan could get on with their lives. "I don't have a problem with that," Franks responded, "but bin Laden and his lieutenants *must die*." A nicotine addict who was simultaneously dipping tobacco and smoking, Franks stubbed out his cigarette in an ashtray as he emphasized the last two words.

Dostum was perplexed. He wanted to project the image of statesman rather than warlord, but Franks seemed to be suggesting he was too soft. Justin looked enviously at the dipping tobacco. Before leaving K2, he and his Green Beret friend Jim, now part of a CIA team in the Panjshir Valley, had procured a large tin of Copenhagen, brought in from the US by another soldier. As they prepared to fly into Afghanistan, they had solemnly opened the tin to divide it between them only to discover it had dried to sawdust after being stored improperly. Outside the guesthouse, everyone lined up to meet the general and receive a commemorative coin from a bag carried by a colonel, an aide-de-camp to Franks. Justin knew Franks from when the general had commanded a division in South Korea. Franks gave the bearded Green Beret in Afghan garb a quizzical look, shook his hand without asking any questions, and moved on.

Another arrival in Mazar-i Sharif was Rear Admiral Bert Calland,

154

the SOCCENT commander and Colonel Mulholland's boss. Calland had been sent in by Franks over the objection of Mulholland, who was bemused that a two-star Navy SEAL was essentially being made the mayor of an Afghan city. Calland was replacing Bowers, a lieutenant colonel, as the main link with Dostum. Just eleven days earlier, Bowers had taken over that role from Nutsch, a captain, who was beloved by Dostum. To add insult to injury for Nutsch, his men were tasked by Bowers with guarding Calland, who had arrived with a Master Chief SEAL who was carrying a starched uniform hanging in plastic. The battle for northern Afghanistan was not yet won, but some in the Pentagon seemed to believe that the fighting and the military rituals of peacetime could begin.

Calland himself had been blindsided by Franks on a November 13 video conference call when he was told that he should fly from K2 directly to Mazar-i Sharif that day rather than returning to his forward headquarters in Qatar. His role, Franks told him, would be to stop Dostum, Atta, and Mohaqeq "from killing each other," and to open both the Friendship Bridge and Mazar-i Sharif airport. This undercut the CIA and confused Bowers, who asked Calland upon the admiral's arrival, "Sir, what's your mission here?"

The day after General Franks had visited Mazar-i Sharif, President George W. Bush appeared at Fort Campbell, visiting the headquarters of the 5th Special Forces Group to mark Thanksgiving Eve. Wearing a green flight jacket labeled Commander in Chief, Bush told more than 15,000 cheering troops, "I believe good triumphs over evil." Declaring twenty-seven of Afghanistan's thirty-four provinces liberated, he compared the War on Terror, barely two months old, to the American War of Independence and World War II. "Wars are won by taking the fight to the enemy," Bush proclaimed. "America is not waiting for terrorists to try to strike us again. Wherever they hide, wherever they plot, we will strike the terrorists." He added that some enemies "seek weapons of mass destruction" and that "Afghanistan is just the beginning of the war against terror...across the world and across the years, we will fight these evil ones, and we will win." That morning, Bush had buttonholed Donald Rumsfeld in the White House to ask, "Where do we stand on Iraq planning?"

* * *

The CIA was stretched thin across northern Afghanistan. Even with the three members of Team Bravo merging with Team Alpha under J.R., there were just eleven Agency officers covering a vast swathe of territory. After the move from Qala-i Jangi, Andy and Mark split off to form what the team called Alpha South, a sub-unit in Kayan, close to Pol-i Khomri, a strategic crossroads in Baghlan province, 120 miles southeast of Mazar-i Sharif. Their task was to work with a young warlord named Sayed Jaffar Naderi—a leader of Ismailis, a Shia sect. He had agreed to form a blocking force to intercept Taliban and Al-Qaeda fighters fleeing Kunduz. Andy and Mark, dressed in Afghan clothes, sat in the back of a van driven by Hazaras and provided by Mohaqeq. There was no translator and the Hazaras did not speak any English; the CIA officers glanced uneasily at each other, holding their pistols beneath their robes, as the van kept being stopped by armed men along the road. By the time they got to Kayan, they had been through more than a dozen checkpoints.

Andy and Mark were expecting to meet a cleric. They were greeted at Kayan, however, by a man in his midthirties wearing traditional Afghan dress but holding a bottle of Jack Daniel's whiskey in one hand and a cigarette in another. He spoke fluent English in an amalgam of an American and British accent. This was indeed Sayed Jaffar Naderi. The son of an Ismaili warlord, at age ten he had been sent to live in Birmingham, England, and three years later moved to Allentown, Pennsylvania. In the US, he had been known as Jeff Naderi and worked in a McDonald's. After returning to Afghanistan, he and his father became power brokers between the mujahideen and the Soviets. In 1989, Naderi appeared in a National Geographic documentary titled *Warlord of Kayan,* clad in leathers and riding a motorcycle to the strains of AC/DC's "Highway to Hell." Now, he commanded 3,000 troops and the CIA wanted him to fight the Taliban. Offered a plentiful supply of weapons and ammunition, help negotiating with the local Tajik tribes, and a pallet of cash, Naderi had agreed.

"You guys made really good time," Naderi told Andy and Mark. "I didn't expect you for at least a couple days. What road did you take?" He was astonished to learn that the Hazaras had driven along the most direct route, straight through enemy territory. "You realize we don't own that road?" the young warlord chuckled. "All those checkpoints you went through were Taliban."

Two days later, Naderi came to tell the CIA men that 600 Taliban fighters had massed in a nearby valley, with an old Soviet tank. Naderi had only a few dozen men at hand and although there had been a CIA airdrop of Kalashnikovs, they were otherwise lightly armed; the Green Beret ODA assigned to Naderi had yet to arrive. With trepidation, Andy and Mark headed over to the valley to discover that the Taliban group had gathered to surrender. The CIA men and Naderi were vastly outnumbered and could easily have been slaughtered en masse had the Taliban reconsidered. Andy told Mark to put the radio to his ear, look up at the sky, and act as if he was talking to American jets. Mark obliged with a string of call signs, grid coordinates, and curt acknowledgments of the armaments with which the imaginary aircraft were prepared to bombard the valley. The Taliban commanders, deeply fearful of American air power, fell for the charade and Andy duly accepted their surrender. It was a heady moment for the young CIA officer, barely three months out of The Farm. "You are now Chief of the Valley," Mark told him.

The 600 Taliban were mostly fighting for money and were content to switch sides and kill their erstwhile comrades. Their commanders knew that the Taliban regime was about to collapse; it was an Afghan tradition to change allegiance and join forces with the victors once it was clear the alternative was death and defeat. But Andy and Mark, who were soon joined in Kayan by Alex, also encountered Al-Qaeda fighters who had been captured by Naderi. These men, mainly Arabs, would fight to the death rather than make common cause with the infidels, as they regarded the Shia. More than 100 miles from the rest of Team Alpha and with Al-Qaeda as well as Taliban forces near Kayan, Andy told himself, "We are right on the edge here."

*   *   *

At Qala-i Jangi late on the night of November 21, Day 36 in Afghanistan for Team Alpha, Dostum sat in a low-ceilinged reception room in the headquarters building on the fort's north side, taking tea with the Taliban. True to his word to General Franks, the warlord was negotiating terms for an end to the war in northern Afghanistan. Encircled in Kunduz since November 13, the Taliban was presented with a choice: surrender or die. Alongside Dostum, perched on battered sofas and armchairs, were Atta, Mohaqeq, and the Northern Alliance commanders who had fought with the Americans in the Darya Suf and Balkh valleys. Facing them were Mullah Fazl, the Taliban's Deputy Minister of Defense and commander of its forces in the north, and Mullah Norullah Noori, political commander of the Taliban's Northern Zone. The mullahs had arrived in a Land Cruiser, its windows blackened, and its panels smeared with mud to mask the white color. It was part of a heavily armed thirty-nine-vehicle convoy that had raced through the night after being granted safe passage from Kunduz. The meeting was at Fazl's request.

Fazl, plump and wearing a loose, white robe along with his black turban, sometimes used the name Mazloom, meaning "the meek." In fact, he exuded a scowling arrogance and had a reputation as a merciless slayer. Fazl had studied Islam for six years while a refugee in Quetta, Pakistan, before traveling to Kandahar to join the Taliban at its founding. He had risen from foot soldier to command more than 10,000 Taliban, as well as 3,000 Al-Qaeda fighters in Brigade 21, which was controlled by the anti-Karimov IMU. The CIA believed Fazl, who had lost his left leg on the battlefield years before, was responsible for the genocide of Hazaras across northern Afghanistan.

Also present was the mysterious former Taliban commander Amir Jan Naseri, who had defected to the Northern Alliance before 9/11 and had been with Dostum in the Darya Suf Valley. Dostum was using him as an intermediary with the Taliban, but some Uzbek commanders feared that Naseri was playing a double game. After the talks, Mullah Dadullah, who had also lost a leg, fighting with the mujahideen, stayed at Naseri's home in Balkh. An important Taliban commander, he was known as Dadullah Lang—Dadullah the Lame. He had stayed away from the Qala-i Jangi negotiations, claiming he was "sick." J.R. and David were in the headquarters building and saw the Taliban leaders but did not take part in the talks. J.R. judged that the Kunduz surrender was a matter for the Northern Alliance. It had been an Afghan fight and it would be their peace deal, no matter how imperfect.

The negotiations went late into the night. Fazl and Dostum did most of the talking. Mohaqeq stared silently at the men he blamed for the slaughter of thousands of his fellow Hazaras. Fazl's pitch played subtly to thirst of Dostum and Atta to assume national roles in the new Afghanistan. If they didn't accept a Taliban surrender, Fazl argued, they would have to fight house-to-house in Kunduz. It would be a bloodbath, and Dostum and Atta would be branded as the men who destroyed the city. Dostum knew that if he took part in a slaughter as the world's media looked on, it would confirm his reputation as a murderous warlord. Fazl was also able to exploit the divisions between the Uzbeks and the Tajiks within the Northern Alliance. The previous day, Fazl and Dadullah had negotiated with allies of Fahim, the Tajik commander in the Panjshir Valley. If Dostum struck a deal with Fazl—the Taliban commander intimated—the Uzbek warlord would be able to outflank the Tajiks and enter Kunduz as the conqueror of the Taliban's last stronghold in northern Afghanistan.

The sticking point was Al-Qaeda. Dostum knew that the CIA would not allow him to let large numbers of foreign fighters slip away. Fazl realized that offering Al-Qaeda fighters was a major bargaining chip. Knowing that J.R. was in the wings, he dangled the possibility that he could help find Osama bin Laden. Pakistan was also pulling strings; President Pervez Musharraf did not want to deal with Tajiks in the Northern Alliance, who were implacably opposed to Islamabad's influence. So Musharraf had called Dostum, appealing to the Uzbek leader's vanity: Dostum was now an international figure, Musharraf suggested, and could be the most important power broker in Afghanistan. Fazl was acting on orders from Taliban leader Mullah Omar, who was supported by elements of the ISI.

Exactly what Fazl offered—and just what Dostum agreed to—was murky. The Americans became alarmed when Dostum seemed to give Fazl too much information, including the routes and date of the planned attack on Kunduz. Dostum also told Fazl: "Lay down your weapons, and then you're going to be transported to the airport in Mazar." Specifying where prisoners would be taken appeared to be a basic mistake, though it could have been deliberate misinformation from Dostum because there was no holding facility at the airport. Close to midnight, Dostum called in a group of Western reporters to hear Fazl capitulate. Some stood on the sofas to get a better view. Fazl and Dostum shook hands and announced a deal that included all foreign fighters. "They are all under my command and they will all surrender," Fazl said. "They will accept my word."

Dostum declared that he would send 5,000 of his soldiers to Kunduz to disarm the Taliban fighters and ensure security. The Afghan Taliban would be allowed to return to their home villages, but foreign fighters would be brought to Mazar-i Sharif, where they would be separated into terrorists and ordinary fighters. "The problem will be resolved without fighting," Dostum promised. "The Kunduz people will surrender the foreigners to the [Northern] Alliance." Dostum assured the Americans he had not been outwitted: "Don't worry...we will use him [Fazl] if he can help surrender Kunduz, and if he can't, he will die." In yet another layer of intrigue, the CIA later learned that the Taliban had paid Dostum $500,000 for the safe passage of Fazl, several other senior Taliban, and an undetermined number of Arab fighters.

Afterward, J.R. held a separate meeting with Fazl and Noori inside Qala-i Jangi. Fazl pretended he did not speak Dari, so everything had to be translated to Pashto and back. The defiant Taliban commander had little interest in talking to the CIA. "We have made an Afghan agreement," he said.

Nutsch, who was providing security, stared at Fazl, who glowered back. Nutsch thought he had never seen a person so filled with hate. He could tell Fazl wanted to kill him—and the feeling was mutual. "He's the reason we're here," he told himself. J.R., too, did not trust Fazl—or believe he would carry out the surrender quite as promised. But the fate of Kunduz was at stake. As much as the Americans wanted to arrest Fazl on the spot, they could not scuttle Dostum's deal. J.R. looked at Fazl and told him, "If this is fake, it will lead to your destruction."

12

NOT SURRENDERED

6:10 p.m. (GMT -7), November 22, 2001;
Wawona, Yosemite National Park, California

FOR SHANNON SPANN, something felt off about her Thanksgiving Day phone call with Mike. She was with Jake, deep in the woods of Yosemite, an annual tradition for her family, who had rented the same cabin for the holiday since Shannon was two. It was still Thanksgiving in California, but it was 6:40 a.m. the following day in Afghanistan. Calling from the Turkish school on a satellite phone, Mike broke some good news. Team Alpha's replacements were due to be in Mazar-i Sharif soon, and he expected to be back in the US in mid-December. He was looking forward to being home for Christmas and had decided to buy his daughters new bicycles.

Shannon and Mike had spoken every few days since he had landed in Afghanistan. Others in Team Alpha talked to their families rarely, if at all, fearing it would distract them from their mission and the fewer details shared the better. David found that phoning home made him feel vulnerable, introducing an element of ambiguity that he did not want to have to deal with. He and his wife, Rosann, had talked only once and had agreed that the conversation was desultory. Justin had decided on a whim to call his girlfriend in Florida from Dostum's command post at Cobaki mountain. The problem was he had left the US without telling her where he was going or calling her for more than two weeks. She was unimpressed to learn that he was in northern Afghanistan.

The newly wed Spanns usually spoke when it was early morning in Afghanistan and dusk in the United States. They had kept a diary of thoughts for each other to share once they were together again. "One thing has troubled me," Mike wrote on one occasion. "I'm not afraid of dying, but I have a terrible fear of not being with you and our son…I think about holding you and touching you. I also think about holding that round boy of ours….It would be cool to have a slow dance with you…"

During the Thanksgiving call, they did their best to keep their conversation light. Mike's daughters, Alison and Emily, were spending the holiday with his ex-wife, Kathryn; her cancer treatment was failing and she was now gravely ill and being cared for by Mike's mother, Gail. Shannon reported that Jake, now five months old, was smiling a lot and had discovered his feet. The couple talked about the moon, marveling how they could see what Shannon called "some little piece of the same" despite being more than 7,000 miles and 12.5 time zones apart. There was nothing bad about the conversation and Shannon had no conscious foreboding, but it was as if her body sensed that she might never speak to her husband again. When Shannon put the phone down, she began to cry.

That morning, November 23—Day 38 for Team Alpha—Mike drove with Justin to Pol-i Khomri to meet with a local Hazara warlord. Their task was to persuade him to work with Northern Alliance forces as they moved on Kunduz. They proposed that while Dostum's forces moved from west to east, he should cut off the Taliban escape route toward Kabul—the local warlord, however, was having none of it. "You must step up and fight," Mike told him, dismayed that an ally whose country the Americans had helped liberate would not follow his instructions. "Would you like some more tea?" the warlord replied. He had seized a strategic crossroads in an area where Hazaras and Ismailis could carve out territory and protect it from the Tajiks. Kunduz was Pashtun, and offered him nothing.

With the Taliban regime in its death throes, tribal and ethnic competition in Afghanistan was returning to the fore. Pol-i Khomri had been built by the Germans as a model town for textile workers before World War II, and the two CIA officers spent a comfortable night in a middle-class house. On the walls were 1970s photos of Afghan women wearing bell bottoms—not a hijab or burqa in sight. Mike was intensely frustrated by the local warlord's refusal to act against the Taliban; some Afghans were gutless, he vented. Justin just shrugged. The warlord's position made sense to him—Afghan priorities would not always align with America's. He and Mike decided to return to Mazar-i Sharif.

After speaking to J.R., Mike had known that Al-Qaeda prisoners were expected, and that he would be questioning them. He was eager to carry out the task, fearing a second Al-Qaeda attack on America could be in the offing. Back in the US, the nation was consumed by the threat from bin Laden. A fifth person had died from anthrax inhalation after a series of letters, some citing the 9/11 attacks, had been sent through the mail. The CIA had received intelligence about possible use of "dirty bombs"—makeshift biological or chemical devices—and perhaps even a nuclear weapon.

As well as overseeing the war in Afghanistan and making early preparations for Iraq, CIA chief George Tenet was grappling with scores of intelligence reports about terrorist attacks each day. Many believed that being hit by Al-Qaeda was a result of a failure of imagination—a later finding of the 9/11 Commission—and there was a consensus across the country that another attack, perhaps more devastating than 9/11, was in the offing. Mike Spann was determined to stop it.

Mike arranged to meet Alex in Pol-i Khomri, principally to brief him about the plans for Kunduz. Communications were a constant issue and Alex could not establish radio contact with J.R. But Mike also wanted to discuss questioning the Al-Qaeda prisoners. Alex was surprised because Mike seemed to be asking his permission, which was not required. "These aren't your regular Taliban guys," Mike said. "They're foreigners, maybe Al-Qaeda. This can't wait until after Kunduz." Alex told Mike that he should go ahead, but he did not realize that ODA 595 would be in Kunduz. Alex had left Mazar-i Sharif before the move from Qala-i Jangi to the Turkish school, so he was unaware just how overstretched the US forces were. It was what he had worried about in the Darya Suf Valley: when you divide your forces, communications become difficult and all manner of problems can follow.

The same day, Mike spoke by radio with Brian, his Farm classmate. The fellow former Marine was with his Jawbreaker element and Tajik forces on the east side of Kunduz. Mike discussed his concerns about the danger the prisoners presented. Brian urged him to take care, because a Tajik commander had warned Jawbreaker to be wary of prisoners; whisperings among the Taliban indicated something might be brewing. The two CIA men also discussed the reliability of their Afghan allies. Brian's team had nearly been wiped out when Tajik forces ran away in the face of a Taliban surprise attack. Fortunately, a B-52 on station had prevented Brian's team from being outflanked. "You can't be sure the Afghans will stand and fight," Brian said. Balanced against the risk, however, was the urgent need to gain intelligence as quickly as possible to stop the next attack on America. Mike's experience with Dostum, moreover, had been much more positive than Brian's tribulations with the Tajiks, who had swung from reluctance to recklessness with alarming unpredictability. Mike knew there was no perfect answer to any of this. "Yeah, man, I got it," he told Brian.

Alex and Brian would replay these conversations in their heads for years afterward.

* * *

By the night of November 23, tension was mounting inside Mazar-i Sharif. Dostum's, Atta's, and Mohaqeq's forces were now on the streets, vying for hegemony over the city. Fears of a Taliban return had ramped up. Captain Anthony Jarrett was commanding a three-vehicle convoy to pick up new arrivals at Dehdadi airfield when he heard the distinctive boom boom boom of a DShK .50-caliber heavy machine gun. It was close. In the rearview mirror of his SUV, he saw tracers lighting up the sky.

Jarrett was driving along a straight, elevated road. At the start of his Army career he had been an "88 Mike," or Army truck driver. He later served as a Green Beret weapons sergeant before becoming an officer. During the Cold War, he had trained in an armored Mercedes at speeds up to 150 miles an hour against the Baader-Meinhof threat in Germany. He knew the best way to survive an ambush: accelerate out of the kill zone. Even as a routine, speed was a convoy's friend because it gave any potential aggressor less time to think. The driver in the lead vehicle, however, had slowed to a crawl. Suddenly, Jarrett, in the trailing vehicle at the rear, saw in his wing mirror a DShK-mounted truck on the shoulder below, bearing down on him from behind. "Oh shit, this dude's trying to kill us," he thought.

As his mind raced, time seemed to freeze. "There's no way for me to turn off," Jarrett thought. "If this guy gets an angle on me, we're dead. But if I go off the road, we'll be stuck and he'll kill us." He redlined the SUV, pushing the engine up to 7,000 rpm and roaring past the other two vehicles, trusting they would follow his lead. "Okay, what's in front of me?" Jarrett thought. "The airport, where there are French forces. But I don't think I can make it." He could see his life passing before him. "My God, I'm never gonna see my sons again," he thought, then caught himself: "Stop thinking about that. Focus. You're not dead yet."

Jarrett had been on the road before, so he knew a building was coming up on the left beside a track leading into the desert. He decided to take the track and execute a Rockford turn—a 180-degree maneuver that would leave him facing the enemy and able to open fire on him. At the last moment, however, the captain realized he did not have time to complete the turn before the truck reached him. "I've got to keep going," he thought. Thankfully, the truck soon fell far enough behind for a change of tactic: Jarrett stopped the SUV and jumped out.

He ordered the other drivers to switch off their lights and follow him on a dogleg into the desert. "Whatever you do," he said, "don't hit your brakes—if they see our brake lights, we're dead." Jarrett drove slowly, praying he didn't hit a mine or unexploded bomb. Then he turned to face the DShK truck, cut his engine, and grabbed his rifle, ready to shoot the driver as he approached. He could hear the truck out in the desert. Then it stopped and waited. He held his breath as he heard voices. Several minutes later, the truck turned around and drove off.

Later that night, Jarrett learned that the DShK truck had belonged to Dostum's men, who had assumed the three American vehicles were a Taliban convoy. He felt sick to his stomach: he had nearly been killed by Dostum's men. Even worse, he felt, he had almost killed them.

*   *   *

Driving back to Mazar-i Sharif with Mike on the morning of November 24—Day 39 for Team Alpha in Afghanistan—Justin spotted a Russian-made Mi-17 helicopter in the distance, flying south from Kunduz toward Kabul. He had read intelligence reports of the Pakistani ISI evacuating its officers who had been fighting with the Taliban and wondered whether this might be one of those flights. It later emerged that the White House had authorized the Pakistani evacuations after discussions with Musharraf.

Mike and Justin were hungry for action. They had been in Afghanistan for more than a month and had yet to experience close combat; neither man had fired his rifle or pistol. On the way back from Pol-i Khomri, they stopped and spoke to locals to glean intelligence. Occasionally, they asked villagers if they had seen Osama bin Laden. It seemed a stretch even at the time, but the American public was fixated on the Al-Qaeda leader, and Cofer Black had told CIA team leaders he wanted "bin Laden's head shipped back in a box filled with dry ice."

As Mike and Justin neared Mazar-i Sharif, an old man told them: "I don't know where bin Laden is, but there are about 200 Chechens up there about to surrender." Mike asked Justin what he thought they should do about the Chechens. He seemed to be probing to find out how determined Justin was to kill the enemy. Justin pondered the question, trying to reconcile his desire to decimate Al-Qaeda with his duty to follow the Law of Armed Conflict. "Maybe we get up there and they'll shoot at us, giving us a reason to call CAS [Close Air Support], and then we can destroy them," Justin said carefully. "OK, sounds like a plan," Mike responded.

It turned out that this was not to be the opportunity Mike and Justin had hoped for. Instead they encountered a standoff: outside the east gate into Mazar-i Sharif, an encampment of prisoners by the main road was being guarded by the Northern Alliance. On a small hill over-looking the prisoners, the bulk of the city's Green Berets—including Nutsch's ODA 595, Lieutenant Colonel Bowers, and most of Boxer—was preparing to head east to Kunduz with Dostum and his forces. They had assembled what looked like a Mad Max convoy of tanks, armored personnel carriers, artillery pieces, pickup trucks, ATVs, and SUVs. Justin was eager to go to Kunduz, where a major battle was expected, but was ordered by J.R. to remain in Mazar-i Sharif with Mike and David. J.R. and Scott would join the Mad Max convoy in their UAZ truck.

The prisoners had arrived unannounced at 3 a.m. in five open trucks and three pickups, then waited until daybreak to surrender. They were foreign fighters—Al-Qaeda, not Taliban—and numbered more than 400. After fighting in Takhar province, they had walked fifty miles to Kunduz and been driven west from there. Fighters from every part of the Muslim world and beyond seemed to be represented. Many were Arabs, from Egypt, Saudi Arabia, Yemen, and the Gulf states. But there were also Azerbaijanis, Dagastanis, Filipinos, Indonesians, Kazakhs, Kyrgyz, Pakistanis, Tajiks, Tatars, Turks, Uighurs, and Uzbeks. The group also included Africans from Algeria, Morocco, Nigeria, and Sudan, and even a few fighters who appeared to be white Westerners.

Many of the captives had spent the day sleeping in black tents, while others sat among the desert dunes. Some said they had been instructed to give themselves up to Amir Jan Naseri, the former Taliban commander working for Dostum. It was unclear how they had been selected and why they had traveled to Mazar-i Sharif. They were twenty-four hours early and 100 miles west of the surrender site supposedly agreed upon with Dostum. Some prisoners indicated they had broken with the Afghan leaders of the Taliban because they feared they would be sacrificed in Kunduz. Most looked sullen, angry, and defiant. Some appeared downcast and fearful. Few seemed defeated.

The Northern Alliance guards, most of them Hazaras, were terrified of these foreign fighters. Justin remembered Dostum regaling the Americans with a tale of one Arab fighter who had kept firing his gun even though an explosion had blown off a large chunk of his head. It was, Justin thought, like the stories of the Japanese at the Battle of Tarawa in 1943, who fought so tenaciously they seemed superhuman.

David was on the hill trying to draw out from the Northern Alliance commanders what was going on. "This is a clusterfuck," he thought. Some of the commanders told him it was the Afghan way of surrendering—in which prisoners were not searched as a matter of honor and weapons were relinquished voluntarily. It wasn't perfect, David reasoned, but it was a little like *The Last of the Mohicans,* in which the French allowed British troops to keep their weapons and be escorted away. The problem was that although a deal had been reached between Dostum and Fazl, some of these fighters did not realize they were being taken into custody. They had understood they would be allowed free passage south to Kandahar, or west to Herat—still controlled by the Taliban—and thence to Iran.

Dostum and Atta, accompanied by Naseri, had spent most of the day negotiating the terms of the surrender. Part of the debate centered on whether the prisoners would be held at the nearby airfield, which, after Dostum's negotiations with Fazl, they seemed to expect, or at Qala-i Jangi. Dostum had told Admiral Calland he wanted to set up a temporary detention facility at the airport, and he had requested materials and instruction in how to run a prison camp. But none of that had happened yet; Dostum and the Americans ruled out using the airfield for the prisoners—it was not secure. Thus, Qala-i Jangi became their destination.

By midafternoon, Dostum had lost patience with the intractability of the prisoners. He asked Major Mark Mitchell to call in "the airplane with the laser gun" to put pressure on them. Mitchell, the Boxer operations officer and number three to Bowers, called over to Staff Sergeant Mike Sciortino, his air controller: "Hey, Mike—can you get whatever aircraft you have in the airspace over here?" Sciortino radioed Kmart, the US Combined Air Operations Center (CAOC) in Saudi Arabia, and Bossman, a NATO AWACS E-3A flying out of Germany. Minutes later, two American B-52s, flown from Diego Garcia, arrived overhead. "Let's have a show of force," Mitchell told Sciortino. "They need to know we mean business." The B-52s, fully loaded with bombs, circled over the prisoners, and a deal was worked out. But the details kept shifting. "We will invite the UN representatives, and we'll hand over the prisoners to them," Dostum told a handful of reporters on the scene. "They are not Afghan, but foreign terrorists, and the UN will decide." The UN, however, had refused to take custody of any prisoners.

Naseri said it was a "mistake" that the foreign fighters had traveled to Mazar-i Sharif instead of surrendering at Kunduz and that Fazl had erred by instructing them to give up their weapons while failing to tell them they would be prisoners. Some of the Al-Qaeda fighters were searched cursorily, others not at all. In part this was due to the Afghan custom of accepting the word of fighters who surrendered. But these men were not Afghans, and they instilled such fear that the Northern Alliance wanted as little contact with them as possible. The surrender negotiations over, Dostum and his Mad Max convoy of American and Northern Alliance vehicles departed east for Kunduz.

The convoy of prisoners set off in the opposite direction, along the main road that ran west, right through Mazar-i Sharif. It was led by a huge truck painted in camouflage colors and loaded with confiscated heavy weaponry. Then came seven open trucks jammed full of

Al-Qaeda fighters. Only three of the trucks had been searched. The convoy halted at the Turkish school and the Green Berets looked out at the Al-Qaeda fighters peering over the seven-foot wall from their vantage point on the trucks. "The enemy can see that American soldiers are here," thought Master Sergeant Dave Betz, tasked with guarding the building. "They're casing the joint." The hatred in the eyes of the Al-Qaeda men was palpable. Just as alarming was the mob in the street, blaring horns and surrounding the trucks. Before the convoy moved off, Betz saw several prisoners dragged from the trucks and apparently beaten to death by locals. A veteran of the Gulf War and Somalia, Betz was a balding, thick-set, hard-driving NCO with a penchant for exuberant profanity. His nickname was Ol' Sarge. "Whoever came up with the idea of driving these mother-fuckers right past us hasn't got a fucking clue," Betz muttered.

Major Kurt Sonntag, who had flown in days earlier, was temporarily in command of the Turkish school. A Green Beret and deputy to Bowers, he was concerned that the overall situation in Mazar-i Sharif was becoming unstable. Sonntag had received intelligence reports of a Taliban force commanded by Mullah Dadullah to the west of Mazar-i Sharif. Mohaqeq, whom Dostum had left in charge of security for the city, was also worried. He had heard a BBC report that Mullah Omar was boasting the Taliban would soon recapture an important city in Afghanistan. Mohaqeq wondered if Omar was referring to Mazar-i Sharif.

Tall, blond, and steely-eyed, Sonntag had an ability to soak up pressure and a natural authority that had marked him out as a future general. Many of his contemporaries had been champing at the bit to get into Afghanistan, but Sonntag was in no hurry. He had concluded that years of war lay ahead, and his chance for combat would come soon enough.

Mitchell was Sonntag's nominal subordinate, though both were majors close in seniority. Despite his unassuming demeanor, Mitchell was tough and did not shrink from unpopular decisions. Balding and with jug ears, he was ferociously strong and had been a wrestler and football player in high school, where he had worked two jobs before arriving for classes. The unsentimental Mitchell had come down hard on Mark Nutsch when the captain complained about orders from Bowers. Mitchell, who had been in Afghanistan since landing at Chapchal on November 2, was also destined for the higher ranks of the Army. It would be fortuitous that he and Sonntag were the two majors left behind when Bowers had followed Dostum to Kunduz.

At the Turkish school, Sonntag had plenty of support soldiers, but only a handful of Green Berets—the men who could fight. Betz informed him there were no sandbags and that the building was especially vulnerable because much of its facade was glass.

It was the gloaming by the time the Al-Qaeda trucks drove into Qala-i Jangi, through the center gateway and into the southern compound. There, the prisoners—some plainly surprised to find themselves inside the fort—climbed down from the vehicles. Body searches by the Northern Alliance soldiers were haphazard and disorganized. A young, aquiline-nosed prisoner wearing a black turban and a camouflage jacket over a brown tunic identified himself in broken English to a television crew as Pakistani. "I come from jihad against the terrorism of USA," he said when asked why he was in Afghanistan. But now he was a prisoner in Mazar-i Sharif, the reporter pointed out. "Yeah," he replied cheerfully, his lips curling into a smile. "It's no problem. All is fair in love and war." But there had been no capitulation, the Pakistani insisted: "We are not surrendered. General Dostum give the permission to road for Kandahar. We are not surrendered." At that moment, he wheeled around at the sound of an explosion thirty yards away. A small puff of smoke rose beside a blue truck, still loaded with prisoners, facing north between the Pink House and the fort's center wall. A prisoner being searched had detonated a grenade, shouting "Allahu akbar!"—"God is great!"—as he killed himself.

Sayed Assad, one of Dostum's commanders, staggered back, blood spurting from his chest, and collapsed. He had been mortally wounded by a grenade fragment. A piece of shrapnel embedded itself in the knee of a British television reporter. Nader Ali, a Hazara commander whom Dostum had just appointed as a police chief, lay on his back, his face streaked with blood, lifeless eyes staring at the sky. With his thick green coat, black hair, heavy mustache, and Asiatic features, Ali bore a marked resemblance to Dostum. It was one of the first suicide attacks after 9/11—and its target appeared to have been the Uzbek warlord himself.

David, Mike, and Justin had just arrived at Qala-i Jangi and were in the courtyard by the gatehouse when the grenade went off. The Hazara guards ran around, agitated. Some were cocking their rifles, and Justin felt that a single misunderstanding could set off a frenzy of gunfire. He had already learned that Ramadan fasting made Afghans jumpier and quicker to action, but this was something more.

"Man, this ain't good," said David, who for a moment feared the start of an uprising. "They're really amped up. I don't know what's going on." Naseri ordered the patting down of the more than 400 Al-Qaeda prisoners but hastily abandoned the plan, and directed they be herded into the Pink House cellar instead. Some of Dostum's men feared the former Taliban commander was secretly helping his former comrades; now, he had just made a key security decision.

Close to the Pink House, there was a Kamaz truck with its tailgate down. Walking over to check it, Justin was confronted by the bloodied corpse of a bearded man with a black turban, wrapped in a quilt. It was the suicide bomber. David consulted with Sayed Kamal, a Soviet-trained ethnic Uzbek who was Dostum's intelligence chief in Mazar-i Sharif. Kamal had not been with Dostum and the Americans in the Darya Suf Valley, but he had quickly forged a rapport with David, who regarded him as highly competent—a fellow intelligence officer. David and Kamal agreed that things were too fluid to try to deal with the prisoners. It had grown dark and did not feel safe. "Let's go," David said.

13

THE IRISHMAN

9:10 a.m. (GMT +4.5), November 25, 2001 (Day 40);
Qala-i Jangi, Balkh province, Afghanistan

SIXTY PRISONERS HAD been brought out into the southern compound of the mud-baked fort by the time David Tyson and Mike Spann arrived from the Turkish school the next day. The Al-Qaeda captives were in two lines, kneeling or sitting in the dust and parched grass to the west of the Pink House. Their upper arms had been tied behind them, like chicken wings, with their turbans.

Most of the prisoners were bearded, their hair long and unruly after their turbans had been removed, and they hailed from across the globe. Of the more than 400 captives, all were males of fighting age, with no boys or old men among them. Many wore a *taqiyah*, or Muslim prayer cap, to cover their head. Some rocked back and forth; others were motionless. It would soon become apparent to David that they shared no common language—and, though undoubtedly Al-Qaeda rather than Taliban, it was clear they had not fought as a unit. None of them was Afghan, and this foreign field appeared to mark the end of their jihad. Only the occasional wail or protestation could be heard above the larks singing in the morning sunshine. An uneasy calm had enveloped Qala-i Jangi, the "Fort of War."

This was a chance for the CIA to gain intelligence on Osama bin

Team Alpha at K2 air base in Uzbekistan on October 16, 2001, in front of the Black Hawk that flew them into Afghanistan that night. Back row, left to right: Alex Hernandez, Scott Spellmeyer, J. R. Seeger, Mark Rausenberger, David Tyson, Mike Spann. Front row: Andy, Justin Sapp.

J. R. Seeger (left) and Andy in the Darya Suf Valley. They were the best horsemen in Team Alpha. J.R. had worked with the mujahideen in the 1980s.

Abdul Rashid Dostum (left), J. R. Seeger (center), Alex Hernandez (foreground), and Captain Mark Nutsch (floppy hat) plan the Darya Suf Valley campaign at the Alamo, near Dehi, on the morning of October 20, 2001, just after ODA 595 arrived.

Abdul Sattar, head of security. No aide to Dostum was more loyal—or more feared. David Tyson saw him as the epitome of the "relentless, even cruel" Uzbek fighters.

Mike Spann (left) and Justin Sapp at Band-e Amir in Bamiyan on the 90-mile journey to link up with Karim Khalili's Hazaras.

Dostum (front) on his horse, Surkun, with three of his commanders, Alex Hernandez (right), and Lieutenant Colonel Max Bowers (rear).

Dostum at his command post south of the Tangi Gap, the gateway to Mazar-i Sharif.

ABOVE: Driving through the Tangi Gap, past Taliban vehicles hit by US air strikes.
LEFT: The Magic Bus that Team Alpha acquired at Chapchal.

Dostum's fighters heading north for the decisive battle with the Taliban.

Locals greet Team Alpha's Magic Bus as the Americans liberate Mazar-i Sharif on November 10, 2001, ending three years of Taliban rule.

ABOVE: Dostum's men wave from the northeastern tower of Qala-i Jangi as the Americans arrive on November 10. The tower was later hit by a US bomb.
LEFT: Taliban commander Mullah Fazl at Erganak. His left leg is a prosthetic.

David Tyson, scratching his head, after addressing locals in Qala-i Jangi about US plans in Afghanistan. The old man in front of him struggled to understand where the CIA man was from. They settled on "west of Herat."

The meeting with Uzbek intelligence officers on the Friendship Bridge, on November 13, 2001. Reopening it was a key US war aim, but the Uzbeks were reluctant. Left to right: David Tyson, Captain Mark Nutsch, and Dostum.

Mike Spann singles out "the Irishman" among prisoners assembled to the west of the Pink House as David Tyson walks behind him and in front of the Pink House, which has guards on the roof.

The Irishman is brought from the main group of prisoners by Sharif Kamal.

Mike Spann watches as the Irishman approaches.

"There were several hundred Muslims killed in the bombing in New York City." Mike Spann tries to persuade the Irishman to talk. David Tyson looks on.

The prisoners minutes before the uprising began.

Close to the Pink House, the "fat Arab" Qatari, with white dust on his knees, writhes in apparent pain. Behind him, with white cap, is the Iraqi. The Indonesian (right) cries out for water.

Mike Spann questions the Qatari, who claimed he worked for Mossad, the CIA, and Al Jazeera.

Seconds before the uprising began. Sayed Kamal, Dostum's intelligence chief (right), questions a prisoner who was brought from the Pink House. Mike Spann (top left) walks toward the two doctors.

Laden's operations. David wore a gray Uzbek guppi over pale green pants and black boots. He had no rifle, but the 9mm Browning Hi-Power pistol he had brought from Tashkent was strapped to his thigh beneath the guppi. With his scrubby beard and mix of clothing, he was a hybrid of Afghan and American.

There was little doubt where Mike was from. He had grown a thin mustache, and over his black Columbia fleece was a rifle strap, attaching his AKMS to his back loosely so he could quickly swing it to his shoulder. On the waist of his jeans was his 9mm Glock 17. Neither CIA man had a radio with them; they had left the PRC in the Toyota, parked in the northern compound. Some three dozen armed guards—mostly Uzbeks—were placed along the crenellated center wall that divided the fort, the edge of the greenery fringing the open space, and the roofs of the Pink House and two buildings next to it.

"Is this dude Arab?" Mike asked David as they looked down at the body Justin had seen in the Kamaz truck the night before. The dead suicide bomber had been dumped in a ditch, and an Afghan guard had stolen his shoes. Much of the right side of his upper body had been ripped away. He had large feet and had been wearing thick green socks with red stripes on the day he had chosen to die.

After returning from the fort the previous night, David had conferred with Hank Crumpton via satellite phone. This was by far the biggest number of Al-Qaeda prisoners gathered since 9/11, and the CTC/SO chief agreed that it was essential to talk to them, identify any captives from the West, and separate commanders from foot soldiers. The first day in the fort would be an initial sift. "Do what you need to do," Crumpton instructed.

As with every Team Alpha operation over the previous thirty-nine days, the details of this assignment were left to the CIA officers at the scene. In turn, Team Alpha relied on Dostum. Their lives had been in his hands from the night they landed in the Darya Suf Valley; that was the nature of the mission. With only eleven CIA officers—including the three additions from Team Bravo—in three locations spread across northern Afghanistan, the CIA lacked the manpower to deal with both security arrangements and intelligence collection. The Agency was in Afghanistan to disrupt and gain intelligence on Al-Qaeda. Every day involved risk and placing trust in Afghan allies of uncertain reliability.

The plan had been for three Team Alpha officers to be at the fort. Justin Sapp had been due to go along with David and Mike and was manning the radio at 7 a.m. when a call came in from Alex Hernandez: a 4x4 truck sent by the CIA station in Tashkent had been brought over the Amu Darya by barge and was needed in Kayan, where Alex, Andy, and Mark were working with the Ismailis. After speaking to Alex, Mike told Justin, "Change of plan. I need you and Bob [from Team Bravo] to deliver the 4x4 to Kayan. I'll take Dave to the fort because he speaks the languages."

At the morning meeting of the four CIA men left in the Turkish school, Mike had told Glenn and Greg that they should be the second two-man team to go to the fort in the afternoon. "I know there's wounded there," Mike said to Glenn. "But you come out later and treat them." Justin helped David and Mike pop the clutch to start their Toyota. As they jumped in the vehicle when the engine started, Justin waved them goodbye, telling them: "When you come back, you're going to have to do that yourselves."

At the Turkish school, the CIA men and Green Berets had discussed whether US military backup was needed in the fort. Sonntag said he had no men or vehicles to spare. Unbeknown to the CIA officers, Task Force Dagger had ordered that Boxer was not to send any soldiers to Qala-i Jangi because of the events there the previous evening. A Special Operations Command (SOCOM) report into the subsequent events, completed in 2004, stated: "FOB 53 [Boxer] was directed not to send a security element with the OGA personnel because of the prisoners' suicide grenade attack at the fortress." But David was not worried; he felt Dostum's force was sufficient for security.

Since flying into the Darya Suf Valley three days earlier than ODA 595, Team Alpha had consistently taken on greater risk than the Green

Berets. In the mountains, however, the CIA and military had made decisions on the ground together, usually without reference to superiors. This was different: the priorities of the CIA and Green Berets had diverged since arriving in Mazar-i Sharif, and the two groups were now operating largely independently. The US military's mission was shifting to reconstruction and humanitarian assistance, whereas the CIA continued to glean intelligence about Al-Qaeda. But for the Green Berets to be told not to send soldiers into the fort for safety reasons, when it was known their CIA comrades would be there, was a major departure.

That morning, Admiral Calland was visiting Kodi Barq Hospital, close to the fort, to distribute medical supplies and assess how its facilities could be improved. Protecting him was the Special Boat Service (SBS), the British equivalent of the SEALs. An eight-man SBS unit had arrived unannounced from K2 two days earlier—a welcome asset at Sonntag's disposal. Calland's hospital visit underscored the prevailing sense among the military command that conflict in Mazar-i Sharif was over.

Once inside the fort, David spoke to Sayed Kamal, Dostum's intelligence man, who was overseeing the interrogations. During the night, Kamal explained, there had been gunshots and at least two explosions inside the cellar, killing several prisoners and wounding others. Clearly, the captives were deeply divided about what course to take. Kamal warned that the prisoners had knives, pistols, hand grenades, and even IEDs—Improvised Explosive Devices, homemade bombs. The cellar he said, should be off limits to the Americans. "It's dangerous down there." David knew that the nature and circumstances of the surrender had been ambiguous. Some prisoners probably felt betrayed by Fazl. Dostum's reputation was such that some feared they were about to be executed. While Taliban fighters from southern Pashtun provinces such as Kandahar, Uruzgan, or Helmand could go home and live to fight another day, these Al-Qaeda jihadists would have arrived in Afghanistan expecting—yearning, even—to die. Pausing to take stock of this or waiting for teams of trained interrogators and security personnel to arrive from the US was not an option for Team Alpha.

Kamal had a system in place that appeared to be working. His security men were bringing the prisoners up the stairs from the cellar one by one. At the top of the stairs, in a corridor just inside the north exit from the Pink House, they were being searched for weapons and documents. As part of this process, the turbans of the prisoners were removed and used to bind their arms.

David was pleased to learn that Amanullah, the humane and selfless Tajik intelligence chief he had befriended in the mountains, was overseeing this process. In place of his beard and Afghan clothing, he now wore a trimmed mustache, camouflage uniform, and peaked cap. Weeks earlier in the Darya Suf Valley, Amanullah had given David a penknife from the Dehi market that had been fashioned from bullet casings and plastic from an RPG round. It was already a treasured possession. Amanullah was an experienced professional, but a potential problem was that his preoccupation with treating prisoners well perhaps outweighed his concern for securing them.

The way the prisoners were bound, for instance, left their hands free to untie others. There was no sign of the fetters used in the Darya Suf Valley, and restraining large numbers of prisoners was something new for Afghans. The US military had been using flex-cuffs—single-use plastic restraints resembling zip ties—for well over a decade, and Marines had been training in their use after 9/11. But in all the supply drops into Mazar-i Sharif, apparently no one had thought to include a few boxes of them.

Kamal and Amanullah, who had been near the suicide bomber the night before, were both highly competent, but their expertise was in intelligence, not security. The same could be said of the two CIA officers: David's military record was limited and not recent, while Mike had been a Marine Corps officer and artillery specialist rather than a Green Beret officer, like Justin, or a veteran Special Forces NCO, like Alex. Almost alone among Team Alpha members, David had recent combat experience; Mike had none. Neither man had experience of a situation going badly wrong, as Alex and Scott had in Somalia.

From the Pink House, the security men brought prisoners out in ones or twos to its western side, where they were presented to Kamal. The intelligence chief made an initial assessment of nationality and seniority before the prisoner was taken to join the lines. Working the lines of prisoners were Kamal's Tajik deputy—who had a mustache and receding hairline, and wore a mustard-colored chapan—and a Pashtun deputy, full-bearded, with white robes and a checkered mauve shawl. Between Kamal, the two deputies, and David, just about every regional language was covered. Kamal carried a pistol, but the deputies and the security men—about ten of them—were unarmed because of the risk a prisoner might grab a weapon.

Mike and David calculated that the ring of armed guards surrounding the prisoners and perched high on the fortress walls should be more than enough to deal with any eventuality. The two CIA officers agreed that each of them should stay aware of the other's whereabouts at all times. But the number of guards, combined with Kamal's orderly system, gave a sense of security that was illusory. Mike and David hadn't realized that almost all the hardened Northern Alliance fighters were in Kunduz. This was Dostum's B-team.

One of Dostum's men, acting as a videographer, was already filming as the CIA men turned up. David wanted his own footage to transmit back to CIA headquarters. In addition, Mike had brought one of Team Alpha's Canon Elph digital cameras to take stills of prisoners. "This is Qala-i Jangi," David said as he began filming on his Panasonic video recorder. "We're in Qala-i Jangi today. We have a bunch of prisoners. We got Arabs, we got Pakistanis, we got Uighurs, we got Chechens, we got everybody." Looking down at the shoeless body in the ditch, he added, "As you see right here, we've got a guy who committed suicide yesterday—blew himself up and blew a couple of other friends of ours up."

David and Mike walked up and down the lines, debating with Kamal's deputies, to identify which prisoners they should talk to. Dirty and disheveled, most of the captives had worn the same clothes for weeks, and they reeked. Mike focused on those who spoke English. The first prisoner he talked to was a Qatari the CIA men had immediately nicknamed "the fat Arab." In his early twenties, he was the only prisoner notably overweight—a possible indication of his importance if he had received more than the meager rations most fighters got.

The Qatari was close to the Pink House. On his right stood the aquiline-nosed Pakistani who had been giving an interview during the explosion the night before. To the Qatari's left was an Iraqi, wearing a white *taqiyah* and a multicolored sweater. Easily the most vocal prisoner, the Qatari wheedled and goaded the CIA men in broken English: "I am passport Ameriki," he had shouted before they arrived. At another point he had told the security men, "I am report, TV report from Al Jazeera report. Listen to me. Talk to the commander. I am from Al Jazeera report, I come from Kandahar to here and I have camera and I lose it in Kunduz. I am not a mujahid." Later, he claimed to be an agent for the CIA and Mossad, the Israeli intelligence service.

Mike approached him. "United States?" the CIA man asked skeptically. "Where?" The Qatari replied: "Check me out. I know United States more than you." As Mike walked away to talk to David, the Qatari shouted after him, "Give us a chance to breathe!" David looked over at him. "What did you lose?" the Qatari said. "What did you lose? Son of a bitch." David was irritated. "We see that man blow himself up, kill," David said, using pidgin English so the prisoners would understand him. The Qatari taunted, "Then you are afraid, yeah?" David jabbed back, "Of course." The Qatari, gesturing at the other captives, said, "Not from me. From them." The Iraqi interjected, "They have check our bodies one hundred times. I will do whatever you want. Do a favor for us. I am studying, sir. You can ask Embassy American for Islamabad, you know." David dismissively reassured him, "Okay, don't worry, we ask everybody. We find everything out."

The next prisoner the CIA men focused on was a young white man who insisted he was from Srinagar, in the Kashmir region of India. He said he spoke Farsi, but David quickly established that the prisoner's grasp of the language was no better than his. The man admitted that he had come to Afghanistan "for jihad," but he was clearly concealing his true origins.

Then another prisoner caught the attention of the CIA officers. He had pale skin and was lanky, narrow-shouldered, and young, but with a dark, heavy beard; his straight, floppy hair was parted on the left and fell over his face. Like most of the prisoners he had no shoes, but he walked as if it pained his dainty feet. To David, his mannerisms seemed effeminate; this was not a person who had led a tough life. Mike homed in on the man's commando sweater—a military-style navy-blue pullover with shoulder patches.

"He's got a British sweater," Mike said, walking over to the prisoner. "Hey, you—you right here with your head down. Look at me. I know you speak English. Look at me. Where did you get the British military sweater?" The prisoner kept his head bowed. Almost alone among the captives, he would not engage with the Americans in any way. Most of them talked, even if only to lie or curry favor. But this detainee would not even return a glance. By this time more than 150 prisoners were outside, still in two lines but packed tightly together, with one line snaking into a curve at the end.

David went back and forth among Mike, Kamal, and the two deputies. He was exhilarated by what he was doing. These were Al-Qaeda fighters, and he was able to use all his languages and cultural expertise to begin to answer the riddle of who they were and what their connection might be to foreign plots. This was what he had joined the CIA to do. "This is the smorgasbord—the al-Qaeda buffet," he thought. "Every ethnic group you can imagine. Every language you can imagine." All of them, he surmised, had declared a Bay'ah, or oath of allegiance, to Osama bin Laden.

Despite the gravity of the situation, and the danger, a lighthearted element entered the proceedings. Kamal would say to David, "What do you think this guy is? Uzbek? Kazakh? Tajik?" The CIA man would take his best guess, and then Kamal would ask the prisoner, "Who are you?"

in various languages. If the subject was recalcitrant, Kamal would try to catch him out, crying, "Hey, you dropped your money!" or "There's a wasp on your ear!" in a language he thought they might speak, to see if they reacted. Kamal chuckled when he outwitted a prisoner or established where he was from before David did. Kamal had a particular interest in Uzbek fighters from the IMU. David was fascinated by some of the prisoners' stories and every so often would become engrossed in a tale. The CIA man was feeling good because the procedures seemed to be working: passports and documents were being gathered, weapons confiscated, and the prisoners mostly complying. Some were surprisingly open about who they were, recounting how they had learned about toxins, poisons, and chemical warfare in Afghanistan's Darunta or Al Farouq training camps.

A security man pulled "the fat Arab" Qatari out of line for questioning. It was fruitless. The Qatari was a timewaster—perhaps deliberately trying to distract the CIA officers. He told Mike he had met a man called John at the US consulate in Jeddah, Saudi Arabia. When Mike asked him to describe John, the Qatari replied, "Short—like you." Exasperated but intent on following every lead, Mike took out his camera and said, "I'm going to take a picture of you and show it to John. That way John can know what you look like. We're going to call John."

Mike then moved on to the Iraqi, who had also been pulled out of the line. Taking a knee, the CIA man placed an A4 notepad on his right thigh to write notes. The Iraqi's manner was ingratiating and his story implausible: he was a Christian, he insisted, in Afghanistan to help the United States. He had fled the Iraqi army, he claimed, and made his way to the US Embassy in Islamabad, Pakistan, where he had met "Mr. Venus and Mr. Bob" and "one lady I don't remember name but she speak Arabic." He had warned the embassy staff about a man named Ahmed Rahim, who had been dispatched on a terrorist mission by Osama bin Laden.

Then, lowering his voice, the Iraqi confided that among the prisoners were 120 members of Al-Qaeda. Mike's antennae twitched. "All

Al-Qaeda, all UBL followers?" he asked, using the US government ab-breviation for bin Laden that must have been a mystery to the prisoner. The Iraqi replied, "Yes—but everybody tell Pakistan, Pakistan."

In the thirty minutes or so since he had questioned the prisoner with the commando sweater, Mike had apparently been told that he was Irish. The Iraqi claimed to know the Irishman. "There's a guy here from Ireland, right?" asked Mike. "Yes, Ireland," the Iraqi replied. "Won't speak." Mike hoped he was building a rapport, but he was getting little that was concrete. "How many people like the Irishman?" The Iraqi replied, "Only one. Only this man." As Mike began to move away, the Iraqi whispered to him that "terrorist acts" would occur that day. But he refused to say more unless he was released.

The aquiline-nosed Pakistani gave away even less. His almost jaunty mood of the night before was gone. So, too, was his candor about being on a jihad against Americans. His new story was that he was on the same side as David and Mike. Over the past few weeks, the two CIA officers had developed a double act, with David playing the bad cop and Mike the good. "These men are terrorists, I believe," David impatiently told the Pakistani. "All these men are terrorists. I think you terrorist. You come here to Afghanistan to kill people."

The Pakistani said he was from the North-West Frontier province. He had received no weapons training but had been brought up knowing how to shoot. "When we are a child, we are prepared because weapons is our life," he said. He claimed he had told the mullah who sent him that he did not want to fight Americans because "by the internet there are some Americans and some British are my friends," and that "after the accident of 11 September, I feel very hard because our dearest cousins have been killed."

David cut him off and walked away. "This is goofy shit," he thought to himself. "A Christian? A Mossad agent? Most of these guys are string-ing us along." David was already starting to realize the prisoners had to be separated before they could be questioned properly. They were whispering and many were intensely wary, as if assessing the situation minute by minute. A German-Turkish prisoner had told Mike that he had come to Qala-i Jangi not to surrender but to fight. Sayed Kamal was picking up more information about the deadly disagreements in the cellar the night before. Several bodies still lay down there.

On one level, all this made David less comfortable than he had felt at first. On another, however, the atmosphere remained calm and there had been no surprises. Yes, some of the prisoners seemed to have formed cliques, but David observed little camaraderie between many of them—and no sense that they could act in unison. He was alarmed, however, when he went into the Pink House to talk to Amanullah and saw the cache of weapons that had been confiscated from the prisoners—dozens of rifles, pistols, and hand grenades. The pile included the full spectrum of weapons, from RPGs and PK machine guns to a set of brass knuckles. "Oh shit," David thought. "This is way more than I'd anticipated." He watched the prisoners emerge from the darkness of the cellar, dazed and blinking in the sunlight. The weapons were being removed every five minutes or so, but each new pile grew inexorably. It was plain that the body searches conducted outside Mazar-i Sharif and at the fort's entrances had been ineffectual. "It is not safe for you in here," Amanullah warned.

As David was recognizing the futility of questioning the prisoners at this juncture, Mike was doggedly seeking out the English speakers among them. He was determined to extract information. His top priority was to find out about the Irishman in the commando sweater. "Has he seen any more of these like the Irishman?" Mike asked David as the white prisoner who claimed Kashmiri roots was quizzed again. Close to 250 prisoners were now lined up in the southern compound.

The noise level had risen, and more prisoners rocked back and forth or protested their discomfort. One prisoner resisted having the ties around his arms tightened. Security men pulled him by the hair and kicked him in the back. An Indonesian prisoner kept shouting "Aab, aab"—Farsi for "water"—as if he were delirious. He had long, wild hair and struck David as deranged. By this time, wounded prisoners were emerging from the Pink House. Some had fresh injuries from the grenade blasts in the cellar the night before. "Some of these fucked themselves up real bad," David told Mike. An Uzbek from Tashkent had a grievous wound, stretching from the bottom of his left ear down to his neck, that seemed fresh. A grimacing Arab using a crutch had lost most of his left foot. After discussion with David and Sayed Kamal, Amanullah sent a guard to nearby Kodi Barq Hospital to fetch medical help.

Mike decided to take another crack at the Irishman. His presence in this Al-Qaeda group was baffling. At the time there had been no known instances of Westerners without Muslim family ties joining Islamist groups. Mike's manner made clear that he had been told that the man with the blue sweater was Irish. He was not guessing. That nationality might have made some sense to Mike, too, because Team Alpha had been briefed that it was possible men associated with the Irish Republican Army (IRA)—which had fought the British over Northern Ireland for more than two decades—could have linked up with Al-Qaeda. Until four years earlier, the IRA had been a designated terrorist group; its members had received training in Libya, and the Bush administration was anxious to identify global networks.

The young CIA man's instinct was that this could be a high-value prisoner. He felt sure the man was lying and that he spoke English. The prisoner's unwillingness to interact at all with his captors suggested possible terrorist training. IRA members, for instance, were taught to remain silent during days of interrogation.

The Irishman was frog-marched toward the center wall by Sayed Kamal's brother, Sharif Kamal, and sat down cross-legged on a blanket. At twenty-eight, Sharif was the youngest of six brothers. He was wearing brand-new military fatigues and a camouflage ball cap. It was Sharif's first day working for his brother Sayed, and he had never fired the AK-47 he had been handed that morning. He was a vegetable farmer with no military service and had been brought in as a guard simply because his family connections meant he could be trusted. A gentle, soft-spoken man, he had little idea what he was doing in Qala-i Jangi.

Although David and Mike did not know it, Sharif Kamal's inexperience was typical of the guard force that day.

"I know you speak English," Mike said, his AKMS still hanging from his back, as Sharif pulled up the Irishman's long bangs and tried to tuck them behind his ears so the CIA man could see the prisoner's face. "I know you speak English," Mike said. "Where are you from? Where are you from? Are you from England or Ireland? Do you believe in what you're doing here?" A crow cawed four times, but there was no reply. "Irish, Inglesi," Mike told some of the security men behind him. "Pakistan, Pakistani," replied one, prompting the prisoner to look up briefly. Mike shook his head: "He's Irish—Ireland."

The CIA man spoke in a flat tone, without emotion. He was annoyed, barely pausing between questions to get an answer. "Do you believe in what you're doing here so much that you're willing to be killed here? How were you recruited? Who brought you here?" Mike snapped his left fingers in front of the Irishman's face. "Who brought you here? Hello! Wake up! Who brought you here to Afghanistan? How did you get here?" Mike waved his hand in a vain attempt to capture the attention of the prisoner, who just stared at the ground. "Are you Muslim? Do you believe in the Muslim faith? Hello!" Mike had run out of patience. He took his camera and knelt on his left knee before the man. "Look!" he ordered. "Put your head up. Don't make me have to get them to hold your head up. Push your hair back so I can see your face." Sharif Kamal walked around to pull up the bangs again as Mike took a photo. The crow cawed six times more.

Mike leaned forward and clicked his fingers again, but there was no flicker of acknowledgment from the Irishman. "Are you going to talk to me?" he asked. "All I want to do is talk to you and find out what your story is. I know you speak English." David approached. It was time for the good cop/bad cop routine, the final attempt to make this apparently Western prisoner talk. "Mike!" David called as he strode toward his colleague. "Yeah, he won't talk to me," Mike replied.

David's manner was brusque and tetchy: "Okay, all right," he said.

"We explained what the deal was, man." Mike concurred: "I was telling the guy we just want to talk to him, find out what his story is." The conversation unfolded right in front of the Irishman. "All right, it's up to him," David said. Mike's annoyance was palpable. "He's a fucking white guy," he said. Feigning nonchalance, David gently kicked a rock as he replied, "Well, you know—he's a Muslim." Mike indicated he knew that: "That's what I asked him. I said to him, 'Is your faith that strong?'" David launched into a coarse diatribe that amounted to the CIA men's last throw of the dice. "Well, obviously, it is," he said. "But the problem is, he needs to decide if he wants to live or die, and die here. I mean if he don't wanna die here, he's gonna die here, 'cause we're just going to leave him, and he's going to fucking sit in prison the rest of his fucking short life."

The bad-cop shtick was making little sense. "It's his decision, man," David said. "We can only help those guys who want to talk to us. We can only get the Red Cross to help so many guys. If they don't talk to us, we can't, we can't…" He trailed off and turned his head toward the Pink House, where almost 320 prisoners now knelt, arrayed in five lines.

Something about David's voice was not quite right. Certainly, the way he was speaking was so far removed from the doctoral student David Tyson at Indiana University that former colleagues would have found him unrecognizable. But that could be put down to a shift between tribes. It was the pent-up tension, the impatience, that was off—as if there was a physiological recognition that something was very wrong. David had seen the pile of weapons and realized how unsafe the Pink House was. There had been a suicide grenade attack the night before. The Iraqi had mentioned "terrorist acts." Sayed Kamal had indicated that some of the hardcore prisoners, the Uzbeks, seemed to be the last to leave the cellar. David's brain hadn't put all these elements together yet; his body seemed to be doing so.

Mike snapped his fingers again in front of the Irishman's face. "Hey, look at me," he said. "Do you know the people here you're working with are terrorists and killed other Muslims? There were several hundred

Muslims killed in the bombing in New York City. Is that what the Koran teaches? I don't think so. Are you going to talk to us?" It was a last chance for the prisoner to come clean, but he remained silent. David was done. "Gotta give him his chance," he told Mike. "He got his chance. That's all you can ask for."

Mike's encounter with the Irishman, filmed by Dostum's videographer, had lasted less than six minutes. Shortly after 10:20 a.m., a pair of medics from Kodi Barq Hospital arrived to treat the wounded prisoners. Immediately dubbed "the two doctors," they were young Tajiks delighted with the liberation of Mazar-i Sharif and intrigued by the chance to see Al-Qaeda fighters. Sayed Shah, twenty-seven, wearing a black business suit and loafers, had shaved his beard a few days earlier. He was a surgical nurse and manager of the hospital's operating theater. Though initially the sole volunteer for this Qala-i Jangi task, Shah had persuaded his friend Tamim Ahad, a twenty-year-old medical assistant, to accompany him. Both had ambitions to become qualified doctors. Taking full advantage of the end of the Taliban restrictions on facial hair and dress, Ahad was wearing a bright red shirt and a shiny leather jacket. His hair was combed back from his smooth face like Tony Manero, the disco king played by John Travolta in *Saturday Night Fever*.

The two doctors set up an improvised aid station about a dozen yards from the Pink House, between the building and the mass of prisoners; soon, they were cleaning and bandaging wounds. Shah used a pair of scissors and cotton balls to swab fresh burns on the face of an Arab prisoner while Ahad used Betadine on the captive's left knee, which was skinned and swollen from a compound fracture. More and more wounded prisoners emerged from the cellar. Several lay unconscious on the ground near the aid station. Some refused treatment.

It was now almost 11 a.m., and fewer than three dozen prisoners remained in the cellar. The more junior fighters seemed to have emerged first. Now, more hardened and senior men were coming up. "These are serious guys," Kamal told David. "They're interesting. Let's keep going with this a little longer and see how it goes." A few minutes later, the intelligence chief estimated that twenty men were still in the cellar, but they were resisting coming up. From this he deduced they were hardcore Al-Qaeda men who did not relish being identified. David and Sayed Kamal spoke to a young Crimean Tatar with a high voice who was originally from Russia. He'd been imprisoned by the Taliban in Kabul, he claimed, because he was suspected of being a Russian spy.

"Can you ask the guards to please loosen me up?" he pleaded with David in Russian. "I'm not going to put up any resistance." David took the Tatar from the Crimea off to the far side of the prisoners from the center wall, the opposite side from where the Irishman had been questioned. His was a pitiful tale. The man wept as he recounted being repeatedly raped by Arab men while incarcerated. Over at the Pink House, Mike walked toward the aid station to establish whether there were any more English-speaking prisoners. Dostum's videographer filmed Sayed Kamal questioning a prisoner. In the corner of the frame, Mike could be seen heading over to the two doctors—a final image of him.

The CIA men were almost at the end of their business for the day. In a matter of perhaps thirty minutes they would be calling Crumpton to brief him on the mammoth task ahead: interrogating the captives properly, which would necessitate flying in additional CIA teams and transferring the prisoners to a more permanent facility. "This is way out of our league," thought David.

14

PINK HOUSE

10:50 a.m. (GMT +4.5), November 25, 2001 (Day 40);
Qala-i Jangi, Balkh province, Afghanistan

THE LAST TWO men to be brought out of the Pink House and into
the southern compound were Uzbeks, leaving about eighteen still in
the cellar. Dostum's videographer filmed as the pair stopped in front of
Sayed Kamal. One prisoner was an older man with a light beard and a
two-panel white-and-gray shirt, the other younger and unshaven. Behind them a guard change seemed to be taking place, with three soldiers
leaving their post and walking north toward the center wall as another
three arrived, one of whom climbed the metal ladder to the roof of the
Pink House. Two other guards were on the roof of an adjacent building,
overlooking the north entrance to the Pink House, just inside of which
the prisoners were being searched and their weapons piled up.

The older prisoner—held by a guard with a turban wrapped around
a turquoise *taqiyah*—told Sayed Kamal that he had come to Afghanistan
from Pakistan. As the prisoner spoke, the guard's head spun around at
the sound of escalating shouts from the north entrance behind him.
The filming stopped just as everything in Qala-i Jangi changed, and the
videographer fled.

The two doctors were at the aid station, twenty or so yards away,
when they heard the shouts and a muffled grenade explosion, then shots

190

from inside the Pink House. They hit the ground as all hell erupted around them. Mike Spann, about five yards away from the pair, swung around to face the source of the noise, raising his AKMS rifle to his shoulder. Some of the eighteen prisoners still inside the Pink House were rushing out, straight at him. The doctors saw Mike shoot two or three of them with his Kalashnikov before the "fat Arab" Qatari and others who had been sitting close to the Pink House stood up and jumped on Mike from behind, pushing him to the ground. Mike managed to pull out his Glock pistol and fire one or two shots before he was overwhelmed, disappearing beneath a pile of prisoners desperately trying to seize his weapons.

David Tyson, about forty yards away, was startled by the commotion. Time slowed down as his brain processed what his eyes and ears were telling him. There were muffled explosions inside the Pink House, and shots. A prisoner ran across his field of vision, heading toward the southeast corner of the fort. David did not know it at the time, but as the two Uzbeks were being ushered into the southern compound, the next few prisoners to be brought up from the cellar had shot the guards and Amanullah, probably using pistols they had hidden. Weapons were being grabbed from the pile, grenades were exploding, and the area where Mike had been standing was a melee of bodies. David stared at the chaos, still not quite registering that this was a prisoner revolt.

As the gunfire and explosions continued, David drew his Browning pistol and stared at it. "Fuck, I've never shot this," he thought. "Do I know what I'm doing with this?" He had used a Kalashnikov rifle twice in combat, but had not fired a pistol since his CIA training course four years earlier. He chambered a round and craned his head toward the Pink House. The mass of prisoners to his left seemed also to be trying to work out what was happening. None appeared to be paying attention to him. Everything felt jarringly strange. David was frozen. "I don't have a plan and I'm not doing anything," he thought. "I should do something—but what?" Split seconds seemed to be elongating into minutes.

Now Sayed Kamal's Tajik deputy with the mustard-colored chapan, who had been between the lines of prisoners, was running in David's direction, holding his notebook before his chest and shouting in Dari, "Fier ne kun!"—"Don't shoot!" David thought, "That's crazy. Why would I fucking shoot you?" The deputy paused for a second to cry, "Farar! Farar kun!"—Dari for "Flee! You must flee!" Then he ran toward the southwest side of the fort—where, it seemed, he knew there was an exit. "This is really bad," David realized. "He's not waiting for anybody. It's every man for himself."

The idea of running never crossed David's mind. As well as time slowing, he was conscious of experiencing a physiological transformation: he was losing his hearing and peripheral vision. Everything that was not relevant to his survival and that of his comrade was being screened out. He could see muzzle flashes, but he couldn't hear shots.

He did hear one thing. Mike was yelling his name: "Dave, Dave, Dave!" It was as if David's brain had filtered out the background cacophony to allow Mike's voice through. The yells snapped David back into the moment and gave him purpose and direction—literally. Knowing where Mike was, David began to move toward him, realizing that prisoners were in the way so he would have to head east and then turn left, to the north, to reach him. Probably no more than five seconds had elapsed since the initial shouting. Most of the guards had already fled. Sharif Kamal, who managed to escape, never fired his AK-47.

As David headed toward the Pink House, a young Arab prisoner with a pale face and jet-black hair came running directly at him. David could remember having spoken to the prisoner, who was now scrunching up his eyes and turning his head slightly. "What the fuck is this kid doing?" David asked himself. He rattled off questions and answers but they seemed to take an eternity to form: "Why is he squinting? Why is his arm up? He has a pistol in his hand. He is shooting at me. Why would he want to kill me?"

David registered that the prisoner was firing the pistol incorrectly, angling it to the side. He was now five yards away and David, zooming in on the threat, could see that it was a Russian pistol, probably a

Makarov, and watched an empty cartridge ejecting. The CIA man was jerked out of his trance as his brain processed all this information and reached a conclusion: "Shoot the motherfucker," he told himself.

David stopped, raised his Browning, and shot the man twice—once in the abdomen, once slightly higher. He registered the expression on the prisoner's face at the moment of death: puzzlement, perhaps faint regret, that he had failed to kill the American. David resumed running toward the Pink House. He passed the two doctors, who were flat on the ground praying for the tumult to subside. They had seen Mike disappear under the pile of bodies and had then been attacked by the Arab prisoner with the compound fracture, whom they'd been treating. Shah had kicked him away. David got to the pile of writhing bodies and could see Mike at the bottom, recognizable by his fleece, jeans, and brown boots. Four prisoners were on top of him, including the Qatari whom the CIA men had dubbed "the fat Arab." David used his pistol to shoot each of them once in the torso, finishing with the Qatari, shooting him twice and then each of the others a second time.

Somehow, David managed to grab Mike's AKMS rifle, which the prisoners seemed to have pulled from his comrade. He then kicked Mike's legs and feet hard two or three times. "Mike, Mike, Mike!" he shouted. There was no response or movement and there was blood. Mike Spann appeared to be dead, quite possibly killed by bullets from his own Glock after his assailants had wrested the pistol away. The CIA later concluded that he had died in the first minute of the uprising.

Remembering Justin's instruction on the subterranean firing range in Tashkent, David pushed the AKMS selector all the way down to semiautomatic. Prisoners from the lines in front of the Pink House were now launching themselves at him, shouting, "Allahu akbar!" None of them seemed to be armed, and most still had their arms trussed. He shot at least four at close range—just five to ten feet away—without registering who any of them were. As he fired the first shot from Mike's rifle, David's brain told him he could feel the rifling of the barrel as the bullet spun out and killed a prisoner. A calm had descended as he fought for his life. Fear was absent. He had no real decisions to make and faced no dilemmas. David shot every prisoner who came at him as he tried to move north toward the center gate. He had to kill or be killed.

In the wake of the initial chaos, the southern compound was being reordered. Most of the guards had fled as soon as the uprising started, doing nothing to try to quell it. Of the few who stood and fought, most had been killed swiftly, some with bullets to the head from their own rifles, as they were overwhelmed by the sheer number of prisoners. With nowhere to go, the guards on the roof of the Pink House and some of the outbuildings were doomed. Prisoners untied each other or ran with their arms still bound. It seemed that some were familiar with Qala-i Jangi, having been based there with Taliban forces before the fall of Mazar-i Sharif less than three weeks earlier. Most had spent enough time in the southern compound to orient themselves and formulate a plan about where to run. Some crawled toward the Pink House and sheltered inside or down in the cellar, while others made beelines for the rooms around the compound walls.

Several prisoners ran for the shipping containers, some of which still held the weapons confiscated from them over the past day, as well as outmoded Soviet and British guns and munitions. The southern compound was an arsenal, and the prisoners now had access to all they needed to dig in and fight. A few captives escaped through holes and drainage pipes, intent on taking their chances outside. They were perhaps the wisest, for Qala-i Jangi had become a place where death was the likeliest outcome.

Lying facedown on the ground, the two doctors from Kodi Barq Hospital had to decide whether to try to get away or risk dying where they were. At first they had hoped the guards would regain control, but there was no sign of that happening. Sayed Shah, spotting a Hazara guard beckoning to him from between two containers on the southern side of the compound, opted to run for it. He urged Tamim Ahad to join him, but his younger friend was nearly catatonic.

Shah made it to where the guard was crouching with his AK-47.

"Tamim, Tamim!" Shah shouted back to his friend. "Come here! Run!" Realizing he would die if he stayed by the Pink House much longer, Ahad stood up and ran to the containers. Prisoners were running but most seemed fixated on their own quest for weapons or escape. Ahad made it and he and Shah took a minute to regain their breath. "You have to get out," the Hazara guard told them, pointing toward the southern wall. "Go. I will wait here."

As David moved away from the Pink House, he saw a grenade fly out of a window and spin toward him in slow motion. It bounced off his chest. Then a second grenade was in the air and hit his thigh. Neither one exploded. It was like he was in a silent tunnel, his mind racing through an entire novel in a single second. For some reason, he had picked up an AK-47 with a worn wooden stock and slung Mike's rifle over his shoulder. Prisoners still launched themselves at him. Something thumped his back and David looked over his shoulder to see the wild-haired Indonesian, his hands still tied, screaming and headbutting him. It was as if he were being set upon by an animal. David back-pedaled and then shot the Indonesian in the head and torso with the AK-47. The Prisoner fell to his knees, most of his head blown off. The AK-47 was out of ammunition. David threw it at the dead Indonesian, hitting him in the chest.

Nearing the center gate, David stumbled and hit the ground, his mouth filling with dirt and grit. Next to him lay the corpse of an Uzbek guard he had seen earlier in the day—an older man with a mustache—blood running from the mouth, blue eyes staring at David. The CIA man rolled over on his back and grabbed another abandoned AK-47, then sat up and began firing it one-handed, his left hand still clutching his pistol, as more prisoners rushed at him. He ran out of ammunition, picked up the AKMS, and headed for the center gate once more.

Mostly, David fired his Browning pistol. He had started with one fifteen-round magazine in the pistol and four spare magazines on his belt—seventy-five bullets in all. Mike's rifle, meanwhile, had a thirty-round magazine. David was conscious of changing rifle magazines just

195

once. Dropping the empty one, he told himself, "Don't pick up the magazine—you don't need it," as if he were mimicking his instructor in training. He was operating on muscle memory.

Close to the gate, a prisoner took potshots at David with a rifle, taking cover behind a tree and then a low wall. David fired back with his pistol. It was almost like a comic Western as they missed each other from no more than ten yards away. Bark flew as David's bullets hit the tree, and small clouds of dust kicked up as they slammed into the wall. "This is fucking nuts," he thought. Both men survived the encounter, and David staggered on.

David ran through the gateway, beneath prisoners on the parapet firing down into the northern compound. It felt miraculous that he had got this far: the grenades had failed to explode, he had been fired at but not hit, and at almost any time a prisoner could have walked up behind him and ended it all by shooting him in the head. Yet somehow here he was, still grasping the AKMS—now out of ammunition—and his own pistol.

But David was not safe yet. Ten feet in front of him was a Dagestani prisoner, wearing camouflage pants, whom David had interrogated earlier. In his left hand the prisoner held a guard by the scruff of his neck, in his right a grenade. The Dagestani's mouth was moving, but David couldn't hear any words. David raised his pistol, only to realize that the prisoner had pulled the grenade pin; only his grip stopped it from exploding. For a split second their gazes met. In that moment, the pair seemed to negotiate a deal with their eyes. "If I shoot him, we all die," David thought. He kept heading toward safety.

Behind David, Sayed Kamal approached and shot the prisoner dead with his pistol. The grenade exploded, killing the guard. David was oblivious, his entire focus in front of him. Abdul Latif, an Uzbek guard, lay on the ground in the open, his hand wounded by a bullet. David dragged him behind a truck, helping him reload his rifle just before an RPG round exploded near where they had been.

Suddenly David was in the open, with the headquarters building

196

still 300 yards away. Heavy fire came down from the center wall and through the gate. He thought about running to the entrance courtyard, but decided against it: armed prisoners could be there, or Uzbek guards who would open fire. "If I go there, I will die," David thought. He ran up the center boulevard before cutting across the grass and then a small, paved courtyard to the west side of the building. By now he had fired seventy-five pistol rounds, emptying all five of his fifteen-round magazines. Mike had fired several of the thirty rounds in his AKMS magazine; David had expended the rest. David had also shot prisoners with the AK-47 he had thrown at the dead Indonesian, as well as the one he had grabbed while lying beside the dead guard.

By even a conservative estimate, he had fired more than 100 rounds, killing at least twelve Al-Qaeda fighters and possibly forty or more. "I am dead now," thought David as he ran, clutching his pistol by the barrel in his left hand and Mike's AKMS in his right. "I'm in the open and they can't miss." In truth, the avenue of large plane and pine trees probably gave him more cover than he believed. But the sense of extreme peril involved in every passing second had yet to fade. As he ran, David waited for a bullet to hit him. It did not come.

*　　*　　*

Bursting through the door of the headquarters building, David was immediately confronted by a camera in his face and a gaggle of people sheltering inside. David felt as if he had been beamed into yet another world. Aware that he was being filmed, he realized his cover was blown and he had to be careful what he said. At the same time, he knew he was still in mortal danger—and that if the prisoners took over the northern compound as well, everyone clustered here in the headquarters building would die. His throat was parched and his body shook.

The German television crew, Red Cross workers, and Afghans facing him knew something serious was happening, but they had yet to grasp it was an Al-Qaeda revolt. Arnim Stauth, a forty-four-year-old German reporter for the Berlin-based network ARD, was in Qala-i Jangi after opting not to go to Kunduz, where most journalists had migrated, because he was worried about the safety of his crew. Stauth had a serious mien and was a pacifist who had avoided military service. He had a visceral dislike of war. He viewed himself as a humanitarian and had eschewed connections with intelligence agencies, regarding them as malign forces in the world. In Qala-i Jangi he had hoped to file a report about the treatment of prisoners. He regarded his presence there as a deterrent to the prisoners being abused, as well as a chance to "somehow give a face and a voice to the demonized Taliban enemy" by interviewing them. Stauth, who had been based in Moscow during the 1990s, spoke fluent Russian and English and was eager to explore the rumor that Chechen prisoners had been taken.

Having observed the Al-Qaeda surrender the previous day, Stauth hoped he would be able to film a "good news" story inside the fort but felt a gnawing concern that he had let ARD down by missing the main action in Kunduz. He had been outside in the northern compound smoking a cigarette when the uprising erupted. Simon Brooks, a Red Cross official, had been upstairs arranging access to the prisoners with one of Dostum's commanders when the firing had started. They were in the room where Dostum had negotiated the prisoner deal with mullahs Fazl and Noori. Brooks, also forty-four, was British and a veteran of the Australian SAS. Tall and urbane, with a full head of dark, swept-back hair, he had lived all over the world and was not the type to panic. At first he shrugged off the gunfire as just another day in Afghanistan. It became apparant that a real battle was underway, however, when the commander excused himself, leaving the Red Cross delegation alone in Dostum's meeting room.

As Stauth peppered the CIA man with questions, David fumbled with his pistol, struggling to return it to its holster. Stauth, too, was rattled. Unaware there had been an uprising, he asked where the prisoners had got their weapons from, who David worked for, and whether the Kalashnikov he was holding belonged to him. The questions veered from the basic to the bizarre. "You were supposed to infiltrate them?" Stauth asked. David wanted to evade and lie, but be credible—a part of his job description he was usually able to fulfill with ease. The CIA man thought he was being clever but the result, he later reflected, was fragments of truth floating in a stream of nonsense. David was so flustered it never occurred to him not to answer Stauth at all.

After a minute or so of being quizzed, David pushed past Stauth and walked upstairs to the second, and top, floor of the headquarters building. He squatted down and asked himself, "What the fuck just happened?" In the southern compound, the physiological reaction to the stress had blocked out feelings. Now he was hit by successive waves of emotion crashing into his consciousness. The first was sadness, almost despair. "Mike is dead," he thought. "Am I going to die?" Next came disappointment. For the past thirty minutes or so—he had little concept of time, but it had taken him eleven minutes to reach the headquarters building—he had been adrift in sea of ferment. Now he had to make decisions and deal with reality. The final wave that smacked into him was fear. He began shuddering but was jolted out of his introspection by the sound of a young Uzbek, Stauth's producer, asking him, "What should we do?"

The first thing David needed to do, he realized, was summon help as quickly as possible. Despite what he had just been through, David dismissed trying to get out of the fort. As the only American there, he was needed to guide US forces back inside to quash the uprising and prevent the prisoners breaking out. Also, he didn't want to leave Mike. He knew his comrade was dead, but couldn't abandon him. Surveying the situation from the roof, David ran into Brooks and his Red Cross colleagues. Brooks had seen David a few days earlier at a prisoner-holding facility in Mazar-i Sharif and remembered him as the swaggering embodiment of American power and self-confidence. Now, however, as the two men took cover together behind a small hut, an ashen-faced David kept jabbering, "They've killed him, they've killed him. They killed my partner."

David's state convinced Brooks he needed to get his Red Cross team out. He scouted around the roof and northen tower and saw his opportunity. As Northern Alliance troops exchanged fire with Al-Qaeda, Brooks and half a dozen others made a run for it. They jumped over the ramparts of the northern tower, landing on the powdery slope ten feet below, then slid and tumbled to the ground. From there they were able to run to the road—where, remarkably, a taxi was waiting. Inside the northern compound, the Land Rover that Brooks had borrowed from a colleague in Tashkent and driven into Afghanistan across the Turkmenistan border was ablaze. In it was a backpack containing $30,000 of Red Cross money, along with his passport and laptop.

"Give me your phone," David ordered Stauth. Later, the German would be criticized for putting the lives of other journalists in danger by giving an American "military adviser," as David had described himself, his phone to summon the might of US forces. Though Stauth would later say he had faced an ethical dilemma over the request, there was no quandary at the time as the German thought of his three-year-old daughter. Distinctions of profession or nationality made no difference to the Al-Qaeda fighters trying to take over the fort. Everyone in the headquarters building faced the same plight. The only phone numbers David could remember were those of his home in Tashkent and the US embassy there. It was a Sunday, he realized, and there might not be many people at the embassy. He dialed his house.

"Oh, that's Dad, that's Dad!" Rosann Tyson told her children as the phone rang. Somehow, she knew it was her husband. Kara, eleven, and Mark, eight, sat at the top of the stairs as she answered and said, "Happy Thanksgiving!" As soon as she heard the strain in her husband's voice, however, she knew something was terribly wrong.

"Rose, listen," David said. "There are people dead. Some of our friends are dead." Rosann dropped the phone. Then, gathering herself, she picked it up and grabbed a piece of paper, knowing her husband's life might well rest on her getting this right. "You've got to call Charlie [Gilbert] and tell him where I am," David said. "I'm in Qala-i Jangi."

Rosann had never heard the name of the fort. She wrote down, "Koala Jan Gi."

During the five weeks her husband had been gone, Rosann Tyson had not permitted herself to contemplate the reality of what David was doing. From their one, short phone call, she knew he had been sleeping out in the mountains of Afghanistan, though even that had not been explicit before he left. "There's shooting—can you hear it?" David asked. Rosann had already registered the gunfire in the background. After a hurried goodbye, she hung up and told her children, "That was Daddy. It's all right, but I've got to call Charlie." She phoned Gilbert—the Tashkent station chief lived just minutes from the embassy—and relayed word-for-word what she'd been told.

Next, David Tyson called the embassy. No one had yet arrived in the CIA station, so he was put through to Mike Davison, a US Air Force major who was the air attaché in Tashkent. A former flight-test engineer with the call sign Psycho, he had gone into the office to catch up on paperwork. The Tashkent embassy was small, with only about thirty Americans serving there, so they all knew each other well.

"There's been an uprising and I need help," David told Davison, who immediately tried to establish what the situation was and how many Americans had been killed. David had a habit of not differentiating between Americans and their Northern Alliance allies—they were on the same side, after all—so Davison had to press to nail him down. "There's hundreds of dead here at least—and I'm not...I don't know how many Americans are dead," David said, with Stauth's cameraman filming all the while. "I think one was killed. I'm not sure. I'm not sure." Davison asked how many Americans were in the fort. "There was two—me and some other guy," David said, deliberately vague because he knew he was being recorded.

David had seen the power of American bombs up close at the Sultan Razia school; he feared the headquarters building would be leveled and its occupants killed. There should be no air strikes, he told Davison: "We just need help to free this place up—we can't hit it from the air. We're not talking coming and bombing. Please make that clear."

Davison sprinted through the corridors of the embassy to raise the alarm. The duty watchkeeper thought the major was about to have a heart attack. Within minutes, Davison had raised Colonel Mulholland's staff at K2. The entire focus of the war in northern Afghanistan was now Qala-i Jangi. Inside Tashkent station, Billy Waugh, a legendary CIA paramilitary officer, was soon on the radio trying to get a helicopter down to Qala-i Jangi. A Vietnam veteran about to turn seventy-two, Waugh had prevailed on Cofer Black to send him to war once again. He had been assigned to Team Romeo, due to go into Logar province.

As all this was unfolding, Rosann Tyson turned her attention to reassuring her children. "This is just another weird thing happening in my life," she told herself. Less than half an hour after David's call from Qala-i Jangi, Rosann's phone rang again. It was Gilbert's wife, Terri. "Rose, would you like me to come and sit with you?" Terri asked. Rosann Tyson felt the bottom drop out of her world. "Oh shit," she told herself. "David might not be coming back."

That evening, as Terri Gilbert talked to Kara and Mark Tyson while her four-year-old son played with Legos on the living-room carpet, Rosann packed her children's lunches for school the next day. Placing miniature boxes of pretzel sticks in each one, she told herself, "I might be a widow by tomorrow."

15

TROJAN HORSE

1:48 p.m. (GMT +4.5), November 25, 2001 (Day 40);
Erganak, Kunduz province

ON A MUDDY knoll to the west of the city, J. R. Seeger, Team Alpha's chief, surveyed the Taliban fighters arrayed below. He had arrived at Erganak, west of the city of Kunduz, late the previous night. J.R. and Scott Spellmeyer had been delayed after detaching from the Mad Max convoy when a truck lost a wheel, sheared off by a rock in the desert. Watching the Taliban troops filtering into the desert plain, J.R. had a queasy feeling: these did not look like men about to surrender.

"Scotty, there's something wrong about this," he said to Team Alpha's number three. "I'm just telling you, those guys do not look right to me." As David and Mike were entering Qala-i Jangi, the day in Erganak had started with Dostum and Atta sitting down on a rug with Mullah Fazl, Mullah Noori, and other Taliban commanders to discuss terms for giving up Kunduz. But Fazl raised obstacle after obstacle, dragging the talks out. The surrender had stalled.

J.R. felt his satellite phone buzz. It was Glenn, the Team Bravo medic, calling from the Turkish school, which had been alerted to David's predicament by Task Force Dagger staff at K2. "Mike is MIA, presumed dead," Glenn said. "Dave is trapped in the fort. We're putting a team together to go in there." J.R. was a level-headed, even phlegmatic, character. But he felt his heart race. It began to dawn on him that the surrender of the more than 400 foreign fighters outside Mazar-i Sharif had been a "Trojan horse"—a ruse to infiltrate Al-Qaeda forces behind Northern Alliance lines. He had already seen intelligence reports of Mullah Dadullah's men gathering near Balkh, northwest of Mazar-i Sharif. Within hours, satellite footage would show a separate enemy force of about 800 men and 200 vehicles moving north of Kunduz toward an old smugglers' route to Mazar-i Sharif.

J.R. concluded that Fazl had known that the "surrendered" fighters at Qala-i Jangi—though he expected they would be at the airport—would rebel. Not only that, but Fazl's offer of the larger capitulation at Kunduz appeared to have been a feint as well—a way of luring the bulk of American forces away from Mazar-i Sharif, leaving the Turkish school vulnerable to attack. If the prisoners broke out of the fort, the Turkish school could be overwhelmed by three converging enemy forces. That would mean Mazar-i Sharif falling to the Taliban again, and the battle for northern Afghanistan raging once more.

The immediate priority for J.R. was to protect himself and the fifty or so Americans at the Erganak surrender site. With thousands of Taliban fighters massing and only 100 of Dostum's Northern Alliance troops and 30 Green Berets present, they could be overrun. The force ratios were no better than they had been at Qala-i Jangi. J.R. was now certain that the uprising at the fort was part of a strategic gambit on the part of Al-Qaeda and the Taliban. The American plan had been to trap the enemy between a hammer and anvil: a perimeter around the eastern side of Kunduz and a blocking force, J.R.'s group, from Mazar-i Sharif to the west. But that presupposed Mazar-i Sharif itself was secure.

Almost simultaneously, Dostum had been alerted about the situation at Qala-i Jangi by his commanders in Mazar-i Sharif. He flew into a rage, fulminating about betrayal and dishonor. After placating the warlord, J.R. and Bowers, the Boxer commander, agreed to consolidate the Americans on the ridgeline currently occupied by the Green Berets. It was a more defensible position than the knoll. As the Americans had learned in the Darya Suf Valley, the way for the Northern Alliance to defeat superior Taliban forces was with the might of US air power. Bowers radioed Task Force Dagger and requested whatever aircraft were available.

News of the uprising was being beamed across the world. German television had already aired footage of David Tyson's urgent call to Mike Davison in Tashkent. International wire services were soon reporting that a "US adviser" had been killed. By 8 a.m. in California—12.5 hours behind Mazar-i Sharif—CNN was reporting that "we appear to have the first American combat death of this war." By the afternoon, footage of David was all over American cable-news channels.

There was no television at the cabin in Yosemite rented by Shannon Spann's parents. Unaware that anything was wrong in Mazar-i Sharif, she posed with Jake, about to turn six months, for her sister to take a photograph. Shannon's broad smile, her baby's sparkling eyes, and their mutual happiness captured them in a moment at the end of the Thanksgiving family gathering, before their lives were turned upside down.

* * *

It was a brilliant, sunny day in Washington, DC, when Amy received a call from CTC/SO summoning her into work. "Mike's missing," she was told as she walked into the office. Cofer Black and Hank Crumpton were there, and everyone was scrambling to clarify what was happening at the fort. Escorted into a side room, Amy found herself talking to George Tenet. The CIA director looked unkempt in a T-shirt, jeans, and flip-flops, his hair disheveled. "We need to get the news to Shannon before she sees this on TV," he told Amy.

Tenet was livid when the Pentagon confirmed at a press conference that none of its personnel was dead or missing, signaling to every CIA family that an Agency man was down. "Why the fuck did they just say that?" the CIA director exclaimed. Black ordered: "I want the next of kin of every CIA officer in Afghanistan contacted within 15 minutes and told their son or husband is alive." Amy tried without success to book a flight to California. It was Thanksgiving weekend and everything was full. Tenet cursed, wondering whether the casualty-notification team might have to be delayed until the next day. Amy looked at him and asked, "You're the director of the CIA and you're telling me you can't get a plane?" Within an hour, Amy and two colleagues were boarding a twin-propeller US government aircraft at Dulles airport.

* * *

Shannon pulled onto the shoulder of California's State Route 99 the second her phone rang. She was in the middle of the five-hour drive from Yosemite back to her parents' house in Orange County, with Jake in the baby seat in the back. The caller was Mike's sister, Tonya, who asked if Shannon had spoken to him that day. Tonya had heard on the radio that someone from the CIA had been killed in Afghanistan. Shannon frantically rang different desks at CTC, but it was a Sunday and it took several minutes for someone to answer. "This is Shannon Spann," she said. "I'm hearing stuff on the news and I just want to know what's going on." She was put on hold, and Hank Crumpton came on the line. He told her that something had happened and a team of CIA officers was en route to her parents' home. Shannon was a CIA officer who worked for CTC and knew Crumpton. "Give it to me straight, Hank," she said. "Is it bad?" He replied that it was indeed bad—that Mike had gone down fighting and was missing amid a chaotic scene of continuing combat.

Shannon felt creeping dread when Crumpton informed her that Amy was among the group of CIA officers on their way to California. Shannon knew Mike had designated Amy to inform her of his death. Shortly after Shannon reached her parents' house, there was a knock on the door. She answered it, holding Jake in her arms. "Hey, Amy, come in," Shannon said. Once Amy was through the door, Shannon asked her point-blank: "Is he dead?" Amy replied, "We don't know, Shannon. We really don't know."

Another CIA team was heading for Winfield to be with Mike's father and sisters while a third group was preparing to pick up his mother and daughters from Manassas to fly them to Alabama. Two days earlier, Mike's ex-wife, Kathryn, had been given the news that her cancer treatment had failed and she had weeks to live.

*　　*　　*

It was about 1:45 p.m.—more than two hours after the uprising began—when the first "Eagle Down" radio message from K2, indicating an American was dead or missing, was received at the Turkish school. As Glenn relayed the details to J.R. outside Kunduz, Major Kurt Sonntag, the Green Beret in command of the school, started drawing up a plan to send a rescue squad to the fort. Around the same time, Admiral Calland returned from his visit to Kodi Barq Hospital and reported heavy gunfire coming from Qala-i Jangi. Passing near the fort, Calland and his entourage had been held up at a Northern Alliance roadblock by agitated fighters who told them several prisoners had escaped.

"There's a right old battle going on," remarked Sergeant Paul McGough, one of four SBS troops guarding Calland. With ODA 595 in Kunduz, the SBS had picked up the VIP security task. Soon, an adviser to Dostum—rattled and out of breath—arrived at the school and blurted out, "You need to come to Qala-i Jangi now, with every man you've got!" Sonntag and his number two, Major Mark Mitchell, used a classroom chalkboard to sketch an aerial view of Qala-i Jangi. It was hard to formulate a plan because no one knew the situation there. They had to rescue David and locate Mike, but the priority from the Task Force Dagger perspective was to contain the revolt and prevent the prisoners from breaking out and joining an attack on Mazar-i Sharif. Sonntag had to weigh the urgency of dealing with whatever was happening at the fort against the need to protect the Turkish school if it was assaulted. He feared the enemy's aim was to draw troops away from the school, leaving it more vulnerable.

Glenn was getting agitated by the debate. "Let's just get the fuck out and get Mike," he said. "We don't need a whole fucking Op Order." Sonntag decided that Mitchell, who had lived in the fort for ten days and knew its layout intimately, should lead the rescue team. Mitchell would take Glenn, the CIA medic; Captain Craig McFarland, the battalion surgeon; McFarland's assistant, Sergeant Brad Berry; and Paul Beck, a communications sergeant. Beck would have to call in air strikes; Mike Sciortino, the only combat controller left behind in Mazar-i Sharif, was at the main airfield, helping to repair the runway.

The past few days had seen an influx of new faces in the Turkish school; Mitchell regarded them as military tourists, sent in now that Mazar-i Sharif was deemed safe. "We're not running a hotel here," he had groused to Task Force Dagger staff. Now, two tourists from the DIA would flesh out the rescue force: Oleg, a Ukraine-born US Air Force lieutenant colonel who spoke fluent Russian, and his colleague Bert, an Air Force major.

No one would dare describe the eight SBS men as tourists. They were an elite Special Forces unit, trained in assault and rescue operations. Their journey to Mazar-i Sharif had been a tortuous one, buffeted by British domestic politics as Tony Blair's government—desperate to remain America's staunchest ally, but fearful of the repercussions—blundered into the intrigue that was Afghanistan. Dozens of SBS had flown C-130s into Bagram, the old Soviet air base north of Kabul seized by the Northern Alliance, on November 15. No one had mentioned their imminent arrival to the Tajik leaders of the Northern Alliance, who were furious that the British—who had sought to conquer Afghanistan in three previous wars—had not requested permission.

Colonel Mulholland was informed of their approach minutes before they landed, and his Green Berets had to pull Northern Alliance soldiers off ZSU antiaircraft guns to stop them from shooting down the British C-130s. Lieutenant Colonel Dickie Pickup, the SBS commander, pushed hard to get his men into the Pashtun south along-side an American ODA. When Pickup cited the Queen as his authority and suggested that Mulholland simply order the ODA commander, a captain, to accept the SBS, the American colonel retorted that he could not do that: "She's back in fucking Buckingham Place and we're here." The decision was left to the Afghans at an hours-long *shura,* or council, attended by the ODA captain. When the Afghans refused, Mulholland turned to Pickup and said, "I don't know what you guys did the last time you were here, but they're still fucking pissed."

Tony Blair was stung by public criticism from the Northern Alliance leadership and reports of a rift with the Americans. He wanted to get credit from the US for having British boots on the ground in Afghanistan, but his generals were warning of the potential for massacres in Kunduz. So Blair hedged his bets: he issued a "national caveat" ruling out the use of British troops in offensive operations. Military leaders then imposed Rules of Engagement (ROE) on the SBS, blocking them from opening fire unless they were fired upon first. An enterprising British liaison officer at K2 managed to secure places for an eight-man SBS team, drawn from Z Squadron, on a flight to Mazar-i Sharif. When they arrived, the British troops, to their chagrin, had to tell the Americans they were not allowed to take part in the impending battle at Kunduz. As an indication of what British commanders intended, the SBS had been ordered to paint their two WMIK Land Rovers white so they would look like humanitarian vehicles belonging to the UN or an aid group.

The SBS, based in Poole, Dorset, had long been regarded as the poor cousins of the Special Air Service (SAS), the British equivalent of Delta Force. The much-larger SAS, based in Hereford, tended to attract the glamour and plum assignments, leaving the SBS with chips on their shoulders. Escorting a SEAL admiral on what felt like a PR exercise had not improved their morale. The Poole men in the Turkish school felt they had something to prove to the Afghans, the Americans, the British government, and Hereford. They wanted to fight. The SBS motto was

BY STRENGTH AND GUILE; but the situation at the fort seemed likely to require brute force rather than finesse. When Mitchell reminded them of the ROE restrictions, an SBS man replied, "Fuck that, mate!"

Every man in the SBS contingent had at least five years in Special Forces. They were led by Jess, a redheaded captain who was a former enlisted marine and SBS operator. His most experienced NCO was Sergeant McGough, known as Scruff, who a year earlier had taken part in the rescue of British soldiers held hostage by rebels in Sierra Leone. The medic was Tony, a stocky, no-nonsense corporal who had been on a training exercise in Oman on 9/11 and feared he would miss the war. Despite his decade-plus of service, he had yet to see action. He hadn't even been to Northern Ireland and was beginning to think he was destined to be left out of the action forever.

Four others on the team, also corporals, might have been assembled simply to come up with a range of accents to confound the Americans. Russ was a huge Cornishman who was strong as an ox. Jonno, a Geordie and another giant, was sometimes called "Little John." Pat, lantern-jawed and with a broken nose, hailed from the West Riding of Yorkshire; his bravery in Kurdistan after the Gulf War had earned him the gallantry citation known as a Mention in Despatches. Flip, from the West Country, was wiry and as hard as nails. Whereas the Green Berets dressed in uniform, the SBS wore local scarves called *shamags,* along with jeans and non-issue sweaters, Barbour jackets, and tactical vests. Some of the tactical vests were Afghan knockoffs bearing the Calvin Klein logo. Each SBS man carried a Diemaco 5.56mm rifle and a SIG Sauer 9mm pistol.

To the surprise of the Green Berets, the eighth member of the SBS team was an American. Stephen Bass—everyone called him Steph— was a thirty-two-year-old Navy SEAL on an exchange program with British forces. From Kentucky, he was the son of a Navy veteran of the Vietnam era. In London on 9/11, Bass had witnessed the outpouring of support for America, highlighted by the band of the Coldstream Guards playing "The Star-Spangled Banner" outside Buckingham Palace. Bass personified the much-vaunted "special relationship" between the United States and the United Kingdom, which was deep enough to overcome episodes like the diplomatic dust-up at Bagram. His SBS comrade Pat would later make the reverse journey and serve with the SEALs.

On September 12, the transatlantic flight ban had been waived for Sir Richard Dearlove, head of MI6, to fly to the United States to express his condolences to George Tenet at CIA headquarters and help plan the response to 9/11. The two countries were always together when it mattered. Now, Bass would have the chance to fight alongside the British in a bid to rescue fellow Americans. The Land Rovers may have been painted white, but each was still mounted with a general-purpose machine gun (GPMG)—firepower the Green Berets lacked. "Brits, grab your stuff" came the call.

*   *   *

The addition of the SBS meant fifteen men would be heading to the fort. The SBS men aside, they were essentially a pickup team in which most barely knew the other players and no one was quite sure what game they would be playing.

It took thirty minutes to drive the eight miles to Qala-i Jangi, passing through the center of Mazar-i Sharif and the bustling market surrounding the Shrine of Hazrat Ali. While the rescue team was en route, Sonntag radioed Task Force Dagger from the Turkish school to request "fast movers"—American jets—over the fort: he was told they would be there by 3 p.m. Mitchell drove the lead vehicle, a beaten-up Toyota Forerunner with no suspension and a right-hand drive, manual transmission. Another Green Beret vehicle and the pair of SBS Land Rovers followed.

Mitchell sped past the shrine, weaving his way among Afghan traders selling pistachios, spices, watermelons, and pomegranates. Glenn, wearing a Harley-Davidson baseball cap, rode shotgun. Mitchell drove around several mule carts and was suddenly blocked by a truck that had reversed out of a side street. "It's an ambush," the Green Beret major thought. "We've been set up." He dropped the Toyota into second gear, swerved off the road, and kept going. Mitchell was new to left-hand shifting, but his focus was on avoiding an accident and spotting any prisoners who might have escaped. Glenn, calling out the obstacles ahead and honking the horn, was impressed by the major's rally-driver skills. "Pretty nice job," the CIA man said.

In the back, McFarland, with no seatbelt, placed his feet on the bar behind the front seats and braced himself for a head-on collision. Broad-shouldered and super-fit, the doctor had been with the battalion for nearly two years but was not Special Forces. Flying over to K2, he had hastily read *Guerrilla Surgeon,* the account of a New Zealand doctor who served with the British SOE alongside Yugoslav partisans during World War II and treated the wounded under fire in horrifying conditions. Now McFarland, armed only with a Beretta M9 pistol, was heading toward combat not knowing what he might face. He thought through the procedures for treating gunshot and blast wounds, and spinal injuries. This mental exercise, and the adrenaline coursing through his body, left no space for fear.

*   *   *

The plan to drive through the main gate of Qala-i Jangi fell apart as soon as the fort came into view. Trails of smoke spiraled into the air as mortar and RPG rounds exploded; the sound of incessant gunfire got louder and louder. Braking 200 yards short of the fort, everyone but the drivers got out and the vehicles became shields from the gunfire, edging closer as the troops trotted alongside—a tactic Mitchell dubbed the "Sarajevo Shuffle."

Jess, the SBS commander, jumped out of his WMIK, and addressed a group huddled outside the fort: "Right—anybody here speak English?" Simon Brooks, the Red Cross official, stepped forward: "I do." Jess replied, "Good. What's happening, then?" The prisoners had revolted,

Brooks related, and the Northern Alliance was trying to beat them back. Once in the entrance courtyard inside the gate, the Green Berets and SBS men were confronted by carnage. At least a dozen bodies lay sprawled on a carpet of broken glass and shell casings. With their commander killed, many Northern Alliance fighters were simply milling about, or loosing off rounds erratically, barely aiming—Afghan "spray and pray," the Americans called it. "Why aren't these guys fucking shooting?" Glenn demanded. "Let's fucking go get 'em!" The Al-Qaeda fighters, by contrast, appeared to be disciplined and effective. Clearly, many had received military training.

Mitchell established that the prisoners controlled the southern compound and were firing through the center gate and from the top of the center wall. Now, he could formulate a plan. Dostum had sent Faqir, the cavalry commander David had fought alongside in the Darya Suf Valley, to take charge of Afghan forces in the fort. Faqir confessed to Mitchell that Al-Qaeda was poised to take over the northern compound. Mortars were being fired from the stables on the southeastern side, beyond the center wall, and shells were now hitting the headquarters building. The mortar men had been bracketing their rounds—firing first short of the target and then beyond it before adjusting the tube angle to score a direct hit.

On orders from Mitchell, Scruff and several other SBS men unhooked the GPMGs from the Land Rovers and lugged them up a long staircase to the eastern tower. Scruff crawled over to the low wall overlooking the southern compound, stood up, and unleashed a wall of lead on the enemy fighters below. The SBS men took turns standing up and firing the machine guns. Within minutes they had mowed down dozens of the enemy fighters—and driven the rest back into the Pink House or the outbuildings along the central wall.

The eastern tower also overlooked the northern compound, so the SBS men used their Diemacos to pick off the sprinkling of Al-Qaeda fighters who had made it through the gate. The combination of highly accurate machine gun and rifle fire was already killing the enemy at an astonishing rate. As Tony heard the radio chatter and the rattle of the GPMGs, he thought: "It sounds like they're shooting fish in a barrel."

* * *

Inside the headquarters building, David Tyson had been losing hope. After Brooks and his Red Cross colleagues had slipped away, David had regained his composure and lain prone on the roof firing an AK-47 at the center gateway, where fighters—some of them unarmed—would rush through in groups of ten or so, shouting "Allahu akbar!" David would shoot two or three in each charge while his Northern Alliance comrades took out a few more, but some made it through. "They're the varsity team and we're a load of clowns," David thought. His greatest fear was that a group of Al-Qaeda fighters would gather in the northern compound and storm the headquarters building.

Handfuls of those who got through the center gate managed to escape the fort altogether to try to hide or blend in with the local populace. Some were shot or beaten to death by villagers in the nearby houses—but others, particularly Uzbeks, probably made it to freedom, because they spoke the local language and the border with Uzbekistan was less than forty miles away.

David went down to the second floor and was in a room decorated by a bright mural of palm trees and fountains when, through the window, he saw an RPG round trailing smoke and heading toward him. He watched it, mesmerized, as it hit the front of the building, below him, sending shrapnel into the mural, sizzling and burning off paint. On the eastern side of the building, he looked over to the northeastern tower and spied a Northern Alliance subcommander, a Turkmen he'd spoken to days earlier. The Turkmen sat cross-legged behind a PK machine gun raining fire on Al-Qaeda fighters in the center gateway, which Tony had dubbed "the fatal funnel." The Turkmen glanced over at David and smiled broadly, his finger still depressing the trigger. Exposed and in danger of dying at any moment, the Turkmen seemed without a care in the world. In stark contrast, other Afghans, many of them teenagers, huddled in the basement of the headquarters, weeping and pretending to be injured as they lay beside the dead and wounded. To David, there seemed to be no middle ground in Afghanistan between abject cowardice and astounding courage.

The worst moment for David had come shortly after Sayed Kamal appeared up on the roof, walking over from the west side after taking cover somewhere in the northern compound. Here was a familiar face and a man David respected. Minutes later, Kamal took a bullet to the upper thigh. Two Afghans braved the gunfire to drag him to cover, blood spurting from his leg. David ripped up a piece of cloth, which he used as a tourniquet. Then Kamal, going into shock, was carried to another room, and David grew certain the intelligence chief would die. Just when David was beginning to feel doomed, the arrival of the SBS on the eastern tower started to turn the tide—he didn't know it was the British troops, but he could tell that the GPMGs were not being fired by Afghans. One of the Northern Alliance fighters had given him a radio and he had managed to speak to Dostum and Faqir, who told him more men were on their way. "At least the Afghans are sending reinforcements," David thought.

In the entrance courtyard, Faqir handed Glenn his Motorola. David was on the other end of the line, and brought the CIA medic up to speed: "Last time I saw Mike, it was in the center of the fort and he was under a pile of dead bodies," David reported. "He wasn't moving. I'm in the headquarters building and I'm out of ammo." Glenn took it all in. This was bad. "Shit…shit…okay…shit…okay," he responded. "Hold on, buddy, we're coming to get you." Listening to the bedlam in the entrance courtyard and Glenn's evident concern, David feared he might not have long to live. Glenn turned to Mitchell: "Mike is MIA. They've taken his gun and his ammo."

Mitchell deliberated with Faqir and Jess, the SBS captain. The major's priority was to stop the prisoners from seizing the fort, massacring everyone in the headquarters building, and then trying to retake Mazar-i Sharif itself. Locating Mike was secondary. Mitchell was now almost certain that the CIA officer was dead. And even if Mike was grievously wounded but miraculously alive, the Green Beret calculated, he lacked the troops to attempt a rescue in the southern compound. It was crucial, he concluded, to call in air strikes to hit the Al-Qaeda mortar positions and kill the foreign fighters wherever they had massed.

"I want SATCOM and JDAMs," Mitchell said. "Tell them there will be six or seven buildings in a line in the southwest half. If they can hit that, then that would kill a whole lot of these motherfuckers." Glenn was desperate to get inside the fort. Every minute that ticked by edged the situation closer to disaster. "Shit," he said. "Let's stop fucking around and get in there." He pointed to the sky and added, "Tell those guys to stop scratching their balls and fly. We have a guy in the north, enemies in the southwest, and friendlies in between."

Up on the parapet above the entrance courtyard, Mitchell pointed his Viper laser range-finder binoculars at targets in the southern compound to get coordinates he could relay to the jets. But he also wanted to get into the headquarters building and reach David before the strikes came in. He and Glenn discussed running across the northern compound, but the intense gunfire would have cut them down in ten yards. Glenn could see the bullets stripping branches off the pine trees. It was too far to attempt a low crawl. Al-Qaeda had PK machine guns, mortars, and RPGs, while the Northern Alliance and Americans had rifles and no helmets or body armor. The SBS machine guns were making a difference, but the "good guys," Glenn thought, remained badly outgunned. "We're still getting our asses kicked," he concluded to himself. "We need another plan."

After consulting Faqir, Mitchell put together an improvised maneuver team of five men: himself, Glenn, Tony, Steph Bass, and Faqir. They would edge around the outside of the fort, counterclockwise, to reach the headquarters building and David. They set off through the entrance gate and then along the outside wall, which protected them from gunfire but not the mortar rounds that were skimming over the parapets and landing outside. It was a unique group: a Green Beret, a CIA officer, an SBS commando, a Navy SEAL, and an Afghan commander. Only Mitchell was in a uniform and no one had a blood group or other medical information written on them that could make the difference between life and death if they were unconscious and being treated. Bass had only recently been sent to the SBS and was hardly acquainted with Tony. "Hey, I'm O-positive and I'm allergic to penicillin," Bass called out. Glenn noted the American accent. He had no idea Bass was a SEAL, but had already thought, "That can't be a Brit," when he saw him chewing Copenhagen tobacco.

Tony was in the lead and called a halt after a few minutes when he glimpsed an Italian TS-50 antipersonnel mine a few feet away. Minefields had been sown all over Afghanistan, left behind for decades by different warring forces. Tony didn't know whether the TS-50 had been planted by the Soviets, the Taliban, or Dostum, but he reckoned it wouldn't matter who the culprit was if he stepped on it. The mines meant the group had to slow down, exposing them to more mortar fire. As if underscoring that danger, a mortar shell exploded fifty yards behind them; had it fallen a minute earlier, several of them could have been killed. They crept forward and another mortar landed about eighty yards ahead. The SBS corporal mused that if they hadn't stopped because of the mine they might have been at that spot. "Maybe it's our lucky day," he thought. As they got closer to the northwestern tower, Glenn halted the five-man team to urinate; he didn't want to have to relieve himself during a firefight.

On the southern side of the fort, Sayed Shah and Tamim Ahad, the two doctors, were also feeling fortunate. After being urged by the Hazara guard to run for it, they had ended up on the southern tower, in a shack stacked with ammunition. They had remained there for three hours, praying and dreading the moment when an Al-Qaeda fighter might wrench open the door and shoot them. Shah had apologized to his friend for pushing him to volunteer for the fort assignment. They had been foolish, they agreed, for willingly venturing inside a citadel full of diehard jihadists. Shah had two children and Ahad had recently married. All they wanted was to see their families again.

The arrival of the Americans and British from the Turkish school gave them their chance to escape. With the Al-Qaeda fighters concentrating on the northern compound, the doctors gingerly opened the door of the shack, darted out, and slipped over the southern parapet. Later that afternoon they were greeted back at the hospital with applause and tears from their colleagues, who had assumed they were both dead.

In the absence of the two doctors, the hospital had filled with casualties from the uprising. One of them was the Hazara guard who had saved them. He had been shot through both forearms but would make a full recovery; Shah and Ahad were delighted he was alive. The doctors also learned that Sayed Kamal, the Uzbek intelligence chief who had been shot in the thigh, had been treated briefly at the hospital. He had then been driven over the Friendship Bridge into Uzbekistan—Kamal's intelligence connections enabled him to be allowed across—and all the way to Tashkent. Kamal too would live to tell the tale of what happened in the fort.

16

CLEARED HOT

3:47 p.m. (GMT +4.5), November 25, 2001 (Day 40);
Qala-i Jangi, Balkh province, Afghanistan

DARK PLUMES OF acrid smoke rose over the fort. It was an hour until sunset, and time was running out. Mitchell's five-man maneuver team had taken twenty minutes to loop around to the outside of the northwestern tower. Now they had to negotiate the sixty-foot curtain wall, scramble up the forty-five-degree dusty slope of the glacis above it, and scale a final ten-foot vertical wall leading to the battlements. Only then, while being raked by gunfire, could they drop down onto the tower inside the fort itself.

At the top of the slope, Faqir tilted his head back and yelled in Uzbek. The turbaned head of a Hazara fighter popped up over the parapet and shouted something in reply. Faqir was first up the vertical wall, his years in the mountains helping him find toeholds and handholds. Mitchell was contemplating the crumbling mud wall when two Hazaras tossed over their purple-and-green plaid turbans to use as climbing ropes. The major felt he was in some Afghan adaptation of "Rapunzel." He grabbed the turban with both hands, leaned back, and walked up the side of the fort to the top. The others followed. Bass fell off, injuring his finger. Glenn had a forty-pound medical pack, as well as his AKMS, on his back. As he reached the battlement, he rolled from side to side

219

trying to get his pack off; the others briefly thought he must have been shot. Eventually, they all made it. They were on the northwestern tower of the fort.

Two US Navy F-18 jets were now overhead. Paul Beck was on the eastern side of the fort, above the entrance courtyard. As the sergeant climbed up, Doc McFarland had been handed an M240 machine gun and told to cover his back in case any Al-Qaeda fighters who had made it into the northern compound sneaked up on the Americans. McFarland didn't have a medical role at this point, and he had no qualms about opening fire on the enemy, but being entrusted with the machine gun unnerved him. "It's a really bad day when your doctor has to actively engage in protecting your rear flank," he thought. McFarland checked the M-4 held by Bert, the Air Force major, who was so afraid he seemed no longer to be functioning. It had a magazine, but no round in the chamber. McFarland chambered one. Oleg had his head in his hands. The Green Berets had already concluded that the DIA men were next to useless. Bullets whistled overhead, one landing so close that McFarland scooped it up as a memento.

Glenn spoke to David on the radio: "I think we're right above you," he said. David could not see him. "Where are you?" he asked frantically. Glenn, unfamiliar with the fort's layout, realized he was in the north-western corner but David was in the north. The connection between the two places was an exposed parapet, which Al-Qaeda was blasting with machine-gun fire from the central gateway. Tony wanted to try crossing it, but Glenn and Bass stopped him. An Afghan made a run for it, and they watched as the bullets hit the parapet, sending up puffs of dust, and then hit the sprinting man. He tumbled over the side and landed in a heap in the courtyard, motionless.

"It's past time for the great equalizer," Glenn thought. "American air power." Whether to call in bombs was not an easy decision, because Mike still lay somewhere in the courtyard. From everything David had told Glenn, it seemed highly likely Mike was dead—but David, clearly traumatized, was bordering on incoherence. The CIA man had glimpsed his comrade for perhaps only three seconds amid the chaos. What if Mike was badly wounded, but alive? What if he had been briefly concussed, then managed to crawl to some hiding place? The chances were remote, but everyone knew that Mike was supremely fit and determined. If anyone could survive a perilous situation, it was Mike Spann.

Glenn settled on three possibilities, in descending order of likelihood. First, Mike was dead. If so, it didn't matter if the southern compound was bombed. Second, Mike had been captured by Al-Qaeda and dragged into the cellar or some outbuilding. If so, he would be undergoing unimaginable torture, which would inevitably culminate in death. Third, Mike was wounded and had been undetected. If so, a bombardment might be his best chance of escaping. In each scenario, Glenn concluded, if he were in Mike's shoes, he would have wanted the bombs to be dropped. He got David on the radio. "Listen, man, we need to call in some close air support," he warned him. Afraid that bombs would hit the headquarters building, David replied: "Fuck, don't do air strikes." But David knew he had no sight of the bigger picture and his military acumen was limited. Most of all, he realized that he had no veto power.

On the northwestern tower, Bass and Tony were busy killing Al-Qaeda fighters. Some were badly wounded but still fighting, some were firing RPGs, and a few were hurling grenades. As the SEAL used his Diemaco to pick them off, a machine gun behind him suddenly opened fire. It was Tony, sitting up on a Russian DShK, firing away, his legs off the ground because it had been set up for a taller man. It was the first time Tony had been in combat and, like David earlier in the day, he experienced many of the sounds of battle being filtered out and time decelerating. Despite the ordnance exploding all around, Tommy could clearly hear Bass talking to him, and when an Al-Qaeda fighter ran into view it seemed he had ample time to take aim and shoot him, when really it was just a second or two. There was such clarity in his mind, he felt he could always identify a pathway through the chaos.

Amid the hubbub of battle, two white doves landed on the parapet beside Bass and Tony. The Shrine of Hazrat Ali in Mazar-i Sharif was famed for its doves, said to have been brought to the city in the 17th century from Najaf, a Shia holy city in modern-day Iraq. Somehow this pair had flown eight miles west to roost. The birds cooed contentedly as the two operatives chuckled at the incongruity of these symbols of peace dropping in on a vicious firefight. After a few moments, the whizzing bullets and rumbling explosions prompted the doves to realize their mistake and flap away.

Many Afghans refused to fight, prompting one commander to beat his men with a stick to force them to pick up their weapons. Some wet themselves as they hid. Glenn laughed as a stream of yellow liquid ran down the ramp and soaked Bass, lying prone with his rifle. Bass jumped up and shook himself off. "Get up there and shoot some motherfuckers," he teased Glenn in retaliation. "Pop your cherry!"

The CIA medic was suddenly conscious of his Harley-Davidson cap, with its orange bar and shield logo. "This is the perfect bull's-eye to get shot in the fucking head," he thought, also reminding himself he had a wife and two young children. But he shouldered his rifle anyway, unleashing a volley at the Al-Qaeda position at the center gateway. It was the first time he had fired his weapon since Team Bravo landed.

Tony found himself bonding with the Afghans, who had initially been mystified by the shabby appearance of the SBS men in comparison to the uniformed Americans. It was soon apparent to the Afghans that the SBS knew how to fight. They got down to business without fanfare or histrionics, talking in their distinctive regional accents, using clipped sentences and first names. As Tony passed ammunition to the Northern Alliance fighters, they grew in confidence. One fighter gave him a bowl of steaming rice—the Afghans had rustled up a meal as the bullets flew.

On the parapet over the entrance courtyard—above McFarland—Beck was frantically trying to get the F-18s to drop bombs. Beck and Mitchell were both experienced Green Berets—not given to displays

Steph Bass, the Navy SEAL serving with the SBS, reached the western tower attempting to locate Mike Spann, earning the Navy Cross and Britain's Military Cross.

Glenn, the Team Bravo medic and the only CIA man in the rescue team. Smoke rises from a US air strike on the southern compound.

Tony, the SBS corporal who was awarded the Conspicuous Gallantry Cross for his actions that day.

Major Mark Mitchell, who led the effort to quell the Qala-i Jangi uprising and was awarded the first Distinguished Service Cross since Vietnam.

David Tyson on November 27, 2001, just before returning to the fort, which he had escaped from two days earlier. Beyond him is one of Dostum's T-55 Russian tanks.

Inside the fort on November 27, Justin Sapp inspects a 19th-century Mosin-Nagant, a Russian rifle being used by one of Dostum's fighters.

The entrance to the tunnel that led from the east side of the Pink House. Shortly afterward, the eighty-six survivors of the uprising emerged from here.

John Walker Lindh is taken into the northern compound from the Pink House on December 1, 2001. The metal frame beyond him is all that remained of the bombed central gateway.

A wounded prisoner, one of the eighty-six who survived in the cellar, is carried from the Pink House by two of Dostum's men.

Carnage beside the Pink House. Some prisoners, their arms still tied, were killed at the start of the uprising. The western tower, which Steph Bass reached late on November 25, is top right.

The corpses of an Al-Qaeda fighter and two of Dostum's horses beside Qala-i Jangi's stables. Northern Alliance fighters are on the parapet of the center wall.

John Walker Lindh in the Turkish school on December 7, 2001.

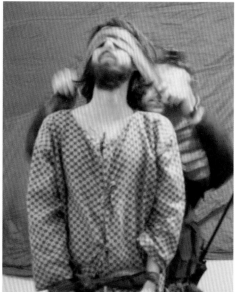

A Green Beret blindfolds Lindh to prepare for his transfer to Camp Rhino.

Members of ODA 592 pose for a "team photo" with Lindh, who has SHIT HEAD written on duct tape over his blindfold. This image led to a US Army investigation.

Shannon Spann and her son, Jake, outside her parents' cabin in Yosemite on November 25, 2001. Hours later, she would learn that her husband, Mike, was missing.

Shannon Spann, hand on heart, looks over her husband's casket at Arlington National Cemetery on December 10, 2001. David Tyson is top left. In front of him, in a beige coat, is Cofer Black. Hank Crumpton, with graying beard, partially obscured, is to Black's right. CIA director George Tenet is bottom left.

The golden dome covers the Mike Spann memorial, next to the west side of the faded Pink House, where the prisoners were lined up in 2001. To the left is the rebuilt center gateway. To the right is the eastern tower, the SBS position. The white structure above the dome, beyond the central wall, is the rebuilt northeastern tower. The stables and other outbuildings have been demolished.

The cellar of the Pink House, looking north. Two rooms are to the left and two to the right. To the right of the Afghan soldier is the entrance to the tunnel to the east of the Pink House, from which the eighty-six survivors surrendered on December 1, 2001.

An Afghan soldier stands inside the Pink House. The window looks out to the west, where the prisoners were lined up and where Mike Spann was killed on November 25, 2001. The hole in the roof was caused by a US air strike.

The memorial to Mike Spann; the star is the same dimensions as the one dedicated to him on the CIA's Memorial Wall, the 79th. By 2021, there were 137 stars.

of emotion, much less panic—but each could detect the tension in the other man's voice as the radio cut in and out. "We're Danger Close," Mitchell told Beck. The jets were at 20,000 feet—clear of shoulder-launched missiles, but too high to see anything—so dropping bombs "Danger Close" required senior-officer permission. But the F-18s were quickly burning through their fuel, reducing their loiter time before a "Bingo" call forced them to return to the carrier.

Perhaps the ideal aircraft to use on the southern compound were AC-130H Spectre gunships, which had just arrived at K2. But their 10,000-foot minimum altitude kept them grounded in daytime. Glenn cursed the Air Force for its reluctance to accept risk. To the Green Berets and SBS, the chances of an aircraft being hit seemed vanishingly remote compared with the immediate threat posed by the Al-Qaeda fighters in the southern compound just twenty yards to Beck's left. On the eastern tower, the SBS men were holding the enemy at bay, killing Al-Qaeda in industrial quantities with their GPMGs. Enemy fighters were flinging grenades at the tower and trying to scale its walls with ladders. Just below the parapet was the body of a Yemeni fighter who had nearly reached the top before an SBS man shot him dead with his pistol. A jammed GPMG or a moment's inattention, and one of the jihadists might get through.

As the minutes ticked by, Beck became increasingly fearful his position would be overrun. Debris showered him and the gunfire was unrelenting. In desperation, he keyed the mic on his MBITR radio, enabling the pilots above to appreciate the fury of the battle below the sanitized cocoon of their cockpits. "Can you fucking hear this?" Beck shouted. "We need help!" As he spoke, a mortar round exploded fifteen yards away. Mitchell demanded that the jets fly lower. "He'll go to 18,000 feet," Beck relayed, explaining with exasperation the pilot's worry of being shot at by Al-Qaeda. "Shot at?" pondered Mitchell. "I can tell him about that." Meanwhile, heavy fire had pinned down the SBS men on the eastern tower.

Beck radioed Bossman, the AWACS controller, and got the minimum altitude brought down to 12,000 feet. Mitchell then used his map and GPS to work out grid coordinates for the first target, which he passed to Beck, who relayed them to the pilots. It took another excruciating twenty minutes for the F-18s to begin dropping 500-pound JDAMs on the southern compound. "Thunder, Ranger," Beck instructed the F-18s. "The coordinates are North 3639984, East 06658945, elevation 1,299 feet." Then he turned to his comrades and began counting down: "Four minutes…three minutes…two minutes…thirty seconds."

At 4:05 p.m., the first metallic, arrow-shaped missile was visible as it plunged through the air, screeching, toward the southern compound. It landed west of the Pink House, the blast waves pulsing outward. The Americans and British took cover behind whatever structures they could, crouching or curling up in fetal balls. When the effects subsided, Northern Alliance soldiers burst into applause.

At the Turkish school, Sonntag breathed a sigh of relief when he heard the first 500-pound JDAM explode. He knew that only US troops on the ground could call in air strikes, meaning some Americans remained alive inside the fort. Everything to do with Qala-i Jangi had been a communications nightmare. On first reaching the fort, Mitchell had switched his AN/PSC-5 satellite radio from the command net—which Sonntag was on—to the fires net so he could coordinate air strikes. For more than two hours, therefore, Sonntag had been unable to determine whether Mitchell and his team were alive or dead. After thirty minutes of silence from Mitchell, Sonntag—preparing for the worst—had contacted Task Force Dagger to activate its Quick Reaction Force (QRF). The QRF was a group of two dozen 10th Mountain Division infantrymen who had been pulling guard duty at K2. Now, Sonntag needed them to defend the Turkish school, which threatened to become a latter-day Custer's Last Stand if Mitchell's fifteen-man rescue team had been killed.

In the meantime, Sonntag had drawn up an evacuation plan for the Turkish school. If Mullah Dadullah's force near Balkh or the 800 Taliban at Kunduz made it into Mazar-i Sharif and moved on the school,

Sonntag and his men would have to evacuate. He had only about eight Americans with weapons pointing out, defending the school, and they had limited fields of fire. The rest were support troops—plus an admiral whose death would be a strategic disaster for the United States. Not enough vehicles were available to get everyone out, so the evacuation would involve bolting for the Uzbek border on foot. Sonntag knew the chances of that working without a bloodbath were slim to none.

In the radio room on the first floor of the headquarters building, David was blown off his feet, suffering a minor concussion, as a JDAM hit the armory in the southern compound and sent bodies flying through the air. The blasts triggered secondary explosions as the arsenal's RPG warheads and mortar rounds cooked off. There was blood all over the radio-room floor, and the wounded were in a corner. One young man with multiple bullet wounds was crying; he had realized he was about to die. David wept too, turning his head away to hide his tears. He lay on the floor, rifle at the ready, imagining jihadists bursting in. "If they come," he thought, "I will kill as many as I can."

Timing their move with the next JDAM strike, Bass and Tony crawled down the ramp in the northwestern corner, protected by only a shallow lip on the side amid bullets flying inches over their heads. At the bottom, two Northern Alliance soldiers ran into the open and were mowed down by withering enemy fire. It made no sense for Bass and Tony to continue. Following the action by radio, David realized it was improbable the team would succeed in reaching him. He sank into despondency once more, especially when Glenn told him over the crackling frequency: "It's going to get dark soon, and at that point we're going to have to leave." Sunset was at 4:47 p.m. and the end of twilight twenty-eight minutes later.

For the past few hours, in his befuddlement and paranoia, David had imagined himself under siege from all sides. It never occurred to him that normal life was carrying on outside the fort. To the north, a main road bustled with traffic as Afghans went about their day unfazed by the enormous explosions.

Arnim Stauth, the German TV reporter, possessed even less situational awareness. He had visited the fort before to conduct interviews but had given no thought to its layout—or how to escape. During the hours of bombardment, Stauth had coped with his fear by switching to work mode, delivering radio reports. Sometime after 3:30 p.m., midday in Germany, he had delivered a live audio broadcast for Sunday's *Wochenspiegel (Mirror of the Week)* one of the country's most-watched television shows. As RPGs and mortar shells hit the headquarters building, Stauth had abandoned his satellite phone to take cover, leaving ARD viewers—among them his parents—listening to the sounds of battle and wondering if the correspondent had been killed. In terms of survival, Stauth had made a conscious decision that his safest option was to follow David's lead. On the roof of the headquarters building, David spotted a wounded Afghan with a crutch slowly making his way over to the northern tower then climb over and disappear. "If he can make it," realized the CIA man, "the rest of us can too." Gunfire from the central wall was now sporadic. It was ten minutes to sunset. "Hey guys, time to go," David told Stauth and his crew. David had promised he would not leave them and was true to his word.

Taking their destiny into their own hands, Stauth and the others overcame their fear of being hit by a bullet or caught by a mortar blast to clamber over the parapet, slide down the slope on the other side, and run across a rutted field to the main road fifty yards away. A taxi van slowed and David stuck Mike's rifle in the driver's face, telling him: "Take me to the Turkish school." The driver raised his hands and agreed. The taxi was already full, but the locals squeezed up, David and the journalists jumped in, and the van drove toward the city.

"Are you American?" the driver asked. Pointing a weapon at someone could easily be pardoned in Afghanistan. As they drove, David became aware of a woman staring at him through the eye slit in her burqa. "Aram," he said—Dari for "Don't worry."

Two JDAMs landed at the entrance of the Pink House, the epicenter of the uprising, but none scored a direct hit on its roof. Despite the devastation around the rest of the southern compound, the mortars, RPGs, and gunfire continued almost unabated. After the sixth JDAM dropped, Glenn watched in awe as a six-man RPG team emerged from the central gate, split into three two-man units, and fired simultaneously at the northwestern, northern, and northeastern sides of the fort. It was like a symbolic middle finger from Al-Qaeda, a defiant salvo to demonstrate what they could still do despite the might of American air power. One RPG flew over Glenn's head and out of the fort. Two scored direct hits on the headquarters building, sailing through the second-floor colonnade and exploding inside. That had been David's last known position and Glenn had no way of knowing that David was now safely in a taxi. In his confusion, David had somehow lost track of the radio he had been using. Glenn tried to raise David. No reply. "Goddamn it," Glenn said to himself. "Not only did we just drop bombs on Mike, now we don't know if Dave got killed by a fucking RPG." He would have to try again to reach the headquarters building.

Glenn and Mitchell decided to make a final attempt before nightfall forced the team to withdraw. As the two F-18s peeled away in the darkening sky, Mitchell called off a B-52 because the pilots could not see any targets through the smoke rising from the JDAMs that had already landed on the fort. Two more F-18s arrived, but the first 500-pounder they dropped sailed off course, landing in a field north of the fort. This alarmed Mitchell. The Americans were one errant bomb away from fratricide and disaster. Mitchell decided to call in a last JDAM and used his laser binoculars to get the coordinates for the center gateway. Machine-gun fire was still coming through the gateway and Al-Qaeda fighters were sheltering behind the vehicles parked nearby—including David and Mike's Toyota.

The plan was for Mitchell and Glenn to use the cover of the final JDAM explosion to leap over the side of the northwestern tower, run along the outside wall, and then jump through a window into the headquarters building. As they waited, Bass told the major he wanted to go forward toward the southern compound to look for Mike. "No," Mitchell answered. "You need to stay here."

But Bass insisted they use the last traces of daylight to find Mike. The JDAM hit exactly where Mitchell had intended, sending up a huge fireball as it set the vehicles alight. Inside the Toyota, David's backpack burned—the PRC radio and the sacred bundle his daughter, Kara, had created for him went up in flames. He had carried the talisman with him throughout his forty days in Afghanistan. Considering the hours of mortal danger he had endured that day, it seemed that the sacred bundle had done its job.

Abandoning their rifles and backpacks, Mitchell and Glenn made a run for the outer wall as the JDAM exploded. They jumped over the parapet, landing on the slope outside, then ran around to the center of the northern side and managed to scale the wall up to the roof. They went down into the headquarters building, their boots crunching on fallen plaster, broken glass, and shell casings. Using their pistols to scan each room for enemy fighters, they searched for David. "Dave, Dave— have you seen Dave?" Glenn asked some Northern Alliance soldiers. The Cheech and Chong pot-fueled comedy riff "Dave's Not Here" flitted incongruously into his mind. "Baba Daoud?" Mitchell called to some Afghans cowering in a corner. They pointed outside, indicating that David had gone.

While Mitchell and Glenn were in the headquarters building, Bass went forward to locate Mike Spann. "Look, we need to try and find him," he told Tony. Before the SBS corporal could talk Bass out of it, the SEAL had jumped over the parapet of the tower and landed outside Qala-i Jangi. Bass crept counterclockwise around the fort, his rifle at the ready in case Al-Qaeda fighters were lurking. Mines were another threat, but the fading light impelled him to cover ground quickly. At the western tower, Bass climbed up and hauled himself over the battlements. On top of the tower, he found four Northern Alliance fighters hiding behind a low wall with the corpses of two of their comrades sprawled a few feet away. Bass took aimed shots with his Diemaco, picking off enemies in the southern compound until they recognized the fresh threat and returned fire. Concerned he was running low on ammo, Bass retrieved an AK-47 from a dead Afghan and fired it instead. As a Navy SEAL firing from an elevated vantage point, Bass was much more accurate than the Al-Qaeda fighters in the compound, and their return fire subsided. He lay on his stomach at the front of the tower, overlooking the southern compound, and scanned the area toward the east. In the distance, just in front of the Pink House on its western side, he picked out a prostrate figure, face-down. It seemed to be clad in pale blue jeans and a black fleece—attire unlike that of any of the other bodies.

The three possible outcomes Glenn had weighed now flashed through the SEAL's mind too. If he saw Mike being tortured, Bass resolved that he would shoot him and explain to the Spann family what he had done. Some things, Bass thought grimly, were worse than death. He fired two shots inches from the figure's feet, to test for a flinch or other sign of life: no movement. Bass felt it was likely that this was Mike Spann—and that he was dead. Bass didn't know it, but the body lay where David had shot the men piled on top of Mike.

Bass jumped over the parapet on the western tower and landed outside the fort. He clambered back up into the northwestern tower—and was confronted by an angry Tony. "You don't go on your own, mate," Tony told him. "We go as a pair. Basic TTPs [Tactics, Techniques and Procedures]." Bass was unrepentant. "I think I saw him," he reported. "There was a body in jeans." Tony had to concede that Bass had gone as far forward as any American or Briton that day. That made the SEAL the only one to have viewed the southern compound from its western side, overlooking where the prisoners had been lined up that morning.

The forays into the headquarters building and to the western tower had taken about thirty minutes. Now, Mitchell, Glenn, Bass, and Tony were back together at the northwestern tower. Mitchell was not confident the Americans and British could hold their positions in the darkness against an assault from Al-Qaeda when it would be hard to distinguish then from Northern Alliance fighters. He ordered all Green Berets and SBS men in the fort: "Let's rally in the entrance courtyard, load up, and get out of here."

Arriving in the courtyard, Glenn brandished a wad of $100 bills and offered $5,000 to any Afghan who could locate his comrades. "Where's Mike? Where's Dave? I got the reward right here." He was immediately regaled with conflicting stories of daring escapes and sightings on parapets. It was typical Afghan bullshit, Glenn concluded.

* * *

Inside a Chinook high above the fort, soldiers from the 10th Mountain Division QRF were throwing up through sheer fear. The vomiting had begun as soon as the pilot announced that the Chinook had crossed into Afghan airspace. It was contagious. Once one had started hurling, another retched and soon there was vomit all over the helicopter. "Thanks a lot, sir," the crew chief told Captain Joe—the gnarled, mustachioed Night Stalker officer and combat veteran who was on the jump seat in the cockpit, leading the mission. "You can help us clean that up later."

Captain Joe had briefed the twenty-three members of the QRF on the tarmac at K2 and tried to steel the young infantrymen for what they would face. "Have you ever been in combat?" he asked them. Silence. "Anybody ever been shot at?" No. "Well, don't worry," he boomed, "you will be today." Captain Joe paused, then added, "But don't worry about it—you're gonna kill them first." One soldier had blubbered as Captain Joe told him, "If you never killed a man, today's the day." Until now, only Special Forces units had been inserted into Afghanistan. These were regular troops, and they were terrified.

Mitchell and his team were leaving the fort as the Chinook descended toward the nearby Dehdadi airstrip. Captain Joe was on the helicopter ramp, ready to liaise with the Green Berets. Beside him was a young lieutenant who had never commanded anything outside training and was petrified by sounds of gunfire and explosions in the fort. The moment the helicopter touched the ground, the lieutenant jumped down and hightailed it away. The first conventional American soldier to set foot in Afghanistan seemed to have gone haywire.

Captain Joe sprinted after him and eventually caught up. "Dude, where are you going?" he asked, wheezing. "I don't know," the lieutenant replied. Captain Joe looked at him and recognized that he was scared out of his mind. He asked the young officer where his platoon sergeant was, and urged him to have a talk with him. "You'll be all right," Captain Joe said. "You've got to lead these boys." The lieutenant began to calm down. "My wife just had our baby girl three weeks ago," he explained. "I've never even seen her." Captain Joe was struck by the dissonance of having what now seemed like a pleasant conversation on a dusty airstrip in northern Afghanistan while a battle raged less than a mile away. "It's okay," he reassured the lieutenant. "You'll see your daughter. It'll be all right. But your job right now is to look after these boys." The lieutenant considered the advice. "If I need you, will you come back?" he asked. Captain Joe looked him in the eye and lied: "Of course—you call, we'll come get you." The lieutenant thanked him and set off to locate his platoon sergeant. The 10th Mountain Division infantrymen loaded up into trucks and were driven to the Turkish school, where they set up their M240 machine guns and stood guard duty through the night.

* * *

By now, David Tyson was in the Turkish school. He was slumped into a chair beside Greg, who was manning the radio, delivering a forty-five-minute stream of consciousness about what had transpired at the fort.

Justin Sapp had returned just after Mitchell's fifteen-man rescue team had departed for the fort. His day had been a debacle. The 4x4 he and Bob had been driving to Kayan had broken down. Stranded, they had to wait for a support mechanic to drive from Mazar-i Sharif. Justin had been pulled off accompanying Mike and David to the fort, only to then miss participating in the rescue mission. When Justin had last seen David, the CIA officer had been his usual assured self; now he was a gibbering wreck. To Justin, David resembled a thoroughbred that had just finished the Kentucky Derby, panting and frothing at the mouth. David was still holding Mike's grime-encrusted AKMS rifle, the action full of dirt.

David was exhibiting another stage of shock. He had said initially he was all but certain that Mike was dead. Now, mumbling about "the fucking Chechens," he was suggesting his comrade might have somehow escaped the fort. When Justin asked him what had happened to Mike, he replied: "He got out. The Uzbek guy told me he got out. He escaped, man." Then, more slowly, David related the full story again. He spoke about the Arab prisoner who had shot at him sideways, Kamal's deputy urging him to flee, Mike shouting out for help, the pile of people on top of Mike, and Mike lying there, not moving. "But you said Mike got away," Justin said. David responded: "That guy told me he saw Mike get away." That made no sense, but David now seemed to be clinging to what an Uzbek guard had told him, probably to try to make him feel better. It offered an irrational hope—running counter to everything he had seen—that Mike could be alive. Justin, aware that David was experiencing severe trauma, opted not to push him any further. He concluded that Mike had been killed. Shortly after midnight, Mitchell transmitted a report to Task Force Dagger at K2, detailing the events of the day and commenting, "Based on Dave's eyewitness account, we believe Mike is dead."

The night at the Turkish school was punctuated by the sounds of explosions from the fort and reports of an enemy convoy of up to 300 vehicles and 800 men approaching the city from the north. After midnight, David received a call from one of Mohaqeq's men advising him to evacuate the Turkish school because prisoners had escaped en masse from Qala-i Jangi and were filtering into Mazar-i Sharif.

A screen of Northern Alliance troops north of Mazar-i Sharif confirmed there was indeed a convoy to the north. In response, Sonntag dispatched Green Berets from ODA 534, who confirmed that an enemy group was approaching. A B-1 Lancer bomber, known as "the Bone," arrived at 20,000 feet overhead. "I need to remove them from the equation," Sonntag thought. He ordered the B-1 to drop its JDAMs, then waited for the countdown to begin. Nothing. Sonntag felt a cold sweat as he strained for the sound that wouldn't come. Instead, the pilot came on the radio to report that his bomb-bay doors were stuck closed. Sonntag had been trained to expect the unexpected, but he couldn't help feeling this was some kind of jinx. Unwilling to divert the F-18s earmarked for the fort after dawn, he had no option but to keep the B-1 on station and have it fly ever lower, hoping it would act as a deterrent to the Taliban below. The bluff worked. The Taliban force converging on Mazar-i Sharif spotted the gargantuan American bomber overhead and came to a halt. For the time being, Sonntag's show of force would keep them away.

*   *   *

Outside Kunduz, J. R. Seeger contemplated two problems. The first was how to survive the night. His hunch was that the prisoners at Qala-i Jangi had jumped the gun, rising up before the 800 fighters north of Kunduz and Dadullah's 200 to the west of Mazar-i Sharif were ready to move. The short time it had taken Mike and David to get into Qala-i Jangi to assess the prisoners might have forced Al-Qaeda's hand, preventing a simultaneous move in Kunduz. But it still left J.R., at Erganak, facing a situation akin to Rorke's Drift, the 1879 battle in which a British force of 150 had to defend itself against 4,000 Zulus. After conferring with Sonntag, J.R. had been able to secure the type of help that had not been available during the Anglo-Zulu wars: two of the AC-130H Spectre gunships newly arrived at K2 were now inbound from the Uzbekistan air base.

The Team Alpha leader's second problem was that Dostum was drunk. After learning of the prison uprising, the Uzbek warlord had grown increasingly incensed that Mullah Fazl had reneged on the surrender deal—and outwitted him. There remained a looming danger that Qala-i Jangi would fall to Al-Qaeda, imperiling the surrender at Kunduz and dashing Dostum's hopes of laying claim to a senior position in Afghanistan's new government.

After visiting the warlord around nightfall, J.R. returned to the UAZ truck and told Scott, "Dostum's hammered—he's hit the vodka. What should we do?" The two CIA men had handled Dostum and Atta for weeks, a delicate dance of massaging their egos, appealing to their better angels, keeping a lid on their rivalry, and nudging them to behave humanely and according to American interests. Dostum was known to enjoy alcohol, but apart from the Johnnie Walker toast at Sheberghan had not been seen to touch a drop in the previous six weeks. If Dostum fell apart, his men would lose heart. Even if Qala-i Jangi didn't fall, Dostum had to be propped up. If not, Atta would press his advantage in Mazar-i Sharif, and the equilibrium the CIA had managed to maintain in the north would be lost. Strife among the groups that had toppled the Taliban regime could only undermine the new Afghan government, which was about to be established at talks in Bonn, Germany.

"You should go down there, slap Dostum around, and tell him it's time to man up," Scott told J.R. The appeal to Dostum's masculinity, a key part of his self-image, was important because it seemed he felt emasculated by Fazl's betrayal. Scott's advice was metaphorical, and J.R.—ever coolheaded and measured—was not about to get into a brawl. He returned to Dostum's tent and told him, "General, you need to stop drinking, get on the radio, and summon reinforcements. We're going back to Mazar, and we're going to retake Qala-i Jangi." In the mountains, Dostum had discussed war with J.R. many times and had grown to value the CIA officer's counsel. Despite the cultural divide, Dostum sensed that the American understood and respected him. He put down the vodka bottle. "Baba Jan, hand me the radio," he said. Team Alpha's leader had managed to coax the Afghan warlord back from the edge.

With the Taliban forces at Kunduz still refusing to surrender, the two Spectre gunships—one on station, the other waiting to relieve the first—arrived to change the enemy's calculus. It was the first time AC-130s—soon dubbed "water buffalo" by the Taliban—had been in action over Afghanistan. "You're cleared hot," the second Spectre was told by Bart Decker, the Boxer air controller, calling in strikes while wrapped in his sleeping bag on a bitterly cold night. "Did you say we're *cleared hot?*" asked a female voice. It was Lieutenant Allison Black, the Spectre's navigator. She could hardly believe they would be engaging enemy targets so soon. Dostum, sobering up, now wanted to decimate the Taliban outside Kunduz while sparing the city itself. Black's Spectre hit a rocket launcher, setting off a huge explosion. Next, the Spectre struck a Taliban building containing at least 100 enemy fighters. The survivors, believing it was a ground attack from machine guns, hid in ditches and beneath trees. The Spectre crew, watching the infrared heat signatures of the fighters, waited for them to regroup in a field before killing them all.

Dostum marveled at the high-powered laser pointer—known to the crew as a "sparkle"—emanating from the Spectre, calling it a "death ray." Hearing another female voice in an American aircraft, he taunted the enemy, just as he had in the Darya Suf Valley. "America is so determined they bring their women to kill the Taliban," he gloated over the radio. "It's the angel of death raining fire upon you."

17

ABSOLUTELY WRONG

6:50 a.m. (GMT +4.5), November 26, 2001 (Day 41);
Mazar-i Sharif, Balkh province, Afghanistan

THE SUN ROSE over the turquoise domes of the Shrine of Hazrat Ali, its first rays reflecting off the gold-flecked walls. White doves stirred, and the first pilgrims of the day glided barefoot across the holy building's frigid marble courtyard. It had been a night of unrest and foreboding. Muffled explosions were audible even as the muezzin's predawn call to prayer echoed through the city. Red tracer rounds lit up the sky as the slaughter continued at the fort. Hours earlier, some faction of the Northern Alliance inside the city had mistakenly opened fire on the convoys bringing the Green Berets back from Qala-i Jangi. Fearful locals barred their doors as an unknown number of escaped Al-Qaeda prisoners roamed free.

At the Turkish school, daylight brought the expectation that the inverted siege at the fort would be ended and the body of Mike Spann retrieved. Faqir's forces had kept a lid on the uprising overnight, with the walls of Qala-i Jangi—originally built to keep enemies out—serving to keep the remaining Al-Qaeda insurgents within.

At Erganak, west of Kunduz, Taliban forces, decimated by the Spectre gunships, prepared—at last and in earnest—to surrender. Debate raged about how to finish off Al-Qaeda at the fort. Captain Nutsch clamored to take his ODA 595 to Qala-i Jangi, but Lieutenant Colonel Bowers, ever a thorn in his side, refused. J.R. and Scott left in their UAZ truck at first light, driving from Kunduz alone—another immense but unavoidable risk. Going into Afghanistan, J.R. had expected to lose some of his men. But that made the reality of it happening no easier. His priority now was to find Mike Spann's body. Until then, he told the rest of the team, Mike was to be considered MIA—Missing In Action—rather than dead.

Inside the Turkish school, Mitchell assembled a fresh team to return to the fort. The two Air Force officers, of negligible value the day before, had made plain their wish to get back to K2 on the first available aircraft. They had no wish to go back to the fort. By contrast, two young Green Beret captains, Kevin Leahy and Paul Syverson, had spent two days at the Turkish school monitoring events from afar, and they were itching to get into combat.

For Leahy, this fight was intensely personal. The weddings of both his brother and his sister had been officiated by Father Mychal Judge, now dead at the hands of Al-Qaeda. The Franciscan priest had been hit by falling debris inside the North Tower of the World Trade Center and designated "Victim 0001" of the 9/11 attacks in New York. That day, Leahy's brother had just moved offices from the World Trade Center, and his father had been in Manhattan. They could have ended up like Father Mychal.

Leahy also had an unusually close connection to the broader military response in Afghanistan: his wife was the daughter of the general leading US Army Special Operations Command—the boss of the Green Berets. Like Sonntag and Mitchell, Leahy had all the makings of a future general. As commander of the battalion's support company, he had been resigned to staying in the rear at K2. Now, he had the opportunity to unleash his anger over 9/11 and take revenge on those who had killed so many New Yorkers that day.

Dave Betz—Ol' Sarge—was Leahy's sergeant major. In the Turkish school that morning, he was concerned that the eagerness of the young officers to kill the enemy was obscuring what he considered to be the primary aim. "Killing these motherfuckers is the SBS's job," he told the planning group. Betz had replenished the SBS ammunition stocks overnight and calculated they had fired 2,000 rounds in the fort the day before from the GPMGs alone. In his view, the SBS men were unmatched killing machines. "Our job as Americans is to recover Mike Spann's body," Betz continued, his voice cracking with emotion. "Our fucking ethos is to never leave a fucking fallen brother behind. If it was me, I would want somebody to take my body back home to my fucking family. It's the right thing to fucking do and it should be our number one mission." There was silence around the room. No one dissented.

Mitchell's plan involved a nineteen-man team divided into three elements to be inside the fort. There would be a command team, led by him, on the northwestern tower, an air-strike team on the northeastern tower, and the SBS machine-gun team on the eastern tower, just as they had been the previous day. A fourth element— a QRF from the 10th Mountain Division—would be outside the fort, 300 yards to the northeast. Once everyone was in place, an F-18 would drop a 2,000-pound JDAM on top of the Pink House, where most of the Al-Qaeda forces had hunkered down.

This JDAM, four times bigger than the bombs dropped the day before, would have a blast radius of 250 yards, meaning it should kill almost every fighter remaining in the southern compound. One JDAM that size should end the uprising; if not, more could be dropped. Once the enemy threat in the southern compound was neutralized, the search for Mike's body could begin.

After a mostly sleepless night the 10th Mountain Division soldiers were still in a state of bewilderment. Now, nine of them were due to be sent to the fort and were being briefed on their QRF duties to rush in if the plan unraveled. At nineteen, Private First Class Eric Andreasen was almost certainly the youngest American soldier in Afghanistan. He had never set foot outside the United States before landing at K2. Until basic training, he had scarcely left his home state of Florida. On 9/11,

Andreasen had been at the Fort Drum base in northern New York state, close to the Canadian border, when a sergeant came running, ordering his men to load up the trucks and shouting, "We've been hit! We're under attack!" When told that night where his unit would probably be heading, Andreasen had asked: "What the fuck is Afghanistan?" In Uzbekistan, he found the old Soviet base at K2 like a place out of time. It was smelly and dirty, and even the horizon looked weird to him. Now, northern Afghanistan struck the teenage soldier as another planet, inhabited not only by old men with turbans and long beards who might have been from the Middle Ages, but also by Special Forces troops, with godlike auras.

Andreasen was so overawed he forgot to listen to the briefing by Sergeant First Class Ken Ashton, a Green Beret, on Mitchell's plan. Ashton had flown into Mazar-i Sharif a few days earlier; he was part of ODB 580, a company support element, but was one of the most trusted combat sergeants in the battalion. Andreasen stared at Ashton and thought: "This is some top-notch super-shooter, door-kicking badass who is way awesomer than I can ever be." Before passing the Q Course and entering Special Forces. Ashton had been in the 10th Mountain Division. Now, fifteen years further on in his military career, he was bearded and wearing items of gear that were not standard issue. The callow young infantrymen, in contrast, were clean shaven and in full uniform, including helmets and body armor. The Green Berets looked like they had gone native, while Andreasen and his comrades could have just stepped off a training exercise back home.

As Andreasen and the rest of the QRF were driven to the fort, one of them began whispering the catchy refrain from the Drowning Pool song "Bodies," which had been dropped by radio stations after 9/11 because playing it was deemed insensitive. Soon, all the 10th Mountain Division soldiers were chanting, "let the bodies hit the floor, let the bodies hit the floor" as they psyched themselves up for combat.

Al-Qaeda was prepared for the return of the Americans. As the QRF was driven around to the northeast side of the fort, Mitchell, the eight SBS men, and eight Green Berets ran into the entrance court-yard. Dead and wounded Northern Alliance troops were already being dragged and carried out. Dave Betz, a combat veteran of the Gulf War and Somalia, was stunned by the noise from the battle raging inside. Six SBS men, hoisting their GPMGs, went up the gatehouse stairs first and set themselves up in the eastern tower to resume the business of the day before. The air-strike team of Betz, Leahy, Syverson, Beck, and Mike Sciortino, the Air Force combat controller, followed. They emerged from the stairs into the daylight—and what felt like a wall of gunfire. "Don't spend a lot of time on the fucking parapet," Betz shouted down. "Get across quick."

The SBS kept the enemy occupied as the five air-strike team members ran around the fort's east pentagon and made the seventy-yard crawl along the exposed parapet to reach the northeastern tower. There the Northern Alliance had situated a T-55 tank, which they had driven up the ramp overnight. Betz and Leahy were the security men, protecting the other three while they set up communications to call in the first air strike. Betz took aim through the center gateway, shooting enemy fighters as they appeared. He scanned the trees in the southern compound, looking for a PK machine-gunner who was firing sporadic bursts. Beck laid out a fluorescent orange VS-17 marker panel so the aircraft could make out the friendly position.

In the meantime, Mitchell led his command team around the outside of the fortress. Mitchell, Captain Jess of the SBS, Captain Anthony Jarrett, Steph Bass, and Tony established their position on the western tower, from where Bass had glimpsed Mike's body the night before. They would coordinate an assault on the southern compound once the JDAMs obliterated the Pink House, the Northern Alliance driving their tank through the center gateway, its fighters dashing in behind as the Americans picked off Al-Qaeda survivors. Bass and Tony used lasers to obtain the coordinates in the southern compound of the Pink House and the ammunition building just west of the gateway.

Back at the Turkish school, David Tyson remained in a state of acute shock. He felt devastated by Mike's presumed death, and was mourning the loss of his friend Amanullah and the many other Afghans who had died. He had spent part of the night drafting a four-page cable to CTC/SO outlining what happened in the fort. The cable used the operational pseudonyms of Mike, David, and Glenn, thereafter referring to them as Officer 1, Officer 2, and Officer 3 respectively. In sixteen paragraphs of dry officialese, David laid out what had occurred during a day that would be seared into his psyche. The cable was sent to CTC/SO, copied to other CIA teams in Afghanistan and Agency stations in the region, at 3:10 a.m. Zulu time, or GMT—7:40 a.m. in Mazar-i Sharif.

David was in no condition to return to the fort, which meant depriving the Americans of their only Uzbek linguist and the man who understood the Northern Alliance fighters best. Along with Glenn, however, he was able to drive to each hospital in Mazar-i Sharif to check in case, by some miracle, Mike had been injured and evacuated from the fort. They saw a lot of dead bodies but found no trace of their CIA comrade.

Justin Sapp and Greg, the former SEAL, had been sent to Qala-i Jangi by J.R. Of the four Team Alpha men left in Mazar-i Sharif, they had the most military experience. But the Green Berets had left the Turkish school early, forcing the CIA pair to speed through Mazar-i Sharif and around the Hazrat Ali Shrine in a Toyota minivan to catch up. As a Green Beret captain detailed to the CIA and Mike Spann's friend, Justin could have been the ideal link between the two American elements, but the need for cohesion seemed to have been forgotten. As he and Greg raced to get to the fort, Justin reflected on how things had gone so wrong so quickly.

In the Darya Suf Valley, Team Alpha, Dostum, and Mark Nutsch's ODA 595 had operated together almost seamlessly. Since getting to Mazar-i Sharif, however, that connection had been lost as more and more Americans filtered in. Dostum had become preoccupied with his rivalry with Atta, and the cast of Afghan characters shifted as scores of new faces joined the core Uzbek group from the Darya Suf Valley. It was too early to draw any conclusions from the horror of Mike's death, but it already seemed emblematic of how danger lurked so close beneath the surface in Afghanistan. More than almost any other theater of war, nothing could be taken for granted. Justin also wondered what difference he might have made had he been at the fort as planned the day before. Would he have been killed? Could he have been able to save Mike? He would never know.

Justin, his AKMS ready, was now on the parapet above the entrance courtyard, the Toyota minivan parked below. "This has to be a better day than yesterday," he thought. On the western tower, Jess asked Jarrett if he could have a look at his M4. "Be my guest," said Jarrett. As Jess peered through the M4's sight, he spotted an Al-Qaeda fighter, took aim, and dropped the man in his tracks. Then he handed the rifle back and thanked Jarrett, who thought: "You are one of the coolest guys in the world."

Over on the northeastern tower, above where the air-strike team had set up, a small group of intrepid Western journalists—mostly young freelancers hungry for excitement—filmed the Northern Alliance fighters. By the back wall, a corpse lay covered by a blanket, its feet bound together with white cord. The T-55 tank fired an occasional round into the southern compound and was resupplied by an SUV that drove up the ramp. Once the tank rounds had been unloaded, the SUV was repurposed as a hearse, driving the corpse away. A Northern Alliance soldier walked over to show off a pair of shoes he had taken from one of the Al-Qaeda bodies lying below.

Dostum's most hardened warriors were still with him outside Kunduz, and many of the young Northern Alliance soldiers left in the fort were undisciplined and treated war like a game. Heavy fire rang out from Al-Qaeda fighters in the southern compound, but the young Afghans expected the American bombs to finish the fight for them. As they awaited this remote deliverance, they played to the journalists' cameras. One Afghan fighter acted as director, instructing his friends how to get into the frame. Another struck a pose as he sauntered toward the journalists. Yet another picked up an RPG launcher, advanced to the edge of the tower, and fired. His commander chastised him, "Hey, why did you fire over there? If you'd hit the ammunition reserve, we would have had a huge explosion!" The fighters began to jostle and argue. "Stop shooting at everything and anything!" the commander screamed. "Don't fire randomly! You're only shooting to show off!" All this was going on under enemy fire. An Al-Qaeda mortar team had set up outside the ammunition store and was raining accurate fire onto the SBS men in the eastern tower. The five SBS men withdrew, running along the four outer sides of the fort's east pentagon and the exposed section of parapet to the northeastern tower, where Betz, Leahy, and the communications team were positioned. This forced withdrawal was a major change from what had been briefed earlier that morning. Once again, things were not going according to plan. British and American forces were now dangerously concentrated in one spot.

*   *   *

Some 30,000 feet above the fort, two US Marine Corps F-18C Hornets from the VMFA-251 Thunderbolts squadron arrived. The single-seat jets were operating from the aircraft carrier USS *Theodore Roosevelt* in the Arabian Sea. Shasta 21 was flown by a highly experienced pilot who a decade earlier had been a ground-based forward air controller—the role Sciortino was performing today. His wingman in Shasta 22, the F-18 carrying the 2,000-pound JDAM, was on his first tour.

"Be advised, you are Danger Close," Shasta 21 told Sciortino, who was using the call sign Boxer 81. "You are about a hundred yards away from the target." Meanwhile, Mitchell was pressuring Sciortino, telling him the bomb should be dropped as soon as possible to neutralize the intensifying mortar fire. Shasta 21, who wanted to drop one of the three 500-pound JDAMs he was carrying, questioned the use of a 2,000-pound bomb. Sciortino confirmed the choice, telling the senior Marine Corps pilot that ground forces were taking enemy fire. Shasta 21 then demanded that the air-strike team pass up its own coordinates; he wanted to be sure he could differentiate them from the coordinates of the Pink House. Mitchell and Sciortino strongly resisted, aware that a mix-up could lead to the bomb landing on American forces. But the Shasta 21 pilot refused to drop the bomb without the friendly coordinates in hand. Sciortino, with Mitchell's consent, reluctantly passed them up.

Catastrophically, both Marine Corps pilots then somehow reversed the two sets of coordinates. Shasta 21 realized his error and corrected it, cross-checking the target visually and through his forward-looking infrared radar (FLIR). But the more junior Shasta 22, focusing on relatively routine wingman duties such as maintaining formation and monitoring the antiaircraft threat, had failed to listen in to his lead pilot's exchange with Sciortino. The senior pilot radioed Shasta 22 on a separate frequency, instructing him how to convert coordinates into the format that would be accepted by the JDAM—a procedure the greener pilot had never executed before. Shasta 22 erroneously programmed in the friendly coordinates, then cross-checked them with Shasta 21.

In the last of a chain of deadly mistakes, the senior pilot wrongly verified that the coordinates his wingman had quoted were the correct ones. The Pink House should have been the target. Instead, now lodged within the JDAM's guidance system were the coordinates for the northeastern tower, 270 yards away. There, five American and six British troops, the T-55 tank crew, and around two dozen Northern Alliance were hunkered down, waiting expectantly for the JDAMs to pulverize their enemies. Sciortino tried to call Shasta 21 but had problems with his radio. So Beck called the senior pilot and cleared the F-18s to drop the JDAM.

At the QRF position outside the fort, the 10th Mountain Division infantrymen took cover behind a mud wall as they too waited for the might of American air power to do its job. Craig McFarland, the doctor, was with them, along with Ken Ashton, two other Green Berets, and a cluster of journalists and Afghans. A few minutes earlier, Andreasen had watched a taxi drive up and three young Northern Alliance soldiers—carrying AK-47s and an RPG—jump out and move toward the fort. "That was the most fucked-up thing I've ever seen," he had thought. They had taken a cab to go to war, acting like a jocular group of friends heading to a skateboard park. "What's a fucking JDAM?" asked Andreasen, overhearing the radio chatter. His sergeant replied: "A big-ass bomb, dude." The moment had come for the Americans and the Northern Alliance to administer the coup de grâce to the al-Qaeda fighters.

"We're about ready to drop," Mitchell said over the radio. As the Shasta 22 pilot prepared to release the JDAM, Mitchell warned the air-strike team: "Mitchell, Syverson—two minutes." When the bomb hit at 10:51 a.m., a huge brown cloud erupted from the fort, shooting 400 yards into the sky like a clutch of gigantic fireworks coalescing. A French journalist gazed skyward, mesmerized by what, to him, was a beautiful sight. But from his position outside the fort, McFarland saw something else entirely: twisted chunks of metal, spinning in the air and arcing toward them. "Shrapnel inbound!" he bellowed, pulling the rapt French journalist to the ground. A young Afghan translator working with the journalists quickly grasped what had occurred: "They shot the wrong one!" he shouted, almost hysterically. "That was absolutely wrong. They shot ours." The translator got in the face of Ashton, who tried to placate him. Ashton knew that there had been a terrible mistake, but he was loath to confirm that, worried that the translator's agitation might whip up the locals who were hanging around, and someone would get shot. Inside, his heart was racing; outwardly, he projected utter calm.

Soon, Northern Alliance fighters covered in what looked like brown talcum powder streamed out of the fort and came trudging down the road, coughing and spitting. "So now I guess we are killing ourselves," one said, almost laughing at the irony. "It missed," said another, blood dripping from his eyes and ears. "I don't know where my friends are." One stunned and speechless Afghan—caked in dust from head to foot, his forehead and eyes bloodied—staggered toward McFarland, his upturned palms outstretched. The wounded man reminded the Army doctor of the spectral figures who emerged from the clouds of debris after the World Trade Center towers collapsed on 9/11.

Minutes earlier, inside the fort, Kevin Leahy had been squinting through the sight of his M4, scanning the center gateway in search of targets. "War is supposed to be the best time of your life," he joked to Dave Betz. As the JDAM was released and reached its terminal velocity, Justin Sapp registered the split-second flicker of its shadow on the fort's western wall and wondered, "What was that?" Betz, who had taken a break from trying to kill the PK machine-gunner, saw the bomb itself—green, with two yellow stripes—as it fell toward him. Paul Beck, looking away as he braced for the impact on the Pink House, heard a swish and a whistle. Mike Sciortino's mind slowed as he looked up and saw the JDAM's vapor trail. He felt he was having an entire conversation in his head. Then, a freeze-frame: "I'm about to die."

When the JDAM hit, the lights went out for Leahy, then nothing. Justin heard the *kaboom* of the bomb's impact with the dry earth and was buffeted by the shock waves bouncing around the northern compound. Clods of mud rained down on him as much of the north-western tower disintegrated and was sent spewing upward. Below him, the door of the Toyota minivan he had driven into the entrance court-yard buckled. The thirty-five-ton T-55 tank flipped over, crushing at least one Afghan; the rest of its crew was blown to pieces. The turret detached and barreled through the air, coming to rest in the rubble. Many of the Afghans who had been mugging for the cameras an hour earlier lay dead.

Betz felt the searing heat on his face as he was propelled into the air. He landed thirty feet below the tower and struggled to stand up, smell-ing the burning flesh of his face. His right eye seemed to be fused shut, while his left cracked open but was full of dust. His Oakley sunglasses had melted, charring his nose. His eyelashes and mustache had been seared off; the watch cap on his head had vanished. Slowly, Betz grew conscious of the body parts of the tank crew scattered around him.

After verifying he still had four limbs, Betz surveyed the churned-up ground for his M4 and found it half-buried. He dug it out with his hands. The rifle had been snapped in two. "I done broke my fucking gun," he thought. "Damn, I'm going to catch fucking hell for this." Then, he realized that someone was shooting at him from the center gateway. "It's that fucking PK," he thought.

Blown forward off the tower and down into the northern compound, Beck bounced along the ground. Each time he hit the dirt, he thought: "I must still be alive." Once his body came to a halt, he could hear nothing but a ringing in his ears. He saw Leahy lying motionless like a crumpled doll, his boots on but his pants shredded around his legs.

Sciortino, after a momentary sensation of heat from the bomb blast, had felt himself being sucked into the air. "I am going somewhere else," he thought, presuming he was dead and heading for the afterlife. Everything around him was dust, and he felt like a tiny particle inside a huge, dark vortex. Sciortino landed on a pile of rubble, with a giant U-shaped hole in the side of the fort marking where the northeastern tower had stood. Anger welled inside him. "How did this land on us?" he wondered. "How could we fail when we were supposed to finish this thing?"

The massive bomb had dropped on the very people it was meant to help and wreaked intense damage. Mercifully, the mud floor and walls of the tower had absorbed much of the blast. That, however, had not saved the tank or its crew. The five SBS men on the northeastern tower had been sheltering around a small hut, affording them some protection. A dusty and bleeding Scruff greeted Tony, who had run around from the western tower, with a relieved smile: "Hello, mate!" Pat, the Yorkshireman, was the worst injured, with ruptured eardrums. Undeterred by the gunfire now resuming from the center gateway, the SBS men jumped down into the northern compound and began tending to the wounded.

When the bomb exploded, Jess, the SBS captain, had felt as if he was in a washing machine before landing beneath a pile of rubble in the northern compound. Betz, Beck, and Sciortino were dazed, bloodied, and singed, but they could walk. Hafizullah Fayez, a former pupil at the Turkish school, had just started working for the Americans as a translator. He had been sheltering behind a mud wall on the north-eastern tower, close to the tank. Now, he found himself being dug out by the SBS; the wall had disintegrated, saving his life but burying him in the process.

At the QRF position, McFarland heard Mitchell on the radio franti-cally trying to contact his comrades. "Syverson, are you okay?" the major asked, desperation in his voice. "Anyone on this net? Anyone on this net?" Another report came in: "We have one down, semiconscious, no external bleeding." It was confirmed this was Leahy. McFarland, the doctor, knew he had to get into the fort to treat the injured. The 10th Mountain Division troops loaded up with him and they all drove toward the entrance to the fort.

On the western tower, Bass feared that the F-18 pilots, flying a loop and intent on returning to drop a 500-pound JDAM on the mortar position, would release a second bomb programmed for the wrong target. "Abort! Abort!" he screamed.

Unable to raise Syverson, Mitchell switched frequencies to speak to Shasta 21, the lead pilot: "Check fire, check fire," he shouted. "Friendly casualties on the ground." Shasta 21, who had tried to contact Sciortino only to be met with silence, was stunned. "Are you sure?" he asked. Mitchell confirmed that he was certain. "Oh my God," the pilot replied in anguish. Shasta 21 asked if he should maintain a holding pattern until the situation became clear and more targets were identified. "Negative," said Mitchell. "We are done for the morning."

Jarrett feared his friend Syverson had been killed. They'd flown in to-gether from K2 just three days earlier, when Syverson had been tasked with bringing in $10 million for the CIA in an A-22 cargo bag. In the entrance courtyard, McFarland and the QRF were met by the SBS man Jonno; the giant Geordie was covered in dust. Jonno steered the group up the gatehouse stairs and back around east pentagon wall. Andreasen, carrying an M240 machine gun, was the first infantryman in the line. As the men reached the exposed section of the parapet, Jonno shouted in Andreasen's ear, "Bad guys on the left, wall on the right. Go to the corner—fast!" Andreasen ran along the parapet as bullets whistled by. Once he was set up on the remnants of the northeastern tower, a Green Beret ordered him, "See that Pink House? Anybody comes out of that, you light it the fuck up!"

Andreasen prayed for an enemy fighter to poke his head around the building, but none did. Part of him was relieved. He might have been the youngest American soldier in Afghanistan, but he could see that an Al-Qaeda assault through the center gateway could easily succeed in killing him and all his comrades. Handed a golden opportunity by the errant JDAM, the Al-Qaeda fighters in the southern compound failed to capitalize on it. They could have attacked the Americans at their most vulnerable, but the jihadists managed only sporadic fire. It was as if they could not quite believe this was a mistake rather than an elaborate trap.

In the entrance courtyard, Ken Ashton saw an Army radio operator, panicked by the gunfire, turn and run, dragging his radio and satellite antennae along the ground by the handset. Ashton drove him back to the QRF point and the pair stood on a van to try to get a satellite signal. But the radio operator was still consumed by fear, pointing his M16 at every Afghan, asking: "Is he friendly? Should we shoot him?" Ashton tried to calm him down. "No, don't shoot anybody," Ashton said. The radio operator was not a Green Beret. Ashton thought to himself: "This is the Special Forces mission. We're among the locals. There's no right, there's no wrong, just a huge gray area. You can't just start shooting people because you're scared."

At the foot of the demolished northeastern tower, McFarland asked Beck where Leahy was. The sergeant couldn't hear properly, so the doctor grabbed his arm and shouted in his ear, "Where's Leahy?" Beck pointed to the hole in the wall. McFarland found Leahy prostrate on the embankment outside the fort; bending over him were Russ, the

Cornishman, and Scruff. The young captain was breathing, but only just. McFarland tried to assess whether he had a brain injury by asking his name, where he was, and what day it was. Leahy knew his name and that he was in the fort, but said it was Sunday. Under the circumstances, two out of three wasn't bad. Leahy would live.

Back inside the fort, Justin saw a medic preparing to fit Syverson with a neck brace. "Hang in there, Paul," Justin said, but Syverson was so concussed he didn't recognize him. Justin and Greg prepared to leave, but the Toyota van's buckled door wouldn't open. Jonno walked over and, in a display of superhuman strength, ripped it off.

As he drove out of the fort, Justin was dismayed to see that the wounded Afghans were not being tended to by the Americans, and that their dead had been left lying in the dirt. By contrast, Leahy, Syverson, Betz, Beck, and Sciortino would all be treated at the Turkish school, then evacuated to K2 and onward to Turkey. Just like David's discomfort over the plight of the wounded commander Tufan in the Darya Suf Valley, the implication that American lives were of greater value than those of Afghans did not sit well with Justin. It was no surprise to him that the Northern Alliance troops were upset and angry: the Americans had killed their brothers, then abandoned them.

*   *   *

In the Oval Office on Monday morning, November 26, George W. Bush was about to receive the President's Daily Brief from the CIA. Vice President Dick Cheney was on hand, along with George Tenet and Condoleezza Rice, the national security adviser. The briefer was Michael Morell, a young analyst who had been with Cofer Black at Camp David on September 15, Morell had placed the four-page cable from David Tyson—sent about eight hours earlier—on top of Bush's folder, highlighting key sentences in his account of the events at Qala-i Jangi. Bush already knew Mike Spann was missing, presumed dead. A somber Tenet had told the president that "it simply boiled down to a case of being in the wrong place at the wrong time."

As Bush began to read David's cable, Morell realized the president was absorbing every word. The description of the chaotic first moments of the uprising was all the more stark because of its simplicity. "Prisoners in the yard began to move en masse toward the guards and the officers," David had written. "Officer 2 [David Tyson] runs to Officer 1 [Mike Spann] and shoots one with his Browning and then shoots the rest— four of the prisoners, one of whom was attempting to take Officer 1's rifle. Officer 2 secures the rifle." It took nearly twenty minutes for Bush to read the whole cable. When he had finished, the president closed the briefing book—ignoring the remainder of its contents about the intelligence picture around the world—and asked if Mike had a family. Tenet responded: "Yes, Mike has a wife named Shannon, who is also an Agency officer, and three children." Tears welled in the president's eyes. "I want to call Shannon," he said.

Later in the week, Team Alpha received a cable marked PERSONAL for David: "DT, On Monday the President very carefully read your account of the insurrection and battle at Qala-i Jangi. The President spent quite some time on the cable and was very moved by the events. On behalf of the President and everyone at CIA, we wanted you to know how proud we all are of you. Our thoughts and prayers are with you and your family. George Tenet."

18

YEAH, BABY!

8:20 p.m. (GMT +4.5), November 26, 2001 (Day 41);
Qala-i Jangi, Balkh province, Afghanistan

A LUMINESCENT GREEN parachute flare spurting through the inky blackness over the fort was to be the signal for Northern Alliance fighters to evacuate. J. R. Seeger had crawled over the remnants of the northeastern tower to get inside, keeping as low as possible as shots from Al-Qaeda pierced the night sky. Next to him was Alex Hernandez. They were leading the first group of Americans to return to Qala-i Jangi after the JDAM debacle. With the CIA men were Major Mark Mitchell, an air controller, and three Green Berets. Their mission in the fort had been agreed when J.R. had conducted a delicate negotiation with their Afghan allies. Now they awaited the AC-130 Spectre gunships.

Some five hours earlier, the Team Alpha leader had arrived back at the Turkish school from Kunduz just as the SBS men returned. The Britons were exhausted and angry, the whites of their glaring eyes highlighted by the dust that covered their bodies from head to toe. J.R. thanked them for risking their lives to find Mike Spann's body. The Team Alpha leader had averted a Dostum breakdown at Kunduz. Now, he had an even greater diplomatic challenge: soothing the Northern Alliance commanders.

"We need to find out what the hell's going on, because we've got a big

252

loss of rapport," Mitchell told J.R. "We destroyed their tank and killed a bunch of their guys. They're ready to just pack up and go home." While the CIA ultimately paid compensation in cash to the families of the dead Northern Alliance fighters, on this day words were the only currency available to J.R. to placate his allies. "I know Commander Faqir," J.R. told Mitchell. "We can patch this up. You just need to get me out to the fort."

Alex had returned separately from Pol-i Khomri, leaving Andy and Mark in the crossroads town 125 miles to the southeast. The Team Alpha deputy spoke to David, who was babbling and appeared to have gone into psychological denial about what had happened to Mike. Alex brought him up short. "Dave, you need to tell me: is Mike dead?" David paused, trying to think straight. "Yes," he replied. "Mike is dead."

At 4:40 p.m., J. R. Seeger and Alex drove with the Green Berets to the east side of Qala-i Jangi, where they parked next to a T-55 tank. They had wanted to get there before dark to lessen the chances of being shot by the Northern Alliance. The atmosphere was predictably tense, almost hostile, with some of Dostum's fighters gesticulating and yelling at them. Yet the Americans were relieved to find that the Afghans had not abandoned the fight inside the fort, which they could hear was still raging. "Don't worry, we're going to iron this out," J.R. reassured a sergeant. The two CIA men crept into Qala-i Jangi to talk to Faqir and his lieutenants about what had happened that morning—and what could be done that night.

As the Americans and the Afghans sat talking in the debris-strewn headquarters building, mortar shells burst in the northern compound outside. Faqir had lost more men during the afternoon after the errant JDAM had dropped. As a warrior, however, he knew that the nature of combat was that things went wrong. More than most Afghans, Faqir appreciated that the first casualty in war was often the plan. He also knew what American air power, applied correctly, could achieve: Mazar-i Sharif would not have been captured without it. J.R. expressed his condolences for the Afghan casualties. Faqir did the same regarding

Mike Spann, whom he had fought alongside in the Darya Suf Valley. Faqir acknowledged that the Northern Alliance had failed to search the Al-Qaeda prisoners properly—a lapse that had led to the uprising.

The niceties dispensed with, J.R. was eager to look forward. "We don't want any more big bombs," Faqir insisted. The CIA man nodded in agreement. "Well, we can do some other things for you that won't be like that," J.R. said. The Americans could send in two Spectre gunships, for example. Faqir was pleased. Dostum had told him of the lethal effectiveness of the Spectres in Kunduz. The gunships would not drop bombs—"No more JDAMs," J.R. promised—but would instead rain down bullets from the sky, killing everything that moved. Faqir grinned. The deal had been reached in twenty minutes. As J.R. and Alex left the fort for a few hours' rest at the Turkish school, Faqir urged them, "Come back soon."

J.R., Alex, and Mitchell's party of five had returned to the fort at 8:10 p.m. The SBS men were not able to take part because their ROE barred them from directing pre-planned or "offensive" air strikes. This was ironic, given that they had probably killed more enemy the day before than any American unit in the war thus far. The Al-Qaeda fighters, still stubbornly embedded in the southern compound, greeted the Americans by pelting the northern compound with small arms, rocket, and mortar fire. Nearly thirty hours after the uprising had begun, a significant enemy force was still in control of half the fort and engaged in combat. The seven Americans had no way of knowing how many of the more than 400 original prisoners were still alive and fighting. Probably half of them had been killed on the first day, the bulk of them by the SBS. Some were undoubtedly wounded, while others had likely been sheltering in the Pink House cellar throughout. A few dozen might have escaped.

During their jihadi mission, these men had subsisted for months on scant sustenance. Before that, most had lived in harsh conditions. And so these former prisoners had managed to survive and keep fighting by exploiting what was available in the fort. Water spigots and streams in the southern compound enabled them to quench their thirst, while flesh carved from slain horses and cooked over fires assuaged their hunger. These hardcore combatants were committed to killing the Northern Alliance forces and their infidel American allies and had easy access to almost unlimited arms and ammunition They were content—even eager—to die for Allah.

But if the Al-Qaeda fighters possessed the will to kill, the Americans had the way. The Spectres, had arrived at K2 in the nick of time after more than two months of delicate talks with the Karimov regime in Uzbekistan. Karimov, wary of alienating Russia, had initially permitted only US reconnaissance, CSAR, and cargo aircraft to operate from his country. The talks about the Spectres had nearly been thwarted on November 4 when Donald Rumsfeld, the US defense secretary, had flown to Tashkent in the hope of finalizing a deal to allow the aircraft to fly into and out of Uzbekistan. The arrangement was that Rumsfeld would meet first with Rustam Inoyatov, head of Uzbek intelligence, and then proceed directly to Karimov's palace for talks with the president. Rumsfeld, however, desired an audience exclusively with Karimov and was irked at being required to meet with "an intel guy."

Charlie Gilbert, the Tashkent CIA station chief and David's boss, patiently tried to explain the situation: Inoyatov was the de facto number two in Uzbekistan, and Karimov deferred to him on military matters. Gilbert then recommended a way for Rumsfeld to frame the argument: yes, the AC-130 Spectres were armed, but they would be deployed only to protect aircraft used for rescue and, therefore, should not be considered attack planes. Rumsfeld, pushing his open palm to within an inch of Gilbert's nose, cut him off: "I know how to brief, son." Rumsfeld grudgingly went to see Inoyatov. Another CIA officer, Tom, translated to and from Russian. Rumsfeld, already famous for his verbal jousting and ruminations about "known unknowns," ignored Gilbert's advice and ad-libbed. The CIA translator, one of the Agency's best Russian linguists, was soon stumped by Rumsfeld's words and found it difficult to follow even the English. Afterward, a puzzled Inoyatov asked Gilbert, "What was *that* about? I thought he was going to ask for planes to be based here." But Rumsfeld—oblivious of his failure to persuade Inoyatov—was already en route to see Karimov, so Gilbert had to salvage the situation on the fly. The station chief explained to Inoyatov exactly what the United States wanted, then quickly called the US ambassador, who was riding in the car with Rumsfeld. "Total fail," Gilbert alerted the diplomat. "Inoyatov needs to be in the meeting with Karimov. He's on his way." Clued in to Rumsfeld's meaning, the Uzbek intelligence chief related it to Karimov and the delegation reached an unofficial agreement. Had Gilbert not intervened, it could have cost American lives in Afghanistan—and perhaps prevented the Northern Alliance recapturing Qala-i Jangi. "Rumsfeld almost ruined that whole fucking thing," thought Gilbert.

Final agreement on the Spectres being based at K2 had been secured only on November 24, almost three weeks after Rumsfeld's meeting with Karimov and just a day before the gunships flew into action over Kunduz. Until that date, four Spectres had sat unused on a runway at Souda Bay, Crete. At the last moment, Uzbekistan cut the number of US gunships allowed to three.

*　　*　　*

With the first Spectre, codenamed Grim 11, due over Qala-i Jangi at 9 p.m., Mitchell prepared to fire the green flare. Five minutes later, amid intensifying enemy fire but no sign of the aircraft, Mitchell radioed Sonntag at the Turkish school; a mechanical problem, he learned, had forced Grim 11 to return to K2. The gunship would not arrive for another two hours.

The delay left the Americans dangerously exposed. Most of the Northern Alliance forces, understandably afraid of being anywhere near Qala-i Jangi when American planes were overhead, had already left. Frantic radio calls between the fort, the Turkish school, and K2 prompted the second Spectre, Grim 12, to be scrambled. It would arrive at 10:10 p.m. For seventy agonizing minutes, seven Americans, practically alone in the fort, lay flat on the ground as Al-Qaeda mortars pounded the northern compound. Sergeant First Class Ken Ashton felt panic well up inside as he realized the mortar's main target was shifting from the headquarters building to the remnants of the northeastern tower, where he and his comrades were hunkered. The mortarman had bracketed their position, and now shells were exploding so close that showers of red-hot metal burned Ashton's hair. Interspersed with the mortar rounds were BM-21 rockets, which the Taliban had briefly used so effectively in the Darya Suf Valley. It seemed only a matter of time before the Americans were hit. Ashton feared that Al-Qaeda would gather a dozen or so fighters, run through the center gateway, and rush the American position. Mitchell, anxious that a single muzzle flash might betray their hiding spot, ordered the Americans to hold their fire.

In training, Ashton had learned to control his fear by recognizing the onset of tunnel vision and hearing loss. Both of those were happening now, but he could identify what his brain was doing and overcome it. He knew that panic was unproductive—the radio operator earlier could have got them both killed. Ashton had a reputation as one of the most unflappable operators in the 5th Special Forces Group. No one knew how hard he worked to achieve that.

Right on time at 10:10 p.m., Grim 12 arrived and Mitchell fired the green flare. Grim 12's crew of fourteen, including two pilots, a navigator, sensor operators, and gunners, went to work. The pilots flew an orbital pattern known as a pylon turn, which enabled its guns, all facing from the port side, to fire continuously into the southern compound. It was soon clear, however, that the two six-barrel 20mm Vulcan guns, each capable of firing an astonishing 7,200 rounds a minute, were faulty. That left Grim 12 with only 100 rounds for its 105mm M102 howitzer—the largest airborne gun in the world—and 250 rounds for its 40mm Bofors cannon.

Grim 12 concentrated its firepower on the Pink House, now

Al-Qaeda's command center within the fort. From 7,000 feet above, the Spectre's thermal-imaging TV operator could see groups of fighters emerging from the tunnel entrance near the Pink House to fire rockets; these men had infantry training.

Until now, the fortified cellar and reinforced-concrete roof of the Pink House had kept those inside safe. Fighters had roamed the southern compound almost at will, with only the sporadic and usually inaccurate fire from Dostum's men to trouble them. But the Spectres were essentially engaged in a turkey shoot. Before the aircraft had lifted off from K2, US military lawyers had pondered whether there might be accusations of the gunships perpetrating a massacre. The verdict was that those in the fort were "enemy combatants"—no longer prisoners— and therefore legitimate targets. Anyone in the southern compound could be eliminated. "We can see thirty-five guys massing around the gate," an AC-130 crewman reported to Mitchell's ground force. "Is that you?" Apparently, the enemy fighters were preparing to execute the surge into the northern compound that Ashton had feared. "Negative," said Mitchell's air controller, who had flown down from K2 as an emergency replacement for Sciortino. "Let them have it." Grim 12 did just that, firing fifty 105mm rounds, felling dozens of Al-Qaeda fighters, and calling "Winchester"—out of usable ammunition—an hour later.

Grim 11, its engine problem fixed at K2, then took over, stepping up the killing with its howitzer and Bofors cannon. After firing sixty-seven 40mm rounds, however, the cannon malfunctioned and had to be shut down. Despite the high death toll, the Al-Qaeda mortar team was still operating. Down on the ground, J.R.'s concerns were mounting. "There are plenty of reasons to hate these guys," he reflected as the insurgents blasted the northern parapet with mortar rounds, starting at the headquarters building and working their way towards his position. "But you've got to admire their skill."

Mitchell radioed Grim 11. "This is a race," he said. "Either you're going to kill them or they're going to kill us." Standing on top of a heap of rubble, Mitchell used his night-vision goggles to point his laser through the center gateway and paint the spot he reckoned was nearest to the mortarman. "Get down!" shouted one of Mitchell's sergeants. "You're gonna get shot!" Mitchell could see mortar shells arcing toward him over the center wall. The Spectre team had still not identified the firing point.

Inside the Spectre, perched behind a blackout curtain separating him from the cockpit, Lieutenant Colonel Greg McMillan, the mission commander, pondered the problem. The Green Berets were reporting mortar-barrel flashes just west of the center gateway, but no one in the Spectre had visually confirmed that. Having been an AC-130 pilot in Panama in 1989, McMillan was familiar with searching in vain for an enemy mortar position. The heat signature of a mortar launch was fleeting, making it difficult to pinpoint, plus this Al-Qaeda team excelled at movement and concealment. With only eight 105mm rounds left, McMillan ordered the pilot to peel off.

Gunners in the stern of the aircraft now had time to reload. The open doors had frozen the ammunition to its holding racks and the pause meant they could fix the problem. But the withdrawal was principally a feint to lure the enemy into thinking the gunship was leaving. As the plane rose, Mitchell supplied McMillan with one crucial additional detail: the trajectory of the mortars was steep. McMillan figured that the Al-Qaeda mortar team must therefore be firing from near the center wall. "Let's go wide on the TV," he ordered, referring to the low-light-level TV camera. Scanning the wall, the TV sensor operator spotted what looked like a Roman candle. It was the mortar tube firing. "So that's where you are," McMillan said to himself. The mortar team had set up between a long, low building west of the center gateway and a smaller building—as if they were in an alleyway. The long building was the main ammunition store, packed with mortar rounds and explosive charges. This proximity to the arsenal, ideal for resupplying the mortarmen, was about to spell their doom.

Spectre 11 fired three 105mm rounds at the "alleyway" position. They missed, sending up a dust cloud and prompting Grim 11 to switch over to its infrared sensor operator, Master Sergeant Jim Patterson. He fired another round, which landed just a few yards away from the mortar tube. Offsetting the miss distance, he fired again, this time scoring a direct hit on the enemy position.

Watching the action through night-vision goggles, the Green Berets saw the mortar tube as it was catapulted into the air. In a stroke of fortune, the blast also sent shrapnel through the wall of the long building, igniting a fire inside. Patterson gazed at his screen, which showed three glowing figures, clearly ablaze, fleeing the building as it spewed flames from its door and windows. Three more rounds—the last of the ammunition in Grim 11—killed two of the fleeing fighters and wounded a third. As Patterson tracked the wounded man, he heard a giant explosion, followed by a chain reaction of other blasts as the arsenal exploded, razing the building and killing everyone nearby. "Yeah, baby!" shouted McMillan in triumph. "That was awesome!" Crouched down at the northeastern corner of the fort, J.R. was transfixed. The exploding arsenal reminded him of the closing-credits scene in the original version of Francis Ford Coppola's *Apocalypse Now:* the sky was bright with munitions shooting out colored trails. Eight miles away, the windows of the Turkish school rattled. From the roof of the headquarters building, David and the Green Berets watched what they joked was a souped-up Fourth of July celebration. Patterson had recorded twenty-seven enemy kills, four buildings damaged, and one building and the mortar position destroyed.

*   *   *

David Tyson balked at returning to the fort the next morning. He had barely slept for the past two nights and was deeply fearful of revisiting Qala-i Jangi, the scene of his recent trauma. "Dave, you need to," coaxed Scott, whom J.R. had appointed to chaperone David. "You can help us find Mike, and you know the language. We can do it quickly, so let's get into the vehicle." David knew this made intellectual sense, but every moment felt like a battle to keep his emotions from overwhelming his rational function. A caravan of CIA men, Green Berets, and SBS stopped short of the fort to liaise with the Afghans and work out a plan to retrieve Mike's body. But first, they would have to run a media gauntlet. Journalists had flocked to Qala-i Jangi after learning of the uprising. On the day Mike was shot and David escaped to the headquarters building, perhaps two dozen reporters were in Mazar-i Sharif. Now, forty-eight hours later, the count had swelled to more than 200.

The CIA group arrived in the Toyota van, driven by Scott. Glenn, holding an AKMS rifle on his lap, was sitting with his foot propped up where the door would have been had Jonno not torn it off the day before. When the CIA officers emerged, they were mobbed by the media. Intent on recovering the body of their fallen comrade and helping the Afghans squelch whatever resistance remained in the fort, the Agency men had no appetite for PR games. "No press," said Scott. "Turn the cameras off."

Alex lost his temper and stormed away. He was pursued by the German journalist Arnim Stauth, who shouted, "You're in Afghanistan. You're a guest like we are. You're not in the United States. You have no right, no authority." Alex struggled to contain his fury and wheeled around. Realizing he was on camera, he told Stauth, "Put that in your notes." Throughout the afternoon on Sunday, the first day of the uprising, Stauth's fate had rested in David's hands and the two had shared a common goal: survival. Now, on Tuesday morning, goodwill had evaporated and the European reporter had reverted to his adversarial stance toward the CIA. The press had captured footage of the confrontation, which would enliven their broadcasts.

With the press now at a safe distance, Commander Faqir explained to J.R. and Mitchell that the Spectres had broken the back of the Al-Qaeda fighters, who had been pushed down into the Pink House cellar or were hiding in outbuildings. The Northern Alliance now had complete control of the northern compound and its soldiers were positioned around the fort's parapets overlooking the southern compound. Only occasional fire came from the enemy. The initiative had shifted decisively. Al-Qaeda had lost its battle to take control of the fort and perhaps only a third of the more than 400 original prisoners were still alive. J.R. told his men that Afghans would lead the operation to deal with the remnants of Al-Qaeda.

From the eastern tower, the Americans viewed a grotesque scene of almost medieval carnage. More than 100 corpses were strewn across the southern compound. Some seemed virtually intact, though bloated or twisted in hideous poses, with limbs jutting out at odd angles, stiffened by rigor mortis. Others had been scythed into pieces by bomb blasts or rounds fired from the Spectre gunships, their brains and entrails spilling out. Scattered around like broken doll parts were severed arms and legs, and the occasional head. On the west side of the Pink House lay about thirty bodies, some with hands tied by turbans, prisoners cut down at the start of the insurrection. A lone, headless dove lay in repose among the corpses. In one area, the ground was carpeted by pine needles, blasted from the trees. Branches hung shredded and limp, or had been ripped off.

Close to the center wall was the smoldering arsenal, detonated by a 105mm round early that morning. The bodies nearby were charred or had been turned to ash. More than a dozen horses lay dead—their legs splayed, their bellies distended to near-bursting. Some appeared to have had flesh ripped off.

Spread among the dead was the detritus of war: shell casings, mortar rounds, broken guns, ammunition boxes, shrapnel. The trucks that had brought the prisoners in on Saturday night were now blackened hulks. Many of the outbuildings had been reduced to rubble, and every square foot of the walls seemed pockmarked by some projectile. A thin film of dust and explosives residue blanketed everything, giving some bodies a translucent, ghostlike aura. The sweet smell of rotting flesh mixed with smoke and cordite pervaded the air. Beholding the scene from the western tower, Justin Sapp wondered how any living thing could have emerged from such destruction. Remarkably, one Northern Alliance guard had managed to survive for more than two days by hiding in an outbuilding, then making a run for the center gateway. Not only had he eluded the Al-Qaeda fighters, he had withstood bombardment by the Spectre gunships. Eyes wide as saucers, he staggered around like a zombie, asking, "Have the Taliban gone?" One of the Green Berets handed him an MRE cracker and the dazed guard wandered off to nibble it, mumbling to himself.

Inside the fort, David was so fear-stricken that all he wanted to do was crawl, grinding his face into the dust and holding his rifle before him commando-style. When he reached the foot of the western tower, David felt certain he would die if he climbed the ladder to view the southern compound. Scott tried to talk him into coming up to describe the layout of the southern compound and the place where Mike had fallen, but David could only offer "Let me tell you from here." That made no sense, even to David as he said it. "I'm really fucked up," he thought.

After Scott had coaxed him up, David pointed out the west side of the Pink House. Bodies were dotted around the place where he had shot the Qatari nicknamed the "fat Arab" and the others on top of Mike, but he couldn't pick out his comrade's body. In the thirty-six hours since Steph Bass, the SEAL, had looked out from the same position and thought he could see the dead CIA officer, the amount of dust and debris around the Pink House had increased exponentially. As the CIA men were surveying the hellish scene below, more gunfire erupted. Al-Qaeda had not given up. "These people just won't die," David thought.

Justin looked down and saw what he presumed was an enemy fighter creeping out with an AK-47 from behind an outbuilding. He raised his AKMS to fire but was stopped by an Afghan, who told him the fighter was "Dost, dost"—Dari for "friend." As Justin hesitated, the armed man below raised his rifle and fired. The bullet hit the wall a foot from Justin's head, kicking up a puff of dust. Justin had been right, and the Afghan's correction had almost killed him. "Keep down!" David shouted wildly. "They saw your fucking white face. You show your turkey neck and they're gonna get you."

Faqir's plan was to climb down ladders from the eastern side of the southern compound and form a line of men who would sweep across to the western side, forcing Al-Qaeda holdouts into the open. But the Northern Alliance marksmanship was haphazard, with bullets zinging past the Americans and Afghans on the western wall. Justin reflected that he was probably more likely to die in the fort from a shot fired by the Northern Alliance than by Al-Qaeda. Before Faqir's men reached the Pink House, three Al-Qaeda fighters emerged from an outbuilding and opened fire. The Northern Alliance panicked and ran, pushing each other out of the way to get to the long ramp leading up to the southern tower. The chaos set the tone for the rest of the day.

The Afghans drove a T-55 through the center gateway, the sides of which had been reduced to rubble by the Spectre gunships. The tank fired five rounds into the Pink House and then looped through the southern compound, crushing dead bodies beneath it. The sight of the corpses being mangled was sickening to the Americans, especially considering that Mike's body might have been among them. Noting Justin's grimace, David told him, "Yeah, the Hazaras and the Uzbeks will do that. When they're mad, they get nasty."

The tank withdrew as soon as an RPG was fired at it, whereupon the Northern Alliance opened up with machine guns and rifles, blasting away at anything that moved. Fighters sprayed rounds from whatever vantage point they could find. One stood on the back of a comrade just outside the fort and raised his rifle aloft to fire it over the battlements without aiming. Another used the prone corpse of an Al-Qaeda fighter as a sandbag, resting his rifle on the dead man, the bare feet poking out from beneath a mat laid over the body. On the fringes of the fort, some fighters ate peanut butter and jelly sandwiches supplied by US forces; others smoked hashish. After shouted negotiations with the prisoners, three Northern Alliance fighters slowly approached the blackened tunnel entrance. When they got there, a grenade thrown by an Al-Qaeda man killed two of them.

Justin looked on, astonished that the Northern Alliance was still falling for the Al-Qaeda ruse of false surrender. He was frustrated that the Americans were not in charge of finishing off Al-Qaeda in the fort. "We should just kill all of them and be done with it," he thought. Instead, with Dostum still in Kunduz, he was witnessing disorganization excessive even for Afghanistan. J.R. and Mitchell, however, were adamant: this was an Afghan operation. The Team Alpha leader ordained that the CIA not open fire even if enemy targets presented themselves.

In some respects, J.R. felt, the Northern Alliance should be given credit for their restraint—not a quality often associated with Dostum or his men. He was surprised that they hadn't simply filled the Pink House with tank rounds and detonated it. By the same token, he gave Dostum some kudos for not summarily executing Mullah Fazl once it became clear that the Qala-i Jangi uprising was a Trojan horse operation of the Taliban commanders' devising. Justin took a more cynical view: the Northern Alliance troops had a thirst for bloody retribution—which in this post 9/11 environment, he shared—but were not competent enough to achieve it.

Emotions were running high for everyone on Team Alpha. J.R. had lost one of his men and was already mentally composing the condolence letter he would send to Shannon Spann. At almost fifty, Alex was close to a generation older than Mike; as a Special Forces sergeant major, Alex had grown accustomed to caring for—and sometimes reining in—young officers like Mike. Neither J.R. nor Alex was the demonstrative type, but Mike's death had hit them hard. Inside the fort, Alex approached Justin and told him: "I saw it in your eyes. You guys had to look over the edge." The implication seemed to be that Justin and Mike had been gung-ho and taking too many risks. Justin sensed that Alex's pain at Mike's loss had prompted him to lash out.

Everywhere around the center gateway, there were dead Al-Qaeda. Team Alpha members resorted to dark humor amid the corpses, which Dostum's men kicked casually. "Some of Dave's friends here from a couple days ago—not," said Justin, as David videoed the bodies. "Guy got run over by a tank. There's Dave. There's a dead guy." David felt no revulsion, only a pull to see those he had killed on November 25. It was as if he wanted it to register, to take responsibility. He wrote in his diary that night: "I was afraid, very much so, but my need to see the dead was very strong." Toward the end of the afternoon, David was kneeling beside a Northern Alliance T-55 tank when he became irritated by a persistent metallic knocking. He tried to work out who could be making the sound, but no one else was there. Looking down, he realized his own hand was shaking rhythmically, banging his AK-47 against the tank. His nerves were wrecked.

That night, Mohaqeq's forces surrounded a house in Mazar-i Sharif where three prisoners, believed to be Chechens, had escaped from Qala-i Jangi and taken a family hostage. Justin was present as the Chechens feigned surrender and then tossed a Soviet F-1 grenade and opened fire. Mohaqeq's men killed them in the exchange and then dumped their riddled corpses on a street corner as an example. Justin saw that the bodies had been shot scores, perhaps even hundreds, of times and felt that he finally comprehended the depth of hatred the Hazaras felt after the genocide their people had suffered. Justin recovered what appeared to be a terrorist training camp notebook, mostly written in Cyrillic, which included details of initiation systems for explosive devices, replete with electrical and engineering formulas for computing resistance in ohms. There was also a diagram of a telescopic sight and a drawing of a US helicopter with crosshairs superimposed on it.

Other intelligence on Al-Qaeda had been gathered in Mazar-i Sharif. Glenn had received permission from CTC/SO to use as an asset an Afghan who had been deported from the US for heroin trafficking. In the post-9/11 environment, such a background was not a dealbreaker. It turned out that the Afghan had valuable information, leading a CIA team to a warehouse that contained a basement, accessible only via a trap door. The basement was stacked with cases of diesel motor oil, boxes of laundry detergent, and bags of ammonium nitrate fertilizer—the major components of Ammonium Nitrate/Fuel Oil (ANFO) explosive mixture.

*   *   *

Just after first light, at 6:15 a.m. on Wednesday, November 28, CIA officers and Green Berets gathered in the northern compound. The Americans were disturbed that Mike Spann's body had lain inside Qala-i Jangi for three nights as the Afghans struggled to regain control of the fort. Now, the Northern Alliance had managed to clear the southern compound using a T-62 tank—a heavier and more modern version of the T-55. After talking to David, Faqir sent a small group of his men to search the area west of the Pink House where the prisoners had overwhelmed Mike late on Sunday morning.

A few minutes later, Faqir came back to David. "Mike was wearing cowboys, right?" he asked. "Cowboys" was the term Afghans used for blue jeans, a symbol of the American West. David confirmed that Mike had worn jeans on Sunday. Faqir told him the body lay exactly where David had described last seeing Mike. Realizing that Mike's body had been found, David involuntarily started to run toward the center gateway. He had momentarily lost control of his senses as he internalized the quest to find his comrade's remains. Over the course of the day, he had swung from almost paralyzing fear to reckless disregard for his own safety. Manzullah Khan, one of Dostum's commanders, saw David running and launched himself at the CIA man, tackling him to the ground. "Daoud, the bad guys are still shooting," he said.

Justin was distressed by the way that four Afghans were carrying Mike's body—each was holding a limb. They moved quickly and in a serpentine pattern in case of any enemy fire. Justin remembered an instructor on his Q Course who was a Green Beret veteran of Vietnam telling him: "Do not mistread the bodies of your slain comrades because one day they will be sitting on your bedpost talking with you." Justin regretted that it was not

267

Americans who had recovered Mike. Glenn said gently that the Afghans were doing their best, pointing out that they had risked their lives to locate Mike's body. The CIA men had feared that a press photographer might capture the scene, but thankfully no media seemed to be present.

J.R. radioed CIA headquarters to report that Mike Spann's remains were safely in American hands. Mike's boots were missing, but he was wearing his Columbia black fleece, sunglasses still tucked in the pocket, and jeans. Given everything that had happened in the southern compound over the past three days, the body was in remarkably good condition. Mike had been shot twice in the head and there were shrapnel wounds, but no signs of torture or abuse.

Mario Vigil—Boxer's sergeant major, who had just returned from Kunduz—stood ready with a body bag. He had also brought an American flag that he had carried into Iraq during the Gulf War. Mike's body was zipped into the bag, then draped with the Stars and Stripes, the emblem he had revered and for which he had given his life. Five CIA men carried Mike's body through the northern compound into the entrance courtyard—J.R. and Alex, who had led Team Alpha; David, who had been with Mike on the day he died; Justin, who had traveled with Mike to Bamiyan; and Glenn, the CIA man in the rescue team on day one of the uprising. Thousands had died on 9/11, and hundreds of Afghans had been killed in the weeks of fighting since then. But this was the first casualty for America on a new, global battlefield. The Iranian Quds Force officer approached Team Alpha to commiserate "from one professional to another."

*   *   *

The past few days had been agony for Shannon as news of the events at Qala-i Jangi had been relayed back. Amy had found herself thinking: "How can this be? With all the military might of the United States, how can we not take this fortress back?" Shannon's milk was drying up and she worried about feeding Jake. Around 9 p.m. on Tuesday in Orange

County, California, where Shannon was still staying with her parents, Amy told her gently that Mike's body had been found. It had seemed impossible that her husband could still be alive, but when told he was missing she had resolved to believe in his survival until definitive evidence proved otherwise. She received the news of his death with silent stoicism. A large part of her being had begun to shut down; Shannon Spann was merely going through the motions of being a person.

*   *   *

On Wednesday evening in Afghanistan, Team Alpha drove Mike Spann's body, still draped in the American flag, from the Turkish school to Mazar-i Sharif airport. In a gesture of solidarity, the eight men of the SBS contingent—the SEAL Steph Bass among them—formed a guard of honor and saluted the CIA man as his remains were loaded onto a Chinook to be flown over the mountains back to K2.

Farther afield, friction between the British and the Americans had ratcheted up. A British military team had angered an ODA in Herat by luring away the Greet Berets' guard force by offering them higher pay. In Islamabad, CIA station chief Robert Grenier found himself having to deal with what he considered a "fraudulent" attempt by MI6 to offer up a wealthy Pashtun exile with the codename Spectre as the new savior of Afghanistan. The British, he lamented, had been "handing up half-truths, exaggerations, and outright fabrications in their effort to gain a place at our side." Where it mattered, however—on the battlefield—British troops had fought heroically and with deadly effectiveness, operating seamlessly with American forces. Never again would the Poole-based SBS be regarded as the poor cousins of their SAS compatriots in Hereford.

19

LUCKY BOOTS

12:15 p.m. (GMT +4.5), November 28, 2001 (Day 43);
Qala-i Jangi, Balkh province, Afghanistan

ABDUL RASHID DOSTUM, clad in a black leather jacket and corduroy tunic, hooked his thumbs in his belt as he surveyed the corpses littering his devastated fort. "It was war," he growled. He had arrived on the fourth day of the battle, hours after Team Alpha had taken Mike Spann's body away. Each morning, Dostum's commanders had prematurely declared victory and an end to the siege, but Al-Qaeda was not finished. Three Afghans working for the Red Cross announced themselves and attempted to descend into the cellar of the Pink House to tend to the injured. They were met with a hail of bullets; two were wounded, one of them fatally.

Dostum had returned to the fort only after the final surrender of thousands of Taliban at Erganak, west of Kunduz. Those prisoners were now being loaded onto trucks for the ten-hour journey further west to the prison at Sheberghan, Dostum's stronghold. The warlord took stock of the calamity at Qala-i Jangi; he had lost four commanders and around fifty soldiers. Amanullah had been killed, along with one of his brothers. Miraculously, two of Dostum's finest buzkashi horses had been found unscathed after they broke free and took refuge in a domed outbuilding. Dostum wept when he realized that his favorite horse was alive.

Later in the day, Dostum brought into the fort Mullah Fazl and Mullah Noori, the Taliban leaders who had negotiated surrender terms in the headquarters building six days earlier. The pair were now in Dostum's custody, but accommodated under guard in his Sheberghan guesthouse. "We tried to treat the prisoners humanely and they took advantage," said Dostum, gesturing towards the two black-turbaned mullahs. Fazl, wearing a camouflage jacket, was impassive while Noori, a white shawl draped over his shoulders, muttered prayers. When Dostum asked the mullahs to speak to the Al-Qaeda fighters still holed up in the cellar of the Pink House, they insisted they did not know them.

The CIA claimed Mike as one of its own. It was a break with precedent, but with so many reporters at Qala-i Jangi the fact that Mike had been in the CIA was an open secret. Mike's parents had wanted their son's affiliation to be made public so it would be known he had been serving his country and was not a mercenary or rogue operator. His career had been short, so dropping his cover would not risk the lives of any clandestine sources.

Now, the world was learning about Mike Spann. At CIA headquarters, George Tenet solemnly gathered staff to inform them of Mike's death. He was unstinting in his praise of Mike's heroism—and unsparing in his condemnation of those who had killed him in Qala-i Jangi. "Although these captives had given themselves up, their pledge of surrender—like so many other pledges from the vicious group they represent—proved worthless," he said.

In Winfield, Alabama, Mike's father, Johnny, stood in front of his house and addressed the media, delivering an eloquent tribute to his only son. "Our son Mike was in Afghanistan on assignment with the Central Intelligence Agency," he said. Asked how he felt about his son being the first casualty in Afghanistan, Johnny Spann briefly groped for words. "I'm his father," he said. "And it couldn't hurt me any worse whether he was the first one or the fiftieth one, I guess." The outpouring of support for their family was something Mike would have expected, his father said. "He knew how people in Winfield were. A small town like this, everybody here knows everybody. And everybody takes care of everybody." Mike, he added, had been "a loving person, a dedicated person, a loyal person, a patriotic person, and a hero."

* * *

Back at Qala-i Jangi, by late Wednesday afternoon, journalists were admitted to the southern compound; they had been told once again that the battle was over. "The situation is completely under control," one of Dostum's men declared. "All of them were killed." Few of the enemy corpses had been removed. The reporters gagged from the stench of rotting flesh. Amid the trees, one fighter was still crouched, rifle in hand, as he had prepared to take aim; half his head was missing. Some were supine, looking almost peaceful; others were twisted in a last agony. Groupings of the dead gave clues to their final actions. Several were sprawled beside a battery of rockets. Inside an outbuilding there was a circle of Arabs, the apparent victims of a suicide blast. The corpses of a dozen young foreign fighters with wispy beards lay close to a bombed kitchen; one wore a San Francisco 49ers sweatshirt, another a knockoff Dolce & Gabbana fleece.

Northern Alliance soldiers turned out the pockets of the dead men, finding bullets, cotton sachets of gunpowder filings, even a small plastic bag of rice. They looted the bodies, scavenging belts and shoes. One of them bent low over a corpse, using a long, thin instrument to pry gold fillings from its teeth. A young Al-Qaeda fighter lay stricken in a ditch, mortally wounded but still breathing. When an Uzbek soldier dropped a rock on him, a horrified reporter begged for compassion: "Hey, why don't you just put a bullet in his head and just kill him, just end it?"

Perhaps Al-Qaeda was not quite finished, Dostum's men conceded. While journalists still roamed the southern compound, the Uzbeks did everything in their power to kill the last fighters in the Pink House cellar. They shot Kalashnikovs through the blackened entrance to the tunnel leading to the Pink House and rolled grenades down staircases inside the building. One commander pushed a six-foot rocket into a drainage pipe leading to the cellar and ignited it, sending flames into the air. There was a dark comedic quality to some of the attempts. Diesel fuel was poured through ventilation holes on the side of the Pink House, but attempts to set it alight failed, because diesel is not flammable.

Amid the carnage was a horse that was still alive, its eyes wild with pain. One of its rear legs had been almost severed. Simon Brooks, the Red Cross official who had escaped from the headquarters building on Sunday, asked a Northern Alliance guard to shoot the whimpering animal and put it out of its misery. After peering into the entrance to the tunnel, from which a stomach-churning miasma drifted up, Brooks motioned a reporter to the eastern side of the compound. "Come and see the stables," he said. "There's a huge pile of bodies there." As the pair walked, four shots rang out from inside the tunnel. Afghans dropped their stretchers, sending bodies tumbling to the ground, and ran.

Brooks and the Red Cross set about their work, recovering 188 corpses. Each dead face was photographed before the bodies were loaded onto a trailer and driven to a desert burial. Brooks noted, "The reality is that behind each one of these bodies is a family. Somebody has to do this." The pictures were destined for a tracing center set up in the hope that relatives might someday trace their missing.

Over the following years, jihadist websites published lists of those who died at Qala-i Jangi, furnishing fragments of lost lives. These lists were translated by the CIA. Three brothers from Riyadh—Yasir, Hakim, and Abdul-Hakim Al-Shahri—were said to have been among the dead. Two Saudis had gone by the noms de guerre Daoud the Chechen and Abu Khalil the Algerian. Walid Al-Hadrami, also from Saudi Arabia, had walked out of a marriage after six months; his father ran several shops selling air conditioners. Faruq Al-Harithi was tall and had a speech impediment. Abu Salah Al-Din Al-Hassawi had a wheaten complexion and a snub nose. Nasir Al-Mutairi gave off a smell of musk; he'd been torn apart by a tank shell, leaving only half his chest and his head. Abu Al-Hasan Al-Abini, imprisoned for eight years "during the socialist period," was a theology student who knew the Koran by heart. For a few, there were hints of a life before jihad: Abu Faruq Al-Maghribi had excelled at kung fu and karate; Khalid Al-Ajami had owned a Toyota Cressida in the 1990s; Abu Haidara Al-Makki was famous for a poem.

*   *   *

On Friday morning, November 30, the fifth day after the uprising and Day 45 for Team Alpha in Afghanistan, Commander Faqir had an idea: his men would divert an irrigation stream into the cellar, literally to flush out the surviving jihadists. By midday, the underground rooms were filled with chest-deep water contaminated with rotting flesh, feces, and fuel. Corpses floated on the surface. Some injured fighters drowned.

About sixty dead bodies lay in the cellar's six rooms. The water slowly receded, but the spirit of the holdouts had been broken: they had no more weapons, and the effluvium enveloping the cellar was overwhelming. Debate among the Al-Qaeda fighters turned from sacrificing themselves for Allah to giving up. "Look, we're going to die either way," said one. "If we surrender, then they'll kill us." Another reasoned: "Is it better to be killed? I mean, if we surrender, the worst that can happen is that they'll torture us or kill us, right?"

At around 10 p.m., a fighter crept from the cellar and called out to Northern Alliance soldiers that he was ready to surrender. A dozen more followed him. Those thirteen were locked overnight in a shipping container brought into the northern compound by Dostum's men for that purpose. Early Saturday morning, a reporter was ushered in to view the piteous scene of the wretched men—some grievously wounded—huddled together in the metal box. They claimed they were Pakistanis and one Afghan.

"Could you ask them to bring us some tea?" one of the fighters asked in perfect English. "We are very hungry. We have had nothing to eat." Another had put a cardboard box on his head in an attempt to stay warm. In the gloom at the back was a man whose nose and mouth had been blown off. For the first time, details of the uprising materialized. "We wanted to surrender on Thursday," said the fighter claiming to be Afghan. "But there was a group of seven Arabs who wouldn't let us."

Remarkably, no American forces remained inside Qala-i Jangi. After Mike's body was recovered, CIA headquarters had issued an order that none of its officers in Afghanistan should enter prisons to talk to Taliban or Al-Qaeda detainees. The Green Berets had decided their mission was over once it was clear the uprising had been suppressed. Mike had given his life to question the group of more than 400 prisoners inside Qala-i Jangi, believing that his duty to avert another attack on the United States could not be delayed. Now, the remnants of those prisoners would be dealt with by Dostum's men, their interrogation by Americans left for a later day. Some Team Alpha members seethed at the implication that David and Mike had erred in going into the fort six days earlier. They also felt that their primary mission in Afghanistan of gathering intelligence on Al-Qaeda—the one Mike had believed in so passionately—was now being jettisoned.

Shortly after 8 a.m. on December 1, the remaining Al-Qaeda men began to emerge from the shattered tunnel entrance. A band of journalists—expecting few, if any, prisoners to be alive—were astonished as seventy-three more sodden, filthy, barefoot jihadists appeared from the Stygian darkness. Dostum's men paraded them past the reporters, one announcing where they were from: "Uzbekistan! Arab! Pakistan! Yemen! Chechnya!" One fighter hopped—his other leg had been broken—while at least twenty were carried on stretchers. Another fighter's jaw had been blown off, while his companion nursed a smashed, gangrenous arm covered in fetid bandages. Some fighters appeared shell-shocked, staring blankly. The fortieth one out seemed to share a joke with a guard.

Most of the fighters ignored shouted questions, but the forty-fourth man stopped and spoke in English. "Where am I from? I was born in America," he responded. A reporter followed up, "Where in America?" The Al-Qaeda man cast his eye over the battle-torn northern compound, as if the answer might somehow lie there. "Baton Rouge," he said. "Baton Rouge, Louisiana—you know it, yeah?" The prisoner was Yaser Esam Hamdi, twenty-one, the son of a petroleum executive who had worked for Exxon in the United States before returning to his native Saudi Arabia when Hamdi was three years old. Months later, it was established that Hamdi was indeed a US citizen.

As the seventy-third and final fighter, a badly wounded Arab, was carried away on a stretcher, an elderly Afghan jumped out from a doorway with a rock. "You killed my son!" he shouted at the Arab, who raised his good arm weakly as the rock was about to crush his skull. Four fingers of his right hand were bloody stumps, the sole remaining digit connected by only a sliver of skin. A reporter rushed forward to intervene, prompting a guard to wrest the rock away from the old man.

The total of eighty-six fighters, now prisoners once again, were coralled together in the northern compound, where their hands were bound and trucks awaited to transfer them to Sheberghan jail. Red Cross officials handed out royal-blue blankets, water, oranges, and bananas, and applied bandages to the captives' wounds. Some of the prisoners talked. Abdul Jabar, from Tashkent, said he was a member of the IMU, and that his leader had been behind the uprising. "It was our commander who began the fighting in Qala-i Jangi," he explained as a Red Cross medic dressed the bullet wound in his foot. "He said, 'It is better to die a martyr than be in prison.' Our commander said we should fight to the last drop of blood."

At first, no one paid much attention to one Al-Qaeda man who tiptoed through the gateway, his shalwar kameez stained, hair matted, and face smeared with grime. He later stated that when the uprising began he tried to stand up but was shot in the leg. The fighter was wearing a blue commando sweater that six days earlier had piqued the curiosity of Mike Spann. He was the Irishman. It turned out this man did indeed have Irish forebears—a grandmother born in County Donegal—but he was no Irishman. He had been told by his commanders to inform his Al-Qaeda comrades he was Irish as a way of deflecting attention from his true nationality: American. He had steadfastly maintained his silence under questioning by Mike and David six days earlier, but now he was talking.

A *Newsweek* reporter was told by his translator that one of the captives—the Irishman—who had stumbled from the cellar had identified himself as American. The reporter found him sitting in a container, arms bound behind his back, right leg and left foot newly bandaged. The prisoner stated that his name was Abdul Hamid. His English was heavily accented, almost mannered, as if he were relearning his native tongue. For six months, he said, he had been in Afghanistan because "the Taliban are the only government that actually provides Islamic law." The reporter asked whether he had supported the 9/11 attacks. "That requires a pretty long and complicated explanation," the prisoner replied carefully. "I haven't eaten for two or three days, and my mind is not really in shape to give you a coherent answer." Pressed again, he stated, "Yes, I supported it."

The Irishman was John Walker Lindh, a twenty-year-old who had grown up in San Anselmo, just north of San Francisco—the city where J. R. Seeger had been working on terrorism issues, and less than 200 miles from the Yosemite cabin where Shannon and Jake Spann had stayed. After a privileged, liberal California upbringing, Lindh had converted to Islam. In the summer of 2001, he had traveled to Afghanistan, where he had trained at Al-Qaeda's Al Farouq camp, which at least seven of the 9/11 hijackers had attended. Weeks before 9/11, Lindh had met with Osama bin Laden at Al Farouq and learned that attacks on the United States were planned.

* * *

The eighty-six survivors from Qala-i Jangi were crammed into two trucks for the three-hour journey to Sheberghan. There, some injured prisoners, including Lindh, were taken to the hospital. Having apparently calculated that his best chances of survival now lay in revealing his true citizenship to whoever he could, Lindh told a doctor he was an American and that his name had been John. An Afghan soldier hurtled back to Dostum's guesthouse to break the news to Captain Mark Nutsch and the rest of ODA 595, who were staying there to assist with prisoners in Sheberghan.

As well as the Green Berets, an adventure-seeking travel writer named Robert Young Pelton was staying at the guesthouse. He was in Afghanistan to write a story for *National Geographic,* with a side gig as a freelance contributor to CNN. Pelton had skillfully insinuated himself into Dostum's entourage; now, he was about to land the scoop of a lifetime. Wrangling his cameraman, Pelton headed to the hospital with Sergeant Bill Bennett, an ODA 595 medic. Lindh again identified himself as Abdul Hamid, saying that "John was my name before," adding that he was from Washington, DC—his true birthplace.

Bennett fitted Lindh with an IV and glucose drip to send calories into his bloodstream and gave him a tetanus shot. "Your wounds don't seem to be very bad," the sergeant told him. "Just fighting is what's made you so tired and weak." Lindh resisted being filmed. "If you're concerned about my welfare, then don't film me and don't take pictures of me," he told Pelton. The journalist deflected. "Okay. Would you like some food, John?" Pelton asked. "I brought some cookies."

Pelton tried to build a rapport with the strange young American by sharing his own experiences with jihadists in Chechnya and the Philippines—and professing respect for Islam. He managed to get Lindh to reveal details of studying Arabic in Yemen and then moving to Pakistan. "The people there in general have a great love for the Taliban, so I started to read some of the literature of the scholars and the history of the movement," Lindh related. "And my heart became attached to them."

But Lindh made clear that he was not an ordinary Taliban fighter. "The Taliban have a separate branch in the army," he explained. "They have Afghan, and they have the non-Afghan. I was with the separate branch of the non-Afghan...it's called Ansar. It means the helpers."

Pelton immediately recognized this as another name for the 055 Brigade, bin Laden's Al-Qaeda troops who fought alongside the Taliban. Lindh explained that "the Arab section of the Ansar is funded by Osama bin Laden," adding, "Also the training camps that the Arabs train in before they come to the frontline are all funded by Osama bin Laden."

When Pelton asked if it was "your goal to be shahid or martyred," Lindh replied that it was "the goal of every Muslim" and elaborated, with passion in his voice, "I tell you, to be honest, every single one of us, without any exaggeration, every single one of us was 100 percent sure that we would all be shahid, all be martyred, but you know, Allah chooses to take a person's life when he chooses."

Perhaps the most revealing answer Lindh offered was to one of the simplest questions. "Was this the right cause, or the right place?" Pelton asked. Lindh replied emphatically, "It is exactly what I thought it would be." Pelton told him that he would be well looked after by Dostum's men, though "they are a little nervous because of the incident at Qala-i Jangi." The reporter added cheerily, "This is Dostum's hometown. You picked a good place to be kept."

An FBI source said that the dark stains on the right side of Lindh's face indicated he had used a weapon at Qala-i Jangi. Lindh, however, was not tested for explosives or firearms residue before he was cleaned up. The Green Berets took Lindh into custody, deciding that a US citizen had to be kept separately from the other prisoners to minimize the chances he would escape or be killed. Lindh spent that night in a bedroom in Dostum's guesthouse with an armed guard stationed outside his room. Pumped with morphine and Valium, the American jihadist was soon comatose.

While Lindh slumbered, Pelton transmitted his report to CNN in the United States, where an astonished public would learn for the first time about a self-radicalized white American who had converted to Islam and carried out acts of war on behalf of his country's enemies. The interview caused widespread outrage and would form a central part of a ten-count federal indictment against Lindh.

At the Turkish school, the Boxer staff and J.R. debated who would be responsible for Lindh. J.R. argued that detainees had never been part of Team Alpha's mission and the legal ramifications of the CIA imprisoning an American citizen were best not tested. No FBI agent was available to fly in from Islamabad to handle the situation, so the CIA concluded that the task fell to the Green Berets. Lindh would now be making a return trip to Mazar-i Sharif. Major Kurt Sonntag, in charge of running the Turkish school, was stunned to learn that there was a US citizen among the men who had killed Mike Spann. "A fricking American Taliban?" he thought. "Are you kidding me?"

ODA 595 bound Lindh's hands with rope, and placed a hood over his head for the drive from Sheberghan back to Mazar-i Sharif. Once the American prisoner arrived at the Turkish school, he was given his own room with a cot, blankets, bedpan, and space heater. The windows had been blacked out to conceal the time of day. For the next week, Lindh would be guarded by the twelve Green Berets of ODA 592, who had been flown from K2 into Mazar-i Sharif after the errant JDAM incident at Qala-i Jangi. A soldier checked on Lindh every hour, logging his condition. Captain Craig McFarland, the battalion doctor, treated Lindh's wounds. They appeared to have been caused by shrapnel, though Lindh insisted the thigh injury was from a bullet that remained lodged there. Lindh's wounds were not infected, and he was hungry but not malnourished. As the American regained his strength, he became more assertive, repeatedly summoning McFarland to complain about his aches, the cold, or tight dressings.

Sonntag believed Lindh had been trained to resist interrogation and was dangerous. Lindh had identified himself as John Philip Walker but had no identity documents and he claimed not to recall his Social Security number. Only when Lindh's parents saw Pelton's interview on television was his identity finally confirmed. When Brooks, the Red Cross official, came to visit Lindh to establish whether he was being treated properly, Sonntag refused to allow the prisoner to have a pen, explaining that it could be used as a weapon. "People aren't all good," Sonntag thought. "If you make the assumption that everyone is good, you're gonna get killed." Lindh dictated a letter for his parents to Brooks. He apologized for having "caused you a lot of grief" and reassured them he was now "in safe hands."

McFarland was anxious to have Lindh transferred—his thigh wound needed surgery—but debate over how the American detainee should be handled extended all the way up to President Bush. Inside the US Justice Department, treason charges were being contemplated.

*　　*　　*

The United States designated Lindh as Prisoner #001—the first American captive in the War on Terror. Now that he was in the custody of the very country he had rejected, his prospects of survival were considerably better than those of his Al-Qaeda and Taliban brothers-in-arms. The plight of the 3,000 inmates of Sheberghan prison, crammed into a facility with a capacity of under 1,000, was desperate. Among them were the remaining survivors from Qala-i Jangi, including Hamdi. As Hamdi was being moved to the prison, he struck up a conversation with a Green Beret who was an evangelical Christian. Sensing an opportunity, the Green Beret suggested to Hamdi that given his current predicament, switching his allegiance from Islam to Jesus might be worth considering. Hamdi listened politely, but declined to convert. It is likely that at least a dozen survivors had died since leaving the fort. Those who made it to Sheberghan alive were the luckier ones. The capture of around 7,000 prisoners in Kunduz had overwhelmed the Northern Alliance, who were still fighting isolated Taliban units.

Dostum was already viewed with deep suspicion by the State Department. What happened next would result in his being barred from visiting the US and treated as a pariah by American diplomats. Kamal Khan, one of Dostum's commanders, was in charge of prisoners at Qala-i-Zaini, a walled compound just west of Mazar-i Sharif. Dostum, concerned that Mullah Dadullah's forces might ambush convoys of prisoners being driven from Kunduz, ordered Khan to provide security. Khan transferred several hundred prisoners from trucks to shipping containers, which were more secure.

For years, containers had been associated with prisoner atrocities, which in turn were a staple of the Afghan way of war. In 1997, Dostum's treacherous deputy, Abdul Malik Pahlawan, had been accused of cramming hundreds of prisoners into containers, where they had been baked alive in the heat. He was said to have buried the bodies in the Dasht-i-Leili desert outside Sheberghan. According to a UN report, a Pashtun faction had murdered Hazara prisoners by locking them in a metal container and then lighting a fire around it, while Malik had dumped a container of Taliban prisoners into the Amu Darya. By Dostum's account, Kamal Khan, who had lost two brothers to the Taliban and was enraged by the events at Qala-i Jangi, was "young and emotional." The warlord later recounted that when some of the prisoners resisted being forced into the containers, Khan's soldiers opened fire. Dostum estimated seventy to eighty captives died in the containers and were buried in the desert.

There were soon allegations of the deliberate slaughter of hundreds or even thousands of prisoners by Dostum's men. Lurid tales metastasized of captives licking the sweat off each other's bodies to prevent dehydration and gnawing at each other's limbs from starvation or delirium. The story of "the convoy of death" became a permanent stain on Dostum's reputation.

* * *

The last thing David Tyson did in Mazar-i Sharif was visit the home of his dead friend Amanullah. Speaking in Uzbek, he lauded Amanullah's bravery and selflessness, his humane treatment of prisoners, and his kindness. He explained why he and Team Alpha had come to Afghanistan—to fight the oppression of the Taliban and Al-Qaeda and prevent another attack like 9/11. With a few dozen Americans and

Dostum's surrounded forces, they had achieved what hardly anyone had thought possible. David admired and respected Afghans, and the intense relationships he had formed with men like Amanullah had enriched his life. Americans were now united with Afghans in victory, and also loss. By the time he had finished, tears streamed down David's cheeks.

At K2, David went through the formalities of identifying the remains of Mike Spann. He then returned to Tashkent with station chief Charlie Gilbert, while Alex accompanied Mike's body onward to Germany. David—still wearing his guppi, with his Browning Hi-Power pistol strapped to his waist—told Gilbert, "I just want to get home."

In Tashkent, David was met by his wife, Rosann, and children, Kara and Mark. He had been silent on the flight from K2, and to Rosann it was as if her husband was a zombie. Gilbert attempted to get David to give up his pistol at K2 and tried again at the airport in Tashkent. "We're here now," the station chief soothed. "You don't need it." David knew he was not being rational, but this was the weapon that had saved his life. "I just don't want to give up my pistol," he said, like a small boy. They compromised by David agreeing to give Gilbert the magazine. That night, David slept with the Browning under his pillow. He carried the pistol everywhere for several days, even as a semblance of his normal life returned.

David had also become attached to his old leather boots, which he had worn nonstop for forty-three days in Afghanistan. Whereas the rest of Team Alpha had been outfitted at CIA headquarters, David had made do with what he could muster in Tashkent. The boots—a pair of Deer Stags, made for leisure—had become so beaten up that Mike had joked they looked like the footwear of his great-grandfather, an impoverished Alabama sharecropper. They'd seen David through the Darya Suf Valley, however, and when he had fought and run for his life inside Qala-i Jangi. When he got back to Tashkent, his son, Mark, dubbed them "Dad's lucky boots."

20

NO SECRETS

11:15 a.m. (GMT +1), December 1, 2001
Landstuhl Army Regional Medical Center, Germany

THE FIRST PURPLE HEARTS of the war in Afghanistan were awarded to victims of friendly fire. Less than a week after they had been hit by a US Marine Corps JDAM on the morning after the uprising began at Qala-i Jangi, the four Green Berets in the air-strike team were called forward to receive their medals. "They paid a price in blood here," the officiating general declared to the TV cameras. "They have given their blood in the war against terrorism." Purple Hearts for those killed or wounded in action would soon be almost commonplace. Over the next sixteen years, more than 57,000 troops would receive them.

Captain Paul Syverson, Captain Kevin Leahy, Master Sergeant Dave Betz, and Sergeant First Class Paul Beck wore desert fatigues with no insignia and were allowed to give only ranks and first names. Staff Sergeant Mike Sciortino, the air controller who was the fifth member of the team, had opted to receive his medal in the US, but attended the ceremony. The Pentagon seized the opportunity to publicize their heroics, holding a press conference afterward. Leahy, still on crutches, was barely well enough to talk and did not face the media. He had regained consciousness only after being flown to Incirlik Air Base in Turkey. Betz—Ol' Sarge—excused himself from the press conference because his ears were ringing. Syverson, Beck, and Sciortino were booked for national TV appearances.

Syverson, with shrapnel grazes and yellow bruising around his left eye, came across as an exemplar of the modern Green Beret. "We had a job to do," he said. "We went and did it. We all know that there's a cost associated with our job." He then mused about where the war in Afghanistan might fit in American military history: "But when you think of what those guys did at D-Day, storming the beaches, when you think of [how] the Marines suffered at Khe Sanh—we think about it. Are we as deserving as them?"

The events of 9/11 were still raw. "The president said from the start that there's going to be a cost involved in this war against terrorism," Syverson said. "Fortunately, we're going to recover from our injuries. Hopefully, we'll be back there in the fight. We need to eradicate terrorists and the organizations and the governments that sponsor terrorists—bottom line." The sacrifice of ordinary Americans on 9/11, they all stressed, eclipsed everything since. "Personally, the thousands of people who from seventy different nations died unexpectedly on September 11, I think they are more deserving," remarked Beck. Sciortino said, "I see the Americans being the heroes. The firefighters, the policemen, and the people all going back to work. Those are the heroes too."

In another part of Landstuhl, a military pathologist performed an autopsy on Mike Spann's remains. She identified the cause of his death as two gunshot wounds to the head "resulting in severe, rapidly fatal injury to the brain." One was a contact wound, indicating a gun had been held to Mike's right temple and a bullet fired through his head, exiting on the left. The other was "intermediate range," meaning that the shot had been fired close enough to the head to leave powder marks; it had entered the right side of his forehead and exited from the back. There were no broken bones or marks to the knuckles to indicate Mike had been able to resist. His back had been peppered with shrapnel after death, probably from JDAM explosions or fire from the AC-130 Spectres. The pathologist noted: "Graze wounds and shrapnel injuries occurring during life are identified on the decedent's arms and legs and right lower back." The grazes were consistent with the struggle witnessed by the two doctors in the fort. Shrapnel injuries could have been caused by bullet fragments—one of the bullets that killed Mike disintegrated on impact—or a grenade. It was a sentence, however, that would prompt Mike's father, Johnny, to cling to the notion that his son might not have been killed immediately.

Alex Hernandez accompanied Mike's body from neighboring Ramstein air base on its final leg home. Their journey was in a forty-five-seat US government Boeing 757-200 jet normally assigned as Vice President Dick Cheney's Air Force Two. George Tenet, the CIA director, had been in Islamabad meeting with President Pervez Musharraf of Pakistan to discuss intelligence about potential follow-up Al-Qaeda attacks on the United States. On his return, Tenet had diverted the plane to Ramstein so it could transport Mike's flag-draped casket, which was placed in an open conference area in the center of the aircraft. The chief of the CIA's Ground Branch, whose assistant on 9/11 had been Mike, was also on board. En route to Washington, DC, Alex related the story of Team Alpha's mission to the two senior CIA officers.

The 757 touched down at Andrews Air Force Base, just outside Washington, DC, on the cold, gray Sunday afternoon of December 2. Shannon Spann; her baby son, Jake; and Mike's daughters, Alison and Emily, boarded the plane for a few private moments. Reporters and television cameras recorded the scene as a six-man Marine Corps honor guard carried Mike's casket to a hearse. Before landing, Tenet had leaned over to the Team Alpha deputy and said, "Hey, Alex, I hate to tell you this, but you're still undercover, and they have a ceremony planned. So I need to ask you to stay on the plane and let us all go off."

While a band played "Amazing Grace," a car drove around the far side of the plane. Alone, Alex descended a separate set of stairs and stepped into a waiting car. At CIA headquarters the next day, Tenet told Alex that Shannon had asked to meet with him to learn more about how Mike had died. "Be candid," the CIA director said. "No secrets."

After Robert Young Pelton's interview with a bedraggled John Walker Lindh had aired on CNN and with Mike Spann's funeral about to be held, the media had fixated on these two very different Americans. The patriot and the traitor, Christian and Muslim—they had become totems of a culture clash between opposing sides in the War on Terror. Later in the week, footage of the CIA officer confronting the Californian jihadist outside the Pink House, shot by Dostum's videographer, was broadcast after it had been sold to a journalist in Mazar-i Sharif. The cinematic scene in the fort ensured that the fates of the two men would forever be entwined. "HERO vs RAT," blared the *New York Post,* which prided itself as the beating heart of the city that had been hit on 9/11.

The two men's life stories were used to fuel a narrative of muscular, small-town conservatism versus effete coastal liberalism—two diametric worlds existing within one country. For some, Mike came to symbolize Bush's America after 9/11—a return to values of service and sacrifice forged by tragedy—while Lindh represented the naivete and permissiveness of Clinton's America before 9/11.

Mike hailed from the fourth generation of a resolutely traditional, Republican family in Alabama. Lindh had grown up in Marin County, across the Golden Gate Bridge from San Francisco, a left-wing enclave in California. Lindh's father, Frank, a former social worker turned wealthy corporate lawyer, had left the family home to live with another man. His son, who was seventeen at the time and had converted to Islam a year earlier, dropped his father's last name and began calling himself John Walker. Shedding and assuming one identity after another, he became Sulayman al-Faris and then Abdul Hamid, the name he used in Afghanistan. Online he went from potty-talk handles such as Hine E. Craque and Doodoo to such sobriquets as Disciple of the Englober, Professor J, John Doe, Brother Suleyman Al-Mujahid, and Mr. Mujahid.

Frank Lindh and John's mother, Marilyn Walker—a photographer who practiced Buddhism and had dabbled in Native American rituals—had supported their son at every turn. They had embraced his religious conversion, allowed him to drop out of school, and, a year later, blessed and funded his solo studies in Arabic and Islam in Yemen and Pakistan, both hotbeds of virulent anti-Western sentiment. Now, he was in US military custody. His parents declined to condemn their son's decision to take up arms on behalf of the Taliban, a regime widely known to have publicly stoned homosexuals, shot women for adultery, and chopped off the hands of thieves.

Although some tried to portray John Walker Lindh as the epitome of California liberalism, in fact he had wholeheartedly rejected it, turning against the almost unfettered tolerance of his parents. He had not spoken to his mother or father for seven months before the evening they saw his blackened, bearded face on television, just as he was arriving at the Turkish school.

*　　*　　*

John Walker Lindh had been a sickly and solitary child who never adjusted after his parents moved from the Washington, DC, suburbs to California when he was ten. He changed schools several times and was tutored at home before ending up at Tamiscal, a progressive high school that held no classes; instead, students attended one-on-one meetings with teachers.

Left to his own devices at age fourteen, he turned to the internet— then in its infancy—and developed an obsessive interest in hip-hop and rap. In one posting, he pretended to be black, mocking "Marin County Caucasians." He even chastised a youth who was black, telling him, "When I read those rhymes of yours I got the idea you were some thirteen-year-old white kid playing smart…Our blackness does not make white people hate us; it is THEIR racism that causes the hate."

Islam soon replaced hip-hop as Lindh's focus—and he approached this new religion with a similar severity and intolerance. He denounced "kaffir [Arabic for "unbeliever"] Zionist owned media outlets" and responded with vitriol to a gay Muslim, telling him that if he rejected the Koran's teachings "to follow your own desires, you are a kaffir and have no claim to Islam." He sought an Islam he considered "pure," and began to wear flowing robes and a turban.

In June 1998, shortly after his seventeenth birthday, Lindh left home, with his parents' blessing, to study Arabic in Sanaa, the capital of Yemen. While there, he embraced anti-American conspiracy theories, writing to his mother that the August 1998 bombings by Al-Qaeda of the US embassies in Kenya and Tanzania were "far more likely to have been carried out by the American government than by any Muslims." He later stated in an email that Saddam Hussein had been "heavily encouraged" by an American official to invade Kuwait in 1990. At the Yemen Language Center, Lindh complained that women were in his classes. Fellow students, mocking his zealotry, nicknamed him Yusuf Islam, after the singer Cat Stevens, who took that name after converting to Islam. Lindh's parents had paid $3,000 for him to attend the center, but he dropped out to attend a fundamentalist Salafi mosque, the Ahl El Kheir, which modeled a version of Islam more to his liking. Next, he studied at the conservative Jami'at al-Iman, or University of Faith, where he met men who had waged jihad in Afghanistan.

After four months in Yemen, Lindh wrote home that he was "not particularly fond of the idea of returning to America," but in April 1999 his visa expired and he flew back to California. He resented being back in the US and headed to Yemen once more in February 2000. He told his mother she should move to England, adding: "I really don't know what your big attachement [sic] to America is all about. What has America ever done for anybody?"

Lindh traveled to Pakistan in October 2000 to continue his Islamic studies—this time at the Madrassa-e-Arabia near Bannu, a town 165 miles southwest of Islamabad. It was the same month that Al-Qaeda attacked the USS *Cole* in Aden, 240 miles south of Sanaa. In emails, Lindh had argued with his father about the attack, justifying it because the very presence of the American ship constituted "an act of war."

Seven months later, Lindh left the madrassa, equivocating about what he planned to do next. He told his parents only that he wanted to go to "some cold mountainous region"—and asked them for money. Frank Lindh wired $1,200 to pay for the next step in his son's quest. On his last day in Bannu in May 2001, John Walker Lindh left a parting note in Arabic in the headmaster's diary, "This is Sulayman al-Faris, from Americastan, who learned seven sections of the Quran." By now, his antipathy toward the United States was plain. In his last emails home, he wrote that "I don't really want to see America again" and life in Pakistan "really makes me look upon American society with pity."

Lindh had been vague with his parents, but he had a specific destination and goal: Peshawar—the largest majority-Pashtun city in Pakistan, just east of the Afghanistan border—and training for jihad. In Peshawar, he went to a recruiting center for Harakat ul-Mujahideen (HUM), a radical Islamist group, and then a training camp near the border with Kashmir, where fighters were battling Indian forces. Lindh underwent twenty days of guerrilla training, including with firearms. Next, he traveled through the Khyber Pass into Afghanistan itself. In Taliban-controlled Kabul, HUM decided Lindh needed training with "the Arab group" before he would be ready for front-line duty against the Northern Alliance. Three months before 9/11, Lindh was among a group of mostly Saudis who arrived at Al-Qaeda's Al Farouq training camp near Kandahar.

The Californian spent June and July 2001 at Al Farouq, receiving instruction in battlefield tactics and the use of weapons and explosives. Osama bin Laden visited the camp three times during this period and on one occasion Lindh and four others were granted an audience with the Al-Qaeda founder, speaking with him for about five minutes.

As Lindh's training drew to a close, Abu Mohammad Al-Masri, an Egyptian senior Al-Qaeda planner, asked him if he wanted to be sent to attack the United States or Israel. Lindh declined, saying that he would prefer to fight inside Afghanistan. The American was transported back to Kabul, where he was issued an AKM rifle, before being ferried to the front lines of Takhar province in July or August of 2001.

Lindh was now part of a band of some 150 fighters, divided

into platoons of twenty-five and operating in shifts against Northern Alliance troops. These Al-Qaeda combatants were rotated out of the front lines every other week. Lindh learned of the 9/11 attacks in the days afterward—he had admitted that to the *Newsweek* reporter—but chose to continue fighting alongside the Taliban forces. He wanted to be part of Al-Qaeda's Brigade 055, even with the knowledge that their Al-Qaeda comrades had slaughtered thousands of innocents under bin Laden. Lindh had found the 7th-century brand of Islam he had yearned for and was waging jihad against the infidels he despised.

Frank Lindh hired James Brosnahan, a top US trial lawyer, and depicted his son as a "decent and honorable" young man pursuing a "spiritual quest" who had never heard of Al-Qaeda. "It was youthful, it was idealistic, it came from a good place," he said later. "It came from a desire to be helpful, to defend innocent people."

*   *   *

While John Walker Lindh was at the Turkish school and his parents and new lawyer were building his defense in California, the military campaign in Afghanistan was reaching its crescendo. With victory in the north and Kabul buttressed by the Kunduz surrender and the failure of Fazl's gambit at Qala-i Jangi, attention had moved to the south and America's principal foe—Osama bin Laden.

United States–led negotiations about the future of Afghanistan had begun in Bonn on November 25, the day Mike Spann had been killed. The Taliban was excluded from the talks, which Mullah Omar vehemently denounced. On December 5, Hamid Karzai, a Pashtun, was declared the country's new president. Three Tajiks from the Northern Alliance would take the top ministries of foreign, defense, and interior. Fahim Khan, whose own reluctance to fight had so frustrated the CIA and Pentagon, was to be defense minister. Dostum, who believed he had been promised the foreign ministry, was apoplectic, declaring: "This is a humiliation for us." Out of twenty-nine government portfolios, the

Uzbeks—whose capture of Mazar-i Sharif on November 9 was the turning point in the campaign—were allotted only agriculture, industry, and mining. So soon after courting him, the US government had decided that while Dostum was the ideal ally to fight a war, he should be kept at arm's length during peace.

For all his obvious flaws, Dostum had come to be revered by Team Alpha and the Green Berets. When Zalmay Khalilzad, an Afghan-American, took over as the Bush administration's envoy to Afghanistan the following month, he met with some of the Green Berets in Mazar-i Sharif. One of the soldiers ventured that the United States should have installed Dostum as president. To Khalilzad, a Pashtun born in Mazar-i Sharif, the notion was preposterous. Rich Blee, the former Alec station chief had become the CIA's chief of Kabul station; he, too, was a Dostum skeptic.

On the day Karzai—America's choice—was named president, a US bomb almost killed him. It had been three weeks since he had been joined in Afghanistan by the CIA's Team Echo and ODA 574. Now, he was in Tarin Kot, north of Kandahar. The town had rebelled against the Taliban on November 17, and Karzai was fighting remnants of the regime with the support of Pashtuns who had rejected Islamic fundamentalism.

In an uncanny repeat of the catastrophe at Qala-i Jangi on November 26, an American B-52 dropped a 2,000-pound JDAM on a US position at Tarin Kot, where Green Berets and the CIA were with Karzai. Aware of what had happened at the fort, the air controller had refused to pass up the friendly coordinates. Unfortunately, the controller had just changed batteries and tested his Viper laser binoculars by pointing them at the ground right in front of him to get coordinates. He did not realize that the Viper had automatically stored those coordinates, and they had been passed up to the B-52.

The 2,000-pound JDAM landed where the coordinates directed it, killing three Green Berets and an estimated fifty Northern Alliance fighters. Greg Vogle, leader of the CIA's Team Echo, flung himself on top of Karzai, who escaped with only cuts and bruises to his face.

Shortly after the Bonn conference, Karzai negotiated a truce with the Taliban that offered the defeated group's fighters safe passage from Kandahar in return for surrendering their weapons to Mullah Naqibullah, a Pashtun former mujahideen commander. The Taliban leader Mullah Omar would be allowed to live in Kandahar under Najibullah's protection if he renounced terrorism. The Bush administration, however, opposed the deal. Donald Rumsfeld, the US defense secretary, rejected it out of hand, stating that "if our goals are frustrated and opposed, we would prefer to work with other people"—a thinly veiled threat to Karzai. The White House said that "those who harbor terrorists need to be brought to justice," emphasizing that this included Mullah Omar. The US government had conflated the Taliban and Al-Qaeda. Although the two groups were certainly allies, the Taliban was deeply divided over Osama bin Laden's presence in their country—a split that Pashtun-oriented officers in the CIA like Robert Grenier, the Islamabad station chief, sought to exploit.

In victory, however, the Bush administration wanted no reconciliation with the Taliban movement, even though this fulfilled the Pashtun practice of *nanawatai*—offering sanctuary to defeated enemies. The model of small numbers of CIA and Green Beret advisors, epitomized by Team Alpha and ODA 595, was being abandoned. Instead of fostering an Afghan solution, the United States switched to imposing an American one. There had been no US invasion of Afghanistan, but one was about to begin as the NATO International Security Assistance Force (ISAF) was established in Kabul and huge American bases built at Bagram and Kandahar. To even moderate Afghans, this looked like a foreign occupation; a nationalist backlash was inevitable. Although the US government and its allies among the exile community favored a centralized regime, most Afghan hands, including J.R. and David, advocated a decentralized one. The deal was jettisoned; it might have failed or been a ruse by Omar, but nearly two decades later some CIA officers regarded it as a lost opportunity to avoid the US fighting and losing a guerilla war, just as the Soviets had done.

*　　*　　*

On December 7, John Walker Lindh was about to be transferred to Camp Rhino, a new US base outside Kandahar, after six days in the Turkish school. He had been carried in on a stretcher; now, he was able to walk on his own. Green Berets from ODA 592 bound his wrists and blindfolded him as a C-130 cargo plane waited at the Mazar-i Sharif airfield. A soldier wrote SHIT HEAD on a piece of duct tape and stuck it on Lindh's blindfold. Five members of the ODA then posed with him for a "team photo." Almost immediately the Green Berets realized the photo was a mistake and tried to delete it. But the incriminating image had already been loaded onto a hard drive and was to be discovered during Lindh's legal case the following year.

Lindh arrived at Camp Rhino on the day Kandahar fell to the Northern Alliance, signaling the end of the Taliban regime. The camp was a remote landing strip in the Registan Desert that had been seized by the US Marines on November 25 and turned into a forward operating base for the assault on Kandahar, ninety miles northeast. Camp Rhino had no washing facilities, and the only food was MREs. All water used in the camp had to be flown in, and the troops operating there slept on the ground in a large, open warehouse building. Chocolate-colored dust filled the air, causing troops to hack up brown phlegm, and Camp Rhino experienced three helicopter accidents amid the brownout conditions.

When Lindh arrived, he was stripped naked, strapped to a stretcher, and placed in a shipping container. As at the Turkish school, Lindh was an object of curiosity and derision at Camp Rhino; at least one photograph of him was taken when he was first put in the container. The weather was warm in the day and chilly—though not freezing— at night, and when Lindh needed to urinate, the stretcher was simply propped up. A few hours after his arrival, Lindh was given a blanket; two days later he was clothed in medical scrubs.

A Marine Corps photograph of Lindh on the stretcher at Camp

Rhino later prompted accusations of torture by his lawyers and an outcry from human-rights groups. Green Berets and Marines argued that the conditions they experienced in the Turkish school and Camp Rhino were worse than anything the Californian endured. It could not be refuted that Lindh was better fed by the Americans than he had been as an Al-Qaeda fighter, or that he had chosen to be in Afghanistan, an austere and dangerous country. But the treatment of Lindh by the American troops underscored how ill-prepared the United States was to deal with prisoners.

At Camp Rhino, Lindh confessed to the FBI that he had learned at Al Farouq during the summer of 2001 that suicide attackers had been dispatched to the United States. That had turned out to be 9/11, which Lindh claimed was the first in three phases of Al-Qaeda attacks against America. Phase two would be a biological weapons strike at the end of the Muslim holy month of Ramadan in mid-December. Phase three, Lindh said, would "finish the United States." The FBI put little stock in the details of Lindh's tale; agents did not view him as a terrorist mastermind or believe that he had known anything specific about the 9/11 plan. But his statements ran counter to his later insistence that he had not heard of Al-Qaeda and was interested only in fighting the Northern Alliance.

Lindh was now on an odyssey that would take him from Camp Rhino to the amphibious assault ships USS *Peleliu* and USS *Bataan,* both in the Arabian Sea, and a military base in Pakistan. From there, he was flown in a C-17 transport plane to Dulles International Airport outside Washington, DC. At the airport, a helicopter waited to fly him on the short trip to Alexandria Detention Center, eight miles from the Pentagon, which was still scarred by a blackened chasm where American Airlines Flight 77 had hit on 9/11, killing 125 people in the building and 64 on board.

*   *   *

A horse-drawn caisson, accompanied by a Marine honor guard in dress blues and the sound of clopping hooves and a snare drum, carried Mike Spann's casket through Arlington National Cemetery. It was 1:15 p.m. on December 10, the eve of the three-month anniversary of 9/11. Amid the leafless trees and white marble headstones stretching into the distance, the caisson halted before grave number 2359 in Section 34.

Mike had visited the cemetery with Shannon and his daughters less than seven months earlier. It was the fitting place, Shannon had decided, for her husband to be laid to rest. Initially, the Pentagon had resisted, arguing that Mike did not meet the criteria because he had not been killed in action while on active duty in the military. A swift series of calls between CIA headquarters, the Pentagon, and the White House cut through the bureaucracy.

Less than a mile from the grave site, the damaged western side of the Pentagon faced the cemetery. Mike's resting place would be in American soil, on a slope bounded by pathways named after his hero, Ulysses S. Grant—a president, and a Union general in the Civil War—and General John Pershing, commander of American forces on the Western Front in World War I. Inside the casket lay a note from Mike's nine-year-old daughter, Alison: "Thank you, Daddy, for making the world a better place. I love you. Everybody's so proud of you—especially me."

Among the nearly 150 mourners were senior CIA officers, including George Tenet, CTC director Cofer Black, and Hank Crumpton, as well as classmates of Mike and Shannon, many of them in disguise to keep their cover intact. Despite it being an overcast December day, there was a profusion of sunglasses, as well as an unusual number of hats. The night before, cars with Russian diplomatic plates had been parked outside the funeral home that hosted Mike's wake, their occupants photographing everyone who arrived and left. For the funeral, Amy wore a long red wig.

As the minister told those gathered that Mike had been "fully committed to his God, his family, and his nation," David Tyson stood grim-faced behind Black. Alex, Scott, Andy, and Justin were also present. Johnny Spann held his wide-awake grandson, Jake, as Shannon prepared to speak. She had finalized her eulogy in Amy's apartment the night before, alone almost for the first time since Mike's death. She had not thought about the media covering the funeral until she looked beyond the casket and saw a wall of press. Even then, she imagined only a few articles and photographs. In fact, the funeral was broadcast live on television.

Her voice quavering only slightly, Shannon told how her heart "broke when it fell to the ground two Sundays ago in a place really far from here." She went on, "I want to tell you that my husband is a hero. But Mike is a hero not because of the way that he died, but rather because of the way that he lived. Mike was prepared to give his life in Afghanistan, because he already gave his life every day to us at home." Her husband had been "in the right place at the right time, doing the right thing in a way that he understood it was his life to do," and if he were alive, he "would ask for all of us to be strong." Above the roar of a plane taking off from nearby Ronald Reagan Washington National Airport, she blew a kiss and closed with the Marine Corps motto: "Semper Fi, my love."

A Marine officer presented Shannon with a United States flag, folded into a triangle. Then seven Marines raised their rifles to fire a twenty-one-gun salute to America's first casualty in Afghanistan.

*   *   *

In the days leading up to the funeral, Shannon had felt as if she was wrapped in a dense fog. It did not occur to her, however, to let anyone else give the eulogy. She had been with Mike for such a short period—speaking at his graveside would be a brief extension of the time she had to represent him as his wife.

Shannon and Mike's friend Amy had run interference for Shannon on every issue—cajoling senior CIA officers, overseeing funeral arrangements, deciding who could speak to her. The day after the announcement that Mike had been in the CIA, it had been reported that Shannon was also an Agency officer. Now, Shannon was besieged by the press, forced to mourn in a media glare. Amy purchased plane tickets for herself, Shannon and her sister, and Jake to fly east from Los Angeles. Since 9/11, when none of the nineteen Al-Qaeda hijackers had been searched before boarding, airport security had become oppressively stringent, with long lines and random screening. As Shannon went through metal detectors at Los Angeles International Airport, struggling with a baby and a stroller, alarms sounded and she was pulled aside. "This is clearly a mom of an infant who is probably not a terrorist," thought Amy, seething at the hard time her friend was being given. On the far side of the checkpoint a supervisor sat reading a newspaper, Shannon's photo on its front page. Amy found herself wanting to scream, "Hey! This is her! Can you not be an asshole?"

At CIA headquarters, one senior Agency officer mistook Amy for Shannon and showered the wrong person with condolences before being corrected. Shannon was gracious, and the senior officer recovered, asking if there was anything he could do for her. When Shannon demurred, Amy interjected, "Well, actually, there is something: we need grocery money." The senior officer opened his wallet and pulled out $400 in cash.

The CIA had no procedures for handling the death of an officer. Amy was told that she could not be reimbursed for all the plane tickets from Los Angeles, and that the ticket cost for Shannon's sister would be coming out of her pocket. "If you are actually going to make a GS-9 pay over $1,000 for a plane ticket to bring a widow's sister back, then I'm ashamed to be an Agency officer," Amy responded. Down the hall, she explained the situation to Frank Archibald, the former Marine who had ripped out the fire-alarm wires in the CTC meeting. "That's a bunch of bullshit," he said. "I will fix this now." Five minutes later, Archibald handed her a container with more than $1,000 in it, donated by CIA staff.

When Shannon met the surviving Team Alpha members, she found herself reassuring them. They seemed extremely nervous about speaking to her, as if she might blame them for living when Mike had died. Such a thought never entered Shannon's head. She was a CIA officer who knew that her husband and their colleagues had been operating on the edge, where every situation was fraught with uncertainty and risk.

Scott and Andy sat down with Shannon, bouncing Jake on her knee, and did their best to talk about the jokes and the goofy moments they had shared with Mike during their forty days together in Afghanistan. They described how they had argued about the moon with the Afghans, who could not believe it was thousands of miles away, or big enough for a man to walk on. In the Darya Suf Valley the Afghans had laughed at how stupid the younger Americans on Team Alpha were, because they were unable to speak Dari when even the smallest child could. Scott and Andy were close in age to Mike and both were married and had young families that were expanding. As CIA paramilitaries in the post-9/11 era, they sensed there would soon be more funerals, perhaps their own. Seeing Shannon in such pain was so gut-wrenching that Andy found himself thinking, "I'd rather get shot at."

Before the funeral, Shannon had met Alex in a diner near CIA headquarters and comforted the hardened Special Forces and Agency paramilitary veteran as he wept for Mike. She was concerned, she told him, that Mike's father, Johnny, believed Mike might have initially survived the uprising, only to be killed by an American air strike. Alex visited Johnny Spann in his hotel, where he was surrounded by relatives. The CIA man gave him an unvarnished account of what had happened, including David's recollections and a description of where Mike's body was found. "I respect you coming here and telling us this," Johnny Spann said. "But I don't believe a damn word you said."

Hank Crumpton made sure he had a box of tissues on hand and steeled himself when Shannon came to see him in CTC/SO. But she was not seeking sympathy. "Mike died fighting," she told Crumpton. "Mike died doing exactly what he wanted. I am so proud of him. This mission is so important. You cannot waver. You must finish the job. You must not relent. Mike would want that." Crumpton briefed her on the fall of Kandahar and how the Taliban and Al-Qaeda leadership was fleeing to Pakistan. She thanked him for leading the CIA teams that had been the vanguard of the war in Afghanistan. After Shannon left, Crumpton sat alone for several minutes, humbled by the fortitude of the young widow and CIA officer.

Mike's death had dampened any sense of jubilation the men might have felt over the success of their mission. After they had picked up gear in Tashkent, Justin and Mark flew back to Washington. At Heathrow airport, they were pulled aside by security when they drew the attention of a sniffer dog that had picked up explosives residue—from the dust on Justin's backpack. "What's this?" the guard asked, holding up Justin's Garmin GPS. "And where are you coming from?" He replied, "It's a camping GPS—we're coming from Central Asia." She smiled. "All you commandos are coming through here now," she said cheerily, waving him through.

Justin was still eager to fight—after having upset his Florida girl-friend by telling her where he was only when he got to Dostum's command post at Cobaki, he had one fewer thing to keep him on US soil. So he volunteered to return to Afghanistan almost immediately on a new team, this time in the Kandahar region. The CIA did not have enough paramilitary officers to form its teams, so more and more Green Berets were being assigned to them. At CIA headquarters, Justin bumped into Sergeant First Class Nathan Chapman, a medic and communications specialist, who was joining Team Hotel, destined for Khost in eastern Afghanistan, right by the Pakistan border. They had both completed dive school at Key West, and Chapman was keen to hear about Afghanistan. On January 4, Chapman would become the first American soldier killed by enemy fire in Afghanistan when three men with Kalashnikovs ambushed his Team Hotel convoy at Khost. A CIA paramilitary officer was hit twice in the chest and survived, but the Green Beret bled to death from a wound to his femoral artery.

The second-guessing of actions taken at Qala-i Jangi soon began. Justin was accosted in the Agency cafeteria by an old colleague of his father's, who said: "What the hell were they doing going in there by themselves?" Similar flak came from some in the Army. A Special Forces major told Justin that Mike and David had been "pretty stupid" on November 25. Justin felt a flash of anger. "I understand that sitting here in the operations center with your cup of coffee, it's easy to say that," he said. "But here's the deal: at the time, we couldn't wait."

On the eve of the funeral, a young CIA officer who had been close to Mike and was serving at headquarters had called Justin. "I just want to ask you a question," the officer said. "What do you think the chances are that Dave's account is true?" Justin cut off the line of inquiry. "Look," he said. "He's the only guy who survived, and you either believe him or not. It's like when you come to a cabin a month after a blizzard and there's only one person left alive. Only he can tell the story. But I spoke to Dave the day it happened, and I believe him. Why would he lie? He's not the type to inflate things or embellish war stories." In Tashkent station during the Qala-i Jangi uprising, legendary CIA paramilitary Billy Waugh—en route to Afghanistan—had told Charlie Gilbert, David's boss, that no Agency officer could have performed better in the fort than David had. But, Waugh added, "people are going to criticize him."

*　　*　　*

Back at the Turkish school, one of the final and most painful tasks had fallen to Glenn, who had offered to sort through Mike's possessions and box them up so they could be sent home to Shannon. That involved reading his notebook to ensure that nothing classified would be divulged about Team Alpha's mission. Glenn choked up as he read a letter that Mike had been composing to Jake. In it, Mike had described finding a mouse in the Turkish school; he was surreptitiously feeding it and had adopted the creature as a pet.

As soon as he read the letter, Glenn, with young children of his own, decided he must get a photograph of a mouse to send back to Shannon so she could keep it for Jake. Glenn crawled around the floor for nearly thirty minutes until he cornered one behind the CIA radio equipment and got the picture. When the new team arrived, Glenn discovered an incoming CIA officer had placed mousetraps all over the fifth floor. Glenn exploded. "You will not kill that fucking mouse!" he screamed, then gathered the traps and threw them out of the window. The time had come, Glenn realized, for him to leave Afghanistan.

21

TOMORROWLAND

5 p.m. (GMT -5), December 29, 2001;
Magic Kingdom, Orlando, Florida

A MONTH AFTER HE had last set foot in Qala-i Jangi, David
Tyson found himself celebrating his daughter Kara's twelfth birthday
in Cinderella Castle. After Mike Spann's funeral, the Tyson family
traveled to Disney World in Orlando, Florida. It was only then that
eight-year-old Mark Tyson realized something was wrong: vacations
usually meant hiking or staying in the woods, and he knew his father
could not abide Disney. David and Rosann, however, had decided to try
something completely different to distract everyone.

For more than a week, the Tysons spent time strolling down Main
Street USA and through Tomorrowland. They rode on Space Moun-
tain and the Magic Carpets of Aladdin, and watched the Christmas
Fantasy Follies. The resort was thronged with tourists who had followed
President Bush's advice on boosting the economy after 9/11: "Fly and
enjoy America's great destination spots. Get down to Disney World in
Florida." Years later, David could barely remember a single moment
of the trip.

Before Disney World, David and Rosann had sat down with Kara
and Mark in Tashkent and told them that their father worked for the
CIA. With TV footage of David in Qala-i Jangi, and a photograph on

303

the front page of the *New York Times* of him clutching a Kalashnikov, they had little option. Mark thought the whole thing was pretty cool, but didn't dwell on it much more. Kara felt betrayed that her father had told her he was going to Tajikistan. "You lied to me," she said.

A few months after Disney World, the Tysons visited Dubai—another break from family tradition—because Kara and Mark wanted to shop at the mall there, a far cry from from Uzbekistan. Checking into their hotel, David hurriedly ushered Rosann and the children behind a huge decorative pillar in the opulent lobby. "You need to stand here while I check in," he told them. "Don't move." For a moment, Rosann wondered if her husband was worried about cultural sensitivity, because her blond hair was uncovered in a Muslim country. Or perhaps he was just being cheap, hiding the kids to avoid paying extra for the room. Then she realized he was hypervigilant about their protection: the pillar could shield them from a terrorist attack.

One day, the family went to a Baskin-Robbins in the Dubai Mall to get ice cream, which David often joked was his main vice because he didn't drink. As David sat in a corner facing the door—a position almost second nature to a CIA operative—he watched a group of Saudi Arabian men enter, wearing white thawb robes and red-and-white keffiyeh headdresses. Suddenly consumed by dread, David instructed Rosann and the children to leave. His bemused family traipsed out as David sat there, transfixed by fear. Melting ice cream ran down David's hand as he waited for the Saudis to leave. "They're going to kill me," he thought. "They know that I'm the guy who shot their brothers."

On a Pakistan International Airlines flight from Karachi in 2003, David found himself sitting next to an Arab man who he sensed was staring at him. David felt sure the man was about to lunge over and try to kill him. When the Arab made his move, David resolved, he would use his thumbs to gouge out his assailant's eyeballs. David sat rigidly the rest of the flight, thumbs ready. The same year, David was walking down a street in Turkey when he saw children lobbing small rubber balls at each other from street-level windows. One of the balls came close to him and he froze. Transported back to the Pink House on November 25, 2001, he recalled, for the first time, the two grenades looping out the window and bouncing off him without exploding.

The CIA flew a psychologist to Tashkent to talk to David. One of the things that haunted the CIA officer was his absent memory of parts of those life-defining eleven minutes. He yearned to view what he called "God's video" of what happened. "It's been deleted or scratched in the hard drive," the psychologist told him, explaining that the brain's response to trauma is often to block some things out. David created more than a dozen scrapbooks about Afghanistan from 9/11 onward, painstakingly pasting in newspaper and magazine articles, computer printouts, photographs, and maps, adding captions in ballpoint pen. Documenting everything he could and trying to create some sort of order from his chaotic, fragmented memories became an obsession.

On the psychologist's advice, David took opportunities to talk to close friends and colleagues about Team Alpha's experiences and what had transpired in Qala-i Jangi. As the years went on, he developed a presentation for CIA recruits on how to keep a situation from spiraling out of control—and how to cope when it did.

David remained stationed in Central Asia until 2009; that insulated him from the Monday-morning quarterbacking about whether he had been reckless. He served out his second tour in Tashkent, continuing to work regularly in Afghanistan, sometimes debriefing prisoners who recognized him from footage shot in Qala-i Jangi. The FBI contacted David whenever a new jihadi video in Urdu or Arabic appeared, featuring images of him and calling for his death. After Tashkent, David became CIA station chief in Ashgabat, Turkmenistan, before taking on the same role in the larger station of Baku, Azerbaijan, where he worked against Russian and Iranian targets. Rather than pursuing station chief positions in larger, more coveted capitals such as Prague or Vienna, David opted to develop his skills as a deep specialist in the CIA. He shunned bureaucratic roles in favor of assignments that allowed him to use his languages and meet assets in the field. In 2010, David was on a secret mission overseas as part of the FBI operation that led to the arrest of ten Russian sleeper agents in the United States.

* * *

On the day of Mike Spann's funeral, Osama bin Laden and 2,000 of his Al-Qaeda fighters were in Tora Bora—literally, "Black Dust"—a complex of caves and tunnels in the mountains of eastern Afghanistan near the Pakistan border. In Kabul, the CIA's Gary Berntsen, Gary Schroen's replacement as Jawbreaker commander, had almost screamed over the phone at Crumpton to get conventional US troops into the area to prevent the Al-Qaeda leader's escape. The head of the CIA's Team Juliet, in Jalalabad, had reported to Berntsen that the Northern Alliance men with him could not be trusted to do the job. During a White House meeting, Crumpton urged General Tommy Franks to send in forces, to no avail, then turned to President Bush, telling him: "We're going to lose our prey if we're not careful."

This time, Bush sided with the Pentagon, deferring to Rumsfeld and Franks, who both believed that the lesson of the Soviet experience was that large numbers of troops alienated Afghans. Just as in the days after 9/11, Franks wanted more time—and more detailed planning—before committing his forces. In the meantime, 1,000 US Marines waited at Camp Rhino, 400 miles to the south, with 3,500 more at sea just off the Pakistan coast. Some 1,000 soldiers from the 10th Mountain Division were available in K2 and at Bagram, along with Royal Marines from Britain, and US Rangers stood ready in Oman. None of these troops were brought forward.

Brigadier General James Mattis, the Marine commander, was furious with Franks, later bemoaning "a culture of pre-briefs, orders, reports, and large staffs." On December 12, to the fury of the Americans, an Afghan commander announced a ceasefire after an Arab leader at Tora Bora promised to capitulate the next morning. It was another surrender ruse. The Al-Qaeda fighters, aided by locals they had bought off, slipped away that night.

Reliance on Pakistan was the fatal flaw of the Tora Bora operation. Although Franks later claimed that 100,000 Pakistani troops had been used to seal the border, bin Laden escaped into Pakistan with apparent ease on or around December 16. Crumpton proposed sending US troops into Pakistan but was curtly rebuffed by the Pentagon. Bush had warned that the Taliban could "run but not hide," but Mullah Omar— his four wives and twelve children in tow—returned to Quetta, from where the Taliban leadership would operate with near-impunity in subsequent years.

There is no indication bin Laden ever left Pakistan after December 2001. The Al-Qaeda leader was shot dead by Navy SEALs during Operation Neptune Spear, a CIA-led raid on his compound in Abbottabad, just north of Islamabad, in May 2011. By then, American mistrust of Pakistan was so intense that its government was not informed of the mission—in its airspace and on its sovereign territory—until it was over. That night, an MH-47G Chinook from the Night Stalkers regiment was the lead aircraft on the mission and flew bin Laden's body to the USS *Carl Vinson,* where it was secretly buried at sea. The same helicopter, then a MH-47E version, had been one of the four Chinooks at K2 in 2001 that took CIA and Green Beret teams into Afghanistan.

In January 2002, the Green Berets held a ceremony behind the Sultan Razia school in which they buried the piece of steel from the World Trade Center that had been carried into Afghanistan by Lieutenant Colonel Max Bowers. The steel, encased in a body bag and wrapped in an American flag, was lowered into a six-feet-deep hole as a dedication was read out. Referring to those killed at the school on November 10, Bowers intoned: "These terrorists were destroyed by the United States and their hiding place is now in ruins, as is their evil dream. The vile cowards who once wielded the lash of terror perished in an ocean of blood and fire."

For a period, Shannon became a public figure. Like Lisa Beamer, whose husband, Todd, had said "Let's roll" just before perishing on Flight 93 on 9/11, Shannon had become a "hero widow." Beamer had been Bush's guest when he addressed Congress on September 20, before Team Alpha left for K2. Shannon was a guest of President Bush at the 2002 State of the Union address, sitting next to Hamid Karzai, the newly installed president of Afghanistan. The chamber gave the CIA officer's widow a standing ovation before Bush turned to her and said, "Shannon, I assure you and all who have lost a loved one that our cause is just, and our country will never forget the debt we owe Micheal and all who gave their lives for freedom." A month earlier, Shannon had stood sobbing on the Lanae Lane sidewalk as she watched Alison and Emily ride their new bicycles, Christmas presents promised by Mike and bought for them by his father.

Jake Spann took his first steps on Father's Day in June 2002, a week after his first birthday. The following month, John Walker Lindh agreed to a plea deal with prosecutors. In return for a reduced sentence of twenty years, he admitted he had "provided my services as a soldier to the Taliban" and "carried a rifle and two grenades." David Tyson, identified in court documents only as the US government's Confidential Source 1 had been on standby to testify against Detainee 001, as Lindh had been designated. Captain Craig McFarland, the military doctor who had treated Lindh at the Turkish school, was also preparing to be called as a witness; he had been instructed to check into a local hotel under the name Mr. White. The prosecution had been unable to establish a direct link between Lindh's actions and Mike's death; the defense had muddied the waters sufficiently to portray Lindh as a misguided youth, motivated by religious reasons to fight against the brutal Dostum.

Shannon had hoped for a treason charge, and even the death penalty, but had known neither outcome was likely. "Being a lawyer, it seemed inevitable to me," she said later. "The thing that was never able to be really factored into it in the way that it should have is the clear, coordinated nature of the uprising as a regional strategy of Fazl. As an intelligence officer, I believe that he [Lindh] couldn't have been ignorant to that, and that he had the opportunity to tell the US officers who were interviewing him about what was going to go down. He certainly chose not to do that."

The Lindh family never wavered in their support for the man who was reviled as the "American Taliban"—even in California, 28 percent of residents in early 2002 believed he should be executed and another 39 percent that he should receive life without parole. After one court appearance, Frank Lindh approached Johnny Spann as he entered an elevator with his ex-wife, Gail, and Shannon. With the media present, the jihadist's father tried to elicit a handshake, saying, "I am sorry about your son. My son had nothing to do with it. I am sure you understand." The Spanns ignored him, and a security guard stepped in. Following the plea deal, Frank Lindh compared his son to the Nobel Peace Prize recipient who helped end apartheid in South Africa, telling reporters, "I told John when he came back from Afghanistan, when I first met him, that Nelson Mandela served twenty-six years in prison. He's a good man, like John."

On December 12, 2002—just after the first anniversary of Mike's death—his parents, Shannon, and Alison were hosted by Dostum at Qala-i Jangi for a ceremony to unveil a marble memorial to the CIA officer. The trip was arranged by Dostum's American friend Charlie Santos and aides to Dana Rohrabacher, a California congressman who had been a Capitol Hill ally of the mujahideen. The trip was opposed by the State Department and CIA's NE Division, and the US Embassy in Kabul pushed the Karzai government to boycott the memorial ceremony, arguing that it "promoted warlordism."

The Spanns were picked up in Tashkent and driven by Dostum's men over the Friendship Bridge, into Afghanistan, in two Land Cruisers trailed by a truck full of armed guards. "What am I doing?" Shannon asked herself as she sped south through Uzbekistan. "It's the middle of the night, we're driving through the desert, and most of the guns seem to be pointed at us." At the bridge, the Spanns were transferred into

Dostum's armored Cadillac, which took them through Mazar-i Sharif to Qala-i Jangi; the Uzbek warlord's soldiers were posted along the route at 100-yard intervals.

During the visit, Shannon was struck by Dostum's optimism, even though he had already been marginalized by the United States. "He truly believed that this was the moment of change for Afghanistan," she later recalled. "There were women who were teachers and nurses coming up to me saying they were prisoners in their own homes before the Americans came. They had pictures of Mike in their purses, and they were grabbing my hands and just crying. Those people, especially the Hazaras in Mazar-i Sharif, were tasting freedom, and it was so powerful."

Beside the Pink House, just to the north of the doorway from which the Al-Qaeda prisoners had been brought out a year earlier, Dostum, Johnny Spann, and Shannon Spann addressed a crowd in pouring rain. Above them hung a sign declaring, in imperfect English: "Afghan nation commemorates immortal heroism of the freedom fighter, purticulary that of United States who sacrificed themselves in liberating Afghanitan." The memorial featured a star 2.5 by 2.25 inches—the exact dimensions of those on the CIA Memorial Wall. Its inscription, composed by Santos, declared:

A hero who sacrificed his life
for freedom
for Afghanistan
for the United States of America

* * *

The Battle of Qala-i Jangi resulted in more gallantry awards than perhaps any other action of the twenty-year war in Afghanistan. After a CIA investigation into the uprising, including testimony from the German reporter Arnim Stauth, David was presented with the Agency's highest award, the Distinguished Intelligence Cross, by George Tenet. On one face of the circular medal was engraved "David N. Tyson," alongside an embossed wreath and "United States of America." On the other was "Central Intelligence Agency" and "For Valor" at the center of the cross, encircling the bald eagle, shield, and sixteen-point compass rose of the CIA seal. In the Agency's fifty-four-year history before 9/11, only thirty CIA officers had received the cross, awarded for "a voluntary act or acts of extraordinary heroism involving the acceptance of existing dangers with conspicuous fortitude and exemplary courage." The citation noted that David had saved the lives of those in the headquarters building on November 25 "through his excellent judgment and great personal courage." It concluded, "In addition, Mr. Tyson did all that he could to determine the status of his colleague, Johnny Micheal Spann, throughout the insurrection and immediately following it, exhibiting the highest standards of professional loyalty, and reflecting great credit upon himself, the Central Intelligence Agency, and the Federal service."

During the same ceremony, the other six CIA members of Team Alpha and the three members of Team Bravo were awarded the Intelligence Star, the CIA's equivalent of the Silver Star. A bureaucratic bungle meant that Justin received only a Bronze Star with a "V" device, denoting valor. Mike's medal was posthumous. In a separate ceremony, a 79th star on the CIA's Memorial Wall was dedicated to him.

Major Mark Mitchell was awarded the Distinguished Service Cross, second in precedence only to the Medal of Honor and the first awarded since the Vietnam war. The citation stated that his "unparalleled courage under fire, decisive leadership and personal sacrifice were directly responsible for the success of the rescue operation and were further instrumental in ensuring the city of Mazar-i Sharif did not fall back in the hands of the Taliban." It was presented to him by General Doug Brown, whose son-in-law, Kevin Leahy, had nearly died in the errant JDAM incident.

In 2003, an SBS operative and a US Navy SEAL were flown back from Iraq to be presented with medals by Queen Elizabeth II at Windsor Castle in a closed ceremony for Special Forces awards. Tony received the Conspicuous Gallantry Cross, while Chief Boatswain's Mate Stephen Bass was awarded the Military Cross, the British equivalent of the Silver Star. Jess, the SBS captain in command of the British contingent at the fort, also received a Conspicuous Gallantry Cross. In the United States, Bass was awarded the Navy Cross—an honor on a par with Mitchell's—for "unlimited courage in the face of enemy fire, and utmost devotion to duty" in attempting to rescue David Tyson and in locating the body of Mike Spann.

After Iraq, Tony was back in Afghanistan with the SBS in 2007 when Mullah Dadullah—Dadullah the Lame—was shot dead by Z Squadron in a raid in Helmand. Dadullah had been part of the plot to recapture Mazar-i Sharif, massing a force near Balkh, but had slipped the net while Fazl and Noori had been taken to Guantánamo. "Six years later, finally got him," thought Tony.

*　　*　　*

By the time Osama bin Laden escaped to Pakistan, President George W. Bush was already fixing his sights on another target: Saddam Hussein. On December 28, 2001, Bush, at his ranch in Crawford, Texas, convened a video conference with officials in the White House Situation Room. General Tommy Franks was at the ranch with Bush, who was wearing jeans and a plaid shirt. Donald Rumsfeld joined from the study of his vacation home in Taos, New Mexico. Franks, with the aura of a triumphant general at ease with the mantle of victory on his shoulders shrugged off a tale of his helicopter dodging a surface-to-air missile in Afghanistan. He had just returned from Karzai's inauguration and gave a brief update. "Two months ago, Afghanistan was a terrorist-sponsored state," the general said. "Today, twenty-six million Afghans have hope for a future." Then, Franks spent an hour outlining a plan for removing Saddam from power in Iraq in a full-scale American invasion with

105,000 troops. When Franks had finished, Bush singled out George Tenet, who was in the Situation Room. "George, your people have done a great job in Afghanistan," the president told the CIA director. "What do you have in Iraq?"

The Pentagon had been unprepared for Afghanistan and subsequently taken a back seat to the CIA. For Bush's second war, Rumsfeld made sure he was ready and in charge. The Iraq War began in March 2003, a conventional invasion rather than the light footprint used in Afghanistan. In the early days of Iraq, Rumsfeld and his generals used the term "catastrophic success" to describe a quick enemy collapse that prompts a humanitarian crisis. The enemy in Iraq did indeed fold swiftly, as it had in Afghanistan.

In May 2003, Bush, clad in a flight suit, landed on the deck of the USS *Abraham Lincoln*. Standing in front of a MISSION ACCOMPLISHED banner, he announced that the combat operations in Iraq were over. A month later, the cover of the *Weekly Standard* magazine featured a beaming Franks, trailing an article with the headline: "How Tommy Franks Won the Iraq War." Nearly eighteen years later, the Tommy Franks Leadership Institute and Museum in Oklahoma was still selling copies of that edition, signed by the long-retired general. The article, based on an interview with Franks at CENTCOM headquarters in Tampa, included a redefinition of "catastrophic success"—that a small, rapid force could achieve victory with fewer troops and fewer casualties by surprising and discombobulating the enemy.

The Iraq War was still viewed as a success three months after the invasion, when Sergeant First Class Bill Bennett, the ODA 595 medic who had treated John Walker Lindh in Sheberghan, took part in a raid on a house in Ramadi, western Iraq. The previous day had been the second anniversary of 9/11. Bennett's team was ambushed in a bomb and gun attack, wounding seven of them. He climbed to the rooftop, where he was shot three times and killed. On the helicopter flight back, Vince Makela, who had also been in ODA 595 in Afghanistan, sat with the body bags containing his friend and another Green Beret, the first

5th Group casualties in Iraq. Bennett, thirty-five, had been scheduled to return home the next day, and his wife had already hung a WELCOME HOME banner at their house in Tennessee. "If he could pick a death, that's one he would choose," said Makela. "He died on the attack, doing what he loved doing, with people he loved."

In the late spring of 2004, Paul Syverson, a newly promoted major whose wife had just given birth to a daughter, their second child, bumped into his friend Anthony Jarrett. By then, Syverson had fully recovered from his JDAM injuries. He told Jarrett, "I'm going back to Iraq—I don't know why." When Jarrett told him to "keep your head down," Syverson responded, "Don't worry. I will."

On June 16, Syverson was walking into the PX store on the American base at Balad, north of Baghdad, to buy a toothbrush. Without warning, a 127mm rocket—one of five fired by Iraqi insurgents—landed less than twenty feet away, the shrapnel killing him instantly. He was thirty-two. Jarrett, who was deeply affected by his friend's death, became disillusioned by his own experience in Iraq. He concluded that the war was unnecessary, and that he—and the country—had been pitched into it before finishing or processing what had happened in Afghanistan. Jarrett had always detested flies and other insects, but these days he can't bring himself to harm one. "I won't kill," he says. "I'll catch it and I'll take it outside and let it go. It's just respect for life, of any kind." Diagnosed with PTSD Jarrett still has nightmares, including flashbacks to his encounter with the DShK truck on the road to Dehdadi on November 23, 2001.

Justin Sapp was among the mourners at the funeral of Syverson, a fellow VMI graduate. The Green Beret was buried in Section 60 of Arlington Cemetery, a stone's throw from Mike Spann's grave. After the burial, Justin found himself talking to a Marine officer who had also been at VMI. As they rehashed the mistakes made by the F-18 pilots who nearly killed Syverson in the JDAM incident, the officer informed Justin, "Don't worry—the clown that did that was cashiered out of the Marine Corps."

Several of those involved in the events around Mazar-i Sharif in 2001 changed the course of their careers shortly afterward. "Maybe I should try something different," thought Mike Sciortino, the air controller injured by the JDAM he had helped call in on his own position. He became a commissioned officer and Physician's Assistant, returning to Mazar-i Sharif as a captain in 2012, when he was stationed at an American base that had been named Camp Mike Spann. Eric Andreasen, the nineteen-year-old 10th Mountain Division soldier who had been pitched into the tumult of the fort after the JDAM exploded, became a combat medic. "I felt like I had a higher purpose than just shooting people in the face," he now quips. Sara Stires, the F-14 radar-intercept officer who had bombed the Taliban convoy on the day Mazar-i Sharif was liberated, switched branches to become a naval dentist. She was the only female in the US Navy to be awarded the Distinguished Flying Cross in the Afghanistan war.

By the summer of 2004, with Sunni and Shia insurgencies raging across the country, President Bush himself used the term "catastrophic success" to sum up Iraq. He described the conflict as one in which the United States was "so successful, so fast, that an enemy that should have surrendered, or been done in, escaped and lived to fight another day." Another two years would elapse before it became clear that something similar had occurred in Afghanistan. There, the remnants of the Taliban had retreated to Pakistan, using that country—and the willing hand of the ISI—as a base to reconstitute itself and fight on in Afghanistan.

Perhaps the most catastrophic facet of the limited victory achieved in Afghanistan in 2001 was that it fed the hubris that regime change in Iraq would be straightforward. Ironically, if lasting success had been possible in Afghanistan, the shift of focus and resources toward Iraq in 2002 probably doomed any chances of it.

Rather than devolving power in Afghanistan to regional ethnic leaders—Dostum included—the United States sought to prop up a central government in a country that had always resisted the writ of Kabul. By the end of the Bush administration, US troop levels in Afghanistan were static at around 30,000. In 2010, under President

Barack Obama, the number reached a high of 100,000—the size of the 1979 Russian invasion force. American deaths peaked at 465 that year, while enemy attacks exceeded 4,000 a month. After the killing of bin Laden in May 2011, troop levels were slashed precipitously; by the close of Obama's second term in January 2017, only 8,400 American forces remained.

For years after 9/11, a sign put up during Cofer Black's tenure at CTC declared: "The date is September 12, 2001." It was designed to encourage CIA officers to act urgently and boldly. The Agency's workforce took the message to heart. At the end of 2009, the CIA's continued determination to penetrate Al-Qaeda—and to take great risks in doing so—was demonstrated when a suicide bomber killed five CIA officers and two contractors at Khost. The device detonated at Camp Chapman, named after Nathan Chapman, the Green Beret killed in 2002, by a Jordanian double agent who had promised access to Ayman al-Zawahiri, bin Laden's deputy.

By 2021, 137 stars were etched into the Agency's Memorial Wall—fifty-six of them added in the two decades since Mike Spann's death, versus thirty-five stars in the two decades preceding it. CIA paramilitary officers have suffered disproportionate casualties, and in 2020 a veteran former SEAL was killed in combat in Somalia. The 121st star on the wall is dedicated to Mark Rausenberger, Team Alpha's medic, who became a CIA paramilitary after 2001. Despite a heart condition, Mark had served in Iraq after Afghanistan, constantly requesting the toughest assignments. He died suddenly at age forty-eight in May 2016 on a CIA mission in the Philippines. The details of his death remained classified.

In 2012, Justin Sapp found himself assigned to the military investigation of a Green Beret unit at a small base near Kandahar. Staff Sergeant Robert Bales, attached to the unit, had walked off the base and been declared DUSTWUN—Duty Status Whereabouts Unknown, or Missing. After he returned, it was revealed that he had massacred seventeen civilians, most of them women and children—while on a mix of alcohol, steroids, and sleeping pills. He burned some of their bodies. It was the worst US atrocity of the war. "How did this happen?" Justin asked himself at the time. "How did we go from this great success, that Sun Tzu would have heralded, to this counterinsurgency quagmire? We've taken our eye off the ball. We focused our attention on Iraq and relegated Afghanistan to the backburner." Even though Bales had previously displayed aggression toward Afghans—he once beat up a local who was delivering supplies to the troops—the Green Beret leadership had not disciplined him.

The most notorious DUSTWUN case of the war was that of Bowe Bergdahl, a soldier with mental-health problems who walked off his base in Paktika province in June 2009. He was captured by the Taliban-aligned Haqqani network, which held him in Pakistan. In 2014, Mark Mitchell—by then a colonel working at the White House on the National Security Council—was involved in exchanging Bergdahl for five senior Taliban prisoners at Guantánamo Bay, among them Mullah Fazl and Mullah Noori. Many of his fellow Green Berets criticized the deal, but Mitchell supported it. "It had been five years and we hadn't been able to find Bergdahl," he said. "Do you think we were going to be able to find him with 10,000 troops in Afghanistan? I would never want to be part of a military organization that made post facto decisions on who is worthy of recovering."

The five surviving CIA officers from Team Alpha went on to long and successful Agency careers. J. R. Seeger, Alex Hernandez, Scott Spellmeyer, David Tyson, and Andy were all promoted to the Senior Intelligence Service (SIS), the CIA's top management tier. Scott became station chief in Kabul at a time when it was the largest CIA station in the world, then retired after working at the White House on the staff of the National Security Council. After retiring, Alex, one of the very few CIA officers to have reached SIS rank after a full military career, rode his motorcycle across the United States. In 2019 he parachuted into Normandy to commemorate the seventy-fifth anniversary of D-Day. J.R. became a prolific novelist. Andy continues to serve in the CIA, alongside Glenn and Greg from Team Bravo. Mike and Shannon Spann's Farm classmates Brian, who is director of the Special Activities Center, and Amy also remain in the CIA. For most of Team Alpha and the Green Berets, Afghanistan and Iraq dominated a decade or more of their lives.

In 2018, Hollywood's version of the 2001 Afghanistan campaign was released. *12 Strong* was adapted from Doug Stanton's 2009 book, *Horse Soldiers*. The movie, produced by Jerry Bruckheimer, focused on the twelve Green Berets of ODA 595 and did not feature Mike Spann or Qala-i Jangi. There was barely a reference to the CIA. One Agency officer appeared briefly in a cameo role, clad in paramilitary garb and a backward baseball cap. He delivered an expletive-laden intelligence brief to the newly arrived ODA men and then bade them farewell with: "I got a fifty-kilometer hike to give a bag of money to another warlord. Who knows, maybe we'll see each other on the battlefield." The legend of ODA 595 in the Darya Suf Valley—first pushed by Rumsfeld's deputy Paul Wolfowitz at the Washington, DC, dinner in November 2001—grew and grew. As the movie was screened in cinemas, Mark Nutsch, the captain who had commanded ODA 595, and Green Beret colleagues launched Horse Soldiers bourbon, made by their American Freedom Distillery, describing it as "our legacy in a bottle." The whiskey label featured the America's Response Monument, an eighteen-foot-high brass statue of a Green Beret on a rearing horse. It had been dedicated on Veteran's Day of 2011 in New York's Liberty Park, next to the 9/11 Memorial Museum. The sculptor had been inspired by the Darya Suf Valley photograph brandished by Rumsfeld shortly after Wolfowitz's speech.

From 2015, there were echoes of 2001 in Afghanistan as the CIA took the lead once again, overseeing up to 90 percent of American operations in the country. Alongside them were the Green Berets, who had stepped into the breach when most conventional troops left. In 2015 the Taliban took control of Kunduz for fifteen days, the first major city it had captured since 2001.

Shortly after the *12 Strong* movie was released, Fazl—the Taliban leader who outwitted Dostum over the surrender that led to the Qala-i Jangi uprising—became a senior Taliban peace negotiator in Doha, Qatar. At the end of that year, the United States stopped issuing statistics about how many provinces were under the control of the Afghan government after the number dropped below 54 percent; since at least 2017, the Pentagon conceded, Afghanistan had been in a state of "strategic stalemate."

The attempt to impose a western-style central government in Afghanistan helped reverse the US victory that Team Alpha spear-headed after 9/11. That victory had been tactical rather than strategic, but it had nevertheless provided an opportunity since squandered.

As ever, the Afghans themselves were caught in the middle, tired of decades of war but fearing a bloodbath and fundamentalist oppression when the Americans departed. The US and the Taliban signed a peace deal in Doha in February 2020. In it, the US government agreed to withdraw all NATO troops from Afghanistan in return for a Taliban pledge to prevent Al-Qaeda from operating. The Afghan government was not party to the agreement. Compared to the potential deal in 2001 with a Taliban that was defeated, demoralized, and in disarry, it was pitiful. Peace talks involving the Afghans began in earnest in Doha in September 2020 and continued haltingly, even as Taliban violence gripped Afghanistan and Mullah Fazl appeared with fighters in a video at a military training camp in Pakistan. This was the negotiator the United States and moderate Afghans were up against. "You just have to wonder, does anybody remember how clever he was?" asked J. R. Seeger, back in his native western New York after retiring from the CIA in 2007. As the end of 2020 approached, no Americans were returning in body bags, but Afghan forces were being decimated, losing soldiers and police at ten times the rate suffered by the US at the height of the war.

22

DAYS OF THUNDER

2:20 p.m. (GMT +4.5), November 15, 2020;
Sheberghan, Jowzjan province, Afghanistan

ABDUL RASHID DOSTUM, his hair and mustache now chalk-white, is both beleaguered and defiant as we talk about Afghanistan, then and now. He sits opposite me in the banquet room of his guesthouse in Sheberghan, almost nineteen years after the uprising at Qala-i Jangi. Nearly two decades earlier, from the same chair, he had feted Team Alpha during the heady days after their victory over the Taliban. The admiration had been mutual. Almost immediately afterward, however, Dostum was blocked from visiting the United States and relegated to the periphery of power by successive administrations.

"I was the one who fought against and defeated the Taliban in 2001," Dostum says plaintively. "My soldiers were killed and wounded, but I was left behind and received nothing. If the Americans had listened to me, they would now have the upper hand on the battlefield and at the negotiation table." He blames the US State Department for his marginalization. "I have no issue with CIA," he says. "They never let me down. But US diplomats have not allowed me to act against the Taliban."

During our conversation, Dostum looks back fondly on the weeks after 9/11, when he had briefly been an American favorite, the man who had won the war. In the intervening years, he has been accused of massacres, rape, and torture; survived several assassination attempts; and twice fled into exile. Dostum was vice president under Ashraf Ghani, Karzai's successor, and has recently been appointed Marshal of the Armed Forces. But these positions are ceremonial. More than two years have passed since he met with Ghani, who still holds office.

Since his return to Afghanistan in 2018 after a year's exile in Ankara, he has lived alone in Sheberghan. His second wife is in Turkey; his third wife, along with his ninth child, lives in Uzbekistan. Many of Dostum's faithful aides remain at his side—including his security chief, Abdul Sattar, the most feared of his men in 2001, who is now a major general in the Afghan National Army. When I ask Sattar about Team Alpha recollections of him shooting an old man stealing supplies, he denies this happened. "The villagers were hungry, so we gave them chocolate and biscuits," he says, his gold teeth glinting as he smiles.

Around Sheberghan are giant posters of Dostum in his new uniform, dripping with gold braid and festooned with medals. The town remains the Uzbek warlord's fiefdom, his name uttered with reverence. Farther afield, however, his power has receded. The Taliban controls the road between Sheberghan and Mazar-i Sharif, turning a ninety-minute drive into a weeklong wait for a military Mi-17 helicopter for visitors, local officials, and anyone associated with the Kabul government. Delays are due in part to the increased need for helicopters to ferry troops to the battlefields. When I am due to leave, the scheduled Mi-17, already carrying the body of a soldier killed by the Taliban, is redirected at the last minute. In Mazar-i Sharif, Atta Mohammed Noor—Dostum's old Tajik sometime rival, sometime ally—holds sway after serving as governor of Balkh for fourteen years until 2018.

Despite all the setbacks for Dostum, he has lived into old age and is still vying for power. Fahim Khan, who became a Marshal in 2005, died of a heart attack in 2014. The same year, Karzai, after breaking with the Americans, left office largely discredited, and slipped into relative obscurity. As we talk, Dostum trumpets his ability to survive, dispatching an aide to bring in a chapan torn by shrapnel; the thick, traditional Afghan coat saved his life when a suicide bomber targeted him in 2009. Dostum is eager to wage unrestrained war once again, promising to rid northern Afghanistan of the Taliban if he is given six months to accomplish the task. But he knows he will not be afforded the chance. At times he seems resigned to the futility of it all: "We Afghans have been fighting with each other for the last forty years," he says. "We have been killing each other for no reason."

The story of the Qala-i Jangi uprising is now part of Dostum lore. The warlord himself prefers not to dwell on the details. Some of his men, however, believe he was betrayed by Amir Jan Naseri— the former Taliban commander who had defected to Dostum before 9/11 but was hosting Mullah Dadullah at Balkh. Naseri was Dostum's liaison with Fazl; he was present when the 400 Al-Qaeda surrendered outside Mazar-i Sharif, and decided that the prisoners should be put in the Pink House cellar without being searched. Some CIA officers share the view that Naseri, who died of natural causes in 2016, played a key role in Fazl's plot.

Qala-i Jangi is no longer Dostum's domain; now, it is occupied by a Pashtun general. There, the northern compound has been extensively repaired and landscaped following—according to a marble plaque— "breakages and fractures" as a "result of bomb hits and also other heavy weapons impacts." Below the rebuilt northeastern tower is displayed the turret of the T-55 tank destroyed by the errant JDAM in 2001. It occupies a metal plinth near two pristine US-supplied MRAP (Mine-Resistant Ambush-Protected) vehicles.

All buildings in the southern compound have been demolished except for the Pink House, its walls pockmarked and crumbling, its color faded to a light blush. Beside it stands a gold-domed gazebo protecting the Mike Spann memorial, in which some white doves are nesting. The land has recently been cleared, with mulberry and cherry trees now planted in neat rows. Below the eastern tower, from which the SBS had machine-gunned scores of Al-Qaeda fighters, is a long, curved overhead trellis, covered with vines. The gateway on the center wall has been rebuilt and a new metal gate installed. On the west side of the Pink House, a few feet from where Mike Spann was killed, sits a pile of rusted metal: the barrels and drum magazines of PPSh-41s, fragments of mortar rounds, PK tripods, Russian ammunition boxes, and intact 80mm shells.

Inside, the Pink House remains almost as it was in December 2001. Part of the metal staircase leading down to the cellar was blown off nineteen years earlier, the remnants now covered in rubble and trash. The walls around the entranceway, where a JDAM landed on the first day of the uprising, are scorched or blasted down to the brick. The cellar is dank and spectral, swathed in darkness except at the foot of the stairs, where a shaft of light penetrates—courtesy of the American munitions that destroyed windows and internal walls above. Its seven rooms, with mud floors, have been cleared of debris and human remains. The ceiling of the long room, along the south side, bears what could be the marks of hand-grenade fragments—a macabre legacy of the prisoner arguments that erupted on the night of November 24, 2001. An unexploded shell remains jammed in a ground-level air vent.

One large hole yawns in the roof, on the southwestern corner. Had the 2,000-pound JDAM landed where intended on November 26, the Pink House would have been obliterated and its occupants entombed. Yet most of the Pink House is structurally intact—an eerie a monument to the carnage that occurred there nearly two decades before.

*   *   *

Of the eighty-six Al-Qaeda fighters who emerged from the cellar of the Pink House at the end of the uprising, the last to be freed from US custody was John Walker Lindh. He was released from federal prison in Terre Haute, Indiana, at the age of thirty-eight in May 2019, with three years lopped off his twenty-year sentence for good behavior. Yasser Esam Hamdi, the other American, had been held without charge as an "enemy combatant" until October 2004, when he was deported to Saudi Arabia as part of a deal in which he renounced his US citizenship. At least fifty of the eighty-six—including twenty-one Saudis, four Yemenis, four Tajiks, and three Uighurs—were incarcerated in Guantánamo Bay, Cuba. The opening of the new military prison there was announced by Rumsfeld a month after the uprising. One Yemeni from the eighty-six died of apparent suicide in 2009 and the remainder of the Qala-i Jangi captives had all been released by 2017.

The Iraqi who had been questioned by David and Mike on November 25 and had intimated that "terrorist acts" were about to take place was a Qala-i Jangi survivor. He was Ali Abdul Motalib Awayd Hassan Al Tayeea. His seemingly implausible claims that he had been a Christian and had tried to give information to the US Embassy in Islamabad turned out to have been largely true. A Shia, he had converted to Christianity, and then back to Islam. In 2009, he was repatriated from Guantánamo Bay, where he had been given the nickname "Pimp Daddy" by American guards.

Lindh had stated at his sentencing in 2002 that "bin Laden's terrorist attacks are completely against Islam." A 2017 report from the National Counterterrorism Center, however, stated that Lindh had continued "to advocate for global jihad and to write and translate violent extremist texts" in prison. In February 2015, Lindh wrote to a California television producer expressing support for the Islamic State, the Islamist group that had recently beheaded three Americans and two Britons in televised executions. Asked if he supported the Islamic State, Lindh—now calling himself "Yahya," an Arabic version of John—replied: "Yes, and they are doing a spectacular job. The Islamic State is clearly very sincere and serious about fulfilling the long-neglected religious obligation of establishing a caliphate through armed struggle, which is the only correct method."

An FBI source stated that Lindh's relationship with his father was increasingly fraught because of his father's homosexuality. The Islamic State executed gay men by throwing them off buildings. A leaked intelligence summary from the Federal Bureau of Prisons revealed that Lindh had been dropped by his long-time lawyer, James Brosnahan. Lindh told his father that he would not reject violence, stating: "I am not interested in renouncing my beliefs or issuing condemnations in order to please Brosnahan or anybody else." Lindh secured Irish citizenship in 2013; he also floated living in Puerto Rico upon his release. Another FBI source divulged that by 2021 Lindh continued to live in Northern Virginia, not far from the Pentagon and CIA headquarters, and was under heavy US government surveillance.

Lindh's embrace of the Islamic State had brought matters full circle. He had been one of the first Westerners to become a self-radicalized jihadist in part via the internet. The Islamic State had leveraged this phenomenon, spurring an estimated 6,000 Westerners to take up arms on its behalf. Among the attacks in its name was the massacre of forty-nine people at a gay nightclub in Orlando, Florida, in 2016.

*　　*　　*

After Mike's death, Shannon Spann resumed her CIA career, returning to work at CTC in 2003. At the end of that year she was posted to the CIA station in Canberra, Australia. Mike's parents contested custody of Alison and Emily, arguing that the children would have more stability in Alabama. But the courts backed Shannon, and the girls, along with Jake, moved with her. In his will, Mike had specified that Shannon should be the guardian of his daughters. She had told Amy at the time: "I prayed to God that He would make us a family, and I meant it. I can't not mean it just because Mike is not here." Looking back, Shannon now says she had been in "a perfect storm of denial" about the difficulties that she, Jake, and her stepdaughters would face. "It turned into a literal court battle. And so, regrettably, a lot of that drove a sense of 'We're going to show everybody that we're a family and that we're fine.'"

In Canberra Station Shannon worked as a counterterrorism liaison. She traveled throughout Southeast Asia, collecting intelligence about

Jemaah Islamiyah, the Islamist group behind the Bali bombings in 2002. Visiting Indonesia on CIA business, she met Thys DeBruyn, a CIA officer stationed in Jakarta. They became a couple after their return to CIA headquarters in 2006 and married the following year, a few days after the sixth anniversary of 9/11. The pull of the Spann family in Alabama remained strong, however, and Alison and Emily ultimately moved to Winfield to live with Mike's parents, Johnny and Gail. After a decade of government service, Shannon left the CIA in 2009 and gave birth to her second son, Lucas, the following year. She now lives in Traverse City, Michigan—her husband's hometown—working as a consultant and, more recently, as a life coach and spiritual director. Her parents, who moved from California, live nearby.

"I feel like my life has been rewritten five times," Shannon, says as the twentieth anniversary of Mike's death approaches. "It never goes in the direction I'm expecting. But the fact that things don't tend to turn out how I expect is part of the mystery of being human to me." In recent years she has developed rheumatoid arthritis, a debilitating and incurable autoimmune disease that causes painful swelling of the joints. After Mike's death, she says she did her best to project that everything was fine, and the pretense had taken a toll. Mike was a hero—revered by his family, the CIA, most Americans, and Shannon herself. But heroes tend to be put on pedestals and their human flaws forgotten. They are frozen in time, untouched by the vicissitudes of age and everyday life. "When you're the one left behind with the bag, you're definitely not on a pedestal," Shannon reflects. "I have realized that just soldiering on is not the best approach. But I learned that the hard way—by becoming totally crippled fifteen years later. I thought I was being strong and all that. But it turns out that being strong is actually turning toward the grief, looking it in the eye and letting it overcome you."

For many years, Jake would say he wanted to become a Marine. But he later chose to pursue writing, securing a place at New York University in 2020. That Christmas, Shannon, Thys, and ten-year-old Lucas welcomed Alison, now a news anchor in Biloxi, Mississippi;

Emily, a recent graduate of her father's alma mater, Auburn; and Jake for the holidays. Life has not been easy over the past two decades, but Shannon—sustained by her faith—has come to accept that. "Suffering is part of the human condition," she says. "It makes us more real and alive. It's not that you wish for it. But the gifts of it are things that I wouldn't want to give away either." She feels a sense of having prevailed, and that Mike would have approved. "Despite everything, we did it," she says. "We're still a family where we bring all of our broken pieces to the table, but we're at the same table."

Justin Sapp remained in the Army after the Team Alpha mission despite overtures to join the CIA as a paramilitary officer—a step his Green Beret friend Jim took. His father, a veteran case officer, dissuaded him from becoming a "gun bunny" for the Agency. In 2021, with multiple tours in Afghanistan and Iraq behind him, Justin is married with three sons and living in New Jersey. Still serving as a colonel, he works in Manhattan for the US Mission to the United Nations, three miles from Ground Zero, where Al-Qaeda brought down the twin towers of the World Trade Center on 9/11.

* * *

On April 14, 2021, President Joe Biden spoke in the Treaty Room of the White House. In was the same room where on October 7, 2001, President George W. Bush announced the opening of the bombing campaign in Afghanistan, declaring "We will not falter and we will not fail." In the intervening period, 2,488 American troops had died in Afghanistan and 20,722 more had been wounded. "I have concluded that it's time to end America's longest war," Biden said. "It's time for American troops to come home." The date by which the withdrawal of the remaining 3,500 US servicemembers would be complete, he declared, would be the twentieth anniversary of 9/11.

The unilateral pullout, based on an arbitrary American timetable rather than a peace deal with the Taliban or a request from the Kabul government, had echoes of the US abandonment of Afghanistan after the ignominious Soviet exit in 1989. It also raised the specter of the disastrous US withdrawal from Iraq in 2011, which left the ungoverned space that ISIS used to establish its murderous caliphate. Team Alpha members fear that the Al-Qaeda sanctuary they had helped destroy in 2001 will be re-created, and global terrorist attacks will once again be launched from a Taliban-controlled Afghanistan. In 2004, Osama bin Laden had boasted that Al-Qaeda was engaged in a "war of attrition to fight tyrannical superpowers"; just as the mujahideen had "bled Russia for ten years, until it went bankrupt and was forced to withdraw in defeat," so too the Americans would leave. When he announced the end of the war, Biden ignored the military truism that the enemy always has a vote. In citing the "cost of billions each year…above the trillion we've already spent," he risked bolstering bin Laden's posthumous status as a prophet. Al-Qaeda declared: "The Americans are now defeated."

*   *   *

David Tyson retired in 2020 as senior case officer for Russian operations. He regards Biden's decision to withdraw from Afghanistan as a "shameful" abandonment of the country and the allies Team Alpha fought alongside in 2001.

As David approached his sixtieth birthday, he and Rosann moved to rural Virginia. They see a lot of their children. For a time, Kara lived off the grid in Maine, harvesting wild rice and tanning animal hides. On his left forearm, David has a primitive tattoo of a parachute that Kara created using hawthorn and charcoal. Mark studied at the Russian East European Institute of Indiana University, where he was taught by some of his father's former professors, and lived for two years in the former Soviet republic of Georgia.

Living in the mountains again, David—his hair and Amish-style beard now snowy white—plans to delve into bluegrass music. Language and idiom retain their fascination. For a time he worked for a local man, building split-rail fences. "He uses verbs and stuff that I hadn't heard since I was a kid in Pennsylvania," David relates. "One day, we're working on a fence and he says to me, 'We sure scared up them rails into those posts, didn't we?'"

In the nearby town, David likes to wander into a repair shop—it seems perfectly preserved from the 1950s—just to chat with the owner. He discovered a long-running dispute between the various businesses that repair chain saws and riding mowers. "The place is full of conflict and antagonism." David chuckles. Once again, he is learning the ways of a new tribe. At the same time, in retirement, he has reconnected with former comrades in Team Alpha and ODA 595. He and Alex have taken part in Horse Soldiers whiskey tastings in Virginia and Florida.

The events in Afghanistan during the fall of 2001—especially those at Qala-i Jangi—are never out of David's thoughts. "It's a shadow that follows me," he says. "It's part of who I am now, and I've tried to embrace that. But I've tried to make it a positive in my life." Sleep remains a problem. He suffers the same nightmare perhaps six nights out of seven, dreaming that Arab fighters are chasing him through woods or dusty streets. Sometimes his pursuers are from the cast of characters lined up outside the Pink House; other times they are the men he killed. Each nightmare ends just as David is about to be slain, and he wakes up trying to scream. Rosann comforts him, telling him it's alright and that he should go back to sleep.

David feels no guilt about the dozens he killed—perhaps forty in Qala-i Jangi, three in the Darya Suf Valley, and several more at the Sultan Razia school. "I've read a lot about killing and I've been surprised to find that a lot of soldiers are obsessed with the idea of killing and who they killed and it haunted them. For me, it's a little bit different because the people I killed were not running away or hiding. I didn't take advantage of them. They were going after me. All the technological advantages of the US government were out the window...I shot them and I remember their faces."

Sometimes, he conducts imaginary conversations with those he killed. "Yeah, man, I was coming at you," a dead man might say to him. "Good on you. It was a fair fight." He bears no animosity toward any of them. "I feel for their families because they were the sons of somebody, and somebody mourned them," he says. "I feel sorry for that."

David still marvels at his ability to function in a situation for which no training could have prepared him. Something seized control of his senses inside the fort during the uprising, forcing him to make decisions in a way that felt automatic. Perhaps the more remarkable thing has been his ability to function so effectively over the subsequent two decades. "You have the choice to be a victim of what happened, or not," he concludes. "I made a conscious decision not to go down the dark path. I have other people that I needed to take care of. One of the things you ask yourself with this is who you are and where did you come from."

Naturally, there is survivor's guilt. "Mike was younger than me. He was stronger and fitter," David says. "He was a tough guy. He was a Marine. If you were to ask who was going to survive a big fight like that, you'd say Mike." But because Mike was right next to the Pink House that day, and because he made the split-second decision to stand and fight rather than to run, he never had a chance. "I lived and Mike died, and therefore it's my job to make my life worth it," David says. "That means not only being a good person, but getting the most out of life—and living it well for Mike."

Sometimes, the tears come. On the three-hour drive to visit his mother in Downingtown, Pennsylvania, where at ninety-four she still lives in the house where she raised David, he will listen to music that takes him back to Afghanistan. "Titanium" by David Guetta, for one, transports him to Qala-i Jangi on November 25, 2001: "I'm bulletproof, nothing to lose; Fire away, fire away." When the Brooks and Dunn country song "Days of Thunder" comes on, David weeps for Mike, the patriotic son of Alabama: "Looking back on those days of thunder; Shake my head and I have to wonder."

David visits Mike's grave at Arlington at least once a year and is also drawn to American war cemeteries overseas. "I just love to read the names of the dead, where they're from, and try to live for them," he says. "I think about Mike all the time and I do believe that there's a sort of judgment out there—that Mike, one day, might comment on what I did. And hopefully he says it was okay. I'm pretty sure he will, but I don't know. I think about Mike's family, the life he would have had. It's all gone."

There is an introspection to David Tyson that has deepened over the years. Pausing in the Virginia woods to watch a globemallow beetle chew an oak leaf, or to gaze at a hickory tree, he finds himself reveling in the beauty of the world, to the point of exhilaration. Again, the tears well. He feels an emotional pull to such things, he ventures, because he has seen so much ugliness; and yet he is alive.

ACKNOWLEDGMENTS

First Casualty has been many years in the making, and I greatly appreciate the encouragement, stimulation, friendship, and practical help of many people involved in my reporting and research. I could not have done this alone.

I want to express my deepest gratitude to everyone who spoke to me. The six surviving members of Team Alpha all agreed to be interviewed for the book; thank you for your trust in me and for seeing what *First Casualty* could be. The frankness, candor, patience, and willingness of people to discuss sometimes painful details of a momentous time in their lives have been humbling. Some people deserve special mention. David and Rosann Tyson and their family were unfailingly open and hospitable, and placed great faith in me. The diaries, photographs, documentation, and video footage David shared with me were immensely useful. More valuable still was David's readiness to answer every question I had and to delve into the depths of his memory and even psyche. Colonel Justin Sapp embraced this project from the outset, was extremely generous with his time; he had a recall of people, places, and events that was a key building block. The grasp of history, strategy, and tribal dynamics provided by J. R. Seeger, Team Alpha's leader, gave *First Casualty* an added dimension. Shannon Spann was a model of kindness and grace as she recalled the tragedy of losing her husband. In Winfield, Alabama, Johnny Spann and Gail Spann could not have been more helpful; their continued pride in their son shines through.

The Green Berets, whom I met with everywhere from a motorcycle repair shop in rural Tennessee to a secure compartment deep inside the Pentagon, were also eager to tell their story. Particular thanks are due to Mark Mitchell, who also made several introductions for me, and Mario Vigil, who gave me a fascinating tour of Fort Campbell. Among the participants who provided photographs were Chris Spence, Ken Ashton, David Tyson, Shannon Spann, Glenn, Mark Mitchell, and Mario Vigil.

The CIA's decision to cooperate in assisting me with Team Alpha's story was a welcome surprise and reflects the Agency's increasing transparency and desire to honor the service and sacrifice of its officers. Sara Lichterman of the CIA's Office of Public Affairs was dogged, cheerful, and extremely resourceful in arranging interviews with serving and retired CIA officers. I am also grateful to the director of Special Forces at the Ministry of Defence in London and the Special Forces Disclosure Cell for their assistance. Ambassador Ayoob Erfani, Marshal Abdul Rashid Dostum's representative in the United States, kindly helped arrange my visit to Afghanistan. I was generously hosted and protected in Afghanistan by Marshal Dostum and his staff, including Humayun Hakbin, Shukoor Rashid, Habib Zalmay, Rustam Dostum, Muner Ghanizadah, and Farhad Dostum. Rohullah Sadat was an invaluable translator and guide in Mazar-i Sharif and at Qala-i Jangi. Back in the US, Ahmad Farid Kohy kindly translated and transcribed my interview with Marshal Dostum.

Those who have helped me in different ways include Kevin Aandahl, Zubair Babakarkhail, Arik Bauriedl, Dai and Denise Bevan, Dan Bolger, Carla Brown, Immi Calderwood, Kevin Carroll, Jonathan Clarke, Devin DeWeese, Laura Ehrsam, Enayatullah Farahmand, Ben Farmer, Kirsten Fleming, Jason Gorey, the late Norman Houston, Simon Huntington, Mark Hyman, Michael Kallenbach, Sean Kanuck, William Knarr, Jonathan L. Lee, Aaron Lewis, Damien Lewis, Brent Lindeman, Deborah MacDougall, Noah Meyers, Johannes Moore, Claudia Morales, Arthur Na, Naiem Naiemullah, Benjamin Runkle, Kalev Sepp, Arnim Stauth,

ACKNOWLEDGMENTS

Robert Tait, Maria Thestrup, Bill Walter, and Patrick Wilson. Advice and expertise on photographs were kindly provided by Annabelle Whitestone, one of London's finest picture editors; Ray Wells, a Fleet Street legend, also stepped into the breach. Eight people read parts of the manuscript and made a variety of suggestions that, in almost all cases, I acted on, improving the final product. Thank you to Maria Romstedt—slayer of the dangling modifier and enforcer of parallel structure—Justin Wilkes, Thomas Braden, Colin Freeman, Kirsty McLean, Andrew Marshall, Peter Levaggi, and Michael McDowell.

I would like to thank Keith Urbahn, the premier literary agent in the United States, for his help in crafting a proposal and in skillfully securing a deal with Little, Brown. I am also grateful to Keith's outstanding colleagues at Javelin, including Matt Latimer, Dylan Colligan, and Matt Carlini. In the United Kingdom, my outstanding London agent Julian Alexander of the Soho Agency delivered once again, negotiating a deal with Welbeck. Both Keith and Julian were a constant source of support and wise counsel. Everything that Little, Brown and Welbeck have done convinced me that choosing them to publish *First Casualty* was the right decision.

At Little, Brown, Vanessa Mobley was the perfect editor, unswerving in her belief in *First Casualty,* encouraging, supportive, demanding, thorough, and deft. Her long hours of editing, our discussions about the characters and the story, her patience, her acceptance of my foibles, and her ability to consider the manuscript with both a literary and a commercial eye have been magnificent. Ben Allen, associate managing editor, was the ever-positive and reassuring calm in the storm. Little, Brown assistant editor Elizabeth Gassman helped in innumerable ways. Gregg Kulick designed a wonderful jacket while Jeffrey L. Ward delivered maps of exceptional quality. Thank you, too, to everyone else in the superb Little, Brown team, including Reagan Arthur (now at Knopf), Bruce Nichols, Katharine Myers, Ira Boudah, and Carolyn Levin. At Welbeck, it has been a pleasure to reconnect with Mark Smith and Wayne Davies, comrades in the trenches a decade ago with

Quercus. Thank you also to Oliver Holden-Rea and the rest of the team at Welbeck, Britain's most exciting and vibrant new publisher.

Thank you to my daughter, Tessa, and son, Miles, for your love, help, and tolerance when I have been tired and preoccupied. Loafer has been this author's best friend, a worthy heir to Finn, and my constant companion even through all-nighters. Ava Papantoniou, thank you for your good humor and irrepressible energy.

My father, Keith, died peacefully on February 10, 2020. During our farewell conversation, I was able to tell him about this book, which I know we would have discussed and debated. I miss your love and encouragement and often feel your presence at my side. Thank you to my mother, Valerie; sisters, Polly and Elizabeth; and brother, William, for everything, always, but especially during a difficult year.

Alexandra, you have supported and loved me every step of the way, living this book in all its stages. You have been my loyal and trusted ally and partner, my first reader, primary editor, and most perceptive critic. Your influence and inspiration are on every page. I love you.

For those interested in supporting the families of fallen CIA officers, I recommend the Third Option foundation, for the CIA paramilitary community, and the CIA Officers Memorial Foundation. The charity No One Left Behind is dedicated to helping Afghan and other interpreters who served alongside US personnel.

Further information about this book and my other work can be found at www.tobyharnden.com. I can be contacted via my website and welcome feedback from readers.

AUTHOR'S NOTE ON SOURCES

I was in Washington, DC, on September 11, 2001, locking the door to our newspaper bureau as the building was evacuated so that we could remain behind to report on the worst terrorist attack in history. One of the first victims named on television was Barbara Olson, whom I knew. In the ensuing months I reported from the Pentagon, New York's Ground Zero, and Shanksville, Pennsylvania, as well as across a changed United States. On the sixtieth anniversary of Pearl Harbor, I met with veterans of a previous attack on America. Shortly before Mike Spann's funeral, I wrote about how he and another CIA officer, then referred to only as "Dave," had questioned a young Californian, John Walker Lindh, in the fort of Qala-i Jangi.

As war enveloped Iraq in 2004, I met journalists there who had been at Qala-i Jangi, and I became fascinated by the events that day—especially by the CIA officer who had managed to shoot his way out of the southern compound. Watching footage of him running through the fort, I wondered what had gone through his mind as he saw his comrade overwhelmed. In 2013, after I had reported extensively as a war correspondent in Afghanistan, I managed to track down "Dave"—David Tyson—who was then living a few miles away from me in Northern Virginia. He was limited in what he could say because he was still a serving CIA officer, but I realized that the story of Team Alpha was one that I wanted to tell.

Turning that aspiration into *First Casualty,* many years later, required a lot of help and thousands of miles in my truck. I interviewed more than seventy people across the United States, traveling to Alabama, Georgia, Kansas, Kentucky, Missouri, New Jersey, New York, North Carolina, Pennsylvania, South Carolina, Tennessee, and Virginia. In addition, I flew to the United Kingdom and the Middle East, and spent five weeks in Afghanistan interviewing Abdul Rashid Dostum in Sheberghan and visiting Qala-i Jangi nineteen years after the uprising. Many people were interviewed several times, resulting in 327 hours of on-the-record interviews. A number of interviews were not recorded, and some people spoke only on the condition of anonymity. I interviewed CIA officers, Green Berets, Special Operations aviators and air controllers, SBS troopers, family members, and others. A full list of interviewees can be found below.

Every author stands on the shoulders of those who have gone before. I am no exception. I owe a particular debt to five foundational books: Doug Stanton's *Horse Soldiers,* an outstanding account of the Green Berets in northern Afghanistan; Steve Coll's *Ghost Wars* and *Directorate S,* magisterial works on the CIA in Afghanistan and Pakistan; Brian Glyn Williams's *The Last Warlord,* the definitive biography of Abdul Rashid Dostum; and Charles Briscoe, Richard Kiper, James Schroder, and Kalev Sepp's *Weapon of Choice,* the official history of US Army Special Operations Forces in Afghanistan.

Memoirs by Gary Schroen, Gary Berntsen, Duane Evans, George Tenet, Hank Crumpton, Robert Grenier, Michael Morell, Tommy Franks, Donald Rumsfeld, Douglas Feith, and Michael DeLong gave me significant insights into the perspective of participants in the events following 9/11. *Bloody Heroes* by Damien Lewis, on the SBS; *"My Heart Became Attached"* by Mark Kukis, on John Walker Lindh; and Richard Mahoney's *Getting Away with Murder* were also important works. The research and writings of William Knarr were an invaluable resource. In addition, I drew on the work of dozens of journalists who were in Afghanistan in the fall of 2001 while I reported from the comfort of the US. Among outstanding contemporaneous accounts were those by Luke Harding, Carlotta Gall, Alex Perry, Robert Young Pelton, Matthew Campbell, Justin Huggler, and Charles Sennott.

First Casualty should be read in conjunction with the notes that follow. These are organized by page number and key phrases. Where no specific source is noted, the information is drawn from interviews with the participants and from contemporaneous documents, such as diaries and video. Some dialogue has been re-created, based on what participants told me was said. Wherever possible, I sought to corroborate these recollections. Where people's thoughts have been quoted or summarized, this is based on what the person told me they thought. The notes contain the short-form references for books and articles—the author's last name and the main title—and relevant page numbers. Full details of the book—subtitle, publisher, and year of publication—are contained in the Select Bibliography, which lists 136 books as well as articles and films. In addition, a General Bibliography of another 150 books, a Glossary of all terms and acronyms, and a Chronology of events can be found on my website, www.tobyharnden.com.

The human memory is not perfect, especially in situations of danger and stress. Often, participants in the same event will have radically different memories of what happened. Rudyard Kipling, no stranger to Afghanistan, wrote of the difficulties of establishing what happened in "the whirlpool of war," when memories are often fragmented and distorted. Reconstructing events twenty years later is immensely challenging. Wherever possible, I have done so by interviewing the participants while also consulting official reports and contemporaneous documents, including diaries, emails, photographs, and videos. *First Casualty* does not seek to pass judgment on those who, to use Theodore Roosevelt's phrase, were "in the arena...marred by dust and sweat and blood." War is chaotic and terrifying and, by its nature, replete with mistakes. Bravery coexists with fear, selflessness with the instinct for self-preservation. Every person who chose to put themselves in harm's way in Afghanistan after 9/11 has my admiration for that act of courage and patriotism.

This account is told principally from the perspective of the members of Team Alpha, their leaders in the CIA, the Green Berets, and America's Afghan and British allies. It has been said that "truth is the first casualty of war"—the first known expression of this was by Ethel Annakin in 1915. From the earliest days after Team Alpha arrived in Afghanistan, false narratives emerged, some of which have endured. In Afghanistan, truth is especially elusive. Westerners, be they intelligence operatives, human rights workers, or journalists, are often supplied with the information they appear to want. In part this is from the Afghan desire to show hospitality toward a guest. Cash is also a factor; information, whether truthful or not, is a commodity that can be monetized.

The following interviews were conducted by the author. Ranks and job titles are those held in 2001. Only first names are used for CIA officers still serving in 2021 and those who requested partial anonymity due to reasons of personal security. In addition, a number of interviews were conducted with people who asked not to be named, including members of the SBS unit.

CIA

George Tenet (director); Cofer Black (head, CTC); Hank Crumpton (head, CTC/SO); Michael Hayden (director, NSA; later CIA director); Rich Blee (chief, Alec station); Michael Morell (President Bush's briefer); Charlie Gilbert (chief, Tashkent station); Robert Grenier (chief, Islamabad station in 2015); Shannon Spann (CTC); Ken Stiles (CTC/SO); Arturo Muñoz (CTC/SO); John Kiriakou (CTC); David Phillips (Jawbreaker); Ned Hubard (Air Branch); Chuck (chief, London station); Bill Harlow (chief spokesman). **Team Alpha:** J. R. Seeger (chief); Alex Hernandez (deputy); Scott Spellmeyer; David Tyson; Captain Justin Sapp (Green Beret, attached to CIA); Andy. **Team Bravo:** Glenn (medic); Greg.

GREEN BERETS

Task Force Dagger: Colonel John Mulholland; Lieutenant Colonel Mark Rosengard; Lieutenant Colonel George Bochain, USAF. **Boxer (ODC 53):** Lieutenant Colonel Max Bowers (in 2014); Major Kurt Sonntag; Major Mark Mitchell; Major Scott Brower; Captain Kevin Leahy; Captain Craig McFarland; Captain Anthony Jarrett; Sergeant Major Mario Vigil; Master Sergeant Randy Emerson; Master Sergeant Dave Betz; Sergeant First Class Ken Ashton; Sergeant First Class Jeff Smith; Sergeant First Class Paul Beck; Sergeant First Class Chris Spence. **ODA 595:** Captain Mark Nutsch; Master Sergeant Andy Marchal; Sergeant First Class Steve Bleigh.

OTHER US MILITARY

US Air Force air controllers: Master Sergeant Bart Decker; Staff Sergeant Mike Sciortino; Staff Sergeant Steve Tomat. **SBS attached:** Chief Boatswain's Mate Stephen Bass. **160th SOAR:** Lieutenant Colonel John Buss; Captain Joe; Chief Warrant Officer Alan Mack; Chief Warrant Officer Andy Sentiff; Mike Cuthbert. **16th Special Operations Squadron:** Lieutenant Colonel Greg McMillan; Master Sergeant Jim Patterson; Master Sergeant Art Ziegler (US Air Force 16th Special Operations Squadron). **10th Mountain Division:** Private First Class Eric Andreasen. **US Embassy, Tashkent:** Major Mike Davison USAF. **USS *Theodore Roosevelt*:** VF-102 (F-14s): Commander Mike Vizcarra; **VMFA-251 (F-18s):** Major Karl Brandt USMC. **USS *Carl Vinson*:** VFA-22 (F-18s): Lieutenant Commander Creighton Holt.

AFGHANS

Abdul Rashid Dostum; Karim Khalili; Mohammed Mohaqeq; Abdullah Abdullah; Faqir Mohammed Jowzjani; Majid Rozi; Abdul Sattar; Haji Bashir; Habibullah Qipchaq; Akram; Ali Sarwar; Habib Zalmay;

Bababek Bekzoda; Chari Rais; Huda Berdi; Mohammed Sami; Hafizullah Fayez; Kal Haci; Sharif Kamal; Tamim Ahad; Sayed Shah; Noor Mohammed Fayez; Kamil Frozenfar; Abdul Latif.

OTHERS

Johnny Spann; Gail Spann; Rosann Tyson; Mark Tyson; Paul Shannon (FBI); Kalev Sepp; Arnim Stauth (ARD TV); Nikolai Pavlov (Reuters TV); Matthew Campbell (*Sunday Times*); Justin Huggler (*Independent*).

SELECT
BIBLIOGRAPHY

BOOKS

Arnold, Anthony. *The Fateful Pebble: Afghanistan's Role in the Fall of the Soviet Empire.* Novato, California: Presidio Press, 1993.

Atkins, Stephen. *The 9/11 Encyclopedia.* Volumes 1 and 2. Santa Barbara, California: Praeger Security International, 2011.

Baker, Peter. *Days of Fire: Bush and Cheney in the White House.* New York: Doubleday, 2013.

Bamford, James. *A Pretext for War: 9/11, Iraq, and the Abuse of America's Intelligence Agencies.* New York: Doubleday, 2004.

Barfield, Thomas. *Afghanistan: A Cultural and Political History.* Princeton, New Jersey: Princeton University Press, 2010.

Barrow, Major E. G. *The Military Geography of Afghanistan. Part II: Afghan Turkistan.* Simla, India: Government Central Printing Office, 1893.

Barzilai, Yaniv. *102 Days of War: How Osama bin Laden, Al Qaeda and the Taliban Survived 2001.* Lincoln, Nebraska: Potomac Books, 2014.

Bearden, Milt, and Risen, James. *The Main Enemy: The Inside Story of the CIA's Final Showdown with the KGB.* New York: Random House, 2003.

Bergen, Peter L. *Manhunt: The Ten-Year Search for Bin Laden from 9/11 to Abbottabad.* New York: Crown, 2012.

Berntsen, Gary. *Jawbreaker: The Attack on Bin Laden and Al-Qaeda: A Personal Account by the CIA's Key Field Commander.* New York: Crown, 2005.

Bierbauer, Alec, and Cooter, Mark. *Never Mind, We'll Do It Ourselves: The Inside Story of How a Team of Renegades Broke Rules, Shattered Barriers, and Launched a Drone Warfare Revolution.* New York: Skyhorse Publishing, 2021.

Blehm, Eric. *The Only Thing Worth Fighting For: How Eleven Green Berets Forged a New Afghanistan.* New York: Harper, 2010.

Bolger, Daniel P. *Why We Lost: A General's Inside Account of the Iraq and Afghanistan Wars.* New York: Houghton Mifflin Harcourt, 2014.

343

Briscoe, Charles H.; Kiper, Richard L.; Schroder, James A.; and Sepp, Kalev I. *Weapon of Choice: U.S. Army Special Operations Forces in Afghanistan*. Fort Leavenworth, Kansas: Combat Studies Institute Press, 2003.

Call, Steve. *Danger Close: Tactical Air Controllers in Afghanistan and Iraq*. College Station: Texas A&M University Press, 2007.

Camp, Dick. *Boots on the Ground: The Fight to Liberate Afghanistan from Al-Qaeda and the Taliban 2001–2002*. Minneapolis: Zenith Press, 2011.

Campbell, Alastair. *The Blair Years: The Alastair Campbell Diaries*. New York: Knopf, 2007.

Cashill, Jack. *What's the Matter with California?* New York: Threshold Editions, 2007.

Chivers, C. J. *The Fighters: Americans in Combat in Afghanistan and Iraq*. New York: Simon & Schuster, 2018.

———. *The Gun*. New York: Simon & Schuster, 2010.

Clarke, Richard A. *Against All Enemies: Inside America's War on Terror*. New York: Free Press, 2004.

Cody, Vicki. *Army Wife: A Story of Love and Family in the Heart of the Army*. Berkeley, California: She Writes Press, 2016.

Coll, Steve. *Directorate S: The CIA and America's Secret Wars in Afghanistan and Pakistan*. New York: Penguin Press, 2018.

———. *Ghost Wars*. New York: Penguin Press, 2004.

Cowper-Coles, Sherard. *Cable from Kabul: The Inside Story of the West's Afghanistan Campaign*. London: Harper Press, 2011.

Crile, George. *Charlie Wilson's War: The Extraordinary Story of the Largest Covert Operation in History*. New York: Atlantic Monthly Press, 2003.

Crumpton, Henry A. *The Art of Intelligence: Lessons from a Life in the CIA's Clandestine Service*. New York: Penguin Press, 2012.

Dam, Bette. *A Man and a Motorcycle: How Hamid Karzai Came to Power*. Utrecht, The Netherlands: Ipso Facto, 2014.

DeLong, Michael. *Inside CENTCOM: The Unvarnished Truth About the Wars in Afghanistan and Iraq*. Washington, DC: Regnery, 2004.

Donati, Jessica. *Eagle Down: The Last Special Forces Fighting the Forever War*. New York: PublicAffairs, 2021.

Draper, Robert. *To Start a War: How the Bush Administration Took America into Iraq*. New York: Penguin Press, 2020.

Duffy, John, and Nowosielski, Ray. *The Watchdogs Didn't Bark: The CIA, NSA, and the Crimes of the War on Terror*. New York: Hot Books, 2018.

Dupree, Nancy Hatch. *An Historical Guide to Afghanistan*. Kabul: Afghan Tourist Organization, 1977.

Durant, Michael, and Hartov, Steven. *The Night Stalkers: Top Secret Missions of the U.S. Army's Special Operations Aviation Regiment*. New York: New American Library, 2008.

Eichstaedt, Peter. *Above the Din of War: Afghans Speak About Their Lives, Their Country, and Their Future—and Why America Should Listen*. Chicago: Lawrence Hill Books, 2013.

Evans, Duane. *Foxtrot in Kandahar: A Memoir of a CIA Officer at the Inception of America's Longest War.* El Dorado Hills, California: Savas Beattie, 2017.

Farrell, Theo. *Unwinnable: Britain's War in Afghanistan, 2001–2014.* London: The Bodley Head, 2017.

Farrow, Ronan. *War on Peace: The End of Diplomacy and the Decline of American Influence.* New York: W. W. Norton, 2018.

Farwell, Matt, and Ames, Michael. *American Cipher: Bowe Bergdahl and the U.S. Tragedy in Afghanistan.* New York: Penguin Press, 2019.

Feith, Douglas. *War and Decision: Inside the Pentagon at the Dawn of the War on Terrorism.* New York: HarperCollins, 2008.

Filkins, Dexter. *The Forever War.* New York: Random House, 2008.

Forsyth, Frederick. *The Afghan.* New York: G. P. Putnam's Sons, 2006.

Franks, Tommy. *American Soldier.* New York: HarperCollins, 2004.

Gall, Carlotta. *The Wrong Enemy: America in Afghanistan, 2001–2014.* New York: Houghton Mifflin Harcourt, 2014.

Gall, Sandy. *War Against the Taliban: How It All Went Wrong in Afghanistan.* London: Bloomsbury, 2012.

Gannon, Kathy. *I Is for Infidel: From Holy War to Holy Terror: 18 Years Inside Afghanistan.* New York: PublicAffairs, 2005.

Gopal, Anand. *No Good Men Among the Living: America, the Taliban, and the War Through Afghan Eyes.* New York: Metropolitan Books, 2014.

Graff, Garrett M. *The Only Plane in the Sky: An Oral History of 9/11.* New York: Simon & Schuster, 2019.

Grenier, Robert L. *88 Days to Kandahar: A CIA Diary.* New York: Simon & Schuster, 2015.

Grossman, Dave. *On Killing: The Psychological Cost of Learning to Kill in War and Society.* New York: Little, Brown, 1995.

Gup, Ted. *The Book of Honor: Covert Lives and Classified Deaths at the CIA.* New York: Doubleday, 2000.

Gutman, Roy. *How We Missed the Story: Osama bin Laden, the Taliban, and the Hijacking of Afghanistan.* Washington, DC: United States Institute of Peace, 2008.

Hardcastle, Nate, ed. *American Soldier: Stories of Special Forces from Iraq to Afghanistan.* New York: Thunder's Mouth Press, 2002.

Harnden, Toby. *Bandit Country: The IRA & South Armagh.* London: Hodder & Stoughton, 1999.

———. *Dead Men Risen: The Welsh Guards and the Real Story of Britain's War in Afghanistan.* London: Quercus, 2011.

Hayden, Michael V. *Playing to the Edge: American Intelligence in the Age of Terror.* New York: Penguin Press, 2016.

Holmes, Tony. *The F/A-18 Hornet Story.* Stroud, Gloucestershire: The History Press, 2011.

———. *F-14 Tomcat Units of Operation Enduring Freedom.* Botley, Oxford: Osprey Publishing, 2008.

Holt, Frank L. *Into the Land of Bones: Alexander the Great in Afghanistan.* Berkeley: University of California Press, 2005.

Jacobsen, Annie. *Surprise, Kill, Vanish: The Secret History of CIA Paramilitary Armies, Operators, and Assassins.* New York: Little, Brown, 2019.

Jenkins, Brian Michael, and Godges, John P. *The Long Shadow of 9/11: America's Response to Terrorism.* Santa Monica, CA: Rand Corporation, 2011.

Jones, Seth. *Counterinsurgency in Afghanistan.* Santa Monica, California: RAND Corporation, 2015.

Kahaner, Larry. *AK-47: The Weapon That Changed the Face of War.* New York: John Wiley & Sons, 2007.

Kakar, Hassan. *Afghanistan: A Study in International Political Developments, 1880–1896.* Lahore, Pakistan: Punjab Educational Press, 1971.

Kessler, Ronald. *The CIA at War: Inside the Secret Campaign Against Terror.* New York: St. Martin's Press, 2003.

Khalilzad, Zalmay. *The Envoy: From Kabul to the White House, My Journey Through a Turbulent World.* New York: St. Martin's Press, 2016.

Kipling, Rudyard. *The Irish Guards in the Great War.* Volumes 1 and 2. London: Macmillan, 1923.

Kiriakou, John. *The Reluctant Spy: My Secret Life in the CIA's War on Terror.* New York: Bantam Books, 2009.

Knarr, William M., Jr. *Mazar-e Sharif Battle Site Survey Support Documents* (revised). Alexandria, Virginia: Institute for Defense Analyses, June 2011.

Knarr, William M., Jr., and Frost, John. *Operation Enduring Freedom Battle Reconstruction: Battle Site Survey and Ground Force Data Reconciliation.* Alexandria, Virginia: Institute for Defense Analyses, December 2010.

Knarr, William M., Jr., and Richbourg, Robert. *Learning from the First Victories of the 21st Century: Mazar-e Sharif* (revised). Alexandria, Virginia: Institute for Defense Analyses, January 2010.

Kolthatkar, Sonali, and Ingalls, James. *Bleeding Afghanistan: Washington, Warlords, and the Propaganda of Silence.* New York: Seven Stories Press, 2006.

Krakauer, Jon. *Where Men Win Glory: The Odyssey of Pat Tillman.* New York: Doubleday, 2009.

Kukis, Mark. *"My Heart Became Attached": The Strange Odyssey of John Walker Lindh.* Dulles, Virginia: Brassey's, 2003.

Kummer, David W. *U.S. Marines in Afghanistan, 2001–2009: Anthology and Annotated Bibliography.* Quantico, Virginia: US Marine Corps History Division, 2014.

Lee, Jonathan L. *Afghanistan: A History from 1260 to the Present.* London: Reaktion Books, 2018.

———. *The "Ancient Supremacy": Bukhara, Afghanistan, and the Battle for Balkh, 1731–1901.* Leiden, The Netherlands: E.J. Brill, 1996.

Lewis, Damien. *Bloody Heroes: The True Story of Britain's Secret Warriors in Afghanistan.* London: Century, 2006.

Lippold, Kirk. *Front Burner: Al Qaeda's Attack on the USS Cole.* New York: PublicAffairs, 2012.

Mahoney, Richard D. *Getting Away with Murder: The Real Story Behind American Taliban John Walker Lindh and What the U.S. Government Had to Hide.* New York: Arcade Publishing, 2004.

Malcomson, Scott L. *Generation's End: A Personal Memoir of American Power After 9/11*. Washington, DC: Potomac Books, 2010.

Mattis, James, and West, Bing. *Call Sign Chaos: Learning to Lead*. New York: Random House, 2019.

Mayer, Jane. *The Dark Side: The Inside Story of How the War on Terror Turned into a War on American Ideals*. New York: Doubleday, 2008.

Mazzetti, Mark. *The Way of the Knife: The CIA, a Secret Army, and a War at the Ends of the Earth*. New York: Penguin Press, 2013.

Moore, Robin. *The Hunt for Bin Laden: Task Force Dagger: On the Ground with the Special Forces in Afghanistan*. New York: Random House, 2007.

Morell, Michael. *The Great War of Our Time: The CIA's Fight Against Terrorism from Al Qa'ida to ISIS*. New York: Twelve, 2015.

Morgan, Wesley. *The Hardest Place: The American Military Adrift in Afghanistan's Pech Valley*. New York: Random House, 2021.

Morgan Edwards, Lucy. *The Afghan Solution: The Inside Story of Abdul Haq, the CIA and How Western Hubris Lost Afghanistan*. London: Bactria Press, 2011.

Moyar, Mark. *Oppose Any Foe: The Rise of America's Special Operations Forces*. New York: Basic Books, 2017.

Myers, Richard B. *Eyes on the Horizon: Serving on the Front Lines of National Security*. New York: Threshold Editions, 2009.

National Commission on the Terrorist Attacks Upon the United States. *The 9/11 Commission Report*. New York: W. W. Norton, 2004.

Naylor, Sean. *Relentless Strike: The Secret History of Joint Special Operations Command*. New York: St. Martin's Griffin, 2016.

Neville, Leigh. *Special Operations Forces in Afghanistan*. Botley, Oxford: Osprey Publishing, 2008.

Packer, George. *Our Man: Richard Holbrooke and the End of the American Century*. New York: Knopf, 2019.

Pelton, Robert Young. *Licensed to Kill: Hired Guns in the War on Terror*. New York: Three Rivers Press, 2006.

———. *The World's Most Dangerous Places* (5th edition). New York: HarperCollins, 2003.

Perry, Alex. *Falling Off the Edge: Travels Through the Dark Heart of Globalization*. New York: Bloomsbury Press, 2008.

Perry, Walter L., and Kassing, David. *Toppling the Taliban: Air-Ground Operations in Afghanistan, October 2001 to June 2002*. Santa Monica, California: RAND Corporation, 2015.

Prince, Erik. *Civilian Warriors: The Insider Story of Blackwater and the Unsung Heroes of the War on Terror*. New York: Portfolio/Penguin, 2013.

Radack, Jesselyn. *The Canary in the Coalmine: Blowing the Whistle in the Case of "American Taliban" John Walker Lindh*. Privately published, 2006.

Rashid, Ahmed. *Descent into Chaos: The United States and the Failure of Nation Building in Pakistan, Afghanistan, and Central Asia*. New York: Viking, 2008.

———. *Taliban*. New Haven, Connecticut: Yale University Press, 2000.

Rausenberger, Mark. *A Somalia Journal*. Mahomet, Illinois: Mayhaven Publishing, 1995.

SELECT BIBLIOGRAPHY

Rice, Condoleezza. *No Higher Honor: A Memoir of My Years in Washington.* New York: Crown, 2011.

Riedel, Bruce. *What We Won: America's Secret War in Afghanistan.* Washington, DC: Brookings Institution Press, 2014.

Rizzo, John. *Company Man: Thirty Wars of Controversy and Crisis in the CIA.* New York: Scribner, 2014.

Rohde, David. *In Deep: The FBI, the CIA, and the Truth About America's "Deep State."* New York: W. W. Norton, 2020.

Rosenberg, Carol. *Guantánamo Bay: The Pentagon's Alcatraz of the Caribbean.* Miami, Florida: Herald Books, 2016.

Rubin, Barnett R. *The Search for Peace in Afghanistan: From Buffer State to Failed State.* New Haven, Connecticut: Yale University Press, 1995.

Rumsfeld, Donald. *Known and Unknown: A Memoir.* New York: Sentinel, 2011.

Sageman, Marc. *Understanding Terror Networks.* Philadelphia: University of Pennsylvania Press, 2004.

Scahill, Jeremy. *Dirty Wars: The World Is a Battlefield.* New York: Nation Books, 2013.

Scheuer, Michael. *Osama bin Laden.* New York: Oxford University Press, 2011.

Schroen, Gary C. *First In: An Insider's Account of How the CIA Spearheaded the War on Terror in Afghanistan.* New York: Presidio Press, 2005.

Shelton, Hugh. *Without Hesitation: The Odyssey of an American Warrior.* New York: St. Martin's Press, 2010.

Smith, Graeme. *The Dogs Are Eating Them Now: Our War in Afghanistan.* Toronto: Knopf Canada, 2013.

Smith, Harvey H.; Bernier, Donald W.; Bunge, Frederica M.; Rintz, Frances Chadwick; Shinn, Rinn-Sup; and Teleki, Suzanne. *Area Handbook for Afghanistan* (DA Pam No. 550-65). Washington, DC: US Government Printing Office, 1969.

Stanton, Doug. *Horse Soldiers: The Extraordinary Story of a Band of U.S. Soldiers Who Rode to Victory in Afghanistan.* New York: Scribner, 2009.

Steinberg, Guido W. *German Jihad: On the Internationalization of Islamist Terrorism.* New York: Columbia University Press, 2013.

Sulick, Michael. *Spying in America: Espionage from the Revolutionary War to the Dawn of the Cold War.* Washington, DC: Georgetown University Press, 2014.

Tapper, Jake. *The Outpost: An Untold Story of American Valor.* New York: Little, Brown, 2012.

Tenet, George. *At the Center of the Storm: My Years in the CIA.* New York: HarperCollins, 2007.

Tomsen, Peter. *The Wars of Afghanistan: Messianic Terrorism, Tribal Conflicts, and the Failures of Great Powers.* New York: PublicAffairs, 2011.

Toynbee, Arnold J. *Between Oxus and Jumna: A Journey in India, Pakistan and Afghanistan.* Oxford, England: Oxford University Press, 1961.

Waldman, Thomas. *Vicarious Warfare: American Strategy and the Illusion of War on the Cheap.* Bristol, UK: Bristol University Press, 2021.

Warrick, Joby. *The Triple Agent: The Al-Qaeda Mole Who Infiltrated the CIA.* New York: Doubleday, 2011.

SELECT BIBLIOGRAPHY

Waters, T. J. *Class 11: Inside the CIA's First Post-9/11 Spy Class.* New York: Dutton, 2006.

Waugh, Billy. *Hunting the Jackal: A Special Forces and CIA Ground Soldier's Fifty-Year Career Hunting America's Enemies.* New York: William Morrow, 2004.

Whipple, Chris. *The Spy Masters: How the CIA Directors Shape History and the Future.* New York: Scribner, 2020.

Williams, Brian Glyn. *Afghanistan Declassified: A Guide to America's Longest War.* Philadelphia: University of Pennsylvania Press, 2012.

———. *The Last Warlord: The Life and Legend of Dostum, the Afghan Warrior Who Led US Special Forces to Topple the Taliban Regime.* Chicago: Chicago Review Press, 2013.

Wise, James E., Jr., and Baron, Scott. *The Navy Cross: Extraordinary Heroism in Iraq, Afghanistan, and Other Conflicts.* Annapolis, Maryland: Naval Institute Press, 2007.

Woodward, Bob. *Bush at War.* New York: Simon & Schuster, 2002.

———. *Plan of Attack.* New York: Simon & Schuster, 2004.

Worthington, Andy. *The Guantánamo Files: The Stories of the 774 Detainees in America's Illegal Prison.* London: Pluto Press, 2007.

Wright, Donald P.; Bird, James R.; Clay, Steven E.; Connors, Peter W.; Farquhar, Scott C.; Garcia, Lynne Chandler; and Van Wey, Dennis F. *A Different Kind of War: The United States Army in Operation Enduring Freedom, October 2001–September 2005.* Fort Leavenworth, Kansas: Combat Studies Institute Press, 2009.

Yakubov, Oleg. *The Pack of Wolves: The Blood Trail of Terror.* Moscow: Veche, 2000.

Zastrow, Scott A. *The Degüello.* Privately published, 2011.

ARTICLES

Anonymous. "Obituary of Sergeant 'Scruff' McGough." *Daily Telegraph,* June 24, 2006.

Backer, Larry Catá. "Emasculated Men, Effeminate Law in the United States, Zimbabwe and Malaysia." *Yale Journal of Law and Feminism* Vol. 17, 2005.

Billingsley, Dodge. "Insurrection at Qala-i Jangi." *Harriman Review,* Columbia University, Vol. 13, No. 4, December 2002.

Campbell, Matthew. "The Fort of Hell." *Sunday Times,* December 2, 2001.

Carr, Rebecca. "Text of Lindh's E-Mails and Letters to his Parents." Cox News Service, February 6, 2002.

Carrier, Scott. "Over There: Afghanistan, After the Fall." *Harper's,* April 1, 2002.

Cicere, Chris, and McMillan, Greg. "The AC-130H Spectre Gunship Over Afghanistan: The Opening Rounds." *Air Commando Journal,* Summer 2014.

Cockburn, Patrick. "The Treacherous General. Profile: Rashid Dostum." *Independent,* December 1, 2001.

Crumpton, Henry A. "On the Front Lines: The CIA in Afghanistan, 2001–2002." *Studies in Intelligence* Vol. 47, No. 3, 2003, Classified Edition.

Dauphin, Gary. "A Portrait of the Jihadist as a White Negro." *Bidoun* Issue 11, Summer 2007.

De Luce, Dan; Gramer, Robbie; and Winter, Jana. "John Walker Lindh, Detainee #001." *Foreign Policy,* June 23, 2017.

Fang, Bay. "'They Were All Fighting to Die.'" *U.S. News & World Report,* December 10, 2001.

Gall, Carlotta. "Alliance Declares Revolt Is Crushed." *New York Times,* November 28, 2001.

———. "At Site of Quelled Prisoner Revolt, Afghan Fort's Walls Tell a Tale of Death." *New York Times,* November 29, 2001.

———. "In Tunnels Full of Bodies, One of Them Kept Firing." *New York Times,* November 30, 2001.

———. "Last Holdouts in Uprising Give Up Fort." *New York Times,* December 2, 2001.

———. "U.S. Bomb Wounds G.I.'s as Battle Rages at Fort." *New York Times,* November 27, 2001.

Godines, Valeria. "Spann's Widow Will Never Forget." *Orange County Register,* September 11, 2002.

Harden, Blaine, and Sack, Kevin. "One for His Country, and One Against It." *New York Times,* December 11, 2001.

Harding, Luke. "Allies Direct the Death Rites of Trapped Taliban Fighters." *Guardian,* November 27, 2001.

———. "Dead Lie Crushed or Shot, in the Dust, in Ditches, Amid the Willows." *Guardian,* November 29, 2001.

———. "Surrender Kills Dreams of Taliban." *Observer,* November 25, 2001.

———. "Taliban Who Came Back from Dead." *Observer,* December 2, 2001.

Harding, Luke; McCarthy, Rory; and MacAskill, Ewen. "Fear of Bloodbath as Alliance Advances on Kunduz." *Guardian,* November 23, 2001.

Harding, Luke; Watt, Nicholas; and MacAskill, Ewen. "Errors Revealed in Siege of Afghan Fort." *Guardian,* December 1, 2001.

Harnden, Toby. "The Spy's Spy: From CIA Officer to Thriller-Writer, the Shadowy World of J. R. Seeger." *Spectator* magazine, August 2020.

Hill, James. "Hope Rises Amid War's Ruin." *National Post* (Canada), March 23, 2002.

Huggler, Justin. "The Castle of Death." *Independent,* November 30, 2001.

Human Rights Watch. "Afghanistan: The Massacre in Mazar-i Sharif." *Human Rights Watch Report* Vol. 10, No. 7, November 1998.

Johnson, Mark. "In the Line of Duty, a Hero Emerges." *Milwaukee Journal Sentinel,* November 14, 2003.

Lichtblau, Eric. "Aboard Flight 11, a Chilling Voice." *Los Angeles Times,* September 20, 2001.

Mayer, Jane. "Lost in the Jihad. Why Did the Government's Case Against John Walker Lindh Collapse?" *New Yorker,* March 3, 2003.

McMurray, Kevin. "Cofer Black, Out of the Shadows." *Men's Journal,* October 17, 2008.

Nieves, Evelyn. "A U.S. Convert's Path from Suburbia to a Gory Jail for Taliban." *New York Times,* December 4, 2001.

Pelton, Robert Young. "The Legend of Heavy D and the Boys." *National Geographic Adventure,* March 2002.

Perry, Alex. "Inside the Battle at Qala-i-Jangi." *Time,* December 1, 2001.

Roche, Timothy; Bennett, Brian; Berryman, Anne; Hylton, Hilary; Morrissey, Siobhan; and Radwan, Amany. "The Making of John Walker Lindh." *Time,* October 7, 2002.

SELECT BIBLIOGRAPHY

Semple, Michael. "The Rise of the Hazaras and the Challenge of Pluralism in Afghanistan, 1978–2011." Carr Center for Human Rights Policy, 2011.

Sennott, Charles M. "The Road to Qala-i-Jangi: Circling Back to America's First Casualty in Afghanistan." *GlobalPost*, April 23, 2015. ·

Shanker, Thom; Dao, James; Myers, Steven Lee; and Schmitt, Eric. "Conduct of War Is Redefined by Success of Special Forces." *New York Times*, January 21, 2002.

Shapira, Ian. "He Was a Baby When His Dad Died in Afghanistan. He's 18 Now, and the War Still Isn't Over." *Washington Post*, November 26, 2019.

Sifton, John. "Temporal Vertigo." *New York Times*, September 30, 2001.

Soloway, Colin. "Tale of an American Talib." *Newsweek*, December 1, 2001.

Somaiya, Ravi. "Why Rebel Groups Love the Toyota Hilux." *Newsweek*, October 14, 2010.

Spectar, J. M. "To Ban or Not to Ban an American Taliban? Revocation of Citizenship and Statelessness in a Statecentric System." *California Western Law Review* Vol. 39, No. 2, 2003.

Starr, Richard. "E-mails from a Traitor." *Weekly Standard*, December 9, 2001.

Thomas, Evan. "A Long, Strange Trip to the Taliban." *Newsweek*, December 17, 2001.

Winn, Patrick. "Lethal Sisterhood: A Small Cadre of Female Airmen Prove Their Mettle in Combat." *Air Force Times*, December 31, 2007.

Wörmer, Nils. "The Networks of Kunduz: A History of Conflict and Their Actors, from 1992 to 2001." *Afghan Analysts Network*, 2012.

FILMS

12 Strong, Warner Bros. Pictures, 2018.

The Afghan Solution, Cowgirl Media Inc., New York, 2011.

Dostum: The Kingmaker, Afghanistan, Australian Broadcasting Corporation, 1996.

CIA Officers Memorial Foundation Mission Statement, YouTube, posted by the CIA Officers Memorial Foundation, May 2016.

Good Morning Afghanistan, Damien Degueldre, 2002.

The House of War: Battling the Taliban, Paul Yule, Berwick Universal Pictures, 2002.

Inside the Afghanistan War, National Geographic, 2013.

Legion of Brothers, Greg Barker, Bergen-Mabile Productions, 2017.

Situation Critical: Taliban Uprising, Rufus Jones, National Geographic, 2007.

Two Young Americans: The Patriot and the Taliban, A&E, 2002.

NOTES

PREFACE

xi **over 3,500 fatalities:** By April 2021 there had been a total of 3,571 military casualties in Afghanistan since 9/11: 2,448 American, 456 British, and 689 from other NATO countries. "Casualty Status," US Department of Defense press release, April 5, 2021; "British fatalities in Afghanistan," UK Ministry of Defence press release, October 12, 2015; "Soldiers Killed in Action in Afghanistan 2001–2020," Statistical Research Department, March 15, 2021.

xi **at least another 18:** By April 2021, the eighteen publicly identified CIA employees who died in Afghanistan after Mike Spann, the first casualty, in 2001 were: Nathan Chapman (2002); Helge Boes, Christopher Mueller, William Carson (2003); Donald Barger (2008); Harold Brown, Elizabeth Hanson, Darren LaBonte, Jennifer Matthews, Dane Paresi, Scott Roberson, Jeremy Wise (2009); Jay Henigan (2011); Dario Lorenzetti (2012); Ranya Abdelsayed (2013); Brian Hoke, Nathaniel Delemarre, George Whitney (2016). Adam Goldman and Matthew Rosenberg, "A Funeral of 2 Friends: C.I.A. Deaths Rise in Secret Afghan War," *New York Times,* September 6, 2017; Ian Shapira, "A CIA Suicide Sparks Hard Questions About the Agency's Memorial Wall," *Washington Post,* May 21, 2019.

xi **trickle after 2015:** By April 2021, there had been ninety-six US military deaths since the start of 2015, when Operation Enduring Freedom became Operation Freedom's Sentinel.

xi **10,000 Afghan civilians:** "Afghanistan: Civilian Casualties Exceed 10,000 for Sixth Straight Year," *U.N. News,* February 22, 2020.

xi **The Taliban:** Pashto for "students." A fundamentalist Islamic group, founded in Kandahar in 1994, that formed the Afghan government from 1996 until 201, imposing Sharia law and attempting to model society on the 7th century ideals of the Prophet Mohammed. Waged an insurgency after 2001, regaining control of much of the country and in 2020 entering negotiations in Doha, Qatar, over a power-sharing deal.

xi **Nearly 3,000 people:** A total of 2,977 were killed on 9/11, plus the 19 hijackers. This number is made up of 2,753 at the World Trade Center, 184 at the Pentagon, and 40 in Pennsylvania. "Breakdown of the 2,977 Victims of 9/11," Agence France-Presse, September 11, 2011.

xi **toll at Pearl Harbor:** 2,403 people were killed at Pearl Harbor on December 7, 1941. Matthew Diebel, Pearl Harbor Remembrance Day 2019: "What Happened During Fateful Attack 78 Years Ago?" *USA Today,* December 6, 2019.

xii **"by, with, and through":** Diana I. Dalphonse, Chris Townsend, and Matthew W. Weaver, "Shifting Landscape: The Evolution of By, With, and Through," *Strategy Bridge,* August 1, 2018.

CHAPTER 1: ZERO HOUR

3 **Settling in:** The account of David Tyson's background and career is drawn from author interviews with David Tyson, Rosann Tyson, and CIA sources.

3 **David Tyson:** Tyson is given the pseudonym Dave Olson in Stanton, *Horse Soldiers;* David Davis in Bolger, *Why We Lost;* Dawson in Berntsen, *Jawbreaker;* and Doug Olsen in Sennott, "The Road to Qala-i Jangi," *GlobalPost.*

3 **flight of seven hours:** The exact flight time was seven hours and twenty-five minutes, departing Tashkent at 4:35 p.m. local and arriving at London Heathrow at 7:55 p.m. local. Information from *Uzbekistan Airways Timetable—Effective until 27 October 2001.*

3 **Mohammed Atta...was about:** Atkins, *The 9/11 Encyclopedia,* 347–59.

3 **most devastating attack:** Francis Temman, "September 11: A Meticulously Planned Operation," Agence France-Presse, September 8, 2002.

3 **"zero hour":** The Al-Qaeda commander was Abu Zubayda. Woodward, *Bush at War,* 40.

4 **separate directorates:** In 2001, the CIA had four directorates: Operations, Intelligence, Science & Technology, and Support.

4 **ass-end of nowhere:** Bierbauer and Cooter, *Never Mind, We'll Do It Ourselves,* 82: "Getting stuck in the ass-end of the world..." The country referred to is identifiable as Uzbekistan.

5 **with a thesis:** The thesis was accepted by Indiana University's Department of Central Eurasian Studies in March 1993.

5 **expert on shrine pilgrimage:** See: David Tyson, "Shrine Pilgrimage in Turkmenistan as a Means to Understand Islam Among the Turkmen," *Central Asia Monitor,* 1997.

7 **seven miles from:** The CIA's Foreign Broadcast Information Service was in Rosslyn, Virginia.

7 **plucked from this backwater:** Tyson was recruited into the DO by Robert Baer, who hired him on the spot when he learned which languages he spoke.

7 **course at "The Farm":** The Farm's location at Camp Peary remains an official secret. "Ex-CIA Agent Tells of Six-Week Peary Course," *Richmond Times Dispatch,* December 28, 1972.

7 **case officer in Pakistan:** The case officer was Chris Wood. He later became chief of Kabul station and director of the CIA's Counterterrorism Mission Center.

8 **Afghans had a:** United Nations High Commissioner for Refugees, "Background Paper on Refugees and Asylum Seekers from Afghanistan," UNHCR Centre for Documentation and Research, Geneva, April 2001.

9 **7 million landmines:** Drew Brown, "One of Biggest Threats Facing U.S. Military in Afghanistan Is Land Mines," Knight Ridder, October 13, 2001.

9 **Pashtuns:** The largest ethnic group in Afghanistan, made up of Sunni Muslims who speak the Pashto language. The bulk of Pashtuns occupy the region stretching from southeast Afghanistan to northwest Pakistan. The Taliban is overwhelmingly Pashtun.

8 **who made up 38 percent:** *The 2001 CIA World Factbook* (Langley, Virginia: Central Intelligence Agency, 2001) lists the ethnic makeup of Afghanistan as: Pashtun, 38 percent; Tajik, 25 percent; Hazara, 19 percent; Uzbek, 6 percent; and minor ethnic groups (Aimaks, Turkmens, Baloch, and others), 12 percent.

9 **Tajiks:** A Dari-speaking Sunni ethnic group native to Tajikistan and Afghanistan. Agmad Shah Massoud, Atta Mohammed Noor, and Fahim Khan were Tajiks.

9 **Hazaras:** A Dari-speaking Shia ethnic group native to central Afghanistan. In 2001, their leaders were Karim Khalili and Mohammed Mohaqeq. The Hazaras suffered ethnic cleansing at the hands of the Taliban, who viewed them as non-Muslims.

9 **Uzbeks:** A Turkic ethnic group native to Central Asia that predominates Uzbekistan and is a minority in northern Afghanistan. Name derives from Öz Beg, a Mongol khan. The Uzbeks are Sunni Muslims who originate from a mingling of ancient Iranian populations and nomadic Mongol or Turkic tribes that invaded the region between the 11th and 5th centuries. Many arrived in Afghanistan as refugees in the 1920s and 1930s to escape repression by the Soviet Union, of which Uzbekistan was part.

9 **Turkmens:** A Turkic ethnic group native to Central Asia, living mainly in Turkmenistan and northern Afghanistan. Closely aligned with Uzbeks—and largely indistinguishable from them to an outsider. Turkmens are Sunni Muslims.

9 **Daoud Khan was executed:** Carlotta Gall, "An Afghan Secret Revealed Brings End of an Era," *New York Times,* January 31, 2009. Daoud Khan was shot dead in the presidential palace along with most of his family and buried in an unmarked grave; his supporters were slaughtered on the streets of Kabul. Khan had become president in a coup against his cousin, the last king of Afghanistan, five years earlier.

9 **with 100,000 troops:** Steve Galster, "Afghanistan: The Making of U.S. Policy, 1973–1990, National Security Archive, October 9, 2001.

9 **over 40,000 Soviet soldiers:** Arnold, *The Fateful Pebble,* 189–90. The official Soviet total was 18,826, but Arnold, a former CIA analyst, concludes there was a "generally consistent estimate of between 40,000 and 50,000 dead."

9 **1.5 million Afghans:** Rashid, *Taliban,* 13.

9 **up to 150,000 fighters:** Tomsen, *The Wars of Afghanistan,* 215.

NOTES

9 **biggest clandestine operation:** Crile, *Charlie Wilson's War,* ix.

9 **the ISI, Pakistan's intelligence agency:** Steve Coll, "Anatomy of a Victory: CIA's Covert Afghan War," *Washington Post,* July 19, 1992.

9 **$4.5 billion in aid:** Rashid, *Taliban,* 13.

10 **Tennessee mules to combat boots:** Mark Fineman, "U.S. Also Helping Afghan Rebels with Mules, Books," *Los Angeles Times,* February 18, 1989.

10 **2,500 shoulder-launched, heat-seeking Stinger missiles:** Coll, *Ghost Wars,* 11.

10 **Massoud, for one, received $200,000:** Bamford, *A Pretext for War,* 178.

10 **35,000 Islamic radicals:** Rashid, *Taliban,* 130.

11 **who arrived in 1984:** Krakauer, *Where Men Win Glory,* 11.

11 **"a few stirred-up Muslims":** Loyn, *In Afghanistan,* 157. The comment was made in 1998 by Zbigniew Brzezinski, President Jimmy Carter's National Security Adviser from 1977 to 1981.

11 **it never funded:** Sageman, *Understanding Terror Networks,* 57.

11 **founding of Al-Qaeda:** Bergen, *Manhunt,* 250.

11 **blocked at Kabul airport:** Tomsen, *The Wars of Afghanistan,* 12–13.

11 **first time in 300 years:** It was also the end of a sixty-three-year interlude in which the city's civilian population had been relatively free from bloodshed. Tomsen, *Wars of Afghanistan,* 215.

11 **Hekmatyar laid siege:** John F. Burns, "With Kabul Largely in Ruins, Afghans Get Respite From War," *New York Times,* February 20, 1995.

11 **Dostum switched sides:** Anwar Iqbal, "Kabul Suffers Another Stalemate," United Press International, January 22, 1994.

12 **new Pashtun group:** Rashid, *Taliban,* 17–30.

12 **Massoud withdrew:** Coll, *Ghost Wars,* 14.

12 **castrated, dragged:** Henry Meyer, "Kabulis Rejoice at Taliban Fall, Cry for Vengeance Against Omar," Agence France-Presse, December 7, 2001.

12 **Northern Alliance was formed:** The Northern Alliance was founded as the "Supreme Council for the Defense of the Motherland" or "United Front." Tomsen, *Wars of Afghanistan,* 542. Though principally Tajik, Hazara, Uzbek, and Turkmen, it also included some Pashtuns.

12 **barred women from:** Kathy Gannon, "Bloody Start for Kabul's New Regime," Associated Press, September 28, 1996.

12 **French perfumes and Russian vodka:** Chris Stephen, "Fight for Mazar: City Waits for the Warlord's Revenge," *Observer,* October 21, 2001.

12 **wore lipstick:** Arthur Max, "In Afghanistan's Other Capital, Women Still Wear Lipstick," Associated Press, October 15, 1996.

13 **once a trading post:** Dexter Filkins, "A Leader of Afghan Rebels Says They Are Near a Crucial Taliban City," *New York Times,* October 16, 2001.

13 **betrayed the Uzbek leader:** Sally Buzbee, "New Afghan Allies No Democracy Poster Boys," Associated Press, October 25, 2001.

13 **Some 2,500 Taliban:** Alex Spillius, "Taliban Closing In on Afghan Opposition," *Daily Telegraph,* August 11, 1998.

13 **massacring 600:** Williams, *The Last Warlord,* 189–90.

13 **2,000 Taliban captives:** Tim Witcher, "Mazar-i-Sharif: City of Blood and Treachery," Agence France-Presse, November 9, 2001.

13 **Dostum returned:** Ann Marlowe, "'Warlords' and 'Leaders,'" *National Review,* February 18, 2002.

13 **fled into Turkmenistan:** "Dostum Re-establishes His Writ over Northern Afghanistan," Deutsche Presse-Agentur, October 21, 1997.

13 **tomb of Abdul Ali Mazari:** Williams, *The Last Warlord,* 196–97.

14 **"Wherever you go we":** Declaration by Mullah Niazi, estimate of Hazaras murdered, and Human Rights Watch statement taken from Michael Sheridan, "How the Taliban Slaughtered 8,000 People in Mazar-e-Sharif," *Sunday Times,* November 1, 1998.

14 **400 of whom were kidnapped:** Rashid, *Taliban,* 75.

14 **eleven Iranian diplomats:** Douglas Jehl, "Iran President Will Not Bar Use of Force on Afghans," *New York Times,* September 10, 1998.

14 **"We must give voice":** Hillary Clinton, "First Lady of the United States Delivers Remarks at Ceremony Observing International Women's Day," *FDCH Political Transcripts,* March 11, 1998.

14 **Mavis Leno:** Bob Herbert, "A War on Women," *New York Times,* October 4, 1998.

14 **State Department report:** "International Narcotics Control Strategy Report," US Department of State Bureau of International Narcotics and Law Enforcement Affairs, March 1998, 229.

14 **had returned to Saudi:** Cameron Stewart, "A New Public Enemy No. 1," August 22, 1998.

15 **revoked bin Laden's citizenship:** Charles J. Hanley, "Militants' Money Man Said to Bail Out of Afghanistan, Back to Sudan," Associated Press, October 3, 1996.

15 **thirty-page fatwa:** Dominic Tierney, "The Twenty Years' War," *Atlantic,* August 23, 2016.

15 **issued another fatwa:** "Compilation of Usama bin Laden Statements 1994– 2004," CIA's Foreign Broadcast Information Service, January 2004. A fatwa is a decree passed down by an Islamic religious leader.

15 **killing 224 and:** Larry Neumeister, "Four Guilty in Embassy Bombings," Associated Press, May 30, 2001.

15 **seventy-five Tomahawk:** Paul Richter, "U.S. Says Raids a Success, Warns of More Strikes," *Los Angeles Times,* August 22, 1998.

15 **around $750,000:** Michael D. Towle, "Tomahawk Missiles Fly Low and Hit Hard," *Fort Worth Star-Telegram,* August 22, 1998.

15 **It was an anemic:** Critics noted that it distracted attention from the Monica Lewinsky scandal, over which Clinton was later impeached; John Lang, "Some Say Clinton's Wagging the Dog," Scripps Howard News Service, August 21, 1998.

CHAPTER 2: BLUE SKY

16 **"Lion of the Panjshir":** The word Panjshir means "five valleys."

16 **vast library:** Ray Rivera, "Legend of a Commander Flourishes, But Can't Repair Afghan Divisions," *New York Times,* September 11, 2011.

17 **a grizzled veteran:** Author interviews with CIA sources. Bierbauer and Cooter, *Never Mind, We'll Do It Ourselves,* 80–86, identifies Fred as the CIA station chief in "a sleepy Central Asian country."

17 **ran to the porch:** Author interview with Rosann Tyson.

17 **"prepared to rip off":** "Uzbek President Vows to 'Rip Off' Heads to Restore Order," Agence France-Presse, April 2, 1999.

17 **Islamic Movement of Uzbekistan:** The IMU was led by Juma Namangani, a former paratrooper in the Soviet Army who had fought in the war against the Afghans, and Tahir Yuldashev.

18 **human rights record:** According to a CIA source, US diplomats had registered dismay at reports that car thieves were being executed. Karimov had responded that the penalty in America for stealing a horse had once been hanging. Just as a horse had been a man's livelihood in the Wild West, so was a car for most Uzbeks.

18 **Alec station:** The predominantly female staff had been labeled "the Manson Family" for their almost cultlike insistence that bin Laden was a mortal threat. Coll, *Ghost Wars,* 453–54.

18 **In June 1999:** Author interview with Blee.

18 **tall, sandy-haired:** Coll, *Directorate S,* 16.

18 **Blee had made the case:** Author interviews with Blee and Tyson. This mission is also described in Crumpton, *The Art of Intelligence,* 129–132; and Coll, *Ghost Wars,* xx.

18 **appointment was a sign:** Blee had been executive assistant to CIA director George Tenet, which gave him influence at senior levels of the Agency.

19 **"This situation is going to change":** Author interview with Blee.

19 **its Northern Alliance Liaison Team:** Coll, *Ghost Wars,* 459.

19 **Massoud in Paris:** Ibid., 554.

19 **mortared Darunta:** Ibid., 487–89.

20 **at Tarnak Farms:** Ben Farmer, "HQ Where Bin Laden Plotted Atrocities," *Daily Telegraph,* September 5, 2011.

20 **Agency's hierarchy:** The decision was made by James Pavitt, Tenet's deputy.

20 **attack on the USS *Cole*:** Lippold, *Front Burner,* 47–48.

20 **"Blue Sky Memo":** *The 9/11 Commission Report,* 196–97.

20 **son of a peasant:** Biographical details of Dostum are drawn from Williams, *The Last Warlord.*

21 **died in bizarre circumstances:** Rod Nordland, "Accused of Rape and Torture, Exiled Afghan Vice President Returns," *New York Times,* July 22, 2018.

21 **behind a refrigerator:** Williams, *Last Warlord,* 159–60.

21 **archetypal Afghan warlord:** The term *warlord* (*Jang salar* in Dari) is controversial and freighted with overtones of corruption, coercion, and human-rights abuses. Since 2001 it has often been used to marginalize and denigrate Afghan leaders. It is used throughout *First Casualty* as a neutral, shorthand term to describe leaders in Afghanistan whose power derives from their military might and reputation as well as their political clout. Brian Glyn Williams has written: "While the word 'warlord' is a relatively recent addition to the English language, based on the German word *Kriegsherr*, the concept itself is not new. It essentially refers to a substate political ruler whose claim to legitimacy is based on his control of military forces." (Williams, *Last Warlord*, 158.) Charlie Santos, the former United Nations official and Unocal oil-company executive, stated in 2001: "If you can tell me the difference between a warlord and a leader in Afghanistan, you should get the Nobel Prize. This is a country at war for 23 years." (Anthony Shadid, "Northern Alliance Divided," *Boston Globe*, November 15, 2001.) Dostum himself has reluctantly embraced the term, stating in 2003: "It's time for a new generation who don't have blood on their hands to build our nation. Perhaps it is fitting that I am my people's last warlord." (Williams, *Last Warlord*, 300.)

21 **secret CIA base at Shakhrisabz:** CIA sources revealed the location of this base to the author.

22 **around 600:** Coll, *Ghost Wars*, 11.

22 **reputedly possessed:** Michael M. Phillips, "Launching the Missile That Made History," *Wall Street Journal*, October 1, 2011.

22 **up to $150,000:** Stephen Graham, "Afghanistan Tries to Round Up U.S. Missiles," Associated Press, January 31, 2005.

22 **Massoud had been slain:** Craig Pyes and William C. Rempel, "Slowly Stalking an Afghan 'Lion,'" *Los Angeles Times*, June 12, 2002.

CHAPTER 3: THIRD OPTION

24 **two scuba divers:** Account of scuba dive and training course drawn from author interviews with Sapp.

25 **A minute before Justin:** Atkins, *9/11 Encyclopedia*, 14–15.

25 **Operational Detachment Alpha:** Usually abbreviated to ODA. A Special Forces unit twelve-men strong, sometimes referred to as an Alpha Team or an A Team. ODAs were given a three-digit number to identify them. A 5 indicated 5th Group. A 1, 2, or 3 as the second number indicated 1st Battalion, 5th Group. A 4, 5, or 6 indicated 2nd Battalion, 5th Group. A 7, 8, or 9 indicated 3rd Battalion, 5th Group. Thus, ODA 534 was from 1st Battalion, 5th Group; ODA 555 was from 2nd Battalion; and ODA 595 was from 3rd Battalion.

25 **Justin had learned:** Details of childhood and early career drawn from author interviews with Sapp.

25 **Sapp's obituary:** "Obituary of Kenneth M. Sapp," *Washington Post*, October 6, 2013.

26 **as he fled:** In 1983, Kenneth Sapp was in the US Embassy in Kuwait when terrorists linked to Iran drove a truck bomb into the compound. More-peaceful postings for the Sapp family included two in India, where Justin had attended British schools in Bombay and New Delhi.

26 **the movie *Patton*:** Sven Mikulec, "*Patton:* A Most Compelling Biopic Worthy of Its Enigmatic Subject," Cinephilia & Beyond, 2017 (https://cinephiliabeyond.org). Coppola's Oscar was for Best Original Screenplay; he received it along with his co-writer, Edmund H. North.

26 **operations against the Al-Qaeda-backed IMU:** Sapp had worked with the Uzbeks in the Fergana Valley, where Uzbekistan, Tajikistan, and Kyrgyzstan converge. The Fergana Valley, home of senior IMU figure Juma Namangani, was one of the most troubled parts of Central Asia.

26 **three infantry divisions:** Williams, *Last Warlord,* 153.

28 **This was not:** Account of Shannon Spann's experience on 9/11, her early life, and her marriage to Mike drawn from author interviews with Shannon Spann.

28 **flight attendant onboard:** The flight attendant was Amy Sweeney. Eric Lichtblau, "Aboard Flight 11, a Chilling Voice," *Los Angeles Times,* September 20, 2001.

29 **The ceremony took place:** Email to author from Phillip Campbell, who was the civil officiant.

29 **born three months apart:** Johnny Micheal Spann was born March 1, 1969. Shannon Joy was born June 14, 1969.

29 **"Silent Mike":** Author interview with Shannon Spann; Klein, "If Anything Happens…," *Parade* magazine, August 18, 2002.

29 **Originally named Needmore:** Calvin Woodward, "Two Americans Come Face to Face on Opposite Sides of War," Associated Press, December 31, 2001.

30 **was christened:** Author interview with Gail Spann.

30 **fished for bass:** Kevin Peraino, "A Dreamer With 'No Fear,'" *Newsweek,* December 10, 2001.

30 **one of only six seniors:** Kim Barker, "Small Town Learns One of Its Own Was a Hero," *Chicago Tribune,* December 2, 2001.

30 **chose Proverbs 13:20:** Winfield City High School Yearbook 1987, 107.

30 **telephoned home to grumble:** Author interview with Gail Spann.

31 **A court hearing:** *Johnny Micheal Spann v. Kathryn Ann Webb Spann,* Case 0204739700, Circuit Court of Prince William County, Virginia. (Hereinafter *Spann divorce file.*)

31 **California farm town:** Scott Martelle and Ray F. Herndon, "Orange County Less Suburban, More L.A.," *Los Angeles Times,* May 15, 2002.

31 **in the pep squad:** Details of Shannon Spann's schooldays drawn from Tustin High School Yearbooks 1986 and 1987.

31 **studied English and American Studies:** Jeff Collins, "Widow Shows Her Resolve," *Orange County Register,* December 13, 2001.

31 **passing the bar in 1995:** The State Bar of California Attorney Licensee Profile Shannon Joy Verleur #179915.

31 **pages of *The Economist*:** Tod Mohamed, "It's No Secret: The CIA Wants Spies,"

Ottawa Citizen, October 1, 1998. A photograph of the CIA job advertisement from *The Economist* accompanied the article.

32 **from more than 20,000 employees:** Tom Raum, "CIA Recruiting Drive Paying Off," Associated Press, January 17, 2000.

32 **into the CIA lobby:** Waters, *Class 11,* 2–4.

32 **77th and 78th stars:** Matt Apuzzo and Adam Goldman, "Raid on bin Laden Compound Avenged CIA Deaths in 1998," Associated Press, May 29, 2011. Molly Huckaby Hardy, fifty-one, was a finance officer. Tom Shah, thirty-eight, was a case officer in Africa Division. Their names were not added to the *Book of Honor,* the goatskin-bound volume in a display case in front of the wall, until 2011.

32 **Art Keller, a former Army:** Details of background and experiences at The Farm drawn from author interviews with Keller.

33 **a CIA assassin:** Kathryn Spann hinted at this claim in court papers. *Spann divorce file.*

33 **Amy, a Californian:** Details of background and experiences at The Farm drawn from author interview with Amy, whose full name is not used because she was still serving undercover in 2021.

34 **alone and celibate:** Klein, "If Anything Happens…," *Parade* magazine.

35 **Brian, who had:** Details of background, experiences at The Farm, and time in Marines with Mike Spann drawn from author interview with Brian, whose full name is not used because he was still serving undercover in 2021.

36 **"Oh my God":** Lichtblau, "Aboard Flight 11, a Chilling Voice," *Los Angeles Times.*

37 **"Let's roll.":** Toby Harnden, "The Quiet Executive Who Defied Hijackers," *Daily Telegraph,* September 18, 2001.

38 **Analysts remembered:** Author interviews with Black, Kiriakov, and Blee.

38 **crashed in Shanksville:** Todd Spangler, "United Jet Crashes in Pennsylvania," Associated Press, September 11, 2001.

38 **the word** EVACUATE: Coll, *Directorate S,* 31.

38 **"why are we leaving":** Author interview with Andy.

38 **White House or the US Capitol:** *The 9/11 Commission Report,* 14.

38 **motto was *Tertia Optio*:** Waldman, *Vicarious Warfare,* 86.

38 **Alison Spann was confused:** "A Daughter's Mission: Special Tribute to American Hero Mike Spann," *SmartHER News* (Jenna Lee Babin podcast interview with Alison Spann, September 9, 2019).

CHAPTER 4: SHOWTIME

42 **Mike had written:** Harden and Sack, "One For His Country, and One Against It," *New York Times.*

42 **Mike had emailed:** Email from Mike Spann to Aaron Catrett, December 30, 1999.

43 **actor Jack Nicholson:** Rizzo, *Company Man,* 176.

NOTES

43 **bin Laden targeted him:** Author interview with Black; Coll, *Ghost Wars,* 271 .

43 **first visited sub-Saharan Africa:** Author interview with Black.

44 **"prudence and fearlessness":** Crumpton, *Art of Intelligence,* 181.

44 **"tried to take Mr. bin Laden":** Susan Page, "Why Clinton Failed to Stop bin Laden," *USA Today,* November 12, 2001.

44 **CIA's legal advice:** Rizzo, *Company Man.*

44 **"This is sometimes a corollary":** Author interview with Black.

44 **preoccupied with:** Crumpton, *Art of Intelligence,* 167: "the new White House team appeared to have even *less* interest in AQ."

44 **Tenet later testified:** *The 9/11 Commission Report,* 277.

45 **Tenet, Blee, and Bleck were prompted:** Author interviews with Black and Blee.

45 **banging his fist:** Author interview with Black; Whipple, *Spy Masters,* 187.

45 **advice went unheeded:** Author interviews with Black and Blee.

45 **On August 6:** *The 9/11 Commission Report,* 260.

45 **"We are going to be":** Coll, *Ghost Wars,* 562.

45 **In an odd coincidence:** Author interview with Black; Lippold, *Front Burner,* xxv.

45 **"So, this has been":** Author interview with Black.

45 **standing on the desk:** Author interview with Kiriakou.

46 **At 9:30 a.m.:** Author interview with Black; Woodward, *Bush at War,* 44–46.

47 **Congress authorized Bush:** Ron Fournier, "Nation Kneels to Pray, President Stirs Passions of U.S. against Terrorism," Associated Press, September 14, 2001.

47 **the lone dissenter:** At the time, Lee faced widespread opprobrium for her vote. By 2019, many in the Democratic Party hailed her as a visionary. Negar Mortazavi, "Biden Breaks from Obama-Era Afghanistan Policy," *Independent,* December 20, 2019.

47 **"rid the world":** Tom Raum, "Anti-Terror 'Crusade' Will Take a While, Bush Says," Associated Press, September 17, 2001.

47 **FBI released the names:** "FBI Releases Names of Hijackers It Says Carried Out Tuesday's Attacks," Agence France-Presse, September 14, 2001.

47 **Mohammed Atta had:** Douglas Frantz, "Germans Lay Out Early Qaeda Ties to 9/11 Hijackers," *New York Times,* August 24, 2002.

48 **Cofer Black, who was there:** Author interview with Black. The account of this meeting also draws extensively from Draper, *To Start a War,* 17–20.

48 **"cut the head off":** Author interview with Black.

48 **the capital of Zaire:** Zaire became the Democratic Republic of the Congo in 1997.

48 **wanted to kill somebody:** Woodward, *Bush at War,* 46.

49 **CENTCOM:** Central Command, the US regional military command covering Afghanistan and the Middle East. Headquartered in Tampa, Florida, and led by General Tommy Franks from July 2000 until July 2003.

49 **remarked acidly:** Donald Rumsfeld, *Known and Unknown,* 358–59.

49 **"I am seeing nothing":** Rumsfeld memo to General Myers and staff, "What Will Be the Military Role in the War on Terrorism?", October 10, 2001.

50 **Hazrat Ali, the cousin and son-in-law of the Prophet Mohammed:** Nancy Hatch Dupree, *An Historical Guide to Afghanistan,* 390.

50 **lobbying for outside support:** Author interviews with Khalili and Mohaqeq.

50 **had noted in 1893:** Barrow, *The Military Geography of Afghanistan,* 9.

51 **In his 2000 book:** Ahmed Rashid's book was *Militant Islam, Oil and Fundamentalism in Central Asia.*

51 **Rashid had added that:** Ibid., 56.

52 **whose interest in Afghanistan:** Author interview with Santos.

53 **accepting a $1 million payment:** Coll, *Ghost Wars,* 329.

53 **message for the US government:** Author interviews with Dostum and Santos; Williams, *Last Warlord,* 68 . Williams identifies Santos only as "an American expat living in Uzbekistan" who "was a former employee of the US oil firm Unocal."

53 **Black chose Gary Schroen:** Author interviews with Black and Crumpton.

53 **medic was Dave Phillips:** Author interview with Phillips.

54 **in which was the key:** Author interview with Gilbert.

54 **$100,000 to return:** Author interviews with CIA sources.

55 **"aggressive philistinism":** Grenier, *88 Days to Kandahar,* 68.

56 **"Fuck diplomacy":** Author interview with Morell; Morell, *The Great War of Our Time,* 60–61.

CHAPTER 5: KILL BOX

57 **"Tenet and Cofer":** Author interview with Stiles.

58 **campaign would be:** Barzilai, *102 Days of War,* 39.

59 **He told General Franks:** Author interview with Crumpton; Feith, *War and Decision,* 77: "CENTCOM believed it could not embed Special Forces with Afghan militias until CIA agents had made face-to-face arrangements with the militia commanders." Feith was the number three official in the Pentagon.

59 **"these dickheads":** Crumpton, *Art of Intelligence,* 227.

59 **leader was J. R. Seeger:** His full name was John Robert Seeger, but from early childhood he had been known as J.R. to differentiate him from his father, who had the same name. Details of his life and career drawn from author interviews with Seeger and other Team Alpha members.

60 **deputy was Alex Hernandez:** Details of life and career drawn from author interviews with Hernandez and other Team Alpha members.

60 **Navy SEAL training instructor:** Hernandez was an instructor on the Basic Underwater Demolition/SEAL (BUD/S) initial training course at the Naval Special Warfare Training Center in Coronado, California. Passing BUD/S is a prerequisite to becoming a US Navy SEAL.

61 **Lawrence "Gus" Freedman:** Gup, *The Book of Honor,* 338–64.

62 **His *Somalia Journal:*** The book was published in 1995 by Mark Rausenberger. The reflection "God has more planned…" is on page 25.

62 **joint session of Congress:** Toby Harnden, "God Bless America—and the President," *Daily Telegraph,* September 22, 2001.

63 **Gallup approval rating:** David W. Moore, "Bush Job Approval Highest in Gallup History, Widespread Public Support for War on Terrorism," Gallup News Service, September 24, 2001.

63 **Lieutenant Colonel Chris Haas:** Haas, commander of 1st Battalion, 5th Group, was sent to the Panjshir Valley with Fahim's forces. He entered Kabul just after it fell to the Northern Alliance.

64 **Dagger would oversee:** TF Dagger was based at K2 and later at Bagram. TF K-Bar, or CJSOTF-South, was responsible for operations in southern Afghanistan. Its headquarters were at Masirah Air Base in Oman and later Kandahar. TF Sword, initially based in Oman but later at Bagram, oversaw forces from the Joint Special Operations Command (JSOC), whose task was to kill or capture senior Al-Qaeda and Taliban figures. Major Denis P. Doty, US Air Force, "Command and Control of Special Operations Forces for 21st Century Contingency Operations," paper submitted to the Faculty of the Naval War College in Newport, Rhode Island, February 2003.

65 **rabbit runs between them dubbed:** Author interview with Kiriakou.

65 **"I don't give a flying fuck":** Duane Evans, *Foxtrot in Kandahar*, 46.

65 **cut the chains off:** Author interview with Kiriakou; Kiriakou, *The Reluctant Spy*, 109.

65 **fire-alarm test:** Tenet, *At the Center of the Storm*, 212. Archibald later became head of the DO before retiring in 2015. He died aged sixty-four in 2020.

65 **beneath twelve feet of debris:** Atkins, *The 9/11 Encyclopedia*, 225–26.

65 **father of Diane Killip:** Berntsen, *Jawbreaker*, 82–83; "Obituary of David Robert Smith," *Daily Press* (Virginia), September 13, 2001.

66 **"I'm taking Dave":** Author interviews with Seeger and Gilbert.

67 **Tashkent station chief:** Gilbert, who took over from Fred, arrived in Uzbekistan on August 30, 2001.

67 **Massie…told one team:** Evans, *Foxtrot in Kandahar*, 63, identifies him as "John, the Deputy Chief of CTC/SO." Crumpton, *Art of Intelligence*, 175, states he was John Massie.

68 **JTV—Jake Terrain Vehicle:** Ian Shapira, "He Was a Baby," *Washington Post*.

68 **so he could feed Jake:** Godines, "Spann's Widow," *Orange County Register*.

68 **was one of his heroes:** Author interview with Shannon Spann; Wayne Drash, "A Child of War, with a Sense of Purpose," CNN.com, September 4, 2013.

68 **pat Shannon's middle:** Godines, "Spann's Widow," *Orange County Register*.

68 **Moochie or Boo-Boo Bear:** Shapira, "He Was a Baby," *Washington Post*.

68 **Marine Corps would do:** Godines, "Spann's Widow." *Orange County Register*.

68 **he emailed her:** Klein, "If Anything Happens…," *Parade* magazine.

69 **morning of October 5:** Last Will and Testament of Johnny Micheal Spann, signed October 5, 2001, document W-10534, Circuit Court of Prince William County, Virginia (hereinafter: *Spann will*).

69 **Manassas to sign his will:** Josh White, "Death Reveals a Willing—but Secret—Hero," *Washington Post*, November 30, 2001; *Spann will*.

69 **salary was $43,059:** Salary Table 2001-DCB, 2001 General Schedule Locality Pay Tables, US Office of Personnel Management.

NOTES

69 **Mike emailed Amy:** Author interviews with Shannon Spann and Amy.

69 **"to sound dramatic":** Klein, "If Anything Happens...," *Parade* magazine; author interview with Amy.

69 **"What everyone needs":** Harden and Sack, "One For His Country, and One Against It," *New York Times.*

70 **"What if every daddy":** Author interview with Shannon Spann.

CHAPTER 6: TALISMAN

72 **from the 1987 movie:** In *The Untouchables,* Jim Malone—a gun-toting Irish-American cop played by Sean Connery—says to a would-be Mafia assassin wielding a knife: "Isn't that just like a wop? Brings a knife to a gunfight."

72 **"bless these crews":** Author interview with Cuthbert.

72 **almost 1.4 million:** *Defense Manpower Requirements Report, Fiscal Year 2003* (US Department of Defense, April 2002) states that 1,387,100 were serving on September 30, 2001.

72 **a silk "blood chit":** Author interviews with Team Alpha members; C.J. Chivers, "A Short History of Blood Chits: Greetings from the Lost, Seeking Help," *New York Times,* March 29, 2012.

72 **at K2 with Brian:** Author interview with Brian.

73 **Sponge 05 and Sponge 06:** After Afghanistan, the DAP call signs were fixed as Chisel and Nail.

73 **chaff and flares:** Chaff, made from millions of tiny aluminum- or zinc-coated fibers, is ejected in tubes from targetable aircraft to lead astray radar-guided missiles. Flares, made of magnesium pellets that ignite when fired, confuse heat-seeking missiles.

74 **Alan Mack:** Mack is given the pseudonym Alex McGee in Stanton, *Horse Soldiers,* and Alfred Mann in Briscoe et al., *Weapon of Choice.*

74 **presented by the crew:** Letter from Colonel John Mulholland and staff and the crews of Sponge 05 and Sponge 06 to President George W. Bush, October 17, 2001. Copy provided to author by US Army source.

75 **The first missile:** Author interview with Gilbert.

75 **Chalked on the Hellfire:** Author interview with Phillips.

75 **"Barbara was a warrior":** Toby Harnden, "'She Asked Me How to Stop the Plane,'" *Daily Telegraph,* March 5, 2002.

75 **fire a Kalashnikov:** Sapp used an AKMS for the instruction. Tyson did not take an AKMS into Afghanistan, instead using an AK-47 from a supply drop. The AKMS and AK-47 had the same firing mechanisms. Andy also gave Tyson some firearms instruction.

76 **clear and moonlit:** Details of this flight are drawn from author interviews with Team Alpha, Cuthbert, Mack, and Buss; see also: Briscoe et al., *Weapon of Choice,* 82–85.

76 **Khazret Sultan:** The mountain had reverted to its original name after being called Peak of the 22nd Congress of the Communist Party by the Soviets.

77 **as the Oxus:** Toynbee, *Between Oxus and Jumna,* 97–8.
78 **village of Dehi:** Author interviews with Team Alpha; Williams, *Last Warlord,* 216.
78 **bottom of a canyon:** Briscoe et al., *Weapon of Choice,* 83.
81 **3,000 Hezb-i-Wahdat fighters:** Ibid., 99.
82 **were no match:** Christopher D. Kondaki, "The Taliban: A Primer," *Defense & Foreign Affairs Strategic Policy,* October 2001.
82 **ex-mujahideen fighter:** Gall, *The Wrong Enemy,* 4.
82 **as a terrorist group:** In October 2007, the US Treasury cited the Quds Force of the Islamic Revolutionary Guard Corps as Iran's "primary arm for executing its policy of supporting terrorist and insurgent groups."

CHAPTER 7: TWO CADILLACS

84 **Tufan had been wounded:** The account of Tufan's plight is drawn from author interviews with Tyson and Andy.
85 **Andy Sentiff:** Sentiff is given the pseudonym Aaron Smith in Stanton, *Horse Soldiers,* and Arthur Solanis in Briscoe et al., *Weapon of Choice.*
85 **Captain Joe:** Full name withheld for personal security reasons at individual's request. In Stanton, *Horse Soldiers,* he is given the pseudonym John Garfield.
85 **apoplectic that:** Author interview with Captain Joe; Stanton, *Horse Soldiers,* 68–69.
86 **Mack called Sentiff:** Author interviews with Mack and Sentiff.
86 **bending the ear of:** Author interview with Mulholland; Stanton, *Horse Soldiers,* 67.
86 **considering firing him:** Author interview with Mulholland.
86 **"little birds in a nest":** Rumsfeld, *Known and Unknown,* 391–92.
86 **"This is the CIA's strategy":** Woodward, *Bush at War,* 243–44.
87 **"select another commander":** Franks, *American Soldier,* 300–301.
87 **"Please hold for…":** Author interview with Mack.
87 **Multi-Mode Radar (MMR):** Author interviews with Mack and Captain Joe; Doug Stanton, *Horse Soldiers,* 86.
88 **Andy Marchal:** Marchal is given the pseudonym Sam Diller in Stanton, *Horse Soldiers,* and in the *12 Strong* movie, in which he is played by Michael Peña.
88 **an hour early:** Author interview with Nutsch.
88 **advance guard of seven riders:** Author interviews with Team Alpha; Stanton, *Horse Soldiers,* 112–13.
88 **his white horse, Surkun:** Williams, *Last Warlord,* 259.
88 **traced their lineage:** Ibid, 44.
88 **Mark Nutsch:** Nutsch is given the pseudonym Mitch Nelson in Stanton, *Horse Soldiers,* and in the *12 Strong* movie, in which he is played by Chris Hemsworth; he is identified as Mike Nash in Briscoe et al., *Weapon of Choice.*
89 **Dostum announced:** Warrant Officer Robert Pennington, in an undated transcript of a PBS *Frontline* interview with members of ODA 595.
89 **"caveman-level Russian":** Author interview with Nutsch; Briscoe et al., *Weapon of Choice,* 126.

89 **called Robin Sage:** Author interview with Mark Nutsch; Major Adam Woytowich, "The Relevancy of Robin Sage," *Special Warfare* magazine, July–December 2016.

89 **real-life Robin Sage:** Author interview with Nutsch; Kalev I. Sepp, "Meeting the 'G-Chief': ODA 595," *Special Warfare* magazine, September 2002.

89 **clans of West Virginia:** Author interview with Marchal; *Legion of Brothers,* documentary.

89 **"and kill the Taliban":** Author interview with Nutsch; Stanton, *Horse Soldiers,* 114.

92 **"the house is quiet":** Shannon Spann eulogy at her husband's funeral, December 10, 2001.

92 **St. Paul's Epistle:** Philippians 4:8, *New American Standard Bible* (La Habra, California: Foundation Publications, 1997), 156.

94 **"bombing for almost fifteen days":** Atta quotations come from interview in Knarr, *Mazar-e Sharif Battle Site Survey Support Documents,* C-24-2.

94 **the title of:** Ibid., III-20.

94 **$250,000 given to Fahim:** Schroen, *First In,* 197.

95 **"Five hundred of my men":** Author interview with Nutsch, to whom Dostum made the comment; Briscoe et al., *Weapon of Choice,* 134; Williams, *Last Warlord,* 219.

96 **the Taliban, who were defending the village of Beshcam:** Stanton, *Horse Soldiers,* 150.

97 **already stood accused:** Rashid, *Taliban,* 56.

98 **Lawrence of Arabia's dictum:** T. E. Lawrence, *The Arab Bulletin,* August 20, 1917, reprinted in *The Arab Bulletin 1916–1919* (Cambridge University Press, 1986).

99 **Escorting them was Abdul Sattar:** In an author interview, Sattar denied shooting anyone on a pallet.

99 **NO BETTER FRIEND, NO WORSE ENEMY:** C. Mark Brinkley, "Marines in Egypt Are Tuning Up—and Bulking Up—for War," *Marine Corps Times,* November 5, 2001.

99 **from a lofty 29,000 feet:** Briscoe et al., *Weapon of Choice,* 132.

99 **$320 million in aid:** "US Cargo Planes Return to Germany after Air Drops in Afghanistan," Agence France-Presse, October 8, 2001.

102 **accompanied Commander Faqir:** This account is drawn from interviews with Tyson and Faqir.

102 **half-Arab and half-Uzbek:** Williams, *Last Warlord,* 34.

102 **Brigade 055:** Daniel Eisenberg, "Secrets of Brigade 055," *Time,* October 28, 2001.

CHAPTER 8: WILD THING

104 **Khalili waited for the CIA:** Details of Khalili's life and experience in 2001 drawn from author interview with Khalili.

104 **Hazaras in central Afghanistan:** Sam Greenhill, "The Warlords Vying for Power," Press Association, November 14, 2001. Khalili led a Hazara coalition of eight Shia Muslim guerrilla groups with the umbrella name Hezb-i-Wahdat.

104 **group of Afghan leaders:** Author interviews with Khalili and Santos.

104 **an inferno:** Fariba Nawa, "Hazaras Willing to Work with Moderate Taliban, despite Massacres," Agence France-Presse, October 18, 2001.

105 **massacred in Yakawlang:** United Nations General Assembly, "Interim Report of the Special Rapporteur on the Situation of Human Rights in Afghanistan," A/56/409, September 26, 2001: 10–11.

105 **One eyewitness reported:** Gutman, *How We Missed the Story,* 228.

105 **who had orchestrated:** "Afghanistan: Three Afghan Commanders Should Be Prosecuted," *Human Rights Watch,* December 3, 2001.

105 **by radio:** Edward A. Gargan, "Taliban Atrocities: Confidential UN Report Details Mass Killings of Civilian Villagers," *Newsday,* October 12, 2001.

105 **Deputy Minister of Defense:** Knarr, *Mazar-e Sharif Battle Site Survey Support Documents,* C-4.

105 **two 6th-century statues of Buddha:** Mohammad Bashir, "Taliban Dynamite Afghan Buddhas as Tide of Protest Rises," Agence France-Presse, March 6, 2001.

105 **did not inspire his soldiers:** Dexter Filkins and David Rohde, "Afghan Rebels Seem a Reluctant Force So Far," *New York Times,* November 4, 2001.

105 **bags of Starbucks coffee:** Schroen, *First In,* 210.

106 **patio chair with a mocha:** Ibid., 260.

106 **"Northern Alliance forces":** Tenet, *At the Center of the Storm,* 216–17.

106 **typed out an explanation:** Full letter is reproduced in Camp, *Boots on the Ground,* 137.

107 **Channeling General Patton:** In the movie version of Patton's speech, the general, played by George C. Scott, says: "We're going to murder those lousy Hun bastards by the bushel." According to Terry Brighton, *Patton, Montgomery, Rommel: Masters of War* (New York: Crown, 2009), 264, Patton said: "We're going to murder those lousy Hun cocksuckers by the bushel-fucking-basket."

107 **around 3,000 Hazaras:** Camp, *Boots on the Ground,* 153–56. The total Hezb-i-Wahdat force under Khalili was estimated at 15,000 to 30,000 fighters.

107 **Steve Bleigh:** Bleigh is given the pseudonym Scott Black in Stanton, *Horse Soldiers,* and in the *12 Strong* movie, in which he is played by Ben O'Toole. The account of his conversation with Seeger is drawn from author interview with Bleigh.

110 **notion of the "savage":** Peter J. Bowler, "From 'Savage' to 'Primitive': Victorian Evolutionism and the Interpretation of Marginalized Peoples." Cambridge University Press, January 2, 2015.

110 **Comanches…had tortured:** The issue of Comanches and torture is examined in S. C. Gwynne, *Empire of the Summer Moon: Quanah Parker and the Rise and Fall of the Comanches, the Most Powerful Indian Tribe in American History* (New York: Scribner, 2010).

110 **the mountain prison:** This account is drawn from author interviews with Tyson and Sapp.

111 **Turkmen-language manual:** David Tyson and Larry Clark, *Turkmen Language Manual* (Washington, DC: Peace Corps, 1993).

112 **"practicable by mules":** Barrow, *The Military Geography of Afghanistan. Part II*, 20.

112 **azure lakes of Band-e Amir:** Heidi Vogt, "Unlikely Vacation Spot? Tourism Blossoming alongside Afghanistan's War Zone," Associated Press, July 5, 2009.

113 **A Chinook from K2:** Author interviews with Team Alpha; Moore, *The Hunt for bin Laden*, 135.

113 **create a signal halo:** This was a technique known as an IR buzzsaw.

113 **Green Berets of ODA 553:** Briscoe et al., *Weapon of Choice*, 99.

116 **D. H. Lawrence's "Self-Pity":** D. H. Lawrence, *Pansies: Poems* (London: Martin Secker, 1929).

116 **Mullah Amir Mohamed:** Knarr, *Mazar-e Sharif Battle Site Survey Support Documents*, III-20, C-24-5, C-24-8.

116 **at LZ Mustang:** LTC David Hilkert and Dr. John W. Partin, "Trojan Horse: Deception at Qala-i Jangi," US Special Operations Command (SOCOM) History and Research Office, May 2005, 3 (hereinafter *SOCOM Report*).

116 **Bob, a case officer:** The officer was referred to as Bob during the deployment because his true first name was the same as that of another member of the team. He recently retired from the CIA but has never been identified publicly.

116 **Greg, the former Navy SEAL:** Still serving as a CIA officer, Greg is identified here only by his first name.

116 **Glenn, a former Special Forces medic:** Glenn is still serving as a CIA officer and is identified here only by his first name. He is given the pseudonym Garth Rogers in Stanton, *Horse Soldiers*; CIA Steve in Lewis, *Bloody Heroes*; and "Harley Davidson" in Perry, *Falling Off the Edge*.

117 **LZ Burro:** *SOCOM Report*, 3.

117 **hanged, and his body riddled:** Kathy Gannon, "Taliban Execute Opposition Leader; Important Pashtun Hanged," Associated Press, October 27, 2001.

CHAPTER 9: DEVIL'S WATER

119 **Fahim had met with:** Author interview with Crumpton; Franks, *American Soldier*, 309–12; Crumpton, *Art of Intelligence*, 228–31.

119 **the 20,000 men:** Rashid, *Descent into Chaos*, 81.

120 **"This is bullshit":** Franks, *American Soldier*, 312.

120 **"Are you sure those":** Blehm, *The Only Thing Worth Dying For*, 164.

120 **pressured Mulholland:** Author interviews with Mulholland and Rosengard. Mulholland said he believed more senior officers were needed to command and control the growing number of ODAs.

120 **Max Bowers:** Bowers is given the pseudonym Marc Bell in Briscoe et al., *Weapon of Choice*.

NOTES

120 **code-named Boxer:** Boxer was an Operational Detachment Charlie, ODC 53. An ODC was the headquarters element of a Special Forces battalion. An ODC commanded three Operation Detachment Bravos (ODBs)—the headquarters element of a Special Forces company—and 18 ODAs.

121 **known as the Third Reich:** Author interviews with former members of 5th Group, who added that Bowers was nicknamed Cinemax. The 2nd Battalion was known as Switzerland.

121 **a nonplussed Dostum:** Photograph by Chris Spence provided to the author.

122 **the Navy fight song:** Earl Kelly, "Navy's unofficial anthem turns 100," *The Capital,* December 2, 2006.

123 **taunted a Taliban commander:** Knarr and Frost, *Operation Enduring Freedom Battle Reconstruction,* III-15.

123 **other Taliban commanders:** Bowers Sitrep of 0845Z, November 3, 2001.

123 **commander Mullah Abdul Razzaq:** Call, *Danger Close,* 20.

123 **Razzaq had been:** Knarr, *Mazar-e Sharif Battle Site Survey Support Documents,* C-23-9.

123 **mistook Nutsch's signal:** Stanton, *Horse Soldiers,* 222–23; Moore, *The Hunt for Bin Laden,* 76–77.

124 **Watching a mushroom cloud:** Author interview with Tomat.

125 **"Israeli bandage":** The Israeli Battle Dressing, a six-inch bandage, was designed to staunch blood flow and stabilize a patient before evacuation or further treatment; Ron Yanor, "High Risk Lifesaver," *Journal of Counterterrorism & Homeland Security International* 12:2 (Spring 2006).

126 **at Pol-e Baraq:** Knarr interview with Commander Haji Chari, Knarr, *Mazar-e Sharif Battle Site Survey Support Documents,* C-2-24.

126 **1968 song by The Who:** Andrew Neill and Matthew Kent, *Anyway, Anyhow, Anywhere: The Complete Chronicle of The Who 1958–1978* (New York: Sterling Publishing Company, 2009), 135.

126 **At a White House meeting:** Author interview with Tenet; Tenet, *Center of the Storm,* 216–17.

126 **New York Times article:** The article was a news analysis by Johnny Apple, who had been a war reporter in Vietnam; R. W. Apple Jr., "A Military Quagmire Remembered: Afghanistan as Vietnam," *New York Times,* October 31, 2001.

127 **"Islamabad Bob":** Grenier, *88 Days to Kandahar,* 170.

127 **"Taliban Bob":** Coll, *Directorate S,* 91.

127 **Tenet admitted:** Woodward, *Bush at War,* 297.

128 **A World War II practice:** C. L. Waller, "Book Chronicles Veteran's World War II Experiences," *Chicago Daily Herald,* January 15, 1999; Paul Richard Huard, "The Combat History of the Condom," War Is Boring website, November 27, 2015.

129 **Bart Decker:** Decker is given the pseudonym Burt Docks in Stanton, *Horse Soldiers.*

129 **Another large Taliban convoy:** Author interview with Stiles.

130 **Taliban had lost 12,000 men:** "The Rout of the Taliban," *Observer,* November 18, 2001.

131 **Some threw money:** Pelton, "The Legend of Heavy D and the Boys," *National Geographic Adventure*.

CHAPTER 10: THE FORT

132 *The Arabian Nights:* Also known as *The Thousand and One Nights*. A collection of Middle Eastern and Indian stories of unknown date and authorship.

133 **"star fort":** Jacob Bogle, "The Lone Star of Afghanistan," *Jacob's Earth* blog, August 21, 2019; D. H. Mahan, *Military Engineering Part I, Comprising Field Fortification, Military Mining, and Siege Operations* (New York: Wiley, 1870), 13.

133 **pride of Abdur Rahman:** Sultan Mahomed Khan, *The Life of Abdur Rahman, Amir of Afghanistan* (London: John Murray, 1900), 69.

133 **first ruler to unite:** Barfield, *Afghanistan*, 155.

133 **a place of treachery:** In 1888, two Afghan colonels—loyal to a commander who had sought refuge with the Russian—had been stationed at Dehdadi with two infantry regiments, six horse-drawn guns, and one mule-drawn gun. After being summoned to Mazar-i Sharif to account for themselves, they promptly switched sides. *The History of Afghanistan: Faiz Mohammad Katib Hazara's Siraaj al-tawarikh,* translated and edited by Mohammad Mehdi Khorrami and Robert D. McChesney (Leiden: The Netherlands, 2016), 156.

133 **Even before the:** This account is drawn from Lee, *The "Ancient Supremacy,"* 390.

133 **a town governor:** Muhammad Sarwar Khan, governor of Akcha, had gone to see General Gulab Haider Khan, governor of Sheberghan, to make peace, but was bound with rope and brought to the site of the new fort. There his captors, led by Mohai al-Din, mutilated him with a knife and killed him; ibid., 289–90.

133 **established the citadel:** Email correspondence between the author and Dr. Jonathan Lee (hereinafter *Lee emails*).

133 **designed by British military engineers:** Ibid.

133 **puppet of the British:** Kakar, *Afghanistan,* 57.

133 **forced labor to build:** Some 3,000 of the forced laborers were Firozkohi Aimaqs, captured during a failed uprising in the remote mountain district of Chaharsada. To feed themselves, the laborers were forced to beg for food on the streets of Mazar-i Sharif. *Lee emails.*

133 **"nearly depopulated":** Lee, *The "Ancient Supremacy,"* 560.

133 **built with British funds:** Demetrius C. Boulger, "Coming Events in Central Asia," *Contemporary Review* LXXXI (January–June 1902), 276.

133 **intended both to defend against:** *Lee emails.*

133 **"the largest and strongest":** Khan, *The Life of Abdur Rahman,* 271–72.

134 **who disguised himself as a Turkmen:** "The Man-thing: General Lavr Kornilov," WeapoNews.com, April 13, 2018.

134 **strongest features included:** Ludwig W. Adamec (ed.), *Historical and Political Gazetteer of Afghanistan: Volume 4, Mazar-i Sharif and North-Central Afghanistan*

(originally *Imperial Gazetteer of Afghanistan by the British General Staff, Calcutta, 1908–14*) Graz, Austria: Akademische Druck- u. Verlagsanstalt, 1973: 174–75.

134 **Soviet forces secretly entered:** This account is drawn from Boris Egorov, "Why Didn't the Soviet Union Support Revolution in Afghanistan?" *Russia Beyond,* May 16, 2018.

134 **300 Russian troops:** Robert Byron, *The Road to Oxiana* (London: Macmillan, 1937), 337–8.

134 **lasted thirty-seven days:** Soviet troops entered Afghanistan on April 15 and were recalled on May 22, 1929.

134 **Primakov described:** Anton Pavlov, "Afghanistan: A Long War History Gives a Timely Object Lesson," *Moscow News,* October 3, 2001.

134 **Mujahideen attacked Qala-i Jangi in 1981:** James W. Hatton, "Rebels Unite Against Soviets," Associated Press, June 30, 1981.

136 **female Muslim ruler:** Seema Kazi, "Women, Islam and Muslim Identity in India," *International Feminist Journal,* April 30, 2000.

136 **They had been shot dead:** Stanton, *Horse Soldiers,* 259.

136 **used as a catchall:** Author interviews with Tyson and Sapp; "Chechens in Afghanistan 1: A Battlefield Myth That Will Not Die," Christian Bleuer, *Afghan Analysts Network,* June 27, 2016.

136 **for just two days:** Doug Struck, "Taliban's Allies Lost in Strange City," *Washington Post,* November 11, 2001.

137 **the district of Malakand:** Author interview with Tyson, who identified Sufi Muhammad as the recruiter.

137 **cleric named Sufi Muhammad:** "Taliban Captures, Kills a Leading Opponent," Knight Ridder, October 27, 2001, which quotes Pakistani government officials as saying 15,000 fighters loyal to Sufi Muhammad were entering Afghanistan.

137 **who used loudspeakers:** Jeffrey Gettleman, "Prisoner of Jihad," *Los Angeles Times,* July 21, 2002.

137 **Members of ODA 534:** Author interviews with Team Alpha members; Stanton, *Horse Soldiers,* 262.

137 **within 500 meters:** *U.S. Army Field Manual 63-1,* Appendix D: USAF Minimum Safe Distance for Surface Targets.

137 **Tomat, the air controller:** This account draws from author interviews with Tyson, Tomat, and Bleigh; the Silver Star citation for Tomat; and Call, *Danger Close,* 21–24.

138 **grabbed by local Hazaras:** Carlotta Gall, "Conflicting Tales Paint Blurry Picture of Siege," *New York Times,* November 20, 2001.

138 **urging Dostum's men:** Damien McElroy, "Surrender Ended in Massacre," *Scotsman,* December 3, 2001.

140 **kept so they could be raped:** Hollie McKay, "Male Rape Emerging as One of the Most Under-Reported Weapons of War," *Fox News,* March 21, 2019; Cécile Allegra, "Revealed: Male Rape Used Systematically in Libya as Instrument of War," *Guardian,* November 3, 2017.

140 **a hard-bitten CIA officer:** The officer was Gust Avrakotos; Crile, *Charlie Wilson's War,* 199–200.

140 **Counterterrorism Pursuit Teams:** The existence of CTPTs was first documented in Woodward, *Obama's Wars,* 8.

141 **worried that large groups of prisoners:** Author interview with Marchal.

142 **allowed her to visit:** Author interview with Shannon Spann.

142 **Mike's favorite candies:** Author interview with Amy.

142 **recited it proudly:** Author interview with Shannon Spann.

142 **spoke at the United Nations:** *Public Papers of the Presidents of the United States: George W. Bush,* 2001, Book II (Washington, DC: US Government Publishing Office) 1375–79.

143 **On November 11:** Berntsen, *Jawbreaker,* 168 .

143 **As darkness fell:** Coll, *Directorate S,* 93.

143 **By dawn on November 13:** Kathy Gannon, "Taliban Leaves Kabul to Opposition," Associated Press, November 13, 2001.

143 **6 p.m. on November 14:** Schroen, *First In,* 351.

143 **last occupied by:** Dan Oberdorger, "U.S. Embassy in Kabul to be Evacuated, Closed," *Washington Post,* January 27, 1989.

143 **Reagan's official photo:** Berntsen, *Jawbreaker,* 168 , 194–95.

143 **The same evening:** Coll, *Directorate S,* 98.

143 **CIA's Team Echo:** Team Echo was led by Greg Vogle, a paramilitary officer.

143 **six CIA teams:** These CIA teams (and their dates of arrival in 2001) were: Jawbreaker, with Fahim (September 26); Alpha, with Dostum (October 16); Bravo, with Atta (November 4); Charlie, with Ismail Khan (November 11); Delta, with Khalili (November 12); and Echo, with Karzai (November 14). Foxtrot, with Gul Agha Sherzai, arrived in Kandahar province on November 19; Juliet, formed from elements of Jawbreaker and military personnel, was put together on November 18 and later went to Tora Bora; Hotel and Romeo deployed in December.

143 **nine ODAs:** These ODAs (and their dates of arrival in 2001) were: 595 with Dostum, and 555 with Fahim (October 19); 585 with Bariullah Khan (October 23); 553 with Khalili (November 2); 534 with Atta (November 4); 586 with Daoud Khan and 594 with Fahim (November 9); 554 with Ismail Khan (November 11); and 574 with Karzai (November 14). Briscoe et al., *Weapon of Choice,* 337–38.

CHAPTER 11: GOAT RODEO

144 **neon-and-glass sculpture:** The sculpture was *Route Zenith* by Keith Sonnier. Bill Adair and Katherine Pfleger, "Ironic Tribute," *Tampa Bay Times,* May 5, 1998.

144 **wielding swords:** John Omicinski, "Special Forces Saddle Up with Northern Alliance," Gannett News Service, November 15, 2001.

144 **released by the Pentagon:** Jim Garamone, "Wolfowitz Shares Special Forces' Afghanistan Dispatches," American Forces Press Service, November 15, 2001.

144 **"saber charges on horseback":** "Media Availability with Secretary of Defense Donald Rumsfeld, Naval Training Center, Great Lakes, Illinois," Federal News Service, November 16, 2001.

144 **fall of Kandahar:** Toby Harnden, "Taliban's Last Stronghold Falls: Mullah Omar Agrees to Surrender," *Daily Telegraph,* November 17, 2001.

145 **looking toward Hamid Karzai:** On November 4, shortly before the CIA flew Karzai temporarily out of Afghanistan to a US base at Jacobabad in Pakistan, Team Echo leader Greg Vogle greeted him enthusiastically as "Your Excellency." Dam, *A Man and a Motorcycle,* 125.

145 **link up with Haq:** Blehm, *The Only Thing Worth Dying For,* 59.

145 **murdered by the Taliban:** Tomsen, *The Wars of Afghanistan,* 549.

145 **bin Laden often posed:** Kahaner, *AK-47,* 1–2.

145 **Alexander the Great:** Holt, *Into the Land of Bones,* 23.

145 **Dostum had been born:** Details of Dostum's early life from Williams, *Last Warlord,* 73, 82, 87.

146 **became a union boss:** John F. Burns, "Afghan Fights Islamic Tide: As a Savior or a Conqueror?" *New York Times,* October 14, 1996.

146 **full of algae:** Sifton, "Temporal Vertigo," *New York Times.*

146 **"Dostum's Castle":** Ibid.

147 **by street transcriptionists:** Karlos Zurutuza, "Living on a Ballpoint Pen in Kabul," Inter Press Service, September 26, 2014.

147 **Taliban had staged:** In the same stadium in April 2000, an accused murderer and robber had been executed by a relative of his victim. In September 2000, a man convicted of adultery had been stoned to death there while his alleged lover, who was pregnant, had been sentenced to 100 lashes. See: "Man Publicly Executed in Faryab," Revolutionary Association of the Women of Afghanistan (RAWA) website, citing *News Network International* report of April 12, 2000; "Afghanistan Country Report on Human Rights Practices 2001," US Department of State's Bureau of Democa racy, Human Rights, and Labor, March 4, 2002.

149 **Merkit were a Mongol tribe:** Bertold Spuler, *The Muslim World: A Historical Survey, Volume 2* (Leiden, The Netherlands: E. J. Brill, 1960), 4.

150 **intense US pressure:** "US Pressing Uzbeks for Quick Re-opening of Termez Bridge to Afghanistan," Agence France-Presse, November 14, 2001.

150 **since May 1997:** C. J. Chivers, "On the Border, a Relief Effort Loaded with Hope and Frustration," *New York Times,* November 12, 2001.

150 **by barge:** Charles M. Sennott, "Taliban Retreat Reopens Key Crossing for Aid," *Boston Globe,* November 15, 2001.

151 **Built by the Russians:** "Karmal's Speech at Opening of Friendship Bridge across Amudarya," *BBC Summary of World Broadcasts,* May 14, 1982.

151 **around November 18:** "Uzbek Islamist Guerrilla Chief Namangani Killed: Dostum," Agence France-Presse, November 19, 2001.

151 **Sector Viper:** *SOCOM Report,* 3. The Panjshir Valley region was designated Sector Cobra.

151 **eighty-room, five-story:** Ibid., 5.

151 **given the top floor:** Ibid., 6.

151 **The Turkish school:** The school was the Afghan-Turk High School, opened in

1996. According to author interviews with former students, it remained in operation under the Taliban until October 2001. "Programme Summary of Afghan Balkh Radio News," BBC Monitoring Central Asia Unit, April 5, 1999.

151 **US Army lawyers had fretted:** Author interview with Mitchell.

151 **the military believed that:** *SOCOM Report,* 5.

152 **the Russians had:** Williams, *Last Warlord,* 123–24.

154 **an affluent suburb:** Christopher Torchia, "Afghan Factory Endures During War," Associated Press, September 13, 2002.

154 **hailed from Midland:** Toby Harnden, "Lone Star General Is 'The Best You'll Ever Meet,'" *Daily Telegraph,* October 10, 2001.

155 **carrying a starched uniform:** Author interview with Betz.

155 **blindsided by Franks:** *SOCOM Report,* 4.

155 **Franks told him:** Ibid, 4–5.

155 **"Sir, what's your mission here?":** Ibid., 5.

155 **15,000 cheering troops:** "Remarks by President George W. Bush to Troops at Fort Campbell, Kentucky," Federal News Service, November 21, 2001.

156 **buttonholed Donald Rumsfeld:** Draper, *To Start a War,* 46; Rumsfeld, *Known and Unknown,* 427.

156 **moved to Allentown:** "From Allentown to the Afghan Mountains: Man Who Spent Youth Here Now Commands Northern Alliance Warriors," *Morning Call,* October 28, 2001.

158 **low-ceilinged reception room:** Author interviews with Dostum and Mohaqeq. The account of the meeting also draws from Gall, *Wrong Enemy,* 1–5.

158 **Mullah Norullah Noori:** Like Fazl, Noori had been sanctioned by the UN for atrocities against Hazaras. "Security Council Committee on Afghanistan Designates Further Individuals, Financial Entities Relating to Resolutions 1267 (1999) and 1333 (2000)," M2 Presswire, January 26, 2001.

158 **thirty-nine-vehicle convoy:** Luke Harding, "Paper Surrender Blowing in the Wind," *Guardian,* November 23, 2001.

158 **at Fazl's request:** Author interview with Dostum. Fazl had contacted him via a Northern Alliance commander in Takhar province, Dostum said.

158 **a reputation as a merciless slayer:** Gall, *Wrong Enemy,* 2–3.

158 **3,000 Al-Qaeda fighters:** Steinberg, *German Jihad,* 186–87.

159 **defected to the Northern Alliance:** Author interviews with Tyson and Majid Rozi; Campbell, "The Fort of Hell," *Sunday Times* Gall, *Wrong Enemy,* 4.

159 **as an intermediary:** ibid.

159 **Mullah Dadullah, who had:** Rahimullah Yusufzai, "Taliban's Most Feared Commander," BBC News, May 13, 2007.

159 **stayed at Naseri's home:** Carlotta Gall, "Northern Alliance Presses for Surrender of Taliban Commander and Troops," *New York Times,* December 4, 2001.

159 **claiming he was "sick":** Luke Harding, et al., "Fear of Bloodbath," *Guardian.* Dostum, in author interview, stated, "Mullah Dadullah was hiding in Balkh district with his fighters."

159 **Mohaqeq stared silently:** Author interview with Mohaqeq.

159 **exploit the divisions between:** Wörmer, "The Networks of Kunduz," Afghan Analysts Network.

159 **sticking point was Al-Qaeda:** Charles M. Sennott and Ellen Barry, "Deal Reached on Surrender; Doubts Linger; Taliban, Qaeda Passage from Kunduz at Issue," *Boston Globe,* November 23, 2001.

160 **dangled the possibility:** Gall, *Wrong Enemy,* 10.

160 **Pakistan was also pulling strings:** Details of Musharraf's overture to Dostum are drawn from Gall, *Wrong Enemy,* 7. She cites Northern Alliance figure Amrullah Saleh, later head of the NDS intelligence service, as her source.

160 **important power broker:** Ibid., 7.

160 **Americans became alarmed:** SOCOM *Report,* 7.

160 **"Lay down your weapons":** Ibid.

160 **Dostum called in:** Gail, *Wrong Enemy,* 9.

160 **Dostum declared that he would:** Details of Dostum's announcement of the deal are drawn from Harding et al., "Fear of Bloodbath," *Guardian.*

160 **allowed to return:** Ellen Knickmeyer, "Taliban Agree to Surrender Last Stronghold in Northern Afghanistan," Associated Press, November 22, 2001.

160 **"resolved without fighting," Dostum promised:** Luke Harding, "Kunduz Ready to Surrender," *Guardian,* November 22, 2001.

160 **"Don't worry":** SOCOM *Report,* 7.

CHAPTER 12: NOT SURRENDERED

162 **something felt off:** Author interview with Shannon Spann.

163 **"had troubled me":** Klein, "If Anything Happens...," *Parade* magazine.

163 **discovered his feet:** Shapira, "He Was a Baby," *Washington Post.*

163 **about the moon:** "Northern Afghan Radio Special Programme on Commemoration of US Officer's Death," BBC Summary of World Broadcasts, December 17, 2002.

164 **built by the Germans:** Smith et al., *Area Handbook for Afghanistan,* 114.

164 **died from anthrax:** Donna Tommelleo, "Home, Mail Scoured in Anthrax Case," Associated Press, November 23, 2001. Although Al-Qaeda was suspected at the time, the FBI later concluded that the perpetrator of the attack was an American government microbiologist.

164 **failure of imagination:** *The 9/11 Commission Report,* 339–48.

165 **Captain Anthony Jarrett:** Jarrett is given the pseudonym Andrew Johnson in Stanton, *Horse Soldiers.*

166 **Baader-Meinhof threat:** The Baader-Meinhof Gang, also called the Red Army Faction, was a radical leftist West German group formed in 1968 and named after two of its leaders, Andreas Baader and Ulrike Meinhof; Stefan Aust, *The Baader Meinhof Complex* (London: Bodley Head, 2008).

166 **Rockford turn:** The term derived from the 1970s TV show *The Rockford Files,* in nearly every episode of which private investigator Jim Rockford (James Garner) performs the maneuver.

167   **It later emerged:** Rashid, *Descent into Chaos,* 91–93.

167   **the American public was fixated:** Jeffrey M. Jones, "Majority Says Military Action Not a Success until bin Laden Captured," Gallup News Service, December 4, 2001.

167   **"box filled with dry ice":** Schroen, *First In,* 38.

168   **a Mad Max convoy:** Author interviews with Sapp and Nutsch. Mad Max was a series of postapocalyptic movies, the first one screened in 1979, that were filmed in the Australian desert.

168   **3 a.m. in five open trucks:** Harding, "Surrender Kills Dreams of Taliban," *Observer.*

168   **Al-Qaeda, not Taliban:** There were no Afghans among the prisoners—and only a handful of Pakistanis. The bulk appear to have been from Brigade 055, the Arab component of Al-Qaeda. It is possible a handful of the prisoners were aligned only with the Taliban, and that a few may have been noncombatants. The prisoners have sometimes been referred to collectively as Taliban, but—given their nationalities and what is known about those who survived—this seems misleading. Throughout *First Casualty,* they are therefore described collectively as Al-Qaeda.

168   **more than 400:** No accurate count of the prisoners was made. From interviews with Team Alpha members and Green Berets, photographs of the surrender site, trucks transporting the prisoners, and video from Qala-i Jangi, it seems there were between 400 and 450.

168   **fighting in Takhar:** Kukis, *"My Heart Became Attached,"* 114.

168   **walked fifty miles:** Mayer, "Lost in the Jihad," *New Yorker.*

168   **give themselves up to:** Gall, *Wrong Enemy,* 11.

169   **twenty-four hours early:** SOCOM Report, 8.

169   **stories of the Japanese:** John W. Dower, *War Without Mercy: Race and Power in the Pacific War* (New York: W. W. Norton, 1986), 99.

169   **like *The Last of the Mohicans*:** In James Fenimore Cooper's *The Last of the Mohicans,* Louis-Joseph de Montcalm of France tells the defeated English officer Major Duncan Heyward that his surrender shall "all be done in a way most honorable to yourselves."

169   **accompanied by Naseri:** Harding, "Surrender Kills Dreams of Taliban," *Observer.* Naseri is described as "the opposition Pashtun General Amir Jan."

169   **Dostum had told Admiral Calland:** SOCOM Report, 7.

169   **Dostum and the Americans ruled out:** Author interview with Mitchell and Tyson; Harding, et al., "Errors Revealed in Siege of Afghan Fort," *Guardian.*

170   **Major Mark Mitchell:** Mitchell is given the pseudonym Mario Magione in Briscoe et al., *Weapon of Choice.*

170   **"airplane with the laser gun":** Author interview with Spence.

170   **in Saudi Arabia:** The CAOC was at Prince Sultan Air Base in Al Kharj, Saudi Arabia. Rebecca Grant, "The Short, Strange Life of PSAB," *Air Force Magazine,* July 1, 2012.

170   **the UN, however, had refused:** Irwin Arieff, "U.N. Says It Can't Handle Taliban Surrender at Kunduz," Reuters, November 20, 2001.

170 **Naseri said it:** Harding, "Errors Revealed in Siege et al., *Guardian.*

171 **The hatred in the eyes:** Author interview with Mitchell.

171 **nickname was Ol' Sarge:** Author interviews with Mitchell and Leahy; Stanton, *Horse Soldiers,* 285 .

171 **Major Kurt Sonntag:** Sonntag was the executive officer of Boxer/ODC 53, deputy to Bowers. He is given the pseudonym Kevin Sault in Briscoe et al., *Weapon of Choice.*

171 **had been a wrestler:** Stanton, *Horse Soldiers,* 49.

171 **He had heard a BBC report:** Author interview with Mohaqeq; Knarr, *Mazar-e Sharif Battle Site Survey Support Documents,* C-24-2.

172 **young, aquiline-nosed prisoner:** Footage of the interview is shown in *The House of War* documentary.

172 **blood spurting:** Author interview with Qipchaq.

173 **a British television reporter:** Andrea Catherwood of ITN. Maggie Brown, "Catherwood Tells of Narrow Escape," *Guardian,* November 30, 2001.

173 **Naseri ordered:** Campbell, "The Fort of Hell," *Sunday Times.*

CHAPTER 13: THE IRISHMAN

174 **Sixty prisoners had been:** This account draws from author interviews with Tyson, Mitchell, Sonntag, Sapp, SBS personnel, Shah, Ahad, Sharif Kamal, *SO-COM Report,* and video shot by Tyson (hereinafter *Tyson Video*) and Dostum's videographer (hereinafter *Dostum Video*).

175 **"Is this dude Arab?":** *Tyson Video.*

176 **"FOB 53 [Boxer] was":** *SOCOM Report,* 10.

176 **OGA personnel:** OGA stands for Other Government Agency, an alternative term for the CIA.

178 **flex-cuffs:** Jim Lewis, "14 Arrested in Protest at Marine Base," *San Diego Union-Tribune,* September 30, 1984.

178 **Marines had been training:** "America's New War: Military Preparedness at Camp Lejeune," CNN Transcript, September 24, 2001.

185 **designated terrorist group:** Elaine Lafferty, "IRA Could Face Return to Terrorist-Group List in US," *Irish Times,* August 18, 2001.

185 **training in Libya:** Harnden, *Bandit Country,* 147.

188 **Both had ambitions:** Sayed Shah and Tamim Ahad indeed both later qualified as doctors.

CHAPTER 14: PINK HOUSE

190 **The last two men:** This account draws from author interviews with Tyson, Sharif Kamal, Ahad, Stauth, Pavlov, Brooks, Rosann Tyson, *Tyson Video, Dostum Video,* and *SOCOM Report.*

191 **Mike Spann, about five yards:** Author interviews with Shah and Ahad.

191 **shot the guards and Amanullah:** Days later, the bodies of the guards and Amanullah were found just inside the Pink House.

192 **angling it to the side:** Author interview with Tyson. Mark Kukis writes that the pistol was "tilted to the side gangland-style"; Kukis, *"My Heart Became Attached,"* 126.

193 **David got to the pile of:** Author interview with Tyson. Shah and Ahad, intent on their own survival, did not see what happened to Spann after he disappeared beneath the pile of bodies.

193 **died in the first minute:** J. R. Seeger, "Northern Afghanistan Operations in the fall of 2001: Continuity, Partnership and Treachery," CIA presentation script provided to the author. It states: "Spann was killed along with a number of senior members of both the Uzbek and Hazara resistance in the first minute of the ambush in Qala-i Jangi."

194 **Lying facedown:** Author interviews with Shah and Ahad.

196 **Dagestani prisoner:** Author interview with Tyson. Dagestan is a Russian republic in the North Caucasus, bordering Chechnya.

196 **Sayed Kamal approached and shot:** Account of Sayed Kamal during CIA investigation, related to the author by Tyson.

196 **Abdul Latif, an Uzbek guard:** Account of Abdul Latif during CIA investigation, related to the author by Tyson.

197 **at least twelve:** A CIA source told the author that Tyson's CIA Personnel Evaluation Report stated that he had killed twelve to fifteen Al-Qaeda.

197 **possibly forty or more:** Tyson has a clear recollection of shooting, almost certainly fatally, six prisoners he could identify: the Arab with the pistol; the four men on top of Spann, including the "fat Arab" Qatari; and the Indonesian. In addition, he is certain he shot at least another three in front of the Pink House. He also shot several Al-Qaeda fighters from the roof of the headquarters building. Handwritten notes made by 5th Group surgeon Craig McFarland (hereinafter *McFarland Notes*), based on his talks with Tyson (but recorded several days after the uprising), read: "He claimed to have shot over 40 Taliban aggressors." Tyson's recollections were, and remain, greatly affected by the intensity and trauma of what he experienced. There is no film footage of what happened, and some of Tyson's targets may have been only wounded. But these recollections, the number of rounds he fired, and the close-quarters nature of the combat make around forty a reasonable estimate.

197 **clutching his pistol by the barrel:** ARD footage shown in *House of War* documentary.

198 **had avoided military service:** Author interview with Arnim Stauth; *House of War* documentary.

198 **"somehow give a face":** Interview with Stauth in *Situation Critical* documentary.

198 **one of Dostum's commanders:** The commander was Mohammad Humayun Fawzi.

198 **the commander excused himself:** The next time Brooks saw Fawzi, the Afghan

commander was standing in plain view atop the headquarters building, barking orders into his radio and seemingly oblivious of the bullets whizzing around him.

199 **eleven minutes:** Author interview with Tyson, who established it from an ARD videotape that recorded when the uprising started.

202 **assigned to Team Romeo:** Jacobsen, *Surprise, Kill, Vanish,* 358–60.

CHAPTER 15: TROJAN HORSE

203 **On a muddy knoll:** This account of the immediate aftermath of the uprising draws from author interviews with Seeger, Spellmeyer, Sonntag, Tyson, Harlow, Glenn, SBS personnel, Bass, Brooks, Faqir, Shannon Spann, *SOCOM Report,* and "Marshal de Boxer 251947Z Nov 01 Freaky. Summary of Actions at the Fortress at Qala-i Jangi" (hereinafter *Mitchell Report*).

205 **reporting that a "US adviser":** "US Adviser Killed in Afghan Prison Revolt," Agence France-Presse, November 25, 2001.

205 **CNN was reporting:** "Unconfirmed Report Indicates First U.S. War Casualty," CNN, November 25, 2001. Interview by Martin Savidge with Alex Perry of *Time* magazine.

205 **It was a brilliant:** The events at CIA headquarters are reconstructed from author interviews with Tenet, Black, Crumpton, Stiles, and Amy.

205 **When the Pentagon:** Author interviews with Harlow and Stiles.

206 **of the five-hour drive:** Author interview with Shannon Spann.

206 **Mike had gone down fighting:** Author interviews with Shannon Spann and Crumpton; also Crumpton, *Art of Intelligence,* 240–45. Spann and Crumpton remember the call differently, with Crumpton writing that Spann intuitively knew her husband was dead.

206 **Mike's ex-wife, Kathryn:** Author interview with Gail Spann.

206 **about 1:45 p.m.:** Briscoe et al., *Weapon of Choice,* 159.

207 **Northern Alliance roadblock:** *McFarland Notes.*

207 **"There's a right old battle":** Author interviews with SBS personnel.

207 **"You need to come":** *SOCOM Report,* 11. The adviser was Alim Razzim, a Dostum aide.

208 **Op Order:** An Op Order (or OPORD) is an abbreviation for "Operations Order," a military directive outlining the plan for a specific task.

208 **Captain Craig McFarland:** McFarland is given the pseudonym Charles Moss in Briscoe et al., *Weapon of Choice.*

208 **Oleg, a Ukraine-born:** Oleg is a pseudonym.

208 **his colleague Bert:** Bert is a pseudonym.

208 **who were furious:** Author interviews with Abdullah Abdullah (a spokesman for the post-Taliban Afghan administration) and Mulholland.

208 **conquer Afghanistan in three previous wars:** The three Anglo-Afghan wars were fought in 1839–42, 1878–80, and 1919.

208 **had not requested permission:** Campbell, *The Blair Years,* 588.

208 **into the Pashtun south:** The British plan was for the SBS to accompany ODA 583 southeast of Kandahar in support of Gul Agha Sherzai.

209 **massacres in Kunduz:** Author interviews with SBS personnel; Lewis, *Bloody Heroes,* 165.

209 **to their chagrin:** Author interviews with SBS personnel.

209 **WMIK Land Rovers:** WMIK (Weapons Mount Installation Kit) typically describes a British Land Rover 110 vehicle that has been hardened into a mobile weapons platform via chassis strengthening and the addition of a roll bar cage and weapons mounts.

210 **McGough, known as Scruff:** Tom Newton Dunn, "SBS Hero Killed on Holiday," *Sun,* June 10, 2006.

210 **had taken part in:** "Obituary of Sergeant 'Scruff' McGough," *Daily Telegraph.*

210 **a Geordie:** A Geordie is someone from Newcastle-upon-Tyne, in England's northeast.

210 **Barbour jackets:** Perry, *Falling Off the Edge,* 14.

210 **Each SBS man carried:** Author interviews with SBS personnel; Lewis, *Bloody Heroes,* 175.

210 **son of a Navy veteran:** "Obituary of Charles J. Bass," *Louisville Courier-Journal,* January 10, 2008.

210 **band of the Coldstream Guards:** Al Webb, "Snapshots of Sympathy," United Press International, September 15, 2001.

211 **much-vaunted "special relationship":** The phrase was coined by Winston Churchill in a speech in Fulton, Missouri, in 1946. David Cannadine, "A Point of View: Churchill and the Birth of the Special Relationship," BBC News, March 11, 2012.

211 **His SBS comrade Pat:** Author interview with SBS personnel.

211 **Sir Richard Dearlove, head of MI6:** Author interview with Tenet; Tenet, *Center of the Storm,* 173–74.

211 **fifteen men would be heading:** Author interviews with Sonntag, Mitchell, Beck, McFarland, Glenn, and SBS personnel; Briscoe et al., *Weapon of Choice,* 160 .

211 **the eight miles:** Google Earth shows the distance as 8.3 miles as the crow flies.

211 **Sonntag radioed:** *SOCOM Report,* 11.

212 **"Sarajevo Shuffle":** Ibid.; David Pratt, "Memories of Sarajevo," *Herald* (Scotland), April 14, 2012.

213 **simply milling about:** Author interviews with Mitchell, Glenn, Beck, and McFarland; *SOCOM Report,* 12.

214 **"the fatal funnel":** Author interviews with SBS personnel; *SOCOM Report,* 13.

215 **"Shit…shit":** Perry, *Falling Off the Edge,* 14.

215 **"Mike is MIA":** Ibid., 14.

216 **"I want SATCOM and JDAMs":** Ibid., 14.

216 **Viper laser range-finder binoculars:** Leica Vipers displayed latitude and longitude coordinates by linking a laser to Global Positioning System receivers. Vince Crawley, "SOCOM Lauded for Its Focus on 'Customers,'" *Air Force Times,* March 25, 2002.

217 **"Hey, I'm O-positive"**: Author interview with Glenn; *SOCOM Report,* 13.

218 **He had been shot:** His name was Javed, he told the doctors, and he was from Balkh; author interviews with Shah and Ahad.

CHAPTER 16: CLEARED HOT

219 **Dark plumes of:** This account of the afternoon and evening of November 25 draws from author interviews with Tyson, Seeger, Spellmeyer, Dostum, Sonntag, Mitchell, Beck, Glenn, SBS personnel, Bass, Faqir, Decker, Sapp, Greg, Captain Joe, Stauth, Pavlov, and McMillan, plus *Mitchell Report* and *SOCOM Report.*

219 **The major felt he was:** Author interview with Mitchell; Stanton, *Horse Soldiers,* 316.

222 **two white doves:** Author interview with SBS personnel; Lewis, *Bloody Heroes,* 216–17.

222 **said to have been brought:** Dexter Filkins, "Doves, Hope Return to Ancient City," *New York Times,* December 9, 2001.

222 **Beck was frantically trying:** Author interviews with Beck and McFarland; *McFarland Notes.*

222 **At 20,000 feet:** *Mitchell Report.*

223 **MBITR radio:** Multiband Inter/Intra Tram Radio, a handheld teactical radio used by NATO forces.

223 **Mitchell demanded:** Author interview with Mitchell; Briscoe et al., *Weapon of Choice,* 161.

223 **"He'll go to 18,000 feet":** Stanton, *Horse Soldiers,* 317 .

223 **"Shot at?" pondered Mitchell:** Ibid., 317.

223 **pinned down the SBS men:** *Mitchell Report.*

223 **Beck radioed Bossman:** Ibid.

224 **his map and GPS:** *SOCOM Report,* 15.

224 **excruciating twenty minutes:** Briscoe et al., *Weapon of Choice,* 161; *Mitchell Report.*

224 **"Thunder, Ranger":** Perry, *Falling Off the Edge,* 15.

224 **At 4:05 p.m., the first:** Alex Perry, "Inside the Battle at Qala-i Jangi."

224 **his AN/PSC-5:** *SOCOM Report,* 15.

224 **Sonntag had been unable to determine:** Author interview with Sonntag; Stanton, *Horse Soldiers,* 321 .

224 **After thirty minutes:** *SOCOM Report,* 15.

225 **cooked off:** Ammunition exploded prematurely because of heat from other explosions.

226 **Two JDAMs landed:** *Mitchell Report.*

228 **"No," Mitchell answered.** Author interview with Mitchell.

228 **Bass insisted:** *SOCOM Report,* 16.

228 **pot-fueled comedy riff:** John M. Glionna, "Decades Later, Dave's Still Not Here," *Los Angeles Times,* December 4, 2015.

232 **"Based on Dave's":** *Mitchell Report.*

232 **up to 300 vehicles:** Author interview with Bass; *SOCOM Report,* 18.

232 **800 men:** Author interview with Sonntag.

233 **known as "the Bone":** Wesley Morgan, "The B-1 Bomber: The Underappreciated Workhorse of America's Air Wars," *Washington Post,* December 30, 2015.

235 **It was the first time:** Author interview with McMillan; Cicere and McMillan, "The AC-130H Spectre Gunship over Afghanistan," *Air Commando Journal.*

235 **"water buffalo":** Jones, *Counterinsurgency in Afghanistan,* 96.

235 **"You're cleared hot":** Author interview with Decker.

235 **a "sparkle":** Winn, "Lethal Sisterhood," *Air Force Times.*

235 **"America is so determined":** Ibid.

CHAPTER 17: ABSOLUTELY WRONG

236 **The sun rose:** This account of the JDAM incident draws from author interviews with Mitchell, Bass, SBS personnel, Andreasen, Faqir, Leahy, Betz, Beck, Sciortino, Ashton, Emerson, Sapp, Tyson, Seeger, Spellmeyer, Dostum, Sonntag, Mitchell, Glenn, and Greg, plus *Mitchell Report* and *SOCOM Report.*

237 **Kevin Leahy:** Leahy is given the pseudonym Karl Latimer in Briscoe et al., *Weapon of Choice.*

237 **Paul Syverson:** Syverson is given the pseudonym Pat Schroeder in Briscoe et al., *Weapon of Choice.*

237 **Father Mychal Judge:** Rick Hampson, "Chaplain Mychal Judge: Victim 0001," *USA Today,* September 2, 2011.

237 **the general leading:** Lieutenant General Bryan "Doug" Brown was head of US Army Special Operations Command (USASOC) from October 2000 to August 2002.

238 **300 yards to the northeast:** Perry, "Inside the Battle at Qala-i Jangi," *Time.*

238 **blast radius of 250 yards:** Mike Toner, "Intelligence Now Applies to Weaponry, Too," Cox News Service, February 21, 2003.

238 **Private First Class Eric Andreasen:** Author interview with Andreasen.

239 **part of ODB 580:** An ODB, or Operation Detachment Bravo, was the headquarters element of a Special Forces company. In 2001, an ODB commanded six ODAs.

239 **was deemed insensitive:** James Sullivan, "Radio Employee Circulates Don't-Play List," *San Francisco Chronicle,* September 18, 2001.

240 **VS-17 marker panel:** Author interviews with Mitchell, Leahy, Betz, Beck, and Sciortino; Briscoe et al., *Weapon of Choice,* 162 ; Mathew Donofrio, "Contemporary Sniper and Observation Post Operations," *Armor,* May 1, 2006.

240 **Bass and Tony used:** *SOCOM Report,* 20.

243 **from the VMFA-251 Thunderbolts:** Holmes, *F-14 Tomcat Units of Operation Enduring Freedom,* 63–64.

243 **Shasta 21 was flown:** Extract of "Review of Report of Investigation into

Friendly Fire JDAM Incident Near Mazar-E Sharif, 26 November 2001," part of document of unknown date provided to author by confidential source.

243 **"Be advised, you are":** Perry, *Falling Off the Edge*, 16–17.

243 **Shasta 21, who wanted:** Extract of "Friendly Fire JDAM Incident."

244 **Shasta 21 then demanded:** Author interviews with Mitchell, Sciortino, and Beck.

244 **Mitchell and Sciortino strongly resisted:** Author interviews with Mitchell and Sciortino.

244 **But the Shasta 21 pilot refused:** Author interviews with Mitchell and Sciortino.

244 **somehow reversed:** Extract of "Friendly Fire JDAM Incident."

244 **two other Green Berets:** These were Captain Aaron Petersen and Master Sergeant Randy Emerson.

245 **His sergeant:** The sergeant was Sergeant William Sakisat.

245 **bomb hit at 10:51 a.m.:** Briscoe et al., *Weapon of Choice*, 162.

245 **a huge brown cloud:** *House of War* and *Good Morning Afghanistan* documentaries.

245 **was a beautiful sight:** Damien Degueldre in *House of War* documentary.

245 **"Shrapnel inbound":** *Good Morning Afghanistan* documentary.

245 **young Afghan translator:** Ibid. The translator was Najibullah Quraishi.

245 **"It missed":** Perry, "Inside the Battle at Qala-i Jangi."

246 **"War is supposed":** *SOCOM Report*, 21.

246 **The thirty-five-ton T-55:** Briscoe et al., *Weapon of Choice*, 162.

246 **Oakley sunglasses:** Author interview with Betz; Stanton, *Horse Soldiers*, 326.

247 **U-shaped hole:** Perry, "Inside the Battle at Qala-i Jangi."

248 **McFarland heard:** Author interview with McFarland; *McFarland Notes;* Stanton, *Horse Soldiers*, 327.

248 **"We have one down":** Perry, "Inside the Battle at Qala-i Jangi."

248 **"Abort! Abort!":** Author interviews with Bass and SBS personnel.

248 **Mitchell switched frequencies:** *Good Morning Afghanistan* documentary.

248 **"Check fire, check fire":** Author interview with Mitchell; Holmes, *F-14 Tomcat Units*, 63–64.

248 **who had tried:** Holmes, *F-14 Tomcat Units*, 64. The crew of a US Navy F-14 was listening in on the radio.

248 **Shasta 21 asked:** Author interview with Mitchell; Stanton, *Horse Soldiers*, 329–30.

250 **saw a medic:** The medic was Sergeant Brad Berry.

250 **George W. Bush was:** Author interviews with Morell and Tenet; this account draws from Morell, *The Great War of Our Time*, 332–34. See also: Tenet, *Center of the Storm*, 221–22.

251 **"DT, On Monday":** Excerpt of cable given to author by CIA source.

CHAPTER 18: YEAH, BABY!

252 **A luminescent:** This account draws from author interviews with Seeger, Hernandez, Emerson, Ashton, and Faqir, plus *SOCOM Report*.

253 **At 4:40 p.m., J. R. Seeger and Alex:** Statements by Petersen, Emerson, and

Ashton accompanying "Narrative Award Justification Data—Bronze Star Medal with 'V' Device" documents provided to author by confidential source.

254 **The SBS men were:** *SOCOM Report*, 24.

255 **had initially permitted only:** Steven Lee Myers and James Dao, "U.S. Stokes the Fire, Adding Gunships and More," *New York Times*, November 22, 2001.

255 **The arrangement was:** This account is drawn from author interview with Gilbert.

255 **verbal jousting:** John M. Donnelly, "Rumsfeld Makes War," *Chicago Tribune*, October 22, 2001.

255 **"known unknowns":** *Larry King Live*, CNN transcript, September 13, 2001.

256 **at Souda Bay, Crete:** The AC-130 Spectres had flown from Hurlburt Air Force base in Florida to Lajes Air Base in the Azores, then to Naval Air Station Sigonella in Sicily, before arriving in Crete—their final stop before Uzbekistan.

257 **For seventy agonizing minutes:** Briscoe et al., *Weapon of Choice*, 162–3.

258 **Grim 12 did just that:** *SOCOM Report*, 26.

259 **"Get down!":** Author interview with the sergeant, Master Sergeant Randy Emerson.

259 **in Panama in 1989:** Author interview with McMillan; Sam Dillon and Andres Oppenheimer, "U.S. Occupiers Move to Quell Panama Mobs," *Miami Herald*, December 24, 1989.

260 **closing-credits scene:** Kenneth Turan, "Like Fine Wine: Francis Ford Coppola Says 'Apocalypse Now' Has Improved with Age," *Los Angeles Times*, May 11, 2001.

260 **Patterson had recorded:** *SOCOM Report*, 26.

261 **"You're not in the United States":** *House of War* documentary.

262 **a lone, headless dove:** Fang, "They Were All Fighting to Die," *U.S. News & World Report*.

264 **One stood on the back:** *House of War* documentary.

264 **Another used the prone corpse:** Photograph by Oleg Nikishin, Getty Images.

264 **others smoked hashish:** Perry, "Inside the Battle at Qala-i Jangi," *Time*.

268 **remarkably good condition:** Reports that Mike Spann's body had been booby-trapped were incorrect.

268 **Mario Vigil:** Vigil is given the pseudonym Marvin Vandiver in Briscoe et al., *Weapon of Choice*.

269 **angered an ODA:** Author interviews with Mulholland and Rosengard.

269 **"fraudulent" attempt:** Author interview with Grenier; Grenier, *88 Days to Kandahar*, 97–103.

CHAPTER 19: LUCKY BOOTS

270 **black leather jacket and corduroy:** Fang, "They Were All Fighting to Die," *US News & World Report*.

NOTES

270 **"It was war"**: Gall, *Wrong Enemy*, 14.

270 **he had lost**: "Speech by General Abdul Rashid Dostum on the Occasion of the Inauguration of the Mike Spann Memorial," November 25, 2002, private collection of Charlie Santos.

270 **finest buzkashi horses**: Azoy, *Buzkashi*, 147.

271 **"treat the prisoners humanely"**: Gall, *Wrong Enemy*, 15.

271 **they did not know them**: Pelton interview in the *House of War* documentary.

271 **The CIA claimed Mike**: John J. Lumpkin, "CIA Officer First U.S. War Death," Associated Press, November 28, 2001.

271 **"Our son Mike was in Afghanistan"**: "America Strikes Back: Wolf Blitzer Reports," CNN Transcripts, November 28, 2001. Johnny Spann's press conference was carried live in its entirety.

272 **gagged from the stench**: Huggler, "The Castle of Death," *Independent*; author interview with Huggler.

272 **"The situation is completely"**: Oliver August, "CIA Blunder Sparked Taliban Revolt That Became a Mass Suicide," *Times* (London), November 28, 2001.

272 **one fighter was still crouched**: Author interview with Huggler.

272 **San Francisco 49ers sweatshirt**: Gall, *Wrong Enemy*, 14.

272 **scavenging belts and shoes**: Hill, "Hope Rises amid War's Ruin," *National Post* (Canada).

272 **One of them**: Huggler, "Geneva Convention."

272 **Al-Qaeda fighter lay stricken**: Perry, "Inside the Battle at Qala-i Jangi," *Time*.

272 **"Hey, why don't you"**: Dodge Billingsley interview in the *House of War* documentary.

273 **Red Cross set about their work**: This account is drawn from author interviews with Campbell and Brooks, and from Campbell, "The Fort of Hell."

273 **188 corpses**: Gall, "Last Holdouts," *New York Times*.

273 **translated by the CIA**: Eleven-page document provided by CIA source.

274 **Commander Faqir had an idea**: Author interview with Faqir.

274 **About sixty dead bodies**: Kukis, *"My Heart Became Attached,"* 134.

274 **"Look, we're going to die"**: Transcript of John Walker Lindh interview with Robert Young Pelton, CNN.com, December 2, 2001.

274 **a reporter was ushered in**: The reporter was Luke Harding. This account is drawn from Harding, "Taliban Who Came Back from Dead," *Observer*.

275 **had issued an order**: Berntsen, *Jawbreaker*, 269–70.

275 **One fighter hopped**: Campbell, "The Fort of Hell," *Sunday Times*.

275 **Another fighter's jaw**: Harding, "Taliban Who Came Back from Dead," *Observer*.

275 **The fortieth one out**: Campbell, "The Fort of Hell," *Sunday Times*.

276 **son of a petroleum executive**: Tony Bartelme, "Born in Louisiana, Captured in Afghanistan, Jailed in Hanahan: Yaser Hamdi Travels Long, Strange Road," *Post and Courier*, March 7, 2004.

276 **"You killed my son!"**: Campbell, "The Fort of Hell," *Sunday Times*.

276 **A reporter rushed forward**: The reporter was Matthew Campbell. Author interview with Campbell; Campbell, "The Fort of Hell," *Sunday Times*.

276 **that his leader:** Northern Alliance commanders said at the time that the leader was Tahir Uldosh, who had taken over from the IMU commander Juma Namangani when he was killed in a US air strike in November.

276 **"It was our commander":** Harding, "Taliban Who Came Back from Dead," *Observer.*

276 **"It is better to die a martyr":** Gall, "Last Holdouts," *New York Times.*

276 **He later stated:** Affidavit of Anne E. Asbury, Special Agent, Federal Bureau of Investigation, dated January 15, 2002, in the case of *United States of America v. John Philip Walker Lindh* (herein after *Asbury affidavit*).

276 **grandmother born in County Donegal:** De Luce et al., "John Walker Lindh, Detainee #001," *Foreign Policy.*

276 **told by his commanders:** *Asbury affidavit.*

277 **now he was talking:** This account is from Soloway, "Tale of an American Talib," *Newsweek.*

277 **A *Newsweek* reporter:** The reporter was Colin Soloway.

277 **at least seven:** *The 9/11 Commission Report,* 234.

278 **"John was my name":** Kukis, *"My Heart Became Attached,"* 143.

278 **a tetanus shot:** "Medical Examination and Treatment of American Citizen," report by Captain Craig McFarland, MD, battalion surgeon (hereinafter *McFarland Report*), contained in Brigadier General David P. Burford, "Report of Proceedings of 15-6 Investigation," February 3, 2003, released to American Civil Liberties Union in July 2005 following a Freedom of Information request.

278 **"Your wounds don't":** Kukis, *"My Heart Became Attached,"* 145.

279 **"they are a little nervous":** Ibid., 153.

279 **An FBI source said:** Author interview with FBI source.

279 **morphine and Valium:** *McFarland Report.*

280 **rope, and placed a hood:** "Proffer of Facts in Support of Defendant's Suppression Motions," filed June 13, 2002, in Case CR 02-37-A, *United States v. Lindh.*

280 **ODA 592, who:** Briscoe et al., *Weapon of Choice, 163.*

280 **Sonntag refused to allow:** Author interviews with Sonntag and Brooks.

281 **"caused you a lot of grief":** Author interview with Brooks; Kukis, *"My Heart Became Attached,"* 158 .

281 **treason charges:** "Apparent US Citizen Fighting with the Taliban May Be Tried on Treason Charges," *All Things Considered,* NPR transcript, December 3, 2001. The reporter was Tom Gjelten.

281 **the 3,000 inmates:** Carlotta Gall, "Witnesses Say Many Taliban Died in Custody," *New York Times,* December 11, 2001.

281 **capacity of under 1,000:** "A War Crime in Afghanistan: Dead on Arrival," *Economist,* August 22, 2002.

281 **an evangelical Christian:** Author interview with Marchal.

281 **around 7,000 prisoners:** Author interview with Dostum.

281 **had overwhelmed:** Ibid.

282 **Malik Pahlawan had been accused:** Gretchen Peters, "Ethnic Divide Massacres Intensify Rifts in Afghanistan," Associated Press, February 7, 1998.

282 **had been baked alive:** Chris Stephen, "The Day Mazar Prison Became a Slaughterhouse," *Irish Times,* December 1, 2001.

282 **According to a UN report:** Human Rights Watch, "Afghanistan: The Massacre in Mazar-i Sharif."

282 **By Dostum's account:** Author interview with Dostum.

282 **gnawing at each other's limbs:** Farrow, *War on Peace,* 194.

282 **"convoy of death":** Dan Lamothe, "The Bloody History of Kunduz, from Afghanistan's 'Convoy of Death' to Now," *Washington Post,* September 28, 2015.

283 **"Dad's lucky boots":** Twitter thread by CIA, June 16, 2019.

CHAPTER 20: NO SECRETS

284 **would receive them:** Barbara Salazar Torreon, "The Purple Heart: Background and Issues for Congress" (Congressional Research Service, June 2020), cites an October 2017 estimate by the Military Order of the Purple Heart of 21,939 recipients from the war in Afghanistan and 35,438 recipients from the war in Iraq.

285 **"We had a job to do":** "Injured Servicemembers Receive Purple Heart," US Air Forces in Europe News Service, December 3, 2001.

285 **"I see the Americans":** Jill Noelle Cecil, "Purple Hearts Come Home," *Leaf-Chronicle,* December 5, 2001.

285 **military pathologist performed:** Extract from "Final Report of Postmortem Examination" A01-92 conducted by LTC Kathleen M. Ingwersen, Armed Forces Regional Medical Examiner, November 30–December 1, 2001.

286 **Cheney's Air Force Two:** Jerod MacDonald-Evoy, "John McCain's Body Will Fly on Air Force Two, Planes Reserved for VPs and VIPs," *Arizona Republic,* August 30, 2018. The same aircraft was used to fly Senator John McCain's body to Andrews Air Force base from Phoenix, Arizona, in 2018.

286 **had been in Islamabad:** Tenet, *Center of the Storm,* 223–4.

286 **cold, gray Sunday afternoon:** "Body of Slain CIA Officer Arrives in US," Agence France-Presse, December 3, 2001.

286 **Marine Corps honor guard:** John J. Lumpkin, "Body of CIA Officer Returned from Battlefront of Secret War," Associated Press, December 3, 2001.

286 **played "Amazing Grace":** "Body of CIA Agent Killed in Mazar-e-Sharif Fortress Returned to U.S.," Associated Press Video Archive, December 2, 2001.

287 **"HERO vs. RAT":** John Lehmann, "HERO VS. RAT: Just Hours Before His Death, CIA Patriot Grilled the Taliban Turncoat," *New York Post,* December 7, 2001.

287 **former social worker:** Fredrick Kunkle, "Lindh Never Betrayed Homeland, Parents Say," *Washington Post,* July 16, 2002.

287 **corporate lawyer:** Nieves, "A U.S. Convert's Path," *New York Times.*

287 **with another man:** Frank Lindh and Brian Johnson became a couple in 1998 and married in 2008.

287 **Shedding and assuming one identity:** Michael Ellison, "American Taliban: 'Traitor' Warns of Imminent Attack on US," *Guardian,* December 13, 2001.

287 **a photographer:** Nieves, "A U.S. Convert's Path," *New York Times.*

287 **Native American rituals:** Timothy Roche et al., "The Making of John Walker Lindh," *Time.*

288 **Washington, DC, suburbs:** The family lived in Takoma Park and Silver Spring, both in Maryland.

288 **"Marin County Caucasians":** James Best, "Black Like Me: John Walker Lindh's Hip-Hop Daze," *East Bay Express,* September 3, 2003.

288 **"When I read those rhymes":** Starr, "E-Mails from a Traitor," *Weekly Standard.*

288 **to a gay Muslim:** Helen Kennedy, "Internet Traces His Path to Taliban," *Daily News,* December 11, 2001.

289 **considered "pure":** Justin Pritchard, "The Roots of the 'American Taliban,'" Associated Press, December 21, 2001.

289 **wear flowing robes:** Kukis, *"My Heart Became Attached,"* 8.

289 **"far more likely to":** "Government's Filing in Support of Detention for John Walker Lindh," US District Court for the Eastern District of Virginia, February 6, 2002.

289 **met men who had:** Kukis, *"My Heart Became Attached,"* 24.

289 **not particularly fond:** Carr, "Text of Lindh's E-Mails and Letters," Cox News Service.

289 **"I really don't know":** Ibid.

289 **"an act of war":** Thomas, "A Long, Strange Trip to the Taliban," *Newsweek.*

290 **"This is Sulayman al-Faris":** Hamza Hendawi, "Letters Show Mom's Search for Lindh," Associated Press, January 24, 2002.

290 **asked him if he wanted:** Federal indictment in case of *U.S. vs. John Phillip Walker Lindh,* US District Court for the Eastern District of Virginia, February 5, 2002.

291 **"decent and honorable":** "Father of a U.S. Taliban Fighter Speaks Out," Associated Press, January 20, 2006.

291 **begun in Bonn:** Mary Dejevsky, "Factions Gather in Bonn to Discuss New Government," *Independent on Sunday,* November 25, 2001.

291 **Three Tajiks:** Abdullah Abdullah, Yunus Qanuni, and Fahim Khan took the Foreign, Interior, and Defense posts respectively.

292 **"This is a humiliation":** Marcus Warren, "'Humiliated' Warlord Boycotts Government," *Daily Telegraph,* December 7, 2001.

292 **should have installed Dostum:** Khalilzad, *The Envoy,* 134 ; author interview with Dostum.

292 **on November 17:** Wright et al., *A Different Kind of War,* 103.

292 **air controller had refused:** Blehm, *The Only Thing Worth Dying For,* 174.

292 **three Green Berets:** Michael A. Fletcher, "Victims Were Professional Soldiers," *Washington Post,* December 6, 2001. Master Sergeant Jefferson Davis, 39, Sergeant 1st Class Daniel Petithory, 32, and Staff Sergeant Cody Prosser, 28, were killed.

292 **an estimated fifty:** Blehm, *The Only Thing Worth Dying For,* 174.

293 **cuts and bruises to his face:** Schroen, *First In,* 277.

293 **Shortly after the Bonn:** This passage draws extensively from author interview with Muñoz and Arturo Muñoz, "A Long-Overdue Adaptation to the Afghan Environment," in Jenkins and Godges (eds.), *The Long Shadow of 9/11,* 23–24.

293 **Karzai negotiated a truce:** Brian Knowlton, "Taliban Fighters Agree to Surrender Kandahar," *International Herald Tribune,* December 7, 2001.

294 **remote landing strip:** Kummer, *U.S. Marines in Afghanistan,* 14.

294 **had been seized:** The Marines flew 441 miles from the USS *Peleliu* in the Arabian Sea to seize the landing strip. Ibid., 15.

294 **All water used:** Mattis and West, *Call Sign Chaos,* 67.

294 **Chocolate-colored dust:** Kummer, *U.S. Marines in Afghanistan,* 19.

294 **hack up brown phlegm:** Mattis and West, *Call Sign Chaos,* 67.

295 **when Lindh needed to urinate:** Richard A. Serrano, "Lindh Lawyers Allege Threats, Abuse," *Los Angeles Times,* June 15, 2002.

295 **Lindh confessed to the FBI:** At Camp Rhino, an FBI agent questioned Lindh, who signed a waiver form and made multiple admissions. Katharine Q. Seelye, "Lindh Sentenced to 20 Years in Prison," *New York Times,* October 5, 2002; Kukis, *"My Heart Became Attached,"* 161–62.

295 **hit on 9/11:** Toby Harnden, "Special Bonds Forged in the Fires but for Many the Pain Lingers On," *Daily Telegraph,* September 11, 2002.

296 **grave number 2359:** Jabeen Bhatti, "Farewell to 'Hero': Arlington National Cemetery Burial Honors CIA Officer Spann's Sacrifice," *Washington Times,* December 11, 2001.

296 **swift series of calls:** Author interview with Tenet. The calls were among John McLaughlin, Tenet's deputy; Wolfowitz; and Andy Card, the White House chief of staff. See also: Tenet, *Center of the Storm,* 224.

296 **Inside the casket lay:** Drew Jubera, "Alabama Town Bids Brave Son Goodbye," Cox News Service, December 6, 2001.

296 **many of them in disguise:** Author interviews with CIA officers, who also revealed that cars with Russian diplomatic plates staked out the wake.

298 **reported that Shannon:** Greg Miller and Jeffrey Gettleman, "Boyhood Focus Led Him to CIA," *Los Angeles Times,* November 29, 2001.

298 **none of the nineteen Al-Qaeda:** *The 9/11 Commission Report,* 1–4.

299 **Hank Crumpton made sure:** Author interview with Crumpton; Crumpton, *Art of Intelligence,* 245–46.

300 **joining Team Hotel:** Thomas Gibbons-Neff, "After 13 Years, CIA Honors Green Beret Killed on Secret Afghanistan Mission," *Washington Post,* April 17, 2016.

CHAPTER 21: TOMORROWLAND

303 **"Fly and enjoy":** David Ivanovich, "Tourism Taking a Hit," *Houston Chronicle,* October 5, 2001.

306 **2,000 of his:** Mattis and West, *Call Sign Chaos,* 75.

NOTES

306 **"We're going to":** Baker, *Days of Fire,* 179.

306 **3,500 more at sea:** Mattis and West, *Call Sign Chaos,* 69.

306 **announced a ceasefire:** Tomsen, *Wars of Afghanistan,* 611.

307 **they had bought off:** Berntsen, *Jawbreaker,* 309.

307 **slipped away that night:** Tomsen, *Wars of Afghanistan,* 611.

307 **on or around December 16:** Mary Anne Weaver, "Lost at Tora Bora," *New York Times Magazine,* September 11, 2005.

307 **shot dead by Navy SEALs:** Toby Harnden, "I Fired Twice and bin Laden Crumpled," *Sunday Times,* February 7, 2015.

307 **an MH-47G Chinook:** An MH-47E with the tail number 91-00499 was one of the four Chinooks used by the 160th SOAR in Task Force Dagger. It was flown during the hunt for Osama bin Laden in the Tora Bora campaign of 2001. It was later converted by Boeing into MH-47G, 08-03783, the lead helicopter during Operation Neptune Spear in 2011 and the aircraft that took bin Laden's body out of Pakistan. Information from confidential US Army source.

308 **Like Lisa Beamer:** "'Hero Widow': The Making of Lisa Beamer's 9/11 Celebrity," *American Studies Journal* No. 62, 2017.

308 **"Shannon, I assure you":** Jeffrey McMurray, "Alabama Delegation Praises Bush's Message," Associated Press, January 29, 2002.

308 **agreed to a plea deal:** Larry Margasak, "Lindh Pleads Guilty, Faces 20 Years," Associated Press, July 15, 2002.

308 **US government's Confidential Source 1:** *Asbury affidavit.*

308 **even in California:** Jim Doyle, "Californians Have No Mercy for John Lindh," *San Francisco Chronicle,* January 28, 2002.

309 **"sorry about your son":** Katharine Q. Seelye, "In Court, a Not-Guilty Plea. Outside, the Real Drama," *New York Times,* February 14, 2002.

309 **"I told John when":** Helen Kennedy, "He's a Patriot, Says His Dad," *Daily News,* July 16, 2002.

309 **ceremony to unveil:** Details of the ceremony and memorial are drawn from author interviews with Santos and Johnny Spann.

309 **"promoted warlordism":** Author interview with Santos.

311 **thirty CIA officers:** Email to author from Sara Lichterman, Office of Public Affairs, Central Intelligence Agency, April 20, 2021. Team Echo leader Greg Vogle was also awarded a Distinguished Intelligence Cross. At least eight crosses were awarded for actions between 9/11 and April 2021.

311 **"a voluntary act":** *CIA Factbook on Intelligence,* Office of Public Affairs, Central Intelligence Agency. Washington, DC, April 1999: 30.

311 **citation noted:** Text of citation provided to author by CIA source.

311 **since the Vietnam war:** Mark Johnson, "In the Line of Duty, a Hero Emerges," *Milwaukee Journal Sentinel,* November 14, 2003.

311 **"unparalleled courage":** Camp, *Boots on the Ground,* 176.

312 **Queen Elizabeth II at Windsor Castle:** Author interviews with SBS personnel.

312 **awarded the Military Cross:** Author interviews with SBS personnel; "Obituary of Seargeant 'Scruff' McGough," *Daily Telegraph.*

312 **awarded the Navy Cross:** Otto Kreisher, "SEAL Honored for Bravery in Afghanistan," Copley News Service, October 30, 2003.

312 **"unlimited courage":** Wise and Baron, *The Navy Cross,* 12.

312 **shot dead by Z Squadron:** Kim Sengupta, "Taliban Factions May Be Using British Forces to Assassinate Rival Commanders," *Independent,* July 25, 2008. Information that Z Squadron carried out the raid from SBS source.

312 **convened a video conference:** Franks, *American Soldier,* 46–54; Woodward, *Plan of Attack,* 52–66.

313 **105,000 troops:** Woodward, *Plan of Attack,* 62.

313 **"catastrophic success":** Rumsfeld used the term during an appearance on a PBS show, *The NewsHour with Jim Lehrer,* on February 20, 2003: "U.S., Coalition Forces Called Ready for Iraqi Operations," Washington File, Office of International Information Programs, US Department of State, February 21, 2003. Franks wrote that he briefed Bush and others on the concept in August 2002: Franks, *American Soldier,* 392.

313 **MISSION ACCOMPLISHED:** Scott Lindlaw, "Bush: Allied Forces Prevailed in Iraq," Associated Press, May 1, 2003.

313 **"How Tommy Franks Won":** Fred Barnes, "The Commander: How Tommy Franks Won the Iraq War," *Weekly Standard,* June 2, 2003.

313 **still selling copies:** "The *Weekly Standard,* Autographed by General Tommy Franks, Featuring an Exclusive Interview" ($15). http://www.tommyfranksmuseum.org/store.

313 **included a redefinition:** The redefinition was by General Peter Pace, then Vice Chairman of the Joint Chiefs of Staff.

313 **house in Ramadi:** "Three Soldiers, Many Mourners: Scott Pelley Reports on Soldiers Killed in Iraq," CBS News Transcripts, March 3, 2004.

314 **In the late spring:** Chivers, *The Fighters,* 59–66.

315 **when he was stationed:** Gretchen N. McIntyre, "A Living Hero," *Defense Visual Information Distribution Service,* November 10, 2012.

315 **the only female:** Twitter message by Admiral Michael Gilday, Chief of Naval Operations, March 31, 2021.

315 **"so successful, so fast":** Nancy Gibbs and John F. Dickerson, "Inside the Mind of George W. Bush," *Time,* September 6, 2004.

316 **sign put up:** Hayden, *Playing to the Edge,* 218; author interviews with Tenet and Hayden.

316 **By 2021, 137 stars:** "CIA Honors Its Fallen at Annual Memorial Ceremony," CIA press release, May 25, 2021.

316 **killed in combat:** Julian E. Barnes, Eric Schmitt, and Adam Goldman, "C.I.A. Officer Is Killed in Somalia," *New York Times,* November 25, 2020.

316 **The 121st star:** "The CIA Book of Honor—Star 121: Mark S. Rausenberger." *Intel Today* blog, February 25, 2020.

316 **died suddenly:** "Obituary: Mark Sherman Rausenberger, November 7, 1967–May 23, 2016," www.dignitymemorial.com; "CIA Honors Its Fallen in Annual Memorial Ceremony," *U.S. Federal News,* May 24, 2017.

316 **Staff Sergeant Robert Bales:** "US Soldier to Be Charged with 17 Afghan Murders," Agence France-Press, March 12, 2012.

317 **successful Agency careers:** Details of careers from CIA sources.

318 **overseeing up to 90 percent:** Author interview with CIA source.

318 **left in 2015:** Donati, *Eagle Down.*

318 **Kunduz for fifteen days:** Rod Nordland, "Taliban End Takeover of Kunduz After 15 Days," *New York Times,* October 13, 2015.

319 **stopped issuing statistics:** Thomas Joscelyn and Bill Roggio, "US Military Ends Reporting on Security Situation in Afghanistan's Districts," *Long War Journal,* April 30, 2019.

319 **"strategic stalemate":** Clayton Thomas, "Afghanistan: Background and U.S. Policy," Congressional Research Service, November 10, 2020.

319 **Mullah Fazl appeared:** "Afghanistan Expresses Concern over Videos of Taliban Leaders Visiting Members in Pakistan," Radio Free Europe/Radio Liberty, December 25, 2020.

319 **ten times the rate:** Morgan, *The Hardest Place,* 490.

CHAPTER 22: DAYS OF THUNDER

321 **twice fled into exile:** Jason Straziuso, "U.S. Blasts Warlord's Return to Afghanistan," Associated Press, August 17, 2009; Mohammad Jawad, "At Least 14 Dead in Kabul Airport Bombing as Exiled VP Returns Home," Deutsche Presse-Agentur, July 22, 2018.

321 **awarded the rank:** Emma Graham-Harrison and Akhtar Mohammad Makoii, "Afghan Power Deal Hands Top Military Post to Man Accused of Torturing Rival," *Guardian,* May 17, 2020.

321 **heart attack in 2014:** Matthew Rosenberg, "Warlord Who Tamped Conflicts as Afghan Vice President Dies," *New York Times,* March 9, 2014.

321 **left office:** Tim Craig, "Afghan President Hamid Karzai Slams U.S. Government Policy in Afghanistan," *Washington Post,* September 23, 2014.

322 **Some of his men:** Author interviews with Dostum commanders.

323 **released from federal prison:** Nancy A. Youssef, "'American Taliban' John Walker Lindh Released After 17 Years," *Wall Street Journal,* May 23, 2019.

324 **deported to Saudi Arabia:** Tony Bartelme, "Hamdi's Return to Saudi Ends Test of Power," *Post and Courier,* October 12, 2004.

324 **fifty of the eighty-six:** Worthington, *The Guantánamo Files,* 9–18.

324 **month after the uprising:** Matt Kelley, "U.S. to Bring Taliban, al-Qaida Prisoners to Navy Base in Cuba, Rumsfeld Says," Associated Press, December 27, 2001.

324 **of apparent suicide in 2009:** David McFadden and Danica Coto, "Military: Gitmo Detainee Dies of Apparent Suicide," Associated Press, June 3, 2009.

324 **a Qala-i Jangi survivor:** Worthington, *Guantánamo Files,* 9–18.

324 **"Pimp Daddy":** Thomas Joscelyn, "It's Hard Out Here for an Iraqi," *Weekly Standard,* March 27, 2006.

324 **"bin Laden's terrorist attacks"**: Michael Kilian, "Lindh: 'I Condemn Terrorism,'" *Chicago Tribune,* October 5, 2002.

324 **"advocate for global jihad"**: De Luce et al., "John Walker Lindh, Detainee #001," *Foreign Policy.*

324 **beheaded three Americans**: Ben Farmer, "Peter Kassig May Have Defied Captors over Beheading Video Statement," *Daily Telegraph,* November 16, 2014.

324 **calling himself "Yahya"**: Graeme Wood, "I Wrote to John Walker Lindh. He Wrote Back," *Atlantic,* May 23, 2019.

324 **"doing a spectacular job"**: Mary Harris, Marina Perelman, and Conan Nolan, "Prison Letters from 'American Taliban' Underscore Concerns over His Supervised Release," NBC Los Angeles, May 22, 2019. Lindh's correspondence was with Harris.

324 **An FBI source**: Author interview with FBI source.

324 **executed gay men**: Ishaan Tharoor, "The Islamic State's Shocking War on Gays," *Washington Post,* June 13, 2016.

325 **"I am not interested in"**: De Luce et al., "John Walker Lindh, Detainee #001," *Foreign Policy.*

325 **Another FBI source**: Author interview with FBI source.

325 **leveraged this phenomenon**: Daniele Valentini, Anna Maria Lorusso, and Achim Stephan, "Onlife Extremism: Dynamic Integration of Digital and Physical Spaces in Radicalization," *Frontiers in Psychology,* March 24, 2020.

325 **estimated 6,000 Westerners**: Hearing before the US Senate Permanent Subcommittee on Investigations of the Committee on Homeland Security and Governmental Affairs, "ISIS Online: Countering Terrorist Radicalization and Recruitment on the Internet and Social Media," July 6, 2016.

325 **massacre of forty-nine people**: Hayley Tsukayama, Mark Berman, and Jerry Markon, "Gunman Who Killed 49 in Orlando Nightclub Had Pledged Allegiance to ISIS," *Washington Post,* June 13, 2016.

327 **2,488 American troops**: David A. Blum and Nese F. DeBruyne, "American War and Military Operations Casualties: Lists and Statistics," Congressional Research Service, July 2020.

327 **remaining 3,500**: Missy Ryan and Karen DeYoung, "Biden Will Withdraw All U.S. Forces from Afghanistan by Sept. 11, 2021," *Washington Post,* April 13, 2021.

323 **perhaps forty**: See note for "possibly forty or more" on pages 379–80.

AUTHOR'S NOTE ON SOURCES

339 **"the whirlpool of war"**: Kipling, *The Irish Guards in the Great War,* Vol. 1, 7.

340 **Ethel Annakin in 1915**: "Truth Is the First Casualty in War," QuoteInvestigator.com, April 11, 2021. This phrase had been attributed to Aeschylus, Samuel Johnson, Senator Hiram Johnson, and others. The final word, however, seems to come from QuoteInvestigator.com. In a paper presented at an education

conference in August 1915, Ethel Annakin cited the phrase, but provided an anonymous attribution: "Someone has finely said that 'truth is the first casualty in war'; and never was a greater untruth spoken than that war is waged for the protection of women and homes." The following year, her husband, Philip Snowden, a member of Parliament in Britain, wrote in an introduction to the book *Truth and the War* by E. D. Morel: "'Truth,' it has been said, 'is the first casualty of war.' When hostilities break out the one object of each belligerent nation is victory."

PHOTOGRAPHY CREDITS

PHOTOGRAPHY CREDITS

Page 8

8.1 Prisoners gathered in front of the Pink House: Author's private collection/Polaris.

8.2 The prisoners closest to the Pink House: Author's private collection/Polaris.

8.3 Mike Spann questions the Qatari: Author's private collection/Polaris.

8.4 Seconds before the uprising began: Author's private collection/Polaris.

INSERT TWO

Page 9

9.1 Steph Bass, the Navy SEAL: Author's private collection/Polaris.

9.2 Glenn, the Team Bravo medic: Author's private collection/Polaris.

9.3 Tony, the SBS corporal: Author's private collection/Polaris.

Page 10

10.1 Major Mark Mitchell: Author's private collection/Polaris.

10.2 David Tyson in the northern compound: Courtesy of David Tyson.

10.3 Justin Sapp inspects a Mosin-Nagant: Author's private collection/Polaris.

Page 11

11.1 The entrance to the tunnel: Matthew Campbell.

11.2 John Walker Lindh, just after surrender: Matthew Campbell.

11.3 Wounded prisoner is carried from the Pink House: Matthew Campbell.

Page 12

12.1 Carnage beside the Pink House: James Hill

12.2 Corpses of an Al-Qaeda fighter and horses: Courtesy of David Tyson.

Page 13

13.1 John Walker Lindh on December 7: Author's private collection/Polaris.

13.2 A Green Beret blindfolds Lindh: Author's private collection/Polaris.

13.3 Members of ODA 592: Author's private collection/Polaris.

Page 14

14.1 Shannon Spann and her son, Jake: Courtesy of Shannon Spann.

14.2 Shannon Spann, hand on heart: Getty Images.

Page 15

15.1 The golden dome of Qala-i Jangi in 2020: Toby Harnden/Polaris.

15.2 The cellar of the Pink House in 2020: Toby Harnden/Polaris.

Page 16

16.1 Afghan soldier stands inside the Pink House: Toby Harnden/Polaris.

16.2 Memorial to Mike Spann: Author's private collection/Polaris.

INDEX

INDEX

Qala-i Jangi fort and, 133, 135–36, 139, 148–49

Qala-i Jangi uprising and, 204, 212, 215, 254, 270–71, 322

Salam's ransom paid by, 109

Santos and, 52–53, 104, 309

secularism of, 141

Sheberghan prison and, 270

Soviet alliance with, 10, 134

Spann's memorial and, 309–10

Stinger missiles returned by, 22

strength of, 26, 107, 108, 127

Sultan Razia school bombing and, 136, 138

supplies for, 121

surrender negotiations with, 157–60, 169–70, 172, 198, 203

Taliban's view of, 105

Tangi Gap battle and, 126, 128–29

Team Alpha and, 58, 66, 71, 78, 80–82, 175

troop rally of, 97–98

Tufan and, 84

US relations with, 21, 51–52, 54–55, 95, 151–52, 281, 292, 315, 320

Uzbek warriors of, 10, 11, 67

victory tour of, 145–47

videographer of, 179, 189, 190, 287

wives and children of, 321

Dostum, Khadija (first wife of Abdul Rashid), 21

Elizabeth II, Queen, 208, 311

F-14 Tomcat, 96, 118, 122–23, 129, 315

F-18 Hornet, 129–30, 137–38, 220–24, 227, 233, 238, 243–48, 314

Faqir, Mohammed Jowzjani

Al-Qaeda firefight with, 102–3, 138

Qala-i Jangi uprising and, 212–13, 215–19, 236, 253–54, 261, 264, 267, 274

Faris, Sulayman al-. *See* Lindh, John Walker

Farm, The (CIA training facility), 7, 28–29, 32–35, 43, 59, 62, 67, 72, 156, 165, 317

Fayez, Hafizullah, 247

Fazl, Mullah Mohammed

Bergdahl exchange for, 317

bin Laden and, 146

Dostum's custody of, 270–71

Guantánamo imprisonment of, 312, 317

Hazaras massacred by, 105, 158

peace negotiations by, 317, 319

Qala-i Jangi uprising and, 204, 265, 308

Seeger's meeting with, 160

surrender negotiations with, 158–60, 169–70, 177, 198, 203, 234, 322

FBI (Federal Bureau of Investigations), 40, 47, 295

Flight 11 (9/11), 3, 25, 28, 36

Flight 77 (9/11), 37, 75, 295

Flight 93 (9/11), 37, 38, 308

Flight 175 (9/11), 37

Flight 201, 3–4, 22

Fort Campbell, 27, 40, 63, 153, 155–56

Franks, Tommy

Afghanistan plan of, 49

Bowers criticism of, 121

Calland and, 154, 155

at Dostum's guesthouse, 153–54

Iraq war and, 312, 313

Khan meeting with, 119, 120

pessimistic progress report and, 107

Special Forces officers and, 120

team insertion delays and, 59, 86–87

Tora Bora operation and, 306, 307

Freedman, Lawrence "Gus," 61

Genghis Khan, 88, 149

Ghani, Ashraf, 321

GI Jane (movie), 116

Gilbert, Charlie, 67

AC-130 Spectre deal and, 255–56

Tyson and, 127, 200, 201, 283, 301

Gilbert, Terri, 202

Glenn (Team Bravo), 125, 266

later career of, 317

performs amputation, 125–26

Qala-i Jangi uprising and, 203, 207, 211–12, 215–23, 225–30, 261, 267–68

Spann's death and, 241, 301–2

Glock pistols, 72, 175, 191

Grant, Ulysses S., 68, 295

Green Berets, xiii

CIA teams with, 58

Dostum and, 292

"kill box" campaign of, 58–59

Kunduz and, 233, 235

Lindh and, 279–80, 294–95

ABOUT THE AUTHOR

Toby Harnden is a winner of the Orwell Prize for Books. A former foreign correspondent for the *Sunday Times* of London and the *Daily Telegraph* who reported from thirty-three countries, he specializes in terrorism and war. Born in England, Harnden was imprisoned in Zimbabwe, prosecuted in Britain for protecting confidential sources, and vindicated by a $23 million public inquiry in Ireland. A dual British and US citizen, he spent a decade as a Royal Navy officer before becoming a journalist. He holds a First Class degree in modern history from Oxford and is the author of *Bandit Country: The IRA & South Armagh* and *Dead Men Risen: An Epic Story of War and Heroism in Afghanistan*. Previously based in London, Belfast, Jerusalem, Baghdad, and Washington, DC, he lives in Virginia.

@tobyharnden
tobyharnden.com